Final Freedom

This book examines emancipation after the Emancipation Proclamation of 1863 and during the last years of the American Civil War. Focusing on the making and meaning of the Thirteenth Amendment, *Final Freedom* looks at the struggle among legal thinkers, politicians, and ordinary Americans in the North and the border states to find a way to abolish slavery that would overcome the inadequacies of the Emancipation Proclamation. The book tells the dramatic story of the creation of a constitutional amendment and reveals an unprecedented transformation in American race relations, politics, and constitutional thought. Using a wide array of archival and published sources, Professor Vorenberg argues that the crucial consideration of emancipation occurred after, not before, the Emancipation Proclamation; that the debate over final freedom was shaped by a level of volatility in society and politics underestimated by prior historians; and that the abolition of slavery by constitutional amendment represented a novel method of reform that transformed attitudes toward the Constitution.

Michael Vorenberg is Assistant Professor of History at Brown University.

CAMBRIDGE HISTORICAL STUDIES IN AMERICAN LAW AND SOCIETY

Editor

Christopher Tomlins   *American Bar Foundation*

Final Freedom

The Civil War, the Abolition of Slavery, and the Thirteenth Amendment

MICHAEL VORENBERG
Brown University

CAMBRIDGE
UNIVERSITY PRESS

PUBLISHED BY THE PRESS SYNDICATE OF THE UNIVERSITY OF CAMBRIDGE
The Pitt Building, Trumpington Street, Cambridge, United Kingdom

CAMBRIDGE UNIVERSITY PRESS
The Edinburgh Building, Cambridge CB2 2RU, UK
40 West 20th Street, New York, NY 10011-4211, USA
10 Stamford Road, Oakleigh, VIC 3166, Australia
Ruiz de Alarcón 13, 28014 Madrid, Spain
Dock House, The Waterfront, Cape Town 8001, South Africa

http://www.cambridge.org

First published 2001

Printed in the United States of America

Typeface   Sabon 10/12 pt.   *System*   MagnaType [AG]

A catalog record for this book is available from the British Library.

Library of Congress Cataloging in Publication data

Vorenberg, Michael, 1964–
   Final freedom : the Civil War, the abolition of slavery, and the Thirteenth
Amendment / Michael Vorenberg
      p. cm.
   Includes bibliographical references and index.
   ISBN 0-521-65267-7
      1. United States. President (1861–1865 : Lincoln). Emancipation Proclamation.
2. Slaves – Emancipation – United States. 3. Afro-Americans – Civil rights – History –
19th century. 4. United States – History – Civil War, 1861–1865. 5. United States.
Constitution. 13th Amendment. 6. Constitutional history – United States. I. Title.

E453 .V67 2001
973.7′14 – dc21   00-063028

ISBN 0 521 65267 7 hardback

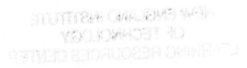

For Dan and Tom, my best teachers

Contents

Illustrations

Acknowledgments

This book exists in large part because of the generosity of friends, scholars, and institutions. Financial assistance was provided by fellowships from the Julian Park Fund of the State University of New York at Buffalo, the Indiana Historical Society, the Henry E. Huntington Library, the Everett M. Dirksen Congressional Research Center, the Mark DeWolfe Howe Fund of the Harvard Law School, the Graduate Student Council of Harvard University, the Charles Warren Center of Harvard University, and the Department of History of Harvard University. A fellowship from the Mrs. Giles Whiting Foundation enabled me to complete the dissertation on which this book is based. Frank Smith of Cambridge University Press and the anonymous readers who evaluated the book for the Press have been patient and helpful in the transformation of the manuscript into the final product.

I benefited immeasurably from the assistance of research librarians and archivists at roughly thirty-five repositories across the country. Limitations in space prevent me from mentioning all of them, but I would like to note in particular the helpfulness of the staffs of the manuscripts division of the Library of Congress and the special collections division of the Henry E. Huntington Library. Also, at the Illinois State Historical Library, Mr. Thomas F. Schwartz, now the State Historian of Illinois, offered much valuable advice and made available to me unpublished Lincoln material. Mary-Jo Kline at the John Hay Library of Brown University came to my rescue in a last-minute search for photographs.

Many scholars have assisted me in the final preparation of the book. I must thank in particular Jeffrey P. Moran, an immensely talented historian and a devoted friend. Jeff read early drafts of many chapters, and he is more than likely responsible for any well-turned phrase that somehow found its way into the final version. Thomas J. Brown and Heather Cox Richardson were also generous with their time and editorial assistance. Their incisive critiques of the manuscript have saved me from many missteps. Special thanks are also due to Michael Green, who lent me valuable notes and shared with me his own work in progress on the Republican party during the Civil War. Many historians have offered valuable comments on parts of the book or on papers derived from it. These include Guyora Binder, David W. Blight, Frederick J. Blue, Paul Finkelman, Sally Hadden, Laura Kalman, David E. Kyvig, Michael A. Morrison, Donald G.

xiii

Nieman, James D. Schmidt, Robert J. Steinfeld, Lea S. VanderVelde, Wang Xi, and the members of the SUNY-Buffalo history department. I also appreciate the helpful comments of Richard Newman, Randall Burkett, and other members of the W. E. B. Du Bois Institute, where I enjoyed a year as a postdoctoral fellow. Thomas Cox, Anna Galland, and Carmen Washington provided valuable research assistance. Before the research began, James M. McPherson, Harold M. Hyman, and Herman Belz offered early encouragement and advice. Other historians played a crucial role, even if they did not always realize they were doing so. A telephone conversation with LaWanda Cox helped me through a particularly bleak period in the work. Bernard Bailyn was not directly involved in the making of this book, but without his guidance and inspiration during my first years in graduate school, I would never have begun a book, much less completed one. Sam Bass Warner, an old family friend, welcomed me into the profession with his typical good humor and generosity. Thomas A. Underwood has been a steady role model in ways that extend well beyond the sphere of scholarship.

Three historians deserve special recognition. David Herbert Donald helped transform a confused and ignorant first-year graduate student into a would-be Civil War scholar. By employing me as a research assistant for his biography of Abraham Lincoln, Professor Donald gave me the opportunity to see firsthand how much fresh work still could be done on Civil War subjects. I continue to be inspired by his scholarship and his empathy for his subjects and students alike. I was lucky that Harvard University hired Professor William E. Gienapp just as I began work on my doctoral dissertation. Always patient and helpful, he listened kindly but never uncritically to my ideas and strategies. Working in conjunction with the staff of the Harvard library, he arranged the purchase of many research materials essential to the dissertation. As my dissertation director, he repaired much faulty logic and muddled writing. Michael Les Benedict deserves more credit than I can possibly give. He offered encouragement early on and then valuable advice once the project was underway. He also gave the manuscript its most thorough reading, saving me from numerous errors and forcing me to sharpen my thinking in many places. Many flaws remain, I am sure, and I take full responsibility for them all.

Without the help and hospitality of many friends and family members, the completion of this book would have been a joyless task. Peter Rosenthal lent much support throughout – support here defined as merciless ridicule and ceaseless torment, with an occasional helping of ribs. Other friends and family members took a more active role by offering me a place to stay as well as good company while I was on the research road. These include Eliza Vorenberg and Barnaby Jackson, Joseph Brenner, Eliot

Codner, Paul Vittimberga, Melinda and John Byrd, Susan Huhta, Elizabeth and John Neiva, Ira Wool and Barbara Mirecki, and Ann and Robert Jones.

My immediate family has been my steadiest source of support and diversion. My mother has offered unflagging and unconditional assistance throughout. My father, a historian at heart, helped me with the bibliography and was surely the book's biggest fan. I only wish he had lived to see it in print. Throughout my life, my brothers Dan and Tom have reminded me of the need to broaden my perspective while being careful not to take things too seriously. They have been my greatest advocates, my tireless protectors, and, of course, my best teachers. I have much to learn from them still.

My wife Katie and my daughter Emma deserve the final word. Katie has suffered my anxieties and time demands with endless patience. I cannot and need not list all that she has done. We both know the leading role she has played in helping me to complete this book while making sure I had some fun along the way. Emma, now three years old, thinks my time spent with this project instead of with her has been time wasted. In this, as in all things, I defer to her judgment, and so bid farewell to the book.

Abbreviations

BC	Special Collections, Bowdoin College, Brunswick, Maine
CG	*Congressional Globe*
CHS	Chicago Historical Society
CiHS	Cincinnati Historical Society
ColU	Butler Library, Columbia University, New York City
CW	Roy P. Basler, ed., Marion Dolores Pratt and Lloyd A. Dunlap, asst. eds. *The Collected Works of Abraham Lincoln.* 9 vols. New Brunswick, N.J.: Rutgers University Press, 1953–55
EM	Eleutherian Mills Historical Library, Wilmington, Delaware
HEH	Henry E. Huntington Library, San Marino, California
HL	Houghton Library, Harvard University, Cambridge, Massachusetts
HSD	Historical Society of Delaware, Wilmington
HSMd	Historical Society of Maryland, Baltimore
HSPa	Historical Society of Pennsylvania, Philadelphia
IHS	Indiana Historical Society, Indianapolis
ISHL	Illinois State Historical Library, Springfield
ISL	Indiana State Library, Indianapolis
LC	Manuscripts Division, Library of Congress, Washington, D.C.
MaA	Massachusetts State Archives, Boston
MdA	Maryland State Archives, Hall of Records, Annapolis
MHS	Massachusetts Historical Society, Boston
MSS	Manuscripts
NA	National Archives, Washington, D.C.
NJH	New Jersey Historical Society, Newark
NYH	New York Historical Society, New York City
NYP	New York Public Library, New York City
NYS	New York State Library, Albany
OHS	Ohio Historical Society, Columbus
RG	Record Group
RTL	Robert Todd Lincoln Collection, Manuscript Division, Library of Congress, Washington, D.C.

UR   Rush Rhees Library, University of Rochester, Rochester, New York

WRH   Western Reserve Historical Society, Cleveland, Ohio

Introduction

By itself, the Emancipation Proclamation did not free a single slave. That fact, well known by generations of historians, does not demean the proclamation. The proclamation was surely the most powerful instrument of slavery's destruction, for, more than any other measure, it defined the Civil War as a war for black freedom. Most Americans today would name the proclamation as the most important result of the war. Had the original document not been destroyed by fire in 1871, it would no doubt reside alongside the Declaration of Independence and the Constitution as one of our national treasures. Even those who contend that slaves did more than white commanders and politicians to abolish slavery tend to see the proclamation as the brightest achievement of slaves' efforts on behalf of their own freedom.

But the fact remains: the Emancipation Proclamation did not free a single slave. And that fact hung over the country during the last years of the Civil War. Many Americans during this period would have considered today's veneration of the proclamation misplaced. They knew that the proclamation freed slaves in only some areas – those regions not under Union control – leaving open the possibility that it might never apply to the whole country. They knew that even this limited proclamation might not survive the war: It might be ruled unconstitutional by the courts, outlawed by Congress, retracted by Lincoln or his successor, or simply ignored if the Confederacy won the war. Americans understood that the proclamation was but an early step in putting black freedom on secure legal footing. Abolition was assured only by Union military victory and by the Thirteenth Amendment, which outlawed slavery and involuntary servitude throughout the country. Congress passed the amendment more than two years after the proclamation, and the states ratified it in December 1865, eight months after Union victory in the Civil War.

Historians have written much about the fate of African Americans after the Emancipation Proclamation, but they have not been so attentive to the process by which emancipation was written into law. In part, the inattention is a natural consequence of the compartmentalization of history. Because emancipation proved to be but one stage in the process by which enslaved African Americans became legal citizens, historians have been prone to move directly from the Emancipation Proclamation to the issue of legalized racial equality. In other words, historians have skipped

quickly from the proclamation to the Fourteenth Amendment, ratified in
1868, which granted "due process of law" and "equal protection of the
laws" to every American. Within this seamless narrative, the Thirteenth
Amendment appears merely as a predictable epilogue to the Emancipation
Proclamation or as an obligatory prologue to the Fourteenth Amendment.

The course of events leading from the Emancipation Proclamation to
the Thirteenth Amendment was anything but predictable. After Lincoln
issued the proclamation, lawmakers, politicians, and ordinary Americans
considered a variety of plans for making emancipation permanent and
constitutional. The abolition amendment was simply one of many
methods considered and, in the early going, was by no means the leading
choice. Only during the course of political struggles in late 1863 and early
1864 did the amendment emerge as the most popular of the abolition
alternatives. By mid-1864, the amendment had become a leading policy of
the Republican party, which wrote the measure into its national platform.
As an avowed Republican policy, the amendment should have dominated
the political campaign of 1864, but unforeseen circumstances and changing party strategies drove the measure from public debate. Nevertheless,
supporters of the amendment claimed the Republican victories of 1864 as
a mandate for the amendment, and they successfully carried the amendment through Congress in January 1865. A number of states quickly
ratified the measure, and ratification was complete by the end of that year.

The sequence of events is crucial: the amendment became a party policy
before its merit or meaning was precisely understood. For those historians
seeking to recover one original meaning of the Thirteenth Amendment,
the premature transformation of the measure into a party policy represents a real problem. As a party policy, the amendment attracted support
from people with similar political objectives but different notions of freedom. Because of the diverse constituencies behind the amendment, some
of its supporters allowed the meaning of the measure to remain vague. If
they had instead assigned a precise meaning to the amendment, they
would have alienated some of those constituencies and jeopardized the
measure's adoption.[1]

This book is not a brief for or against one specific reading of the
Thirteenth Amendment. Instead, it is an attempt to place the amendment
in its proper historical context by recreating the climate in which the
measure was drafted, debated, and adopted. To understand this climate, I
have read through congressional and state legislative proceedings but have

1   William E. Nelson and others have noted a similar problem confounding efforts to
    determine the original meaning of the Fourteenth Amendment. See Nelson, *The Four-
    teenth Amendment: From Political Principle to Judicial Doctrine* (Cambridge, Mass.:
    Harvard University Press, 1988), 1–12.

also cast my eye far beyond these deliberative bodies. Because legislative activity was simply one part, albeit the most visible part, of a social and political process of law making, I also have read more than twenty Union newspapers published during the Civil War years, dozens of pamphlets and published diaries, and the manuscripts contained in almost three hundred collections in more than thirty archives across the country. Drawing together such disparate pieces as a local abolitionist society's petition, an African American newspaper editorial, or a private letter between two legal scholars, I have tried to give as much texture as possible to the story of the amendment's creation.

To understand the making of the amendment is to understand the fluid interaction between politics, law, and society in the Civil War era. The amendment was not originally part of a carefully orchestrated political strategy; nor was it a natural product of prevailing legal principles; nor was it a direct expression of popular thought. Political tactics, legal thought, and popular ideology were always intertwined, and, at every moment, unanticipated events interceded and led to unexpected consequences. The Thirteenth Amendment was, above all, a product of historical contingency. Americans glimmered the revolutionary potential of the amendment only after the measure emerged as an expedient solution to the problem of making emancipation constitutional. The "true" meaning of the amendment was thus destined to be controversial. Even today, historians and legal scholars struggle over the measure's original meaning, usually in order to understand its relevance to the present. Did it simply prohibit America's peculiar form of racialized chattel slavery, or did it promise in addition a full measure of freedom to all Americans? Was it the brainchild of conservative politicians, progressive abolitionists, or the slaves themselves?

Those who enter this book looking for simple answers to these questions will leave frustrated. I offer no single, original meaning of the amendment. Nor do I provide a single, clear answer to the increasingly stale question, Who freed the slaves? Histories that seek mainly to identify the primary agents of emancipation tend to emphasize divisions among those who strove for black freedom rather than acknowledging some of the common goals. The story of the Thirteenth Amendment is one of cooperation as well as discord, of achievements by one person as well as concerted efforts among many. The search for any measure's origins is always a perilous venture, and it is especially so in the case of the Thirteenth Amendment. The amendment was not the product of any one person or process, and its meaning was contested and transformed from the moment of its appearance. Thus there is a paradox in this book's title: despite the amendment's promise to make freedom final, Americans were left to work out the origins and meanings of freedom long after the measure was adopted.[2]

Rather than thinking of the amendment as a well-planned measure with an agreed-upon purpose, it is best to see it as a by-product of, and a catalyst for, three distinct but related developments. The first was Americans' ongoing confrontation with the realities of emancipation. Struggles to attain and define freedom began with the period of European settlement of North America and continue today, but, as Eric Foner and other historians have demonstrated, they were most fierce during the Civil War and Reconstruction. Prior to the Civil War, Americans agreed upon only two facts about freedom: slaves were not free, and free people were not slaves. Once the Civil War began, Americans facing the prospect of constitutional abolition had to rethink emancipation. If the Constitution came to outlaw slavery, would it make everyone equally free? The struggle over the Thirteenth Amendment thus enlarged and enlivened the debate over freedom.[3]

The Thirteenth Amendment played a critical role in a second development: political transformation. One of the most remarkable phenomena in the Union during the last years of the Civil War was the fluidity of party politics. Prior to the Civil War, Republicans were primarily known as a northern party that abhorred slavery – or at least slavery's extension into the territories. During the last years of the Civil War, however, the prospect of reunion under the antislavery amendment forced Republicans to reconsider their objectives. Would the party now explicitly demand equal

2 For the search for original intent, especially the original intent of the Civil War amendments, see Herman Belz, *Abraham Lincoln, Constitutionalism, and Equal Rights in the Civil War Era* (New York: Fordham University Press, 1998), 170–86, which contains references to other important works on the subject. Also see Belz, "The Civil War Amendments to the Constitution: The Relevance of Original Intent," *Constitutional Commentary*, 5 (Winter 1988), 115–41. For debates over agency in emancipation, see Ira Berlin, "Who Freed the Slaves? Emancipation and Its Meaning," in David W. Blight and Brooks D. Simpson, eds., *Union and Emancipation: Essays on Politics and Race in the Civil War Era* (Kent, Ohio: Kent State University Press, 1997), 105–21; and James M. McPherson, "Who Freed the Slaves?" *Reconstruction*, 2 (1994), 35–40. Despite the opposing thrusts of these essays, both authors are aware of the pitfalls of focusing on one person or group to the exclusion of all others. Lerone Bennett, *Forced into Glory: Abraham Lincoln's White Dream* (Chicago: Johnson, 1999), a powerful attack on the myth of Lincoln as "Great Emancipator," is the latest work to weigh in on the question of agency. Because Bennett's book was published when my own book was already in production, I was unable to attend to its argument and evidence in the pages that follow. The omission is not grave: like most works on Civil War emancipation, Bennett's book is focused almost entirely on the coming of the Emancipation Proclamation, whereas mine examines the fate of emancipation after the proclamation.

3 The best, most succinct discussion of emancipation, with citations to the literature on the subject, is Eric Foner, "The Meaning of Freedom in the Age of Emancipation," *Journal of American History*, 81 (September 1994), 435–60.

rights as well as freedom for African Americans? Would it try to make inroads into the South? Meanwhile, northern Democrats began to divide over their party's traditional stance against emancipation. While conservative Democrats deployed increasingly vicious attacks against Republican antislavery initiatives, more moderate Democrats tried to take the party in a new direction by embracing emancipation – at least emancipation in the form of a constitutional amendment. For some observers and political insiders, the appearance of a new coalition behind the amendment portended the creation of a new party system. Recent examinations of Civil War–era politics slight the fluidity in party politics during the period, either by looking at only one party in isolation or by treating the Republicans and Democrats as two well-defined entities constantly locked in battle. The real nature of politics during the period, the unpredictability and occasional incoherence, is better revealed by studying the complexity both within and between parties on one issue – in this case, slavery – over a brief period time. If one premise of the book is that politics can be understood only by examining all the parties at once, another is that political history must include as wide a population as possible. I follow the lead of recent scholars of political history who look to actors beyond candidates and voters and actions beyond campaigns and elections. But I also believe that political institutions such as Congress and the parties have an internal life of their own that can profoundly affect those at the peripheries of the political universe. To be as inclusive as possible, this book tries to attend to a broad population of political actors and ideas as well as to the inner workings of the institutions of power. It moves between the contemplations of the nonelite and the deliberations of the congressional committee and party caucus.[4]

The making of the Thirteenth Amendment was part of a third pivotal

---

4 The goals articulated here echo many of those described in Michael F. Holt, "An Elusive Synthesis: Northern Politics during the Civil War," in James M. McPherson and William J. Cooper, Jr., eds., *Writing the Civil War: The Quest to Understand* (Columbia: University of South Carolina Press, 1998), 112–34, esp. 133–34. My conception of politics has been enriched by recent scholars who have expanded the scope of political history along two different axes. The first expansion, which involves treating nonelites, including nonvoters, as crucial players in politics, is described in Jean Harvey Baker, "Politics, Paradigms, and Public Culture," *Journal of American History*, 84 (December 1997), 894–99. The second expansion, which involves treating institutional evolution as crucial to democratic development, is discussed with references to relevant works in Richard R. John, "Governmental Institutions as Agents of Change: Rethinking American Political Development in the Early Republic," *Studies in American Political Development*, 11 (Fall 1997), 347–80. On the specific issue of political fluidity during the last years of the Civil War and the first years afterward, see Michael Les Benedict, *A Compromise of Principle: Congressional Republicans and Reconstruction, 1863–1869* (New York: W. W. Norton, 1974); and LaWanda Cox and John H. Cox, *Politics, Principle, and Prejudice, 1865–1866: Dilemma of Reconstruction America* (New York: Free Press, 1963).

development: Americans' reconceptualization of their Constitution. More than any measure since the Bill of Rights, the Thirteenth Amendment allowed Americans to conceive of the Constitution as a document that could be altered without being sacrificed. In the fifty years leading up to the Civil War, Americans had come to regard the constitutional text as sacred. They rarely contemplated constitutional amendments, opting instead to alter constitutional doctrine through judicial and legislative interpretation. On the issue of slavery in particular, Americans had resisted tampering with constitutional provisions drafted by the founding generation. The Thirteenth Amendment took the nation in a different direction. It signaled that the venerated constitutional text needed revising, forcing Americans to confront the profound implications of rewriting the original Constitution. Historians have often looked to the Gettysburg Address as the document that "remade" the Constitution, but it was the Thirteenth Amendment, not Lincoln's address, that Americans of the Civil War era saw as the transforming act. Yet, although the Thirteenth Amendment represented a turn against the nation's fathers, it was no act of patricide. By altering the Constitution without eviscerating it, Americans could remain firm in the belief that they were building on the founders' structure rather than tearing it down. The movement toward an amendment did not signal a clear, fundamental shift in constitutional ideology. Rather, the shift was subtle, and its full effects would be realized only slowly. Amending the Constitution was nothing new in American history, but amending it to achieve a major social reform was. Unexpectedly, then, the discussion of the amendment opened up an even broader debate about the nature of amendment and the fundamentality of the Constitution. Through this dialogue, Americans rediscovered the amending device as a cure for constitutional paralysis. The amendment helped redirect Americans' attention to the concept of a living Constitution and set the stage for the drama of constitutional revision during the next seven decades.[5]

5   On constitutional development during the Civil War, see Phillip S. Paludan, *A Covenant with Death: The Constitution, Law, and Equality in the Civil War Era* (Urbana: University of Illinois Press, 1975); Harold M. Hyman, *A More Perfect Union: The Impact of the Civil War and Reconstruction on the Constitution* (New York: Alfred A. Knopf, 1973). On the Gettysburg Address, especially the role that the address played in incorporating into the Constitution the doctrine of the Declaration of Independence that "all men are created equal," see Garry Wills, *Lincoln at Gettysburg: The Words That Remade America* (New York: Simon and Schuster, 1992), and Pauline Maier, *American Scripture: Making the Declaration of Independence* (New York: Alfred A. Knopf, 1997), 154–208. On the patricide theme, see George B. Forgie, *Patricide in the House Divided: A Psychological Interpretation of Lincoln and His Age* (New York: W. W. Norton, 1979). On the constitutional amending process in American history, see David E. Kyvig, *Explicit and Authentic Acts: Amending the U.S. Constitution, 1776–1995* (Lawrence: University Press of Kansas, 1996), esp. 154–87, which offers the most balanced treatment of the

The use of a constitutional amendment to abolish slavery was a distinguishing feature of emancipation in the United States. In other areas of the Western Hemisphere during the nineteenth century, abolition was accomplished by statute, edict, or judicial action. The peculiar form that abolition legislation took in the United States may not be as important as the extraordinary process by which slaves actually became free citizens, but the distinctiveness of this method nonetheless deserves attention. That Americans chose to graft abolition onto their most cherished legal document showed a desire not merely to eradicate slavery but to make a break with the past. Historians may continue to debate the extent to which slavery caused the Civil War, but one fact remains certain: it was slavery, more than anything else, that forced Americans to confront the imperfection of their Constitution. It was slavery, too, that gave rise to the modern notion of the amending power. Once they had amended the Constitution to abolish slavery, Americans felt more comfortable endorsing other amendments that could not have been adopted during the time of the framers. Reformers were more likely to accept the Constitution as an aid rather than an impediment to change, and they increasingly cast their proposals in the form of constitutional amendments. It is no small irony that slavery, the most antidemocratic institution sustained by the Constitution, unleashed one of the greatest democratizing forces to transform the Constitution.

significance of the Civil War amendments in reshaping Americans' attitudes toward amendments in general. Bruce Ackerman argues more forcefully than Kyvig for the significance of these amendments as moments of constitutional change; see Ackerman, *We the People,* vol. 2, *Transformations* (Cambridge, Mass.: Harvard University Press, 1998), 99–252. For an interpretation somewhat different from my own, one that views the Thirteenth Amendment merely as a "completion" of the Constitution, see Michael P. Zuckert, "Completing the Constitution: The Thirteenth Amendment," *Constitutional Commentary,* 4 (Summer 1987), 259–84. For the literature on the "living Constitution," see Howard Gillman, "The Collapse of Constitutional Originalism and the Rise of the Notion of the 'Living Constitution' in the Course of American State-Building," *Studies in American Political Development,* 11 (Fall 1997), 191–247.

1

Slavery's Constitution

On July 4, 1854, the abolitionist William Lloyd Garrison observed Independence Day by burning a copy of the United States Constitution. He was disgusted that the Constitution not only permitted the continued enslavement of 4 million African Americans but also required federal officials to return fugitive slaves to their masters. The gesture earned Garrison both praise and scorn, as did his declaration that the founding document was a "covenant with death" and "an agreement with hell."[1] Today, in an era when burners of the American flag are routinely hauled before the courts, Garrison's destruction of another national icon seems radical in the extreme. The act seems even more poignant when contrasted with today's constitutional politics. When reformers today run into the roadblocks of constitutional provisions, congressional legislation, or judicial decisions, they are much more likely to demand a constitutional amendment than the abandonment of the entire Constitution. Garrison and other abolitionists, however, failed to embrace the amendment alternative.

Ultimately, of course, opponents of slavery did come to regard a constitutional amendment as the best method of ending slavery, but they did so only after the conflict over slavery had erupted into a shooting war. When Congress finally adopted the antislavery amendment in January 1865, Garrison announced that the Constitution, formerly "a covenant with death," was now "a covenant with life."[2] Garrison's praise suggested that the amendment had always been the abolitionists' goal, but, in fact, the measure appeared rather late on the antislavery agenda. Contrary to what abolitionists said after the amendment was adopted, and what historians have accepted ever since, the amendment was never the expected outcome of the conflict over slavery.

Nevertheless, in the years leading up to the Civil War, and in the first years of the war itself, Americans laid the groundwork for an abolition amendment, even if that particular measure had been little contemplated by either the early opponents or champions of slavery. Only the ante-

---

1 Phillip S. Paludan, *A Covenant with Death: The Constitution, Law, and Equality in the Civil War Era* (Urbana: University of Illinois Press, 1975), 1–3.
2 *Liberator,* February 10, 1865, p. 2.

bellum failure to resolve slavery disputes under the existing Constitution, followed by the wartime struggle to set the Union on new constitutional foundations, made it possible at last for Americans to contemplate an antislavery amendment.

The Constitution, Slavery, and the Coming of the Civil War

Americans of the nineteenth century, though often frustrated by the ambiguities of the Constitution, usually accepted the document's vagaries as the price of Union. "Nothing has made me admire the good sense and practical intelligence of the Americans," wrote the French social theorist Alexis de Tocqueville in 1835, "more than the way they avoid the innumerable difficulties deriving from their federal Constitution."[3] In a sense, the Civil War erupted because the American people refused any longer to overlook their competing conceptions of their founding charter.

The most difficult of the "innumerable difficulties" noted by de Tocqueville was the Constitution's ambiguity on slavery. The word "slavery" did not appear in the Constitution of 1787 – the framers opted for the less offensive expression "person held to service or labor" – but the institution nonetheless permeated the document. In five places slavery was directly indicated, and in as many as ten others it was implied.[4] Most important among the explicit concessions to slavery were the three-fifths clause, which counted each slave as three-fifths of a person for the purpose of representation in the House of Representatives; the fugitive slave provision, which decreed that escaped slaves had to be "delivered up" to their original state; and the perpetuation of the African slave trade to at least 1808. Of the implicit concessions to slavery, the most important was the absence of any mention of congressional authority over slavery in the enumeration of congressional powers. Because Congress was given only enumerated rather than plenary powers, and because it was not explicitly granted the power of emancipation, most Americans came to believe that Congress could not abolish slavery in the states. In the years after the Constitution was ratified, Americans generally regarded the document's protection of slavery as part of a necessary compromise. Yet there was no single compromise over slavery, no identifiable bargain in which northerners "sold out" the slaves to southern whites. Rather, there

---

3 Alexis de Tocqueville, *Democracy in America*, ed. J. P. Mayer (Garden City, N.Y.: Anchor Books, 1969), 165.
4 Paul Finkelman, "Slavery and the Constitutional Convention: Making a Covenant with Death," in Richard Beeman, Stephen Botein, and Edward C. Carter II, eds., *Beyond Confederation: Origins of the Constitution and American National Identity* (Chapel Hill: University of North Carolina Press, 1987), 188–225.

was a series of agreements, which, in the words of historian Don E. Fehrenbacher, formed a pattern "acknowledging the legitimate presence of slavery in American life while attaching a cluster of limitations to the acknowledgment."[5]

More than simply an exercise in coalition building, the framers' acceptance of slavery was, in part, a product of their vision of a Constitution open to improvement. The essence of that vision appeared in Article 5, which outlined the procedures for amending the Constitution. The amending provision was hardly revolutionary, for it had deep roots in Anglo-American legal tradition, and it prevented the Constitution from being whimsically rewritten.[6] The country could change its charter through two different methods. In the first, two-thirds of both houses of Congress approved the amendment, and then three-fourths of the states ratified it. In the second method, which has never been successful, two-thirds of the states petitioned Congress to call a national convention, and three-fourths of the states ratified any amendments proposed by the convention. No matter which method was used to amend the Constitution, Article 5 prohibited any amendment from depriving a state of its equal suffrage in the Senate.

At first, the new nation embraced the founders' notion of an adjustable Constitution. In the fifteen years after the Constitution's ratification in 1789, Congress proposed and the states ratified twelve amendments. The first ten, the Bill of Rights, James Madison pushed through Congress himself as concessions to the Antifederalists. These amendments, at least in Madison's view, made explicit those rights that the original Constitution had only implied. Both the eleventh and twelfth amendments rectified oversights by the framers of the original Constitution. The Eleventh Amendment made it clear that suits against individual states by private or foreign citizens would take place in state rather than federal courts, a matter that the Constitution and Judiciary Act of 1789 had failed to resolve. The Twelfth Amendment, adopted in the wake of a deadlocked presidential election between two candidates of the same party, adjusted

5 Don E. Fehrenbacher, *The Dred Scott Case: Its Significance in American Law and Politics* (New York: Oxford University Press, 1978), 27. See Earl M. Maltz, "The Idea of the Proslavery Constitution," *Journal of the Early Republic,* 17 (Spring 1997), 37–59; and Peter Knupfer, *The Union As It Is: Constitutional Unionism and Sectional Compromise, 1787–1861* (Chapel Hill: University of North Carolina Press, 1991), 45–47.
6 David E. Kyvig, *Explicit and Authentic Acts: Amending the U.S. Constitution, 1776–1995* (Lawrence: University Press of Kansas, 1996), 19–65; Richard B. Bernstein with Jerome Agel, *Amending America: If We Love the Constitution So Much, Why Do We Keep Trying to Change It?* (New York: Times Books, 1993), 3–30; John R. Vile, *The Constitutional Amending Process in American Political Thought* (Westport, Conn.: Praeger, 1992), 1–46.

the electoral system to conform to the unanticipated development of a two-party system. Although lawmakers argued over the form of these first twelve amendments, they generally saw the amendments as supplementing or clarifying the Constitution rather than revising it.[7] The difference between a supplement, which made explicit something implicit or remedied something unforeseen, and a revision, which seemed to challenge original doctrine, might seem trivial, but it was precisely this difference that would trigger a furious debate over the Thirteenth Amendment.

After the adoption of the first twelve amendments, constitutional doctrine evolved solely through judicial decisions, not constitutional amendments. In fact, the amending process generally fell into disuse. Between 1810 and 1860, congressmen proposed fewer constitutional amendments than had been proposed during the much shorter span between 1789 and 1810. And in the later period, no amendment was adopted by the nation or even approved by Congress.[8]

The atrophying of the amendment process during the antebellum era is remarkable considering how often during this period abolitionists spoke of the inadequacy of the proslavery Constitution. Prior to 1808, the year that Congress outlawed the African slave trade by statute, abolitionists in and out of Congress only occasionally proposed antislavery amendments, and after that date they almost never did. Those who aimed to outlaw slavery tended instead to target the legal system of individual states. That strategy had been successful in the northern states during the late 1700s and early 1800s, though in most of these states emancipation was gradual and slavery lingered on well into the nineteenth century. Meanwhile, in the southern states during the antebellum period, slavery became increasingly entrenched, and those rare moments when a statewide initiative for emancipation took hold passed quickly. By the 1830s most abolitionists had given up on state-level legislation in the South and opted instead to try to shame slaveholders into emancipating their own slaves. At the same time, they appealed to the federal government to abolish slavery in one of the few areas where it had exclusive jurisdiction: Washington, D.C. Rare was the abolitionist who proposed abolishing slavery everywhere by constitutional amendment.[9]

7 Kyvig, *Explicit and Authentic Acts*, 87–116. In a technical sense, the Twelfth Amendment was a genuine revision, rather than a mere supplement, because it changed explicit electoral procedures outlined in the original Constitution. But because these procedures had proved to be wholly impractical, people did not object to the Twelfth Amendment because it challenged "original" doctrine.

8 See Herman Ames, *The Proposed Amendments to the Constitution of the United States during the First Century of its History* (1896; repr., New York: Burt Franklin, 1970), 306–55.

9 Most of the proposed amendments attempted to abolish slave importation. One pro-

An important exception was John Quincy Adams. In 1839 the Massachusetts congressman and former president proposed amendments that prohibited slavery in the District of Columbia, banned the admission of more slave states, and abolished all hereditary slavery after 1842. The House of Representatives, which had imposed a gag rule on all antislavery petitions, refused to consider the amendments. Adams, who had been fighting the gag rule for years, knew that his proposals would never be debated, much less adopted. His hope had been to use the amendment method to keep the slavery issue before Congress and to push abolitionists to demand the emancipation of slaves everywhere, not merely in Washington, D.C. After Adams's failed effort, no one in Congress proposed an antislavery amendment until the outbreak of the Civil War; even outside of Congress, abolitionists rarely considered the amending strategy.[10]

The idea of writing emancipation into the Constitution did not fit well into most abolitionists' thinking about the Constitution. Antislavery activists tended to take one of three approaches to the Constitution, none of which led naturally to an abolition amendment. The first approach, which the historian William M. Wiecek labels "radical constitutionalism," assumed that the Constitution was a purely antislavery document that, from its inception, empowered the federal government to abolish slavery everywhere.[11] Radical constitutionalists believed that the framers' genuine attitude toward slavery was expressed in the Declaration of Independence, which declared that "all men are created equal," and in the Fifth Amendment, which prohibited the deprivation "of life, liberty, or property, without due process of law." Also demonstrating the founders' antislavery leanings was the Northwest Ordinance of 1787, an early version of which

posed amendment in 1818 prohibited slavery everywhere. See ibid., 193, 208–9. On abolitionism in general, see Paul Goodman, *Of One Blood: Abolitionism and the Origins of Racial Equality* (Berkeley: University of California Press, 1998); Aileen Kraditor, *Means and Ends in American Abolitionism: Garrison and His Critics on Strategy and Tactics, 1834–1850* (New York: Pantheon Books, 1969). On emancipation in the North, see Joanne Pope Melish, *Disowning Slavery: Gradual Emancipation and "Race" in New England, 1780–1860* (Ithaca: Cornell University Press, 1998); Arthur Zilversmit, *The First Emancipation: The Abolition of Slavery in the North* (Chicago: University of Chicago Press, 1967).

10 Kyvig, *Explicit and Authentic Acts*, 144; William Lee Miller, *Arguing about Slavery: The Great Battle in the United States Congress* (New York: Alfred A. Knopf, 1996), 353–54; and William W. Freehling, *The Road to Disunion: Secessionists at Bay, 1776–1854* (New York: Oxford University Press, 1990), 343–44. David L. Child and Henry B. Stanton were two of the exceptional abolitionists who proposed antislavery amendments; each hoped to use this method to build popular support for the antislavery cause. David L. Child, *The Despotism of Freedom* (Boston: Young Men's Anti-Slavery Association, 1833), 25; and William M. Wiecek, *The Sources of Antislavery Constitutionalism in America, 1760–1848* (Ithaca: Cornell University Press, 1977), 256.

11 Wiecek, *Sources of Antislavery Constitutionalism*, 259–63.

had been drafted by Thomas Jefferson. Radical constitutionalists looked to the ordinance's ban on slavery in the Northwest as proof that the framers envisioned a nation free of slavery (though they chose to ignore the fact that the ordinance was only infrequently enforced).[12] Radical constitutionalists rarely argued for an antislavery amendment. For them, such a measure would be, at best, redundant and, at worst, an admission that the original, unamended Constitution was proslavery – precisely the interpretation that they disputed.[13]

The second abolitionist reading of the Constitution, a reading made popular by William Lloyd Garrison and his allies, regarded the Constitution as thoroughly proslavery. Garrison himself had arrived at his position slowly. In the early 1830s, he contemplated constitutional solutions to slavery, even an antislavery amendment.[14] But during the latter part of the decade, antiabolitionist violence and legislative inaction on slavery turned Garrison against the Constitution and in favor of a sectional break with slave owners. After 1841 he never seriously contemplated revision of the Constitution, although Wendell Phillips, Garrison's main ally, seemed to lean in this direction when, in an 1847 pamphlet attacking the radical constitutionalist position, he wrote, "the Constitution will never be amended by persuading men that it does not need amendment."[15] But Phillips never suggested an antislavery amendment, not even as a long-term goal. He wanted an immediate break with slavery, and because no amendment could be adopted in the short term, the only path was "over the Constitution, trampling it under foot; not under it, trying to evade its fair meaning."[16] Many African American abolitionists joined Garrison in the proslavery reading of the Constitution, but just as many, perhaps even more, took the radical constitutionalist position that the Constitution *as it was* authorized abolition as well as equal rights for African Americans.[17]

12 Paul Finkelman, *Slavery and the Founders: Race and Liberty in the Age of Jefferson* (Armonk, N.Y.: M. E. Sharpe, 1996), 34–79; Peter S. Onuf, *Statehood and Union: A History of the Northwest Ordinance* (Bloomington: Indiana University Press, 1987).

13 See, for example, Amos A. Phelps, *Lectures on Slavery and its Remedy* (Boston: New-England Anti-Slavery Society, 1834), 192–96.

14 Garrison to Thomas Shipley, December 17, 1835, in Walter M. Merrill and Louis Ruchames, eds., *The Letters of William Lloyd Garrison*, vol. 1, *I Will Be Heard!, 1822–1835* (Cambridge, Mass.: Harvard University Press, 1971), 584.

15 Wendell Phillips, *Review of Lysander Spooner's Essay on the Unconstitutionality of Slavery* (Boston: Andrews and Prentiss, 1847), 4.

16 Ibid. 35. See Louis S. Gerteis, *Morality and Utility in American Antislavery Reform* (Chapel Hill: University of North Carolina Press, 1987), 48–51.

17 See the 1857 debate between Frederick Douglass and Charles Lenox Remond in John W. Blassingame et al., eds., *The Frederick Douglass Papers* (New Haven: Yale University Press, 1985), ser. 1, 3:151–62 (Remond argued that the Constitution was proslavery, while Douglass argued that it was antislavery, a position that he had newly adopted in the early 1850s). Also see Vincent Gordon Harding, "Wrestling toward the Dawn:

Alongside the radical constitutionalist and Garrisonian readings of the Constitution was the more moderate free-soil reading, which was made popular by Salmon P. Chase, an Ohio lawyer who had gained fame by defending fugitive slaves. Originally a Whig sympathizer, Chase joined the antislavery Liberty party in the early 1840s and then helped create the Independent Democrats (or "Free Democracy," as he called it), a coalition of Liberty men and free-soil Democrats that elected him to the Senate in 1848. Chase eventually joined the fledgling Republican party in the 1850s and helped shape that party's stance on slavery. The problem with slavery, explained Chase and other Republican leaders, was that it violated the free-labor ideal of workers exchanging their labor for appropriate wages.[18] Here Republicans followed the ideology not only of established abolitionists but of most Americans in the market-oriented society of the North. Where Republicans differed from prior antislavery activists was in their free-soil approach to the Constitution. Instead of seeing the Constitution as wholly proslavery or antislavery, Chase and the Republicans argued that the framers of the Constitution meant for slavery to be prohibited from the territories but protected in the states. The way to abolish slavery, then, was by federal legislation where slavery did not yet exist and state legislation where it already existed.[19]

Republicans, along with other antislavery activists, seemed unable even to contemplate another constitutional route to emancipation: a federal abolition amendment. Perhaps some Republicans feared that proposing such a measure would give the party too radical a reputation. Critics could charge that the Republicans, despite their promise not to touch slavery where it existed, meant to abolish it everywhere. Yet this explanation for the absence of an amendment works only for moderate and conservative Republicans. We should still find calls for the measure from those radical Republicans who were openly committed to prohibiting slavery everywhere. But no faction of the party seems to have discussed, much less proposed, an abolition amendment. Perhaps antislavery groups saw the

The Afro-American Freedom Movement and the Changing Constitution," *Journal of American History,* 74 (December 1987), 721–23.

18 John Ashworth, "Free Labor, Wage Labor, and the Slave Power: Republicanism and the Republican Party in the 1850s," in Melvyn Stokes and Stephen Conway, eds., *The Market Revolution: Social, Political, and Religious Expressions* (Charlottesville: University Press of Virginia, 1996), 202–23; Eric Foner, *Free Soil, Free Labor, Free Men: The Ideology of the Republican Party before the Civil War* (New York: Oxford University Press, 1970), 11–39.

19 Michael A. Morrison, *Slavery and the American West: The Eclipse of Manifest Destiny and the Coming of the Civil War* (Chapel Hill: University of North Carolina Press, 1997), esp. 58–59; John Niven, *Salmon P. Chase: A Biography* (New York: Oxford University Press, 1995), esp. 99–113; Foner, *Free Soil, Free Labor, Free Men,* 73–102; Wiecek, *Sources of Antislavery Constitutionalism,* 191–93, 216–20.

impossibility of securing the requisite number of congressional votes and state ratifications to adopt the amendment. The unlikelihood of the amendment's adoption hardly explains why almost no one proposed it, however. Abolitionists could have proposed an antislavery amendment simply to keep the subject of universal emancipation before the public. That had been the strategy of John Quincy Adams in 1839 when he offered his antislavery amendments. Abolitionists had not been deterred from proposing other antislavery solutions by the unlikelihood of their adoption (Garrison's radical call for secession from slaveholders was the most obvious example), so it seems doubtful that the difficulty of securing an abolition amendment alone explains the absence of such a proposed measure.

The deeper reason for the absence of antislavery amendments was the widespread belief among all Americans that the constitutional text should remain static. This belief stemmed, in part, from the symbolic role that the Constitution had played as the defining emblem of the nation. Few Americans could cite specific provisions of the Constitution, yet almost all assumed that its alteration would stain the national character and render life rudderless.[20] No one better reflected this attitude than Abraham Lincoln, who in his now-famous "Lyceum address" of 1838 identified the Constitution as a central tenet in the nation's "political religion."[21] As a congressman in 1848, Lincoln opposed a constitutional amendment providing for internal improvements. "New provisions," he argued, "would introduce new difficulties, and thus create, and increase appetite for still further change. No sir, let it [the Constitution] stand as it is."[22] During the political convulsions over slavery's extension into the territories in the mid-1850s, Lincoln told an audience: "Don't interfere with anything in the Constitution. That must be maintained, for it is the only safeguard of our liberties."[23] Historians have rightly contended that Lincoln saw the Constitution as evolving, that he maintained the old Whig belief that federal power under the Constitution should expand in order to develop the country's natural resources and to ensure people's natural rights. But it is important to remember that he did not see this evolution occurring through constitutional amendments. In Lincoln's view, the Constitution needed only to be interpreted along proper Whig, then Republican, lines; it did not need revision.

Even when the Supreme Court issued a decision contrary to Republican

---

20 Michael Kammen, *A Machine That Would Go of Itself: The Constitution in American Culture* (1986; repr., New York: Vintage Books, 1987), pt. 1, esp. 101–4.
21 *CW,* 1:112.
22 *CW,* 1:488.
23 *CW,* 2:366.

doctrine in the *Dred Scott* case of 1857, Lincoln and other party members
failed to propose a constitutional amendment as a corrective. In his majority decision, Chief Justice Roger B. Taney ruled that a slave residing temporarily in a free state or territory remained a slave and that any act
prohibiting slavery in the territories was unconstitutional. He also declared that African Americans could not be citizens of the United States.
Because of a persistent confusion in the country about the nature of
freedom and citizenship, Taney could claim that freedom was in itself no
guarantee of either state or national citizenship. Free blacks born in free
states, therefore, were not necessarily citizens – a remarkable claim, not
only because of the country's long-standing tradition of birthright citizenship, but because free blacks in a number of northern states had been
living as citizens of those states for many years.[24] Taney justified his
position by reading the clause of the Constitution declaring that "citizens
of each state shall be entitled to all the privileges and immunities of
citizens in the several states" as saying that citizens of one state were not
necessarily citizens of the nation, but citizens of the nation were citizens of
every state. Republicans preferred the contrary interpretation of the dissenting Justice Benjamin R. Curtis. Curtis equated state and national
citizenship even as he agreed with Taney that freedom alone was not a
guarantee of citizenship and that states had the power to deny state and
national citizenship as well as civil rights to its native-born residents.
Lincoln called Taney's ruling something less than "a settled doctrine" and
hoped for a time when the Court would overrule its own decision.[25]
Republicans in general joined Lincoln in blaming the *Dred Scott* decision
on a defective Court rather than a flawed Constitution. So committed
were Republicans to the Constitution's original text that they did not urge
the adoption of a constitutional amendment to override Taney's decision,
even though Taney himself thought that Republicans might take precisely
such a course.[26]

24 Paul Finkelman, "Rehearsal for Reconstruction: Antebellum Origins of the Fourteenth
    Amendment," in Eric Anderson and Alfred A. Moss, Jr., eds., *The Facts of Reconstruc-
    tion: Essays in Honor of John Hope Franklin* (Baton Rouge: Louisiana State University
    Press, 1991), 1–27; Robert J. Cottrol, "The Thirteenth Amendment and the North's
    Overlooked Egalitarian Heritage," *National Black Law Journal*, 11 (1989), 198–211;
    James H. Kettner, *The Development of American Citizenship, 1608–1870* (Chapel
    Hill: University of North Carolina Press, 1978), 287–333.
25 *CW*, 2:401.
26 That Taney considered the possibility of Republicans proposing an antislavery amend-
    ment is suggested by that part of his decision pointing out that "if any of its [the
    Constitution's] provisions are deemed unjust, there is a mode prescribed in the instru-
    ment itself by which it may be amended." "Dred Scott v. John F. A. Sandford," *United
    States Reports*, 19 (October 1857), 426. On the facts and resolution of the case, see
    Fehrenbacher, *The Dred Scott Case*.

Democrats were at least as devoted as Lincoln and the Republicans to preserving the text of the Constitution. Although Democrats during the antebellum era had been the leading proponents of constitutional change at the state level – a position that paralleled their preference for codification over judge-made law – their belief in the need for constitutional revision when governments abused their power rarely carried over to their view of the federal Constitution.[27] State constitutions never inspired the same awe, the same expectation of permanence, as the federal Constitution, and in no state was there a tradition of honoring the state constitution that compared with such traditions surrounding the federal Constitution. Democrats may have seen state constitutions as pliable, but the words that they used to describe the federal Constitution – "a rock," "a sheet-anchor," "the rubicon of our rights," and "the ark of safety" – connoted permanence.[28] Despite their significant ideological differences with Republicans, Democrats in the antebellum era shared with Republicans a belief in the sanctity of the Constitution's text. Regardless of their political persuasion, Americans prior to 1860 were likely to see any amendment to the Constitution as an admission that the American national experiment had failed.

The proposal of an antislavery amendment in particular was unlikely, for most Americans assumed that a compromise on slavery was essential to the maintenance of the Union. Indeed, the amending device was invoked during the antebellum era more frequently to preserve rather than to abolish slavery. The proslavery statesman John C. Calhoun in particular did more than any northern abolitionist to popularize the amendment method.[29] Because a supermajority of the states was needed to ratify an amendment, Calhoun reasoned, a similar consensus should be required to adopt a federal law that went against a state's interests. In the anonymously authored *Exposition and Protest* of 1828, Calhoun argued that a state convention could nullify a law such as a tariff or, implicitly, a restriction against slavery. Congress then had to rescind the law or resubmit it to the states in the form of a constitutional amendment. Calhoun's theory enjoyed a powerful legacy, and Americans were likely during the antebellum years to associate the amendment method with the protection of

---

27 Harold M. Hyman and William M. Wiecek, *Equal Justice under Law: Constitutional Development, 1835–1875* (New York: Harper and Row, 1982), 3–5; Michael F. Holt, *The Political Crisis of the 1850s* (1978; repr., New York: W. W. Norton, 1983), 106–9.

28 Jean H. Baker, *Affairs of Party: The Political Culture of Northern Democrats in the Mid-Nineteenth Century* (Ithaca: Cornell University Press, 1983), 153; Joel H. Silbey, *A Respectable Minority: The Democratic Party in the Civil War Era, 1860–1868* (New York: W. W. Norton, 1977), 70–79.

29 Kyvig, *Explicit and Authentic Acts*, 139–43; Vile, *The Constitutional Amending Process*, 79–93.

slavery and states' rights. Some of the most frequently proposed amendments during this period were those ensuring that slaveholding and non-slaveholding sections had an equal say in the election of the president. Calhoun himself suggested an amendment establishing a dual executive – one president from the North, and one from the South.[30] During the antebellum era, as antislavery northerners devised every method *except* a constitutional amendment to end slavery, proslavery southerners established the precedent of proposing amendments that preserved slavery forever.

The election of 1860 should have awakened more of slavery's opponents to the possibility of using an amendment to abolish slavery. The victory of Lincoln and the Republicans, followed soon after by the secession of the seven states of the deep South and the departure of most of the southerners from Congress, provided an ideal opportunity to push through an abolition amendment. A number of southerners predicted that this would be the Republican strategy in the months to come.[31] From the perspective of today, when proposals for constitutional amendments have become commonplace, we might assume that southern fears of an abolition amendment were well founded, especially since we know that such an amendment was adopted in 1865. But, in fact, Lincoln and his party did not begin to consider an abolition amendment until they had fought more than two years of war. Instead, the amendment that most Republicans contemplated in the wake of the 1860 victories was yet another proposal for preserving slavery forever.

The Secession Crisis: Amending the Constitution to Protect Slavery

The surge of proposed amendments during the secession crisis was staggering. Whereas only a handful of amendments concerning slavery was proposed in Congress between 1789 and December 1860, roughly 150 slavery amendments were proposed between December 1860 and March 1861, when Lincoln took office. Not only national leaders but ordinary citizens offered revisions. A Rochester man wrote to his local paper that the key doctrines of the *Dred Scott* decision should be added to the Constitution, while a Baltimore resident suggested an amendment prohibiting the succession of two northern presidents.[32] Not since the creation of

---

30 Bernstein, *Amending America*, 80–81; Ames, *Proposed Amendments*, 103–4.
31 See, for example, the speech of Henry L. Benning, November 19, 1860, in William W. Freehling and Craig M. Simpson, eds., *Secession Debated: Georgia's Showdown in 1860* (New York: Oxford University Press, 1992), 119.
32 *Rochester Democrat and American*, December 29, 1860, p. 2; Neilson Poe to Thurlow Weed, December 19, 1860, Thurlow Weed MSS, UR.

the Constitution had the nation witnessed such a torrent of proposed revisions.

Almost all of the proposed slavery amendments during the secession crisis sought to protect rather than abolish slavery. The proposals thus resurrected older proslavery efforts to use amendments to preserve slavery forever. This time, however, the amendments attracted much northern support, mainly because of fears of disunion. Senator Stephen Douglas of Illinois, Abraham Lincoln's longtime Democratic foe, promised a friend that a compromise amendment took "the slavery question out of Congress forever . . . and gives assurance of permanent peace."[33]

None of the amendments proposed early on in the secession crisis, however, did very well. In his last annual address to Congress in December 1860, President James Buchanan proposed one amendment that recognized the right of property in slaves, another that protected slavery in the territories, and a third that acknowledged the right of masters to recover escaped slaves.[34] No one in Congress pushed hard for the president's proposals. Senator John J. Crittenden of Kentucky offered a similar package of compromise measures, although his included an amendment creating a permanent boundary between slavery and freedom that ran along the old Missouri Compromise line, which extended west from Missouri's southern border. Southern moderates and northern Democrats welcomed Crittenden's solution, but the Republicans, who held a majority in both houses of Congress, refused to consent, for the measure directly violated their commitment to freedom in the territories. "Let there be no compromise on the question of extending slavery," Lincoln told Lyman Trumbull, a former Democrat but now a Republican senator from Illinois.[35] Only the most conservative Republicans supported Crittenden's solution, and the remaining members of the party easily blocked the measure's passage.[36]

The president-elect, who had counseled fellow Republicans to reject compromises such as Crittenden's, could see that such a strategy might make things worse. If Lincoln and his party refused to endorse a compromise, southern unionists might assume that the new administration meant to abolish slavery and trample on states' rights, just as the secessionists had predicted. As long as they seemed intractable, Republicans

33 Douglas to Charles H. Lanphier, December 25, 1860, Charles H. Lanphier MSS, ISHL.
34 R. Alton Lee, "The Corwin Amendment in the Secession Crisis," *Ohio Historical Quarterly*, 70 (January 1961), 7.
35 *CW*, 4:149.
36 Kenneth M. Stampp, *And the War Came: The North and the Secession Crisis* (Baton Rouge: Louisiana State University Press, 1950), 166–70; David M. Potter, *Lincoln and His Party in the Secession Crisis* (New Haven: Yale University Press, 1942), 108–10, 181–200.

risked the secession of the slave states of the upper South. Long before he took office, therefore, Lincoln began thinking of his own compromise measures to keep these so-called border states in tow. He shared his ideas with Thurlow Weed, the editor of the *Albany* (New York) *Evening Journal,* during a conversation in Springfield, Illinois, on December 20, 1860. Weed was the best-known and most influential wire-puller in the party. He was also the eyes and ears of New York senator William Henry Seward, Lincoln's choice for secretary of state. The president-elect gave the New York editor some written compromise measures that Seward might introduce to Congress. Although historians disagree about what Lincoln wrote on this occasion, his proposals most likely did not take the form of constitutional amendments and probably included only the modest concession of a guarantee to uphold the Fugitive Slave Law of 1850. Lincoln must have assumed that Weed would pass the proposals to Seward, and perhaps he hoped that Seward would introduce the measures to Congress. But the New York senator, who still stung from being denied the Republican presidential nomination, believed himself a much better judge than Lincoln of the political situation. So Seward took the liberty of rewriting Lincoln's proposals. The new plan called for a constitutional amendment that prohibited the adoption of any future amendment interfering with slavery in the southern states.[37] Such a proposal, Seward thought, would put an end to secessionist propaganda that Republicans planned to abolish slavery by constitutional amendment. Upper South unionism would then flourish, and secessionism would wither and die.

Seward's steering of his amendment through Congress was the first legislative success of the embryonic Lincoln administration. In the House, Seward's ally Charles Francis Adams of Massachusetts proposed a version of the amendment that was taken up by the "Committee of Thirty-Three," a body formed to consider and propose compromise measures. The head of the committee, Congressman Thomas Corwin of Ohio, reported out the amendment in January 1861, and from then on the measure was known as the Corwin amendment.

At first, it seemed that Republicans would oppose the Corwin amendment as they had blocked the previous compromise measures. A petition of Massachusetts Republicans proclaimed that the Constitution "needs to be obeyed rather than amended."[38] Other Republicans opposed the amendment because they, like most Americans, assumed that the constitutional text should remain static. Congressman Schuyler Colfax of Indiana

---

37 Lee, "The Corwin Amendment," 12–17; and Potter, *Lincoln and His Party in the Secession Crisis,* 166–70.

38 John M. Forbes to Charles Francis Adams, February 2, 1861, Adams family MSS, MHS.

announced that "our battle cry ought to be 'the Constitution as our fathers made it,'" while Senator Trumbull admitted an uneasiness with "tinkering with the Constitution unnecessarily."[39] Early Republican opposition to the amendment convinced Corwin himself that the measure was doomed.[40]

Slowly, moderate and radical Republicans began to change their minds. They grew to see the wisdom of using the amendment to hold onto the border states and thwart secession. Also, they rightly interpreted Seward's lobbying for the measure as a sign that Lincoln supported it even though he publicly backed no compromise. Finally, they were satisfied by the claims of other Republicans that the amendment, rather than making a genuine change to the Constitution, merely prevented "misconstruction of existing provisions."[41] On February 28, 1861, enough Republicans swung to the amendment to carry it through the House of Representatives. Three days later, under the leadership of Stephen Douglas, the Senate approved the measure.[42] President Buchanan then signed it and Congress submitted it to the state legislatures, two of which voted for ratification.[43]

The actions of the president and Congress showed a cavalier if not defiant attitude toward the written rules of amendment. The Constitution did not require the president to sign an amendment – indeed, most of the framers probably expected the president to be absent from the amending process – and it specified that Congress submit amendments to state legislatures *or* conventions. Buchanan's signature, though technically improper, was not a significant challenge to constitutional doctrine: the president simply wanted to demonstrate his support for the Corwin amendment. The congressional resolution limiting ratification to state legislatures was a more serious infraction, for it curtailed the express right of the states to determine the mode of ratification. Most likely, the resolution was a deliberate attempt by congressmen to keep the amendment out of southern state conventions that had met to decide on secession. Those

---

39 Schuyler Colfax to Orville Hickman Browning, January 13, 1861, Orville Hickman Browning MSS, ISHL; Lyman Trumbull to William Jayne, February 17, 1861, cited in Mark M. Krug, *Lyman Trumbull: Conservative Radical* (New York: A. S. Barnes, 1965), 179.
40 Anna Ella Carroll to T. H. Hicks, January 24, 1861, Anna Ella Carroll MSS, HSMd.
41 Congressman Albert Porter, cited in Lee, "The Corwin Amendment," 21.
42 Stephen Douglas to August Belmont, December 25, 1860, Stephen Douglas MSS, CHS; Roy Franklin Nichols, *The Disruption of the American Democracy* (1948; repr., New York: Free Press, 1967), 479–82.
43 The two states were Maryland and Ohio. Illinois also voted for ratification, but the vote was technically invalid because it was done by state convention, whereas Congress specified ratification by state legislatures. See Lee, "The Corwin Amendment," 25.

conventions so far had been dominated by prosecessionists, who denounced all compromise measures. The Corwin amendment would not
do well there. Also, congressmen may have wished to avoid the thorny
question of whether a state convention called to consider secession had
the authority to vote on the separate matter of a compromise amendment.
Regardless of the motives behind Buchanan's signature and the congressional ratification resolution, few people questioned the two actions. But
both were significant because they served as precedents: four years later,
Congress imported the same ratification resolution to the amendment
abolishing slavery, and Lincoln followed Buchanan's lead by signing this
final Thirteenth Amendment.

On March 4, 1861, the day after Congress adopted the Corwin amendment, the new president took office. In his inaugural, Lincoln once again
invoked the Constitution as the icon of stability. "Continue to execute all
the express provisions of our national Constitution," the president advised, "and the Union will endure forever." To this he added a lukewarm
endorsement of the Corwin amendment, the only specific compromise
measure that he mentioned. Because the amendment did not alter the
Constitution but simply made explicit what was already "implied constitutional law," he had "no objection to its being made express, and
irrevocable."[44]

The secession crisis had so unnerved Lincoln and other Republicans
that they were willing to take seriously an unamendable amendment.
Harold Hyman has accurately assessed the amendment as a "measure of
how low secession had brought the constitutional ethics of many Americans."[45] Then again, the amendment had little to do with constitutional
ethics. Lincoln and his party thought of the amendment not as a genuine
constitutional change, but rather as an expedient tool to preserve the
loyalty of the upper South and to breed unionism in the deep South.

On April 12 the fantasy of constitutional compromise was shattered by
Confederate guns aimed at Fort Sumter. When, three days later, Lincoln
called for seventy-five thousand militia to put down the insurrection, the
states of the upper South – Virginia, North Carolina, Arkansas, and
Tennessee – joined the Confederacy. The Constitution as it was had failed
to prevent the Civil War.

44 CW, 4:264–65, 270.
45 Harold M. Hyman, *A More Perfect Union: The Impact of the Civil War and Recon-
    struction on the Constitution* (New York: Alfred A. Knopf, 1973), 41. See Mark E.
    Brandon, "The 'Original' Thirteenth Amendment and the Limits to Formal Constitu-
    tional Change," in Sanford Levinson, ed., *Responding to Imperfection: The Theory and
    Practice of Constitutional Amendment* (Princeton: Princeton University Press, 1995),
    215–36.

Preserving the Constitution in the War for Emancipation

Susan Arnold Wallace, the wife of a Union commander, could see the future. Only eight months after the Civil War began, Wallace told her mother: "However we may go into this war, we shall come out of it abolitionists."[46] For most northerners, the war that ended slavery began only as a war to restore the Union. Unforeseen events and influences ultimately drove the Union side to embrace emancipation as a war aim, but the progress toward that point was never steady, rarely clear, and always resisted. No one person or group of people was solely responsible for turning the Civil War into a war for black freedom. Rather, the Union war policy of emancipation emerged in a haphazard fashion as a response to competing motivations and initiatives. And always, the movement toward emancipation was constrained by the idea of a fixed Constitution.

Some of the first northerners to embrace the Civil War as an abolition war were, unsurprisingly, the abolitionists. "Thank God!" wrote Frederick Douglass after the firing on Fort Sumter. "The slaveholders themselves have saved our cause from ruin! They have exposed the throat of slavery to the keen knife of liberty, and have given a chance to all the righteous forces of the nation to deal a death-blow to the monster evil of the nineteenth century."[47] For the next two years, abolitionists battled public opinion and badgered the Lincoln administration to acknowledge emancipation as a higher cause than Union.

Meanwhile, the slaves themselves did their part to convince northerners to make this a war for emancipation. From the moment of the firing on Fort Sumter, slaves knew freedom was at hand.[48] The presence of Union armies in the South offered the opening they sought. But when slaves fled to Union lines, they discovered that most northern commanders returned them to their masters or banned them from the lines. Concerned about keeping the border states in the Union, military officials were especially protective of slavery in Missouri, Kentucky, Maryland, and Delaware. General Benjamin F. Butler, stationed at Fortress Monroe in Virginia, took a different approach. When three African Americans arrived at his post in May 1861, Butler declared them "contraband" of war and refused to return them unless their masters pledged loyalty to the Union. Some

---

46 Susan Arnold Wallace to "My Dear Mother," December 22, 1861, Lew Wallace MSS, IHS.
47 *Douglass' Monthly*, May 1861, in Philip S. Foner, ed., *The Life and Writings of Frederick Douglass* (New York: International Publishers, 1952), 3:90–91.
48 David W. Blight, "They Knew What Time It Was: African-Americans and the Coming of the Civil War," in Gabor S. Boritt, ed., *Why the Civil War Came* (New York: Oxford University Press, 1996), 53–77.

Union commanders refused to follow Butler's lead, but many more began taking "contrabands" into their lines. That Butler had started the practice was ironic, for he was no abolitionist. Prior to the war, he was known as a "doughface" – a northern Democrat who defended slave-owning rights – and when the war broke out, he offered to put down a rumored slave rebellion in Maryland. The realities of war changed Butler's heart. War had brought the slaves face-to-face with Butler and other northern commanders and forced them to see the necessity if not the morality of emancipation.[49]

Congress lagged behind the army on the slavery issue. When the Thirty-seventh Congress convened in July 1861, it voted in favor of Congressman John J. Crittenden's resolution to uphold "the *supremacy* of the Constitution" and the preservation of the "Union with all the . . . rights of the several States unimpaired."[50] Congress strayed from these principles in August 1861, when, following the lead of Butler and other generals, it passed the First Confiscation Act, which allowed federal authorities to confiscate slaves used by Confederates for military purposes. Almost a year later, in July 1862, Congress strayed even further by adopting the Second Confiscation Act, which emancipated all slaves owned by rebel masters. But, despite the fact that the confiscation acts helped to undermine slavery, congressmen could still claim that they had held to the principle of noninterference with slavery in the states, for the acts targeted slaves of certain masters, those who were disloyal, rather than slavery in specific states. Clearly, confiscation did not deliver the deathblow to slavery. Even the legal means of emancipation was left vague in both acts. The first act failed to promise permanent freedom to the contrabands, and the second, while declaring confiscated slaves "forever free of their servitude," provided freed people with no legal mechanism such as the right to sue for their freedom in court. Moderate and radical Republicans had asked for such provisions, and a House version of the Second Confiscation Act contained them. But the final act, rather than offering ex-slaves measures to uphold their freedom, simply declared that they could be used by the president "in such manner as he may judge best for the public welfare," a signal that former slaves could be enlisted into military service and that the act was more about military necessity than permanent abolition. Henry Winter Davis, a former Maryland congressman who would reenter the House a year later, criticized the Second Confiscation Act for

---

49 Ira Berlin et al., eds., *Freedom: A Documentary History of Emancipation*, ser. 1, vol. 1, *The Destruction of Slavery* (Cambridge: Cambridge University Press, 1985), 1–56.
50 *CG*, 37th Cong., 1st sess. (July 22, 1861), 222–23. The Senate passed a similar declaration three days later.

"the entire absence of *all legal* provisions for the security of the freedom given to the negroes."[51]

In contrast, congressional emancipation policy outside of the slave states was clear and comprehensive. In April 1862, three months before passing the Second Confiscation Act, Congress approved a measure freeing the three thousand slaves of the District of Columbia, where the federal government had exclusive jurisdiction. Unlike the confiscation acts, this law made no distinction between slaves of disloyal and loyal owners, and it left no ambiguity about the legal process of emancipation. Ex-slaves had the right to testify in special emancipation hearings and received passes certifying their new status. Republicans also carried a bill prohibiting slavery in the territories, thus repudiating a crucial element of the *Dred Scott* decision. In their first year in power, Republicans had pressed freedom to the edges of constitutional constraint.[52]

Although the early blows against slavery by Congress represented forward steps, they included two regressive provisions: compensation for former owners and colonization for ex-slaves. Under the act of emancipation in the District of Columbia, the federal government paid loyal owners the value of their slaves; and in both the district act and the Second Confiscation Act, Congress appropriated funds for the voluntary colonization of ex-slaves. Lincoln supported compensation and colonization, and it was in part because of his urging that Congress included these provisions in its emancipation legislation.

Indeed, in all matters concerning slavery, Lincoln was more restrained than most of his Republican colleagues. Although he allowed Butler to practice his contraband policy, he cut short General John C. Frémont's effort in August 1861 to free by military order all rebel-owned slaves in Missouri. Lincoln first asked Frémont to modify the order, and when the general refused, Lincoln revoked it. Again the president moved against freedom in May 1862, when another independent-minded general, David

---

51 Henry Winter Davis to Samuel F. DuPont, undated, group 9, series B, box 42, W9–17209, Samuel Francis DuPont MSS, EM. Herman Belz, "Protection of Personal Liberty in Republican Emancipation Legislation," in *Abraham Lincoln, Constitutionalism, and Equal Rights in the Civil War Era* (New York: Fordham University Press, 1998), 101–18; Patricia Allan Lucie, *Freedom and Federalism: Congress and Courts, 1861–1866* (New York: Garland, 1986), 26–45; Mary Frances Berry, *Military Necessity and Civil Rights Policy: Black Citizenship and the Constitution, 1861–1868* (Port Washington, N.Y.: Kennikat Press, 1977), 19–48; Louis S. Gerteis, *From Contraband to Freedman: Federal Policy toward Southern Blacks, 1861–1865* (Westport, Conn.: Greenwood Press, 1973); James G. Randall, *Constitutional Problems under Lincoln* (1926; rev. ed., 1951; repr., Gloucester, Mass.: Peter Smith, 1963), 275–370.

52 George H. Hoemann, *What God Hath Wrought: The Embodiment of Freedom in the Thirteenth Amendment* (New York: Garland, 1987), 33–61; Michael J. Kurtz, "Emancipation in the Federal City," *Civil War History*, 24 (September 1978), 250–67.

Hunter, ordered all slaves in Florida, Georgia, and South Carolina to be freed and armed. Lincoln rescinded the order and proclaimed that only he, as commander in chief, had the power "to declare the Slaves of any state or states, free."[53] (Lincoln's sympathetic biographers see this statement as a sign that Lincoln was already thinking of the Emancipation Proclamation, though the evidence for that conclusion is scant.) Lincoln also restrained congressional emancipators. He objected to the Second Confiscation Act because it contained the "startling" phrase "that congress can free a slave within a state."[54] Only by changing the language of this and other provisions of the act did Congress avoid a presidential veto.

Lincoln lagged behind some commanders and congressmen on slavery mainly because he adhered more closely than other northerners did to a southern strategy. Prior to the war, Republicans' southern strategy aimed at driving a wedge between southern slave-owning leaders, who wanted all territories left open to slavery, and southern non-slave-owning whites, who were generally resistant or at least indifferent to slavery's expansion. By keeping the issue of slavery focused on expansion, Republicans hoped to detach southern yeomen from southern planters, thus destroying the slave South from within and perhaps gaining a new constituency in the bargain. Lincoln tinkered with this strategy after the war began. His plan was to keep southern unionists exempt from federal emancipation legislation while simultaneously cultivating state-level emancipation movements that would undermine Confederate loyalty.[55] The border states were the natural place for Lincoln to apply the strategy, because antislavery sentiment had always been stronger there than in the deep South. Of course, a single, humiliating military victory over the Confederates would be an equally effective method of undermining secession.

Neither of these strategies for weakening southern morale succeeded during the first year of the war. Instead of scoring a stunning military victory, the Union armies, particularly those in the East, suffered a string of embarrassing defeats or stalemates. The prospects for border state emancipation looked equally dismal. In late 1861 Lincoln targeted Delaware, a state with only eighteen hundred slaves, as a test area for a compensated emancipation scheme. When unionist congressmen from Delaware presented Lincoln's plan to their state, their constituents reacted skeptically, and their Democratic opponents denounced the effort "to

53 *CW*, 5:222.
54 *CW*, 5:329.
55 See Richard H. Abbott, *The Republican Party and the South: The First Southern Strategy, 1855–1877* (Chapel Hill: University of North Carolina Press, 1986), 3–41.

place the negro on a footing of equality with the white man."[56] Similar results awaited Lincoln's proposed resolution to Congress of March 1862, which pledged federal funds to any state freeing its slaves. Although Congress approved the resolution, border state congressmen received the measure coldly, and no state ever adopted an actual scheme of subsidized emancipation.[57] In a desperate final meeting just before Congress adjourned in July 1862, Lincoln told border state congressmen: "if the war continue long, as it must, . . . the institution [of slavery] in your states will be extinguished by mere friction and abrasion – by the mere incidents of the war."[58] That was a poorly cloaked threat, and it suggested that the president was ready to experiment with a new approach to slavery, and to the war. Ten days later, on July 22, 1862, he presented the first draft of the Emancipation Proclamation to the cabinet.

The proclamation signaled an important shift in Lincoln's conception of the war, but it represented no sea change in his approach to emancipation. Having failed to precipitate a quick, internal collapse of the rebellion, the president now resorted to more aggressive methods. Along with his proclamation, which targeted only those slaves in rebel-controlled areas, was an order from Lincoln allowing military and naval officers in rebel areas to recruit male African Americans, free or enslaved, as noncombat soldiers. The order followed the lead of Congress, which had authorized military service for blacks in the Second Confiscation Act and the Militia Act of 1862, and it made official a policy already practiced by such officers as David Hunter in South Carolina and James H. Lane in Kansas. Eventually, the recruitment policy, which exempted the border states as well as Tennessee and North Carolina, came to encompass all the slave states. And the African American recruits, who initially were confined to drudge work, lobbied successfully to see combat service. In the spring of 1863, with Lincoln's approval, the War Department created the Bureau of Colored Troops.

Yet, despite the Union's move to a more aggressive war, the president never relinquished his border state strategy. He still hoped to divide the Confederacy. His preliminary proclamation of September 1862 promised the southern states full restoration of their rights (including, implicitly, slaveholding) if they would give up rebellion. Knowing that few states would bite at the offer, Lincoln sweetened impending emancipation with a

56 H. Clay Reed, "Lincoln's Compensated Emancipation Plan and Its Relation to Delaware," *Delaware Notes*, 7th ser. (1931), 27–78 (quotation at 51); for drafts of Lincoln's bill, never submitted, for compensated emancipation in Delaware, see *CW*, 5:29–30.

57 William E. Gienapp, "Abraham Lincoln and the Border States," *Journal of the Abraham Lincoln Association*, 13 (1992), 33.

58 *CW*, 5:317–18.

pledge, aimed particularly at the border states, that he would continue to push Congress toward gradual, compensated emancipation coupled with the voluntary colonization of *all* persons of African descent, not only ex-slaves. Most important, the president maintained that he still abided by his constitutional obligations to slavery. The proclamation's ultimate goal, said Lincoln, was not universal emancipation but the restoration of "the constitutional relation between the United States, and each of the states, and the people thereof."[59] By imposing black recruitment and emancipation only on those who had rejected the Constitution – that is, the secessionists – Lincoln could claim to have held true to the hallowed principle of noninterference with slavery.

His opponents were unconvinced. On September 23, 1862, the day after Lincoln issued the preliminary Emancipation Proclamation, the Democratic *Chicago Times* scoffed at the order as an underhanded initiative to "save the Union . . . by overriding the constitution."[60] Military emancipation, declared the Democrats, undermined not only the country's Constitution but its racial composition. Everywhere in the Union, but especially in the Midwest, the opposition warned that, as one Illinois Democrat put it, "our people are in great danger of being overrun with negroes set free by our army or by the President's proclamation."[61] By playing on the theme of impending constitutional and racial chaos, the Democrats scored major victories in the fall elections of 1862. Republicans in the next Congress (the Thirty-eighth) would still have a firm hold on the Senate but only narrow control of the House of Representatives. Buoyed by their gains, the Democrats in later electoral contests would continue to harp on the racial and constitutional consequences of Lincoln's emancipation policy.

Republicans struggled to meet the opposition's objections to military emancipation. All but the most radical party members were quick to deny that ex-slaves would migrate north and become equals with whites. Some Republicans joined Lincoln in promising that colonization would avert further comingling of the races. Others thought colonization infeasible but believed nonetheless that African Americans could not survive long in the country. Typical was an editorial in the *New York Evening Post*, generally considered a radical organ, that promised that emancipation would trigger the immigration of thousands of Europeans followed by the

---

59 *CW*, 5:433–436.
60 *Chicago Times*, September 23, 1862, p. 2.
61 James C. Allen in *Quincy* (Illinois) *Herald*, cited in Bruce Tap, "Race, Rhetoric, and Emancipation: The Election of 1862 in Illinois," *Civil War History*, 39 (June 1993), 116. As Tap shows, comments such as Allen's were a reaction not only to the proclamation but to a simultaneous order by Secretary of War Edwin M. Stanton resettling some of the freed people throughout Illinois and the Midwest.

disappearance of African Americans: "as the Indians were crowded westward, and out of our bounds, by the irresistible advance of the white man, so will the blacks be, whenever that powerful protective system with which the slave-holders have guarded them is removed."[62] Meanwhile, to counter the opposition's constitutional objections to emancipation, Union leagues, those organizations formed by Republicans to rally proadministration sentiment, circulated pamphlets justifying the proclamation as a necessary and legal act of war. The author of one of these tracts, the New York lawyer Grosvenor P. Lowrey, argued that the Constitution, "the proximate source of light, and authority" for all, contained implicit "war powers" authorizing the federal government to enact military emancipation.[63] Although Republicans were forced to rely on implicit rather than explicit constitutional powers, they insisted that they were preserving rather than defying or altering the Constitution.

At the heart of the Republicans' defense of military emancipation was their assertion that the policy was only temporary. "When the rebellion is suppressed," argued a proadministration paper in Ohio, "the same Constitution will be operative as before. . . . Although every Slave in the South be emancipated, the 'institution' in its legal sense would not be destroyed. The Slaves, if they remained in the States, could all be re-enslaved as soon as the army that liberated them was removed."[64] Some Republicans objected to such a stance because it suggested that a free person could be reenslaved. But, as Lincoln often observed, an unfriendly Congress or Supreme Court could indeed strike down the effects of wartime emancipation once the war was over. At the very least, party members conceded that the surrender of the Confederacy might leave in bondage those slaves not yet free. According to the *New York Tribune,* "were the Rebel States to say to the Federal Government to-morrow, 'Withdraw your Proclamation of Freedom, and we will each return to loyalty,' . . . we hold that the President would be at perfect liberty to accept the offer if he saw fit."[65]

If permanent emancipation rather than Union victory had been the Republicans' primary objective, they might have explored more seriously the possibility of abolishing slavery by constitutional amendment. But

62 *New York Evening Post,* November 13, 1862, p. 2. For a similar Republican editorial in the Midwest, see *Ohio State Journal,* October 15, 1862, p. 4.

63 Grosvenor P. Lowrey, "The Commander-in-Chief: A Defence upon Legal Grounds of the Proclamation of Emancipation," in Frank Freidel, ed., *Union Pamphlets of the Civil War* (Cambridge, Mass.: Belknap Press, 1967), 1:474–502 (quotation at 480). See also Charles P. Kirkland, *A Letter to the Hon. Benjamin R. Curtis, Late Judge of the Supreme Court of the United States* (New York: Latimer Bros. and Seymour, 1862).

64 *Toledo Blade,* reprinted in *Cincinnati Gazette,* October 17, 1862, p. 2.

65 *New York Tribune,* March 16, 1863, p. 4.

Republicans in the early years of the war rarely considered amending the Constitution for any purpose. A number of Republican lawyers, politicians, and treatise writers griped about the "inadequacy" of the Constitution to handle such wartime phenomena as confiscation and disloyalty. The remedies they prescribed, however, were not long-term amendments but instead short-term actions whose constitutionality rested on the principle of wartime necessity.[66] Only the most radical Republicans pondered an antislavery amendment. Lydia Maria Child, for example, wrote in 1862 that the people should "modify" the Constitution to "get *rid* of the virus infused throughout the blood of our body politic." But Child herself foresaw the main obstacle to an antislavery amendment. "Wholesale lauding of the Constitution has made it an object of idol-worship," wrote the reformer; Americans would never consent to changing a word of it.[67] In early 1863 a few antislavery politicians toyed with the idea of having Senator Charles Sumner propose some antislavery amendments, but they eventually decided that it was "unwise to raise at this moment any new question that may distract the public mind or interfere with the practical legislation."[68] "If we had the Constitution to make, we should probably have it otherwise," wrote Horace Greeley. "But we must take it as it is."[69]

Despite the unfavorable climate for constitutional change, Lincoln proposed three amendments in his annual message to Congress of December 1, 1862. The first offered federal compensation to states abolishing slavery by 1900; the second promised compensation to slave owners for the loss of freed slaves; and the third authorized Congress to appropriate funds for the voluntary colonization of blacks outside the United States. The amendments fell well short of outright abolition. States were only encouraged, not required, to emancipate their slaves by 1900. Moreover, permanent liberty would be limited to those slaves "who shall have enjoyed actual freedom by the chances of the war, at any time before the end of the rebellion."[70] The president was simply shaping his border state policy into the form of constitutional amendments. As the day approached when he was to sign the Emancipation Proclamation aimed at rebels, he wanted to reassert his more benign emancipation program for loyal citizens.

No one took the president's amendments very seriously. The only people who welcomed the proposals were a smattering of Lincoln's oppo-

66 Hyman, *A More Perfect Union*, 99–123.
67 Child to George W. Julian, January 30, 1862, in Milton Meltzer and Patricia G. Holland, eds., *Lydia Maria Child: Selected Letters, 1817–1880* (Amherst: University of Massachusetts Press, 1982), 403–4.
68 John Jay to Charles Sumner, January 19, 1863, Charles Sumner MSS, HL.
69 *New York Tribune*, April 17, 1863, p. 4.
70 CW, 5:530.

nents, who wrongly saw the amendments as an admission by the president that the Emancipation Proclamation was unconstitutional.[71] Radical Republicans in particular frowned upon the measures. Henry Winter Davis, the former Maryland congressman who usually favored all measures ending slavery, called Lincoln's proposals "illusory to the loyal states and ridiculous in relation to the disloyal states."[72] Salmon P. Chase, now serving as Lincoln's secretary of the treasury, also recognized the amendments as backward steps. But, refusing to challenge the president on the immorality of gradual emancipation, Chase merely suggested to Lincoln that the measures were inexpedient: they could not be adopted, and thus they would "weaken rather than strengthen yourself and your administration."[73] No one in Congress proposed, much less promoted, the President's amendments.[74]

Lincoln's border state plan still gave some last gasps. In the final session of the Thirty-seventh Congress, from December 1862 to March 1863, loyal Missouri congressmen tried to pass a bill for compensated emancipation in their state. The Senate adopted the measure, but in the House, antiadministration congressmen from the border states joined with northern Democrats to defeat it. Opponents of the bill complained that the administration would never deliver the promised government bonds to slave owners, and even if the government did, Union military losses could make the securities worthless. To this objection the president offered the prediction: "you southern men will soon reach the point where bonds will be a more valuable possession than bondsmen. Nothing is more uncertain now than two-legged property."[75] Despite his frustration with border state unionists, Lincoln exempted from the final Emancipation Proclamation all the border states as well as every Confederate region then under Union occupation. He also excluded Virginia's westernmost counties, which, with Lincoln's help, became the new state of West Virginia, where slavery was to be abolished gradually. Disappointed that the original border states had rejected gradual emancipation, Lincoln gladly helped create a border state that would accept it.[76]

---

71 See, for example, the *New York Evening Express,* December 2 and 3, 1862.
72 Davis to Mrs. Samuel F. DuPont, January 2, 1863, Samuel Francis DuPont MSS, EM.
73 Chase to Abraham Lincoln, Washington, November 28, 1862, RTL.
74 Occasionally a congressman did mention Lincoln's proposed amendments. For example, John Hutchins, a Republican representative from Ohio, remarked in passing that the amendments were "entirely impracticable." CG 37th Cong., 3d sess. (December 11, 1862), 79.
75 James G. Blaine, *Twenty Years of Congress: From Lincoln to Garfield* (Norwich, Conn.: Henry Bill Publishing Company, 1884), 1:448.
76 Dallas S. Shaffer, "Lincoln and the 'Vast Question' of West Virginia," *West Virginia History,* 32 (January 1971), 86–100.

Figure 1. This image, from the December 20, 1862, issue of *Harper's Weekly*, reflects antislavery northerners' dissatisfaction with President Abraham Lincoln's annual message to Congress earlier that month, which recommended constitutional amendments providing for gradual emancipation and voluntary colonization of African Americans, with slavery not to be fully abolished until 1900. The amendments seemed to many a retreat from the Emancipation Proclamation, a preliminary version of which Lincoln had issued on September 22, 1862, and the final version of which he would sign on January 1, 1863.

The final proclamation contained strategic wording besides immunity for the border states. In response to those who had been predicting that the proclamation would provoke a massive slave revolt, Lincoln inserted a clause requesting ex-slaves to "abstain from all violence, unless in necessary self-defence," and to "labor faithfully for reasonable wages." (Significantly, the president had dropped his call for colonization; he now saw the wisdom of using former slaves in Union armies rather than sending them abroad.) Actually, the plea against violence had as much to do with foreign policy as domestic race prejudice. Europeans had suspected Lincoln of fostering a slave rebellion when, in the preliminary proclamation, he restrained military officers from hindering "any efforts" the freed people made for "their actual freedom." The president could not risk alienating Europe with the proclamation. Indeed, he and his secretary of state had hoped to use the proclamation to secure the neutrality if not the support of England and France, both of which had already abolished slavery. Therefore, Lincoln worded the final proclamation to pacify European fears of the United States being transformed into the next Santo Domingo.[77]

One last change of wording distinguished the final proclamation. Whereas the preliminary version had declared the slaves "thenceforward, and forever free," the second simply proclaimed that they "henceforward shall be free."[78] The omission of "forever," though perhaps incidental, highlighted the president's uncertainty about the proclamation's standing once the war was over. Many times over the next two years Lincoln adamantly refused to retract the proclamation, but many times as well did he admit his concern about the permanence of black freedom once the Union was restored.

Americans in early 1863 could already sense that military emancipation was not the same as constitutional emancipation. Soon after Lincoln signed the final proclamation, an Ohio resident wrote to his senator, "If it will aid in putting the rebellion down then I am for it – anything to accomplish that. But can a proclamation, make a slave free? . . . In what way can slaves recognized by the constitution be declared free by the execution [of the same Constitution]. I have not examined the question much; but to a hasty consideration of the matter I can't but entertain

---

77 Mark E. Neely, Jr., *The Last Best Hope of Earth: Abraham Lincoln and the Promise of America* (Cambridge, Mass.: Harvard University Press, 1993), 110–12; Howard Jones, *Abraham Lincoln and a New Birth of Freedom: The Union and Slavery in the Diplomacy of the Civil War* (Lincoln: University of Nebraska Press, 1999), esp. 122–27; Jones, *Union in Peril: The Crisis over British Intervention in the Civil War* (Chapel Hill: University of North Carolina Press, 1992), 162–97.
78 Compare *CW*, 5:434 and 6:29–30.

doubts."[79] The problem, simply put, was that unionists were now supposed to fight two seemingly incompatible wars: one against slavery, and one for a Constitution that supported slavery.

The president was slow to offer solutions to the paradox. With the Union victories at Gettysburg and Vicksburg in July 1863, the prospect of a quick end to the war was brighter, and northerners began to turn more seriously to the question of reconstructing the Union and abolishing slavery permanently. But Lincoln stayed silent on slavery during the last months of 1863. His thoughts on the future of African Americans, free or enslaved, were still unformed. Also, he did not want to make emancipation a central issue in the fall elections, as it had been the year before. Lincoln's one pronouncement during this period, a public letter to the Illinois Republican James C. Conkling, simply affirmed the Emancipation Proclamation as constitutionally and militarily sound. If the black soldiers "stake their lives for us," Lincoln explained, "they must be prompted by the strongest motive – even the promise of freedom. And the promise being made, must be kept."[80] Despite his eloquence and commitment, the president sidestepped the question of *how* to keep the promise.

Privately, however, Lincoln did take some steps toward securing legal freedom for the slaves. In August 1863 he wrote a few recommendations regarding reconstruction to the Union commander in Louisiana, General Nathaniel P. Banks. The president denied any desire to take "direction" of reconstruction, and as an illustration of his restraint, he admitted that Congress, not the president, must decide whether to admit Louisiana's representatives and senators. Nevertheless, the president did offer Banks a proposal for establishing black freedom in the state. Louisiana could make a new constitution "recognizing the emancipation proclamation, and adopting emancipation in those parts of the state to which the proclamation does not apply." Then, state authorities could "adopt some practical system by which the two races could gradually live themselves out of their old relation to each other, and both come out better prepared for the new." Lincoln was vague on the details, although he wrote that the young freed people should receive an education and that all ex-slaves should have some form of labor contract.[81]

In some ways, the president's plan seemed little different from his earlier emancipation schemes for the border states. Slaves would be freed gradually and only by state action. Lincoln still doubted the constitutionality of federal emancipation legislation, particularly when it was aimed at loyal areas. Soon after the president wrote his letter to General Banks, Secretary

79　A. L. Brewer to John Sherman, January 7, 1863, John Sherman MSS, LC.
80　CW, 6:409.
81　CW, 6:365.

Chase asked Lincoln to extend the Emancipation Proclamation to regions not under rebellion. The president shot back, "would I not thus give up all footing upon constitution or law? Would I not thus be in the boundless field of absolutism?"[82] Lincoln was sincere in his desire to see slavery abolished everywhere. Had he not cared about the fate of slavery, had he merely wanted Louisiana's speedy return to the Union, he could have said nothing about a new state constitution abolishing slavery. Yet, despite his ever strengthening commitment to a war for emancipation as well as for the Union, Lincoln still felt beholden to the antebellum principle of federal noninterference with slavery in the states.

By the end of 1863 the president could see that the country might soon be rid of slavery, but he had not yet arrived at a method of ensuring freedom to the enslaved. In his Gettysburg Address of November 19, 1863, Lincoln made his most advanced statement so far on emancipation. He said nothing of the Constitution's protection of slavery but instead invoked the promise of equality in the Declaration of Independence as the basis for a future in which "this nation, under God, shall have a new birth of freedom."[83] The phrase was poetic, but, on closer inspection, it was also frustratingly vague. Lincoln did not yet know the form that the new nation – or emancipation – would take.

Only slowly had the Civil War eroded northerners' assumption that the maintenance of the Union required constitutional safeguards for slavery. As the conflict had evolved, more and more northerners had come to accept the idea that the Union's preservation required emancipation in some of those places where slavery had long existed. But many northerners doubted the constitutionality of emancipation in nonrebellious areas, and even more questioned whether black freedom would be constitutional after the war had ended. Between the black race and its freedom, said Frederick Douglass, "the constitution is interposed. It always is."[84] Even as Lincoln envisioned a "new birth of freedom" for the Union, he did not yet see how the Constitution might be adjusted to secure, rather than to obstruct, black freedom.

---

82 *CW*, 6:429.
83 *CW*, 7:23.
84 Douglass, "The Present and Future of the Colored Race in America," address delivered in New York City, May 1863, in Foner, *The Life and Writings of Frederick Douglass*, 3:354.

2

Freedom's Constitution

The Gettysburg Address offered only the promise of freedom, not a specific plan of emancipation. After the address, in the winter of 1863–64, Lincoln and the new Thirty-eighth Congress finally began to craft legislation that would secure black freedom in the reconstructed Union. Because the antislavery constitutional amendment was ultimately adopted, we naturally assume that Civil War–era lawmakers always had the amendment in mind as the obvious complement to the Emancipation Proclamation. But, in fact, the amendment was not part of a prearranged agenda. Instead, it was born from a complex tangle of party politics, popular antislavery fervor, and constitutional theory. And far from being an obvious supplement to the proclamation, the amendment represented, for many northerners, a critique of the president's emancipation program.

The Popular Origins of Universal Emancipation

As the new Congress prepared to convene, northerners were far from united on a single plan of emancipation, but they seemed more interested than ever in seeing slavery somehow abolished. In the Midwest, a Republican preacher who had complained in the fall of 1862 that "nobody wants any lectures on the slavery question" observed that audiences now clamored for antislavery speakers, especially those recently converted to the cause.[1] Antislavery whisperings could even be heard from some traditionally antiabolitionist newspapers like the *Pittsburgh Post*. When the *Post*, a Democratic paper, reported that "the future peace of this now bleeding and distracted country, requires the *total extinction of slavery among us*," the Republican Indianapolis *Daily Journal* was quick to respond: "that sounds very like 'Abolitionism' to our ears."[2]

A number of factors during 1863 had made universal emancipation, once the cause of a few abolitionists, a campaign embraced by an ever widening circle of northerners. Perhaps most important was the antisouthern hostility born from the unprecedented scale of destruction during the war. At Shiloh in early 1862, twenty thousand men were killed or

---

1 Ichabod Codding to Maria Codding, October 13, 1862, Ichabod Codding MSS, ISHL; Ichabod Codding to Zebina Eastman, August 14, 1863, Zebina Eastman MSS, CHS.
2 Indianapolis *Daily Journal*, December 12, 1863, p. 2. Similar examples were cited in the *New York Tribune*, December 3, 1863, p. 4.

wounded; at Antietam later that year, another twenty thousand; and at Gettysburg in mid-1863, fifty thousand more. Lincoln estimated that the Union was spending $3 million a day on the conflict. The havoc of war aroused northern passions for vengeance, and emancipation was the perfect instrument of retribution. Black freedom, then, was in part the result of a vicarious war fought by northern noncombatants. "We must have some compensation for the blood and treasure which we have been forced to spend," demanded the editor of the Cincinnati *Catholic Telegraph;* "this we find in the abolition of slavery."[3] For combatants as well, antislavery action was often the natural outcome of antisouthern fury. According to one St. Louis editor, "our soldiers take the slave, because they hate the slaveholder, but not because they love the negro."[4]

Especially when coupled with black enlistments, black freedom offered not only vengeance but a military advantage to white northerners. "Among thinking men the impression is becoming daily more general," a Nashville correspondent observed, "that the coming man for whom we have been looking . . . is the negro emancipated, armed, instructed and drilled."[5] First at Milliken's Bend and Port Hudson on the Mississippi River, and then at Battery Wagner in Charleston Harbor, black Americans had proved that they could make good soldiers – and thus good citizens. The abolitionist Angelina Grimké Weld exulted in the "praise that is lavished upon our brave colored troops even by Proslavery papers. . . . Their heroism is working a great change in public opinion, forcing all men to see the sin and shame of enslaving such men."[6] By the end of 1863, the gallantry of African American soldiers and sailors had converted countless northern whites to the abolitionist cause.

Also decisive in turning northern sentiment in favor of emancipation was the budding antislavery movement in the border states. In the recent elections in all of the border states, even in heavily Democratic Kentucky and Delaware, proemancipation candidates had won important victories. In Missouri, the recent state constitutional convention had voted to abolish slavery, although the plan called for gradual instead of immediate emancipation. "It is certain," the *New York Tribune* reported, "that the

3 *Catholic Telegraph,* reprinted in *Ohio State Journal,* December 19, 1863, p. 2. See Charles Royster, *The Destructive War: William Tecumseh Sherman, Stonewall Jackson, and the Americans* (1991; repr., New York: Vintage Books, 1993), 260–64.
4 [Charles L. Bernays] to Montgomery Blair, August 17, 1863, Blair family MSS, LC. See Joseph Allan Frank, *With Ballot and Bayonet: The Political Socialization of American Civil War Soldiers* (Athens: University of Georgia Press, 1998), 67–70.
5 "Granite" to *Cincinnati Gazette,* November 15, 1863, reprinted in Indianapolis *Daily Journal,* November 24, 1863.
6 Angelina Grimké Weld to Gerrit Smith, July 28, 1863, cited in James McPherson, ed., *The Negro's Civil War: How American Negroes Felt and Acted during the War for the Union* (1965; repr., Urbana: University of Illinois Press, 1982), 191.

Administration will have no more hearty support in its Emancipation measures than from . . . the States which it was not long ago deemed necessary to conciliate by halting in Anti-Slavery progress."[7]

The animosity of northerners toward southern whites, the success of African American soldiers, and the increasing hostility of the slave states themselves to slavery – all fueled the drive toward universal emancipation. Yet, as congressmen gathered in the Capitol, there was no clear consensus about the form emancipation might take.

The many petitions demanding abolition, for example, failed to take a consistent position on how to end slavery. Some called simply for abolition, whereas others adopted the familiar language of the Northwest Ordinance and demanded an end to "slavery and involuntary servitude." Conservative petitioners asked Congress "to drop the negro question and attend to the business of the country." Those of a more radical mind-set demanded that Congress not only free the slaves but grant them legal equality. An equally radical measure for the prohibition of "Slavery and involuntary *service*" was proposed by others who probably did not realize that such a measure might outlaw many other oppressive labor systems in addition to slavery.[8]

One petitioning effort in particular attracted national attention to the cause of universal emancipation. The Women's Loyal National League, organized in the spring of 1863 by abolitionists Elizabeth Cady Stanton and Susan B. Anthony, circulated a "mammoth petition" for immediate abolition. Women throughout the Union took up the cause, sometimes venturing into areas where strong Confederate sympathies made their work exceedingly dangerous. One of the league members, H. Tracy Cutler, wrote Governor Richard Yates of Illinois for a pass so that she could carry the petition to some of the hostile regions of Kentucky and Missouri. Yates's secretary mocked Cutler for circulating "a petition for the general emancipation of the Niggers," but the governor granted the pass anyway.[9] By December league members had amassed hundreds of thousands of signatures. Although the League had fallen far short of its objective of a

7 *New York Tribune*, December 8, 1863, p. 4. See J. R. Lowell, "The President's Policy," *North American Review*, 98 (January 1864), 254.

8 Emphasis added. On the legal difference between "servitude" and "service," see Robert J. Steinfeld, *The Invention of Free Labor: The Employment Relation in English and American Law and Culture, 1350–1870* (Chapel Hill: University of North Carolina Press, 1991). For a modern effort to read the Thirteenth Amendment as a doctrine empowering all laboring classes, see Lea S. VanderVelde, "The Labor Vision of the Thirteenth Amendment," *University of Pennsylvania Law Review*, 138 (December 1989), 437–504. For the original petitions, see HR 37A-G7.2; HR 37A-G7.3; HR 38A-H1.2; HR 38A-G10.1, all in RG46, NA. See P. J. Staudenraus, "The Popular Origins of the Thirteenth Amendment," *Mid-America*, 50 (April 1968), 108–15.

9 H. M. Tracy Cutler to Richard Yates, September 11, 1863, Yates family MSS, ISHL.

WOMEN'S

(When this sheet is filled, add others of the same width, to the foot of it, with paste or mucilage, and return to S. B. ANTHONY, room 20, Cooper Institute, New York.)

To the Senate and House of Representatives of the United States:

The undersigned, Women of the United States, above the age of eighteen years, earnestly pray that your Honorable Body will pass, at the earliest practicable day, an Act, emancipating all persons of African descent, held to involuntary service or labor in the United States.

NAME.	RESIDENCE.
Mrs E. B. Maybine	Newark Ohio.
Mrs M. A. Pallon	Kenia O.

Figure 2. This 1863 petition of the Women's Loyal National League was one of the earliest to implore Congress to fortify Lincoln's Emancipation Proclamation with a measure that would secure freedom to all slaves. This early petition did not call specifically for a constitutional amendment abolishing slavery, but in early 1864 league organizers rewrote the petition so that it did. Like many such petitions, signatures were divided between male and female (on the opposite side of the petition pictured here were the male signers). A note at the top of the petition asks the last signer to return the petition to Susan B. Anthony, one of the league's organizers. (Courtesy National Archives)

million signers, the *New York Tribune* could report that, because of its efforts, "the People everywhere – men, women, soldiers, and civilians – seem to be rousing to the work."[10] League organizers planned to present all of the petitions to Congress in early 1864, but even before then their endeavor had made its mark.[11]

Yet, for all its effect in shaping and demonstrating popular opinion against slavery, the petition of the Women's Loyal League, like most of the emancipation petitions, did not at first prescribe a precise law. The league's petition simply demanded that Congress "pass at the earliest practicable day an Act emancipating all persons of African descent held to involuntary service or labor in the United States." The form of the "act" – whether a statute or constitutional amendment – did not matter to league

10 *New York Tribune*, December 19, 1863, p. 10.
11 Susan Marie Zaeske, "Petitioning, Antislavery and the Emergence of Women's Political Consciousness" (Ph.D. diss., University of Wisconsin, 1997), 339–47; Wendy Hamand Venet, *Neither Ballots nor Bullets: Women Abolitionists and the Civil War* (Charlottesville: University Press of Virginia, 1991), 109–22; Mary P. Ryan, *Women in Public: Between Banners and Ballots, 1825–1880* (Baltimore: Johns Hopkins University Press, 1990), 141–55; and Elizabeth Cady Stanton, Susan B. Anthony, and Matilda Joslyn Gage, *History of Woman Suffrage* (1881–1922; repr., New York: Arno and the New York Times, 1969), 2:50–89.

members. For some league members, the nonspecific approach was an act of deference to legislators who knew best how to frame antislavery legislation. But for others, nonspecific petitioning was meant as a subtle protest. The strategy allowed league members, like female antislavery petitioners before them, to act politically while drawing attention to their exclusion from the formal legislative process. The petitioners prided themselves on ruling the province of popular mobilization while leaving the mundane business of law making to the stuffed shirts in office. Only rarely did league members dwell on the problems of making antislavery legislation constitutional or overcoming a Constitution that seemed to sanction slavery. An exceptional instance came at the league's national convention in 1863, when Ernestine L. Rose, a Polish émigré, declared that "a good constitution is a very good thing; but even the best of constitutions need sometimes to be amended and improved." "If written constitutions are in the way of human freedom," she announced, "suspend them till they can be improved."[12]

Proposals such as Rose's smacked too much of radicalism. For lawmakers and most ordinary Americans, the Constitution was still the Union's sacred text, never to be suspended or rewritten. Thus, when Attorney General Edward Bates read in late 1863 that a convention of "Radical Germans" in Cleveland had recommended "a revision of the Constitution in the spirit of the Declaration of Independence," he scornfully denounced them as living in "practical ignorance of our political institutions and of the very meaning of the phrase 'Liberty by Law.'"[13] A healthy dose of nativism informed Bates's opinion – Who were these foreigners to suggest changes in our national charter? – but so did his commitment to the "rule of law," the belief that only unchanging laws could preserve order and liberty.[14] It was fine for Lincoln at Gettysburg to slight the Constitution in favor of the Declaration, but it was a different matter entirely to suggest an actual change in the framers' text.

12   Stanton et al., *History of Woman Suffrage*, 2:75. On female petitioning, see Julie Roy Jeffrey, *The Great Silent Army of Abolitionism: Ordinary Women in the Antislavery Movement* (Chapel Hill: University of North Carolina Press, 1998), 86–93, 214–17; Nancy Isenberg, *Sex and Citizenship in Antebellum America* (Chapel Hill: University of North Carolina Press, 1998), 64–69; Zaeske, "Petitioning, Antislavery and the Emergence of Women's Political Consciousness"; Deborah Bingham Van Broekhoven, " 'Let Your Names Be Enrolled': Method and Ideology in Women's Antislavery Petitioning," in Jean Fagan Yellin and John C. Van Horne, eds., *The Abolitionist Sisterhood: Women's Political Culture in Antebellum America* (Ithaca: Cornell University Press, 1994), 179–99.

13   Washington *Daily National Intelligencer,* October 29, 1863, p. 3; Howard K. Beale, ed., *The Diary of Edward Bates, 1859–1866* (Washington, D.C.: Government Printing Office, 1933), 312.

14   Phillip S. Paludan, *A Covenant with Death: The Constitution, Law, and Equality in the Civil War Era* (Urbana: University of Illinois Press, 1975), esp. 27–30.

Emancipation and Reconstruction, Republicans and Democrats

Most Republicans shared Bates's preference for some method of emancipation that left the constitutional text untouched. Former senator Preston King of New York, though a conservative Republican, captured the feeling of many in his party when he wrote that he longed for "the termination of Slavery whose existence will not permit a permanent peace" but did "not want a single word or letter of our constitution changed."[15]

Republicans generally looked outside of the amending process for ways to abolish slavery constitutionally. Radical Republicans tended to favor one of three strategies. First was Senator Charles Sumner's "territorial" method. The longtime foe of slavery from Massachusetts argued that because secession was a form of state suicide, the rebel states were now territories, and, as such, slavery could be abolished there by federal statute. A second strategy was proposed by William Whiting, the solicitor of the War Department, who opposed Sumner's "state suicide" idea. Whiting preferred to make emancipation an issue between the federal government and the southern *people,* so he suggested legislation requiring former rebels to renounce their slaveholding rights as a condition of resuming allegiance to the Union. The most popular proposal, however, was that of Maryland representative Henry Winter Davis. Davis argued that the Constitution's guarantee of a republican form of government in every state gave Congress the power to redesign the rebel state governments so as to abolish slavery by state action. For all of their technical differences, the radical programs shared two basic tenets. First, emancipation, by way of reconstruction, lay solely within congressional jurisdiction; the president and state governments were excluded. Second, the unamended Constitution provided more than enough justification for congressional legislation abolishing slavery in the southern states.[16]

More conservative Republicans shared with radicals a desire for universal emancipation and an unaltered Constitution, but, unlike the radicals, they resisted interfering with states' rights. Postmaster General Montgomery Blair, for example, delivered a speech in October 1863 that blasted the interpretation of the "guarantee" clause offered by his foe Henry Winter Davis. As Blair explained it, the clause did not empower but rather restrained the federal government from interfering with state laws, includ-

15 Preston King to Orville Hickman Browning, November 7, 1863, Orville Hickman Browning MSS, ISHL.
16 These methods are described in more detail in Herman Belz, *Reconstructing the Union: Theory and Practice during the Civil War* (Ithaca: Cornell University Press, 1969), 168–97.

ing, implicitly, laws upholding slavery. Disrupting the balance in federal-state relations, Blair declared, was part of the radicals' scheme of promoting " '*amalgamation, equality,* and *fraternity.*' " The speech reflected a common juxtaposition of political, racial, and class anxieties: "amalgamation" raised the specter of race mixing, while "equality" and "fraternity," code words for the French Revolution, connoted a massive proletarian revolt.[17] Because members of the Blair family were close to Lincoln, some political insiders, including one correspondent of the *New York Herald*, saw the speech as a sign that the president would "withdraw or modify his emancipation proclamation and recommend a repeal or modification of the confiscation act."[18] Lending credibility to that rumor was a speech delivered soon after Blair's by Secretary of State William Henry Seward, the one time radical now considered Lincoln's most trusted advisor among the conservatives. When Seward said that the rebel states were "verging upon the time when submission, coming too late will leave neither slavery nor slaves in the land," he hinted that seceded states might retain slavery if they surrendered immediately. "The question of slavery," Seward proclaimed, "is their business, not mine."[19]

The basic difference between the radical and conservative solutions was one of means, not ends. Conservatives shared radicals' desire for universal abolition. Seward's offer of a deal to the South – your slaves for your submission – was hollow, for he knew that the Confederates were not about to surrender, and he approvingly expected slavery to be ground down by the Union armies and the slaves themselves. Montgomery Blair, though a personal enemy of Seward's, was equally committed to black freedom. Soon after his infamous speech against the radicals, he wrote a series of healing letters to Sumner arguing that there was "a perfect accord" between them in their desire "to suppress the rebellion and secure emancipation."[20] But conservatives were far more rigorous than the radicals in their commitment to the antebellum principle of noninterference with slavery in the southern states. Moreover, although conservatives still held to the idea that southern whites could be induced to adopt abolition by state action and to join the Republican party, radicals had renounced

17 Montgomery Blair, *Speech of Montgomery Blair, on the Revolutionary Schemes of the Ultra Abolitionists, and in Defence of the Policy of the President* (New York: D. W. Lee, 1863). Montgomery's brother Francis P. Blair, Jr., a Missouri congressman and Union general, simultaneously attacked the radicals and declared that the disposition of slavery should await the end of the war. See William E. Smith, *The Francis Preston Blair Family in Politics* (New York: Macmillan, 1933), 2:165–67.

18 L. A. Whiteley to James Gordon Bennett, October 12, 1863, James Gordon Bennett MSS, LC.

19 *Rochester Democrat and American*, November 2, 1863, p. 2.

20 Montgomery Blair to Charles Sumner, October 24, 1863, and November 28, 1863, both in Blair family MSS, LC.

that goal, preferring instead to force emancipation on the South and to seek a constituency among southern blacks, not southern whites. Both sides, it is important to note, assumed that they could achieve their goals without amending the Constitution. If any constitutional change was to take place, it would happen at the state level. Either, as the conservatives wanted, the southern states would be prodded to revise their state constitutions to outlaw slavery or, as the radicals wanted, they would be forced to do so.[21]

Aside from the reconstruction schemes offered by Republican radicals and conservatives, a third set of proposals surfaced – or, rather, resurfaced – from the Democrats. During the secession crisis, the northern Democrats had backed a program to rebuild the "Union as it was" on the foundation of the Corwin amendment, which prohibited any revision of the Constitution in regard to slavery. Once the war broke out, however, the northern wing of the party remained only loosely united. Some prowar Democrats temporarily joined the ranks of the Republicans and promised to support all administration policies including emancipation. Meanwhile, those party members who remained antagonistic toward the Republicans divided into two groups: the War Democrats, who supported military efforts to suppress the rebellion but opposed emancipation; and the Peace Democrats, who preferred an immediate armistice followed by some settlement restoring the Union and granting southerners permanent slaveholding rights.

In late 1863, with Congress poised to consider reconstruction, Peace Democrats turned once again to the amending process as the means to restore the Union. Already, under the direction of peace men like congressmen Clement L. Vallandigham of Ohio and Fernando Wood of New York, state-level Democratic parties had included in their platforms constitutional amendments protecting slavery. Some Peace Democrats also devised a scheme by which they would use the Constitution's amending provision to call a national convention. Ostensibly, the convention would meet to draft amendments, but its real purpose would be to settle a peace.[22] Other Peace Democrats were genuine in their desire to overhaul the Constitution. Sidney Breese, for example, a judge on the Illinois State Supreme Court and an elder statesman of the Democratic party, believed that "no good results can be reached, without a radical amendment of the Constitution of the United States." Breese drafted a number of amendments for the party's consideration, only one of which promised noninter-

21 Herman Belz, "Henry Winter Davis and the Origins of Congressional Reconstruction," *Maryland Historical Magazine*, 67 (Summer 1972), 137–39.
22 See, for example, the *Cincinnati Gazette*, August 5, 1863, p. 2; and the Springfield *Illinois State Register*, July 31, 1863, p. 2.

ference with slavery. What he envisioned was nothing less than a complete revision of the federal system, including a new method of electing presidents and a new judicial function for the Senate, under which the upper house would be "a court in the last resort, in every case where the rights of the states come in question, or the Constitutionality of a law is to be passed on."[23] Breese tried to publish his proposed amendments, but he found they were coolly received. Even the propeace editor Wilbur Storey, whose *Chicago Times* the government had temporarily shut down, deemed the proposals too radical.[24] Yet, even if most Democrats were not ready for a complete revision of the Constitution, at least they would agree to an amendment protecting slavery in the southern states.

Or would they? In the fall of 1863, for the first time since the war began, a significant number of War Democrats began to grow jittery over the party's position on slavery. Opposition to emancipation had been the linchpin of Democratic political strategy and had helped the party win new seats in the 1862 elections. But by late 1863 an increasing number of War Democrats refused any longer to stomach slavery. Some were swayed by the military benefits if not the morality of emancipation; others saw the defense of slavery simply as a political liability. Those Democrats who had declared for emancipation and joined with coalition Union parties in the state elections of 1863 had met with much more success than those who had held the party line. Most notable among these Democratic turncoats was the Ohio gubernatorial candidate John Brough of Ohio, who had disavowed standard Democratic dogma and asserted that "slavery must be wiped out and the slaves once free must not be re-enslaved."[25] Brough was elected, but many Democrats who took the other side on slavery were not so lucky. An Iowa Democrat rightly blamed the party's setbacks in 1863 on "the votaries of slavery in the North."[26]

Democrats who had already aligned themselves with the Lincoln administration seized the opportunity and tried to nudge War Democrats toward emancipation. The editor of the *Sacramento Daily Union,* a Democratic paper that had lent its support to the president and the war, called on War Democrats to wrest the party from the proslavery element: "the word Democracy has lost its true meaning . . . it has been made the rallying cry of those who advocate and defend slavery as a divine institution."[27] Even in some of the slave states of the upper South, pro-Lincoln

23 Sidney Breese to L. L. Bryan, J. W. Merritt, and H. K. S. O'Melveney, September 15, 1863, Sidney Breese MSS, ISHL.
24 Wilbur Storey to Sidney Breese, December 2, 1863, Breese MSS, ISHL.
25 *Cleveland Leader,* September 19, 1863, p. 3.
26 D. A. Lough to W. H. Lough, December 1, 1863, William Lough MSS, CiHS.
27 *Sacramento Daily Union,* December 1, 1863, p. 2.

Democrats took hold of the abolition banner. But often, they did so as a way to preserve states' rights. Edward L. Gantt, an Arkansas Democrat, explained in a series of speeches throughout the Union that emancipation would undercut the radical plan to "reduce the seceded States to the condition of territories." With slavery abolished, Gantt predicted, radicals would lose the pretext by which they hoped to invade the states: "by thus *formally giving up* what is *already lost,* we will have secured to us, all our rights as equal States in the Union."[28] This argument – that emancipation would thwart rather than fuel radicalism – would eventually drive many Democrats to support the abolition amendment to the Constitution.

The rumblings of antislavery dissent within the Democratic party erupted into open revolt at the meeting of the Northwestern War Democrats at Chicago in November 1863. James W. Taylor of Minnesota led a movement to have the convention resolve that "the American Union, as well as the progress of Democratic principles, require the total divorce of the party of Jefferson and Jackson from all association or sympathy with slavery." Taylor even went so far as to endorse Sumner's state suicide idea by declaring that the seceded states had abdicated "all legitimate State authority." Unprepared to take such a radical step, the convention rejected Taylor's reconstruction plan and invited southern states to return to the Union as states. The War Democrats were agreeable to Taylor's position on slavery, however, and they declared that "we shall not regret if slavery falls as the legitimate consequence of the war."[29]

The Chicago meeting was but the most visible manifestation of a larger phenomenon: the emergence of an antislavery faction of Democrats that threatened to disrupt both party politics and the making of reconstruction policy. It is impossible to calculate the size or influence of this faction. Certainly those Democrats who continued to defend slavery tried to dismiss them. At a Democratic rally in New Jersey, Fernando Wood toasted the War Democrat as "a white man's face on the body of a negro."[30] But Taylor, one of the leaders of the antislavery Democrats, understood that the group could play a crucial role by forming a new coalition with Republicans. Taylor even had a platform designed for the new coalition. To Salmon P. Chase, the secretary of the treasury, Taylor recommended

28 *Ohio State Journal,* December 8, 1863, p. 1.
29 Proceedings of the War Democrat Convention in the *Chicago Times,* reprinted in the *Cincinnati Gazette,* November 28, 1863, p. 2. See G. P. Edgar to John McClernand, December 4, 1863, John A. McClernand MSS, ISHL; Christopher Dell, *Lincoln and the War Democrats: The Grand Erosion of Conservative Tradition* (Rutherford, N.J.: Fairleigh Dickinson University Press, 1975), 259–60.
30 *Cincinnati Enquirer,* November 28, 1863, p. 2. See Springfield *Illinois State Register,* December 5, 1863, p. 2; *Cincinnati Gazette,* November 27, 1863, p. 2.

the slogan "a *Union as it was and the constitution as it is* (or as *it may be amended*)."[31] Here was one of the first proposals for an antislavery constitutional amendment, and it came from a Democrat, not a Republican. Chase received Taylor's platform coolly; like many radical Republicans, he assumed that abolition could be imposed on southern state constitutions without a national amendment. But Chase did agree that antislavery men from both parties might be persuaded to form a new political organization – and, ambitious as ever, he hoped to be at its head. Indeed, he had been trying to foster such an alliance long before he heard from Taylor.[32]

Presidential Emancipation: Lincoln's Reconstruction Proclamation

Lincoln also recognized the pivotal importance of the War Democrats, both for his own reelection and for reconstruction, and he kept this group in mind as he penned his annual message to Congress. According to Lincoln's personal secretary, John Hay, while the president worked on the message, Secretary of State Seward sniffed out ways of "bringing over to our side the honest War Democrats."[33] The Blairs worked independently toward the same end. Francis Blair, Sr., acknowledged that antiradical speeches by his sons Montgomery and Frank, Jr., in the fall of 1863 were designed to promote "a Cordial fusion between patriotic democrats and Republicans."[34] Although Hay regarded War Democrats as nothing more than "foul birds . . . trying to roost under the National Aegis," Lincoln saw them as critical allies.[35] The president hoped to seize the opportunity provided by the current fluidity in politics. By keeping his reconstruction plan conservative, he could perhaps draw more Democrats into his fold. One Washington insider even predicted that the president, in a "bid to the Democracy," would recommend the return of the southern states "with all the powers and benefits of states to be exercised by the people within

31 James W. Taylor to Salmon P. Chase, November 26, 1863, Salmon P. Chase MSS, LC.
32 See, for example, Chase to Benjamin F. Butler, December 14, 1862, Benjamin F. Butler MSS, LC; Thomas Brown to Chase, Salmon P. Chase MSS, LC; Chase to Henry C. Whitman, September 12, 1863, Chase to Joshua Leavitt, October 7, 1863, Chase to John Lorimer Graham, November 2, 1863, all in Salmon P. Chase MSS, HSPa; Chase to Daniel S. Dickinson, November 18, 1863, Daniel S. Dickinson MSS, Newberry Library, Chicago.
33 Tyler Dennett, ed., *Lincoln and the Civil War in the Diaries and Letters of John Hay* (New York: Dodd, Mead, 1939), 129.
34 Francis P. Blair, Sr., to Francis Blair, Jr., October 6, 1863, Blair family MSS, LC. See also Francis Blair, Sr., to Apolline Alexander Blair, October 25, 1863, Blair family MSS, LC.
35 Dennett, *Lincoln and the Civil War*, 129, 130, 137.

them."[36] The ultimate price of such a conservative bid, of course, might
be the continuation of slavery beyond the war.

As it turned out, Lincoln did not propose an antislavery amendment in
his annual message of 1863, but neither did he backpedal on emancipation. He promised never "to attempt to retract or modify the emancipation proclamation," lest he commit "a cruel and an astounding breach of
faith."[37] The *New York Tribune* heaped praise upon the "thoroughly
uncompromising language of the President," while the *Chicago Tribune*,
which had also been needling Lincoln to push forward on emancipation,
congratulated the president for his commitment to "wipe the Confederacy
. . . clean of slavery."[38]

The most important part of Lincoln's message was his Proclamation of
Amnesty and Reconstruction. The proclamation called for a state to be
readmitted to the Union once a minimum of 10 percent of its voters in
1860 swore an oath to the Constitution and the laws and proclamations
passed during the rebellion, including those emancipating the slaves. This
loyal minority would then call a constitutional convention that would
draft a state constitution abolishing slavery. Meanwhile, the federal government would pardon all rebels but those who had served directly in
positions of authority in the Confederate government.

Although the proclamation required that new state constitutions outlaw slavery, it generally took the conservative line on reconstruction. For
example, the program did not specify that all slaves in a state must be
freed immediately. Also, Lincoln left in the hands of the reformed governments the method of dealing with the freed people; some ex-slaves might
well be forced to become apprentices to their former masters. The president said nothing of the future of slavery in the loyal slave states, and he
admitted that any wartime legislation against slavery could be "repealed,
modified or held void by Congress, or by decision of the Supreme Court."
Most important, he urged, rather than forced, emancipation and reconstruction upon the states: his plan was "the best the Executive can suggest
. . . [but] it must not be understood that no other possible mode would be
acceptable."[39]

Lincoln might have offered more secure footing to black freedom by
proposing an abolition constitutional amendment. In mentioning that the
Supreme Court could overturn all emanicipation measures, the president
implicitly acknowledged the need for an antislavery amendment. Yet he
had decided, quite deliberately, against explicitly recommending such a

36 Joseph H. Geiger to Salmon P. Chase, November 18, 1863, Salmon P. Chase MSS, LC.
37 *CW*, 7:51.
38 *New York Tribune*, December 10, 1863, p. 1; *Chicago Tribune*, December 14, 1863, p.
    2.
39 *CW*, 7:56.

measure. Two of his Illinois friends, Congressman Isaac N. Arnold and Leonard Swett, had separately urged him to include an antislavery amendment in his reconstruction program. Arnold assured him that the amendment would "complete the work" and guarantee him reelection, while Swett warned him that some other presidential candidate might back the amendment "to outstrip him in satisfying the radical element." Lincoln was unconvinced, almost uninterested. "Is not the question of emancipation doing well enough now?" he asked Swett.[40]

The president worried that an abolition amendment might foul the political waters. The amendments he had recommended in December 1862 had gone nowhere, mainly because they reflected an outdated program of gradual emancipation, which included compensation and colonization. Moreover, Lincoln knew that he did not have to propose amendments because others more devoted to abolition would, especially if he pointed out the vulnerability of existing emancipation legislation. He was also concerned about negative reactions from conservatives, particularly potential new recruits from the Democrats. Although the president was no doubt pleased to see some of the War Democrats willing to embrace emancipation, he probably feared that they would retreat into the regular Democratic ranks if the administration took steps toward federal action against slavery in the southern states.

If the president thought an antislavery amendment would alienate War Democrats, he may have miscalculated. Democrats, after all, had been the most ardent advocates of constitutional amendments, though admittedly for the preservation rather than the prohibition of slavery. Also, they might have considered the amending process an excellent way of taking the slavery issue out of the federal government and putting it directly into the hands of the people. An antislavery amendment would appeal especially to those War Democrats whose only objection to the president's emancipation policy was that it was, in their opinion, unconstitutional. In the face of the heated political campaign to come, however, Lincoln opted for caution over experimentation. He chose to make the Proclamation of Reconstruction and Amnesty, and not a constitutional amendment abolishing slavery, the opening salvo in the battle to win the allegiance of the War Democrats.

Congress Responds: Proposals for an Abolition Amendment

Congressional Republicans responded to Lincoln's proclamation with their own reconstruction programs, some of which included an abolition

---

40 William H. Herndon and Jesse W. Weik, *Abraham Lincoln: The True Story of a Great Life* (1892; repr., New York: D. Appleton, 1913), 2:241; Isaac N. Arnold to Abraham Lincoln, December 4, 1863, RTL.

constitutional amendment. But, as historians Herman Belz and Michael Les Benedict have demonstrated, these proposals were meant to supplement rather than undercut the president's. The division between congressional Republicans and the president over reconstruction did not develop until long after Lincoln's annual message. Some of the leading radicals in the House of Representatives, including congressmen James M. Ashley of Ohio and Henry Winter Davis of Maryland, seemed to approve of Lincoln's plan.[41]

Soon after the new Congress convened, Ashley proposed a bill that conformed to Lincoln's plan in all but a few significant details. Like the president's plan, Ashley's rejected theories of territorializing the South in favor of preserving the states and guaranteeing them a republican form of government. Similarly, Ashley's program required a pledge of loyalty from only 10 percent of a state's 1860 voters to reform the state. And, as in the Proclamation of Amnesty and Reconstruction, Ashley's bill required as part of the oath of loyalty a pledge to respect all the Union measures regarding slavery. On the issue of suffrage, however, the bill differed significantly with the president's proclamation. It restricted from voting anyone who had fought against the Union or held office in a rebel state. And whereas Lincoln's system restricted voting to loyal white males, Ashley's opened the polls to black men over the age of twenty-one. Despite its radical details, Ashley's bill mainly sought to add specificity to Lincoln's general outline of a reconstruction program. The plan was known more for the general principle it shared with Lincoln's, a rapid reconstruction led by loyal minorities, than for its liberal provisions for African Americans.[42]

What many of Ashley's contemporaries and a number of later historians have overlooked, however, was that the Ohioan's reconstruction bill was really one part of a two-pronged program of reconstruction. Unlike Lincoln, Ashley refused to leave any doubt about the constitutionality of emancipation, and in his reconstruction bill, he referred to the need for a "constitutional guarantee of . . . perpetual freedom."[43] So, at about the same time that he offered his reconstruction bill, he introduced a constitutional amendment abolishing slavery. The Ohioan's bill provided "for the submission to the several States of a proposition to amend the national Constitution prohibiting slavery, or involuntary servitude, in all of the States and Territories now owned or which may be hereafter acquired by

41 Belz, *Reconstructing the Union,* 168–97; Michael Les Benedict, *A Compromise of Principle: Congressional Republicans and Reconstruction, 1863–1869* (New York: W. W. Norton 1974), 70–73.
42 Belz, *Reconstructing the Union,* 176–87.
43 Ibid., 179.

the United States."[44] Ashley's strategy revealed a powerful commitment to African American rights coupled with a keen sense of politics. The congressman hoped to engraft black suffrage onto the malleable state constitutions of the South while simultaneously revising the federal Constitution more moderately, making black freedom, and only black freedom, a constitutional guarantee. Young and opportunistic, the stout, gruff Ashley, who had long idolized radical leaders like Joshua R. Giddings and Salmon P. Chase, also had begun to forge alliances with party moderates like President Lincoln. In his two separate proposals, Ashley sought to satisfy both factions.[45]

Only by understanding the connection between Ashley's reconstruction bill and the abolition amendment can we begin to appreciate the reconstruction bill as an enforcement device for the amendment. Besides specifying how rebel states were to be readmitted to the Union, Ashley's bill outlined legal procedures that protected black freedom. The legislation gave sole jurisdiction in seceded states to federal district courts; it allowed qualified African Americans to sit on juries in those courts; and it mandated stiff fines and jail terms for anyone attempting to reenslave a freed person.[46] These measures were meant to rectify the shortcomings of the confiscation acts, which merely declared certain slaves free without offering specific enforcement provisions. Enforcement measures such as these were what Congressman James F. Wilson of Iowa had in mind when, in his own proposed abolition amendment, he included a clause empowering Congress to uphold emancipation by "appropriate legislation."[47] Wilson, the chairman of the House Judiciary Committee, no doubt expected the current Congress to enact such enforcement legislation by adopting either Ashley's proposal or some other reconstruction bill. As it turned out, and for reasons no one could have predicted, none of the reconstruction bills considered by this Congress would be enacted into law. As a result, when the Thirteenth Amendment was ratified in December 1865, the enforcement legislation that congressmen had in mind when they proposed the measure was nowhere to be found, and enforcement would have to await the Civil Rights Act of 1866.

---

44 CG, 38th Cong. 1st sess. (December 14, 1863), 19.
45 Robert F. Horowitz, *The Great Impeacher: A Political Biography of James M. Ashley* (Brooklyn: Brooklyn College Press, 1979), 89–110.
46 Ibid., 94–95; Belz, *Reconstructing the Union*, 180–81.
47 CG, 38th Cong., 1st sess. (December 14, 1863), 21. The text of Wilson's proposal is as follows: "Sec 1. Slavery, being incompatible with a free government, is forever prohibited in the United States; and involuntary servitude shall be permitted only as a punishment for crime. Sec. 2. Congress shall have power to enforce the foregoing section of this article by appropriate legislation."

Ashley's two-pronged method – a constitutional amendment to secure emancipation, and a reconstruction statute to enforce it – represented a novel approach to the prohibition of slavery. No congressman since John Quincy Adams in 1839 had proposed a constitional amendment on abolition. Most antislavery congressmen sought their objective within the framework of an unamended Constitution, usually by adopting some strategy, like Sumner's territorial method or Davis's use of the guarantee clause, that could be reconciled with the principle of noninterference with slavery in the states. Other congressmen still held to the radical constitutionalist idea that Congress already had the power to abolish slavery in the states. This small minority included the Illinois representative Owen Lovejoy and the New Hampshire senator John P. Hale, both of whom proposed statutes, not amendments, that abolished slavery *and* explicitly guaranteed civil rights to African Americans.[48] The amendments proposed by Ashley and Wilson were not nearly as radical. They said nothing explicitly about equal rights and they implied that the existing Constitution was insufficient to abolish slavery everywhere. Nonetheless, the amendments did represent a new departure: instead of looking for a constitutional loophole that would allow abolition, they corrected the Constitution, making it an unequivocal charter for freedom.

Lawmakers in the Senate were slower than their counterparts in the House to take up the abolition amendment. By the end of 1863, Lyman Trumbull, who, as chairman of the Senate Judiciary Committee, would have an important role in any constitutional revision, still had not taken to the idea of an antislavery amendment. Earlier that year, the Illinois senator had told another Republican that the Constitution could not be changed while the country was still at war.[49] In contrast, Charles Sumner, Trumbull's rival within the party, already had drafted an amendment that declared all people "equal before the law," a phrase borrowed from the French Declaration of Rights of 1791. Sumner hoped to grant the fullest measure of equality for African Americans while adding more luster to his own reputation.[50] But Sumner's friend Francis Lieber, a well-known

---

48 Ibid., 20 (Lovejoy), 17 (Hale). Not only some Republicans but a few Democrats still held to radical constitutionalist doctrine. The historian George Bancroft, for example, thought that Congress could legitimately pass an act of universal emancipation. See Bancroft to Robert C. Schenck, November 18, 1863, Robert C. Schenck MSS, Rutherford B. Hayes Historical Library, Fremont, Ohio.

49 *CG*, 37th Cong., 3d sess. (January 29, 1863), 592.

50 David Donald, *Charles Sumner and the Rights of Man* (New York: Alfred A. Knopf, 1970), 149. Similar amendments were offered in the House, but perhaps the most radical amendment of all was the one proposed by Wendell Phillips outside of Congress, which prohibited states from making any legal distinction according to race. See Andrew Kull, *The Color-Blind Constitution* (Cambridge, Mass.: Harvard University Press, 1992), 55–56.

scholar of law and political science, advised the senator not to propose the amendment lest he destroy the prowar coalition. "If it be too early, and if you do not carry your point," Lieber warned, "it will be a positive retrogression" and would "drive off the 'war democrats.'" Lieber advised that the senator wait for public opinion to turn more in favor of equal rights, and then submit not one but "some 3 or 4" amendments to Congress.[51] Sumner followed his friend's recommendation and looked for a more favorable occasion.

That opportunity came on January 11, 1864, when Senator John Henderson of Missouri proposed a joint resolution for a constitutional amendment that declared, "slavery or involuntary servitude, except as a punishment for crime, shall not exist in the United States." Unlike Sumner's proposal, Henderson's did not explicitly grant equality before the law. Henderson, a former slave owner and longtime Democrat who had helped form the Union party of Missouri, cared little for African American rights. Indeed, like many other Democrats newly converted to antislavery, he hoped that his measure would put an end to the squabbling over slavery and "the negro issue" that had so divided his home state and the Union. After Henderson's measure was referred to Trumbull's Judiciary Committee, Sumner put into play a strategy by which he hoped to take control of the amendment. He persuaded the Senate to create a new committee on slavery and freedmen, which he would chair, that would consider the many abolition petitions flowing into Congress.[52] He planned to use this committee to propose and promote his own constitutional amendment.

Sumner made his intentions clearer on February 8, when he introduced his constitutional amendment to the Senate and asked that it be referred to his new committee. So desperate was he to make his amendment the final version that he challenged the well-accepted custom of sending proposed amendments to the Judiciary Committee. His Republican colleagues would hear nothing of it. Trumbull, the conservative James Rood Doolittle, and the moderate William Pitt Fessenden, Sumner's arch-rival, all confronted the Massachusetts senator and forced him to refer his amendment to Trumbull's committee.[53]

On the next day, the senator once again tried to take charge of emancipation, this time by grandly introducing the "mammoth" abolition petition of the Women's Loyal National League. Sumner carefully arranged for two African American men to carry the impressive document into the

51 Lieber to Sumner, December 4, 1863, Francis Lieber MSS, HEH.
52 Donald, *Charles Sumner and the Rights of Man*, 147–48.
53 CG, 38th Cong., 1st sess. (February 8, 1864), 521–22.

Senate chamber. Because the petition mentioned only an act of emancipation, not a constitutional amendment, the Senate referred it to Sumner's committee on slavery and freedmen.[54] But the Senate's decision was a hollow victory for Sumner. By this point, the senator knew that slavery would most likely be abolished by constitutional amendment. And it would be Trumbull's committee, not his, that Congress would charge with drafting the amendment. So he pocketed his measure with the dim hope that the Judiciary Committee might propose an amendment in line with his own.

The Drafting of the Thirteenth Amendment

The Senate Judiciary Committee began meeting in January 1864 to draft an abolition amendment. It is difficult to reconstruct the committee's deliberations because no record of them survives.[55] Whatever went on in those meetings, the committee had completed its task by February 10. On that day, Trumbull announced that he would report "at an early day" an amendment declaring that "neither slavery nor involuntary servitude, except as a punishment for crime, whereof a party shall have been duly convicted, shall exist within the United States, or any place subject to their jurisdiction; and also that Congress shall have power to enforce this article by proper legislation."[56] It was no coincidence that Trumbull's announcement came only two days after Sumner had proposed his amendment making all persons "equal before the law." The Massachusetts senator had spurred the committee into final action.

In drafting their amendment, the senators on the Judiciary Committee drew from various amendments proposed to both houses of Congress. They built upon Henderson's amendment, incorporating into it some of the language of Ashley's version in the House and adding an enforcement article similar to the one offered by James Wilson.

---

54 Ibid. (February 9, 1864), 536; Donald, *Charles Sumner and the Rights of Man*, 148–49; Venet, *Neither Ballots nor Bullets*, 119; James M. McPherson, *The Struggle for Equality: Abolitionists and the Negro in the Civil War and Reconstruction* (Princeton: Princeton University Press, 1964), 126.
55 The National Archives holds various bills, resolutions, and petitions presented to the Judiciary Committee, but no record of the actual discussions. See 38th Congress, RG 46, sec. 8E2, NA. No newspaper correspondents in Washington – at least none I have found – offered any account of what transpired in the committee room. Also, committee members said nothing of the committee's deliberations. This silence was unsurprising, for congressional committees were expected to keep committee discussions secret unless a dissenting committee member wished to record his objections.
56 *CG*, 38th Cong., 1st sess. (February 10, 1864), 553.

Although it made Henderson's amendment the foundation of the final amendment, the committee rejected an article in Henderson's version that allowed the amendment to be adopted by the approval of only a simple majority in Congress and the ratification of only two-thirds of the states.[57] With this article, Henderson probably hoped to get around two of the thorny questions involved in the amendment process: were the empty seats of southern representatives and senators supposed to count toward the total number of congressmen, and were the Confederate states supposed to count toward the total number of states? If Henderson's language were adopted, the amendment could easily be ratified regardless of whether southern congressional seats and Confederate states were included in the various counts. Indeed, any future constitutional revision would be a fairly simple matter. Ordinary Americans as well as United States senators were reluctant to adopt these or any new rules for constitutional change. A Pennsylvania man pleaded with his congressman not to approve Henderson's modification of the amending process: "The present Constitution is good enough, and should never be touched, other than to prohibit the existence of Slavery in the future in all the states."[58] Committee members agreed, and they scratched Henderson's provision. Recent scholars – most notably Bruce Ackerman – have correctly observed that Civil War–era Americans seemed to take a carefree attitude toward the formal rules of amendment.[59] But the fact remains that, regardless of how *we* might judge their respect for the amendment process, these Americans judged themselves to be formalists. That is, they genuinely believed that they held true to the rules of amendment, and thus they rejected every attempt to change those rules.

Although committee members dismissed Henderson's approach to the problem of the South in the amending process, they did not offer a solution of their own. It is fair to assume, however, that, for the purposes of a vote on an amendment, the committee did not expect the absent southern congressmen to count toward the total number of congressmen. Ever since secession, congressmen had voted as if the Congress assembled was the whole Congress. That same logic did not apply to the southern *states*, however. Because the joint resolution for the amendment said nothing about excluding any states, and because the proscription of states from the ratification process was unprecedented, many legislators must have believed that the rebellious states would take part in ratification. Most Republicans, including Lincoln, refused to acknowledge that southern

57 See ibid. (March 28, 1864), 1313.
58 D. W. Patterson to Thaddeus Stevens, January 14, 1864, Thaddeus Stevens MSS, LC.
59 Bruce Ackerman, *We the People*, vol. 2, *Transformations* (Cambridge, Mass.: Harvard University Press, 1998), pt. 2.

states had left the Union. How could they then exclude those states for the purpose of ratification? Those Republicans who did accept the legitimacy of secession – and thus believed that the seceded states should not count toward the total number of states – were reluctant early on to make a stand on this issue lest they split the party and jeopardize the amendment. Because most congressmen assumed that the southern states would be included in ratification, and because others with contrary views kept their opinions to themselves to ensure the amendment's adoption, there was almost no discussion of southern ratification until after Congress passed the amendment in early 1865.

Perhaps the most important decision of the Judiciary Committee was the rejection of Sumner's explicitly egalitarian language in favor of the language of the Northwest Ordinance, which simply prohibited slavery and involuntary servitude. At first glance, this decision might suggest that the committee did not believe that the amendment secured equality before the law. But, in fact, some committee members may have thought that the final amendment went as far as Sumner's in guaranteeing legal equality. Indeed, two of the committee members later claimed that the final amendment was intended to extend civil rights to black Americans. The occasion for this claim was a debate in early 1866 over the civil rights bill and the Freedmen's Bureau bill. Senators Trumbull and Jacob M. Howard of Michigan, both members of the committee that drafted the Thirteenth Amendment, argued that the two bills were precisely what their committee had in mind when it wrote the amendment in 1864. The amendment, Trumbull said, was meant to abolish "absolutely all provisions of State or local law which make a man a slave. . . . Those laws that prevented the colored man going from home, that did not allow him to buy or to sell, or to make contracts; that did not allow him to own property; that did not allow him to enforce rights; that did not allow him to be educated." Howard went even further. He said that it was in anticipation of southern state discriminatory legislation that the committee drafted an amendment that would give "to persons who are of different races or colors the same civil rights."[60]

Obviously, there was some embellishment here, for committee members in 1864 could not have envisioned all that southern state governments would do to undercut black freedom in 1865 and 1866. It was understandable, then, that a number of lawmakers in 1866 did not accept Trumbull and Howard's story. The Pennsylvania senator Edgar Cowan, a conservative Republican who had served with Howard and Trumbull in

---

60 CG, 39th Cong., 1st sess. (January 19, 1866), 322 (Trumbull); (January 30, 1866), 503–4 (Howard).

the Thirty-eighth Congress, denied his colleagues' version of events. Cowan argued that the amendment was meant only to outlaw traditional forms of bondage; it "never was intended to overturn this government and revolutionize all the laws of the states everywhere."[61]

Trumbull and Howard may have overstated their case, but there was still much truth to their claims. Although the Senate Judiciary Committee rejected Sumner's explicit promise of equality, at least a few members of the committee assumed that the final amendment still carried an *implicit* guarantee of the same rights promised by Sumner's measure. During the Senate debate of the amendment in 1864, Trumbull assured Sumner that the committee's decision against Sumner's language represented a preference in style, not content. "The words we have adopted," Trumbull promised, "will accomplish the [same] object."[62] Sumner himself was persuaded by Trumbull's argument. When later explaining why he preferred his own version to Trumbull's, the Massachusetts senator did not object that Trumbull's bill came up short on equal rights but only that it allowed slavery to exist as a punishment for crime.[63] This clause was indeed an unfortunate flaw, for it allowed involuntary servitude to survive the war in the form of peonage and convict labor.

It seems, then, that Trumbull's claim in 1866 that the Thirteenth Amendment offered the promise of equality was not entirely a later invention.[64] But if members of the Senate Judiciary Committee in 1864 saw their amendment as accomplishing the same object as Sumner's, why did they reject Sumner's wording?

In part, the committee was opting for the simplest language possible. Sumner's phrasing confused even the highest law officer in the Union, Attorney General Edward Bates. Upon reading Sumner's amendment, Bates asked, "What is *equality before the law?* . . . Does *that equality* necessarily prevent the one from becoming the slave of the other?"[65] Much preferable, argued Senator Howard, was "the good old Anglo-Saxon language employed by our fathers in the [Northwest] ordinance of 1787, an expression which has been judicated upon repeatedly, which is

---

61 Ibid. (January 30, 1866), 499.
62 CG, 38th Cong., 1st sess. (April 8, 1864), 1488.
63 Sumner to George William Curtis, April 13, 1864, in Beverly Wilson Palmer, ed., *The Selected Letters of Charles Sumner* (Boston: Northeastern University Press, 1990), 2:233.
64 For a fuller discussion of this point, see Akhil Reed Amar, "Remember the Thirteenth," *Constitutional Commentary,* 10 (Summer 1993), 403–8; VanderVelde, "The Labor Vision of the Thirteenth Amendment"; and Harold M. Hyman and William M. Wiecek, *Equal Justice under Law: Constitutional Development, 1835–1875* (New York: Harper and Row, 1982), 386–438.
65 Beale, *Diary of Edward Bates*, 330.

perfectly well understood both by the public and by judicial tribunals."[66] Whereas Sumner's amendment might take the law in a new direction, the committee's measure simply took the Northwest Ordinance, already a cornerstone in northern antislavery law, and applied it to the South.[67]

In the same way that committee members avoided the appearance of disrupting constitutional norms, they eschewed language suggesting a social revolution. When faced with Sumner's use of a phrase from the French Declaration of Rights, Trumbull explained, the committee decided not to "go to the French Revolution to find the proper words for a constitution. We all know that their constitutions were failures, while ours, we trust, will be permanent."[68] Senator Howard even saw in Sumner's proposal the potential for a dangerous leveling of gender hierarchies. An amendment that made "all persons" equal before the law, said Howard, would naturally lead to legal equality between the sexes, a reform that few of the legislators condoned.[69] The committee's amendment, by contrast, steered clear of the issue of female emancipation.

The committee's choice of language was also the result of personal animosities and short-term political strategy. Sumner's uncompromising nature had alienated many of his fellow senators, including some of those on the Judiciary Committee. "If I could cut the throats of about half a dozen Republican Senators," wrote Senator Fessenden to his cousin, ". . . Sumner would be the first victim, as by far the greatest fool of the lot." To his son, Fessenden added that Sumner "is not a mean but a malignant scoundrel," and he provided a list of ten Republican senators who despised the Massachusetts senator. Four of them were on the Judici-

---

66 CG, 38th Cong., 1st sess. (April 8, 1864), 1489. James Ashley, the amendment's sponsor in the House, also claimed to be aiming for familiarity when he used the Northwest Ordinance as the basis for his own proposed amendment. See J. M. Ashley to Benjamin W. Arnett, November 14, 1892, in Benjamin W. Arnett, ed., *Orations and Speeches: Duplicate Copy of the Souvenir from the Afro-American League of Tennessee to Hon. James M. Ashley of Ohio* (Philadelphia: A.M.E. Church 1894), 331.

67 On the use of the Northwest Ordinance in antislavery legislation and legal opinion, see Peter S. Onuf, *Statehood and Union: A History of the Northwest Ordinance* (Bloomington: Indiana University Press, 1987), esp. 109–52; and Paul Finkelman, *An Imperfect Union: Slavery, Federalism, and Comity* (Chapel Hill: University of North Carolina Press, 1981), 82–87. Prior to the Civil War, it should be noted, the Supreme Court under Roger B. Taney had denied the applicability of the Northwest Ordinance to slaves entering the northwestern states: the ordinance, said Taney, had concerned slaves there only when that region was still a territory. See Finkelman, *An Imperfect Union*, 272–74. The Thirteenth Amendment, then, was a reassertion of the primacy of the Northwest Ordinance in the law of slavery.

68 CG, 38th Cong., 1st sess. (April 8, 1864), 1488.

69 Ibid. See Amy Dru Stanley, "Conjugal Bonds and Wage Labor: Rights of Contract in the Age of Emancipation," *Journal of American History,* 75 (September 1988), 471–500.

ary Committee.[70] Little wonder, then, that committee members rejected Sumner's amendment, even if some of them agreed with the principle of equality that it embraced.

Committee members also understood that the more the amendment was associated with Sumner, the more it would be regarded as dangerously radical. During the early months of the Thirty-eighth Congress, Sumner introduced legislation ending prohibitions against black testimony in federal courts, removing racial discrimination from Washington streetcars, and granting equal pay to black soldiers. All of these measures met with race-baiting blasts from the Democratic opposition as well as disaffection from allies like William Lloyd Garrison, who tried to warn Sumner off these issues and to keep him focused on "the proposition to abolish slavery."[71] The senators on the Judiciary Committee, who consistently voted more conservatively than Sumner on issues involving African American rights, knew that it would be impossible to carry an amendment identified as Sumner's.[72]

The committee had to consider in particular the wishes of the War Democrats. The amendment could receive the necessary two-thirds support of Congress only if a sizable minority of Democrats supported it, and there was good evidence that some of them would. Republican leaders did not forget the light chirping of antislavery sentiment among War Democrats after the elections of 1863, and they must have been aware of the rumors that some Democratic congressmen were preparing to support an antislavery amendment. They were sure to lose that support if they allowed either Sumner's name or his pet phrase, "equal before the law," to become attached to the amendment. The Democratic *Cincinnati Enquirer*, for example, ridiculed Sumner's amendment for promoting "the dogma that the negro is exactly like the white man."[73] By rejecting Sumner's proposal, a decision that one War Democratic sheet called "the wisest thing that could have been done," Trumbull and his committee

---

70 William Pitt Fessenden to Elizabeth Fessenden Warriner, June 1, 1862, Fessenden to William H. Fessenden, March 2, 1864, and May 7, 1864, all in Fessenden family Papers, BC. See Donald, *Charles Sumner and the Rights of Man*, 143–45.

71 Garrison to Sumner, April 19, 1864, in Walter M. Merrill, ed., *The Letters of William Lloyd Garrison*, vol. 5, *Let the Oppressed Go Free, 1861–1867* (Cambridge, Mass.: Harvard University Press, 1979), 199. See Donald, *Charles Sumner and the Rights of Man*, 152–61.

72 Of the six committee members, three – Lafayette Foster of Connecticut, Ira Harris of New York, and John C. Ten Eyck of New Jersey – may be classed as conservatives, and only one, Howard, as a radical. Trumbull defied classification. The final member of the committee, Lazarus W. Powell of Kentucky, was a consistent Peace Democrat. See Benedict, *Compromise of Principle*, 28; Allan G. Bogue, *The Earnest Men: Republicans of the Civil War Senate* (Ithaca: Cornell University Press, 1981), 104–5, 109–11.

73 *Cincinnati Enquirer*, February 17, 1864, p. 2.

kept antislavery Democrats open to the idea of a less explicitly radical amendment.[74] A onetime Democrat himself, Trumbull played to the War Democrats by claiming that the committee simply borrowed the language of Thomas Jefferson, the father of the Democratic party and the author of an early version of the Northwest Ordinance. The "Jeffersonian" label stuck to the amendment throughout the congressional debates.[75]

This short-term strategy for securing the amendment's adoption had an unanticipated, powerful long-term effect on civil rights law. Trumbull and some of his colleagues may have thought that their measure accomplished all that Sumner's did for equal rights, but by rejecting Sumner's language, they unwittingly placed an effective cudgel in the hands of later jurists and legislators who beat down any attempt to broaden the amendment into an extension of civil equality for African Americans.

It is somewhat inappropriate to dwell so long on the difference between the final amendment and Sumner's, because it was not Sumner's proposal but rather Lincoln's Reconstruction Proclamation that the committee had most in mind when it drafted the amendment. The committee's main purpose was to put emancipation on firm constitutional ground, something Lincoln's plan failed to do. Under the Reconstruction Proclamation, Congressman Isaac Arnold explained, there remained the "danger under a state government of the re-establishment of slavery."[76]

The precise nature of Arnold's anxiety must be understood. Like most northerners, the Illinois congressman doubted that slavery could be re-established as a viable system of labor in the South. Nevertheless, the war might end with some black Americans still legally enslaved, and the lingering institution might then create further sectional conflict. Charles Francis Adams, the minister to England, put the matter best when he wrote to his son: "the repentant class of slave owners with their old democratic allies of the north [may] . . . attempt to re-establish the Union as it was. . . . Not that I doubt the fact that in any event slavery is doomed. The only difference will be that in dying it may cause us another sharp convulsion, which we might avoid by finishing it now."[77] The congressional movement toward a constitutional amendment grew in large part from the conviction of congressional Republicans that they knew better than Lincoln how to free the slaves – and thus how to prevent another future civil war.

74 *Rochester Democrat and American,* February 12, 1864, p. 2.
75 See, for example, *CG,* 38th Cong., 1st sess. (April 8, 1864), 1487–88; and the Indianapolis *Daily Journal,* April 13, 1864, p. 2.
76 Isaac N. Arnold to Nathaniel P. Banks, February 14, 1864, Nathaniel P. Banks MSS, ISHL.
77 Charles F. Adams, Sr., to Charles F. Adams, Jr., August 24, 1863, in Worthington Chauncey Ford, ed., *A Cycle of Adams Letters, 1861–1865* (Boston: Houghton Mifflin, 1920), 2:76–77.

But, while congressional Republicans may have differed with Lincoln on the method of emancipation, most shared the president's belief that the future of the Union mattered more than the future of African Americans. Trumbull was a perfect example. He thought Lincoln's reconstruction program was weak and suspected that the president would not be re-elected.[78] What was needed, Trumbull explained in a private letter to his friend General Nathaniel P. Banks, was an abolition amendment: "If this can be accomplished and our arms are successful, it ends all future trouble."[79] Clearly, Trumbull thought of his committee's proposal mostly as a means of removing the cause of the present war. Like Lincoln, Trumbull believed that the primary objective was union, but unlike the president, he assumed that an abolition amendment was just as necessary as military victory to reach that goal.

Sumner was not so sanguine about the amendment's potential. For him, the measure was but an incident in the larger struggle for freedom and equality. Trumbull may have believed that Union victory and the antislavery amendment guarded against "all future trouble," but the Massachusetts senator had the prescience to see that "much else must be done."[80]

78 Trumbull to H. G. McPike, February 6, 1864, Lyman Trumbull MSS, LC.
79 Trumbull to Banks, February 18, 1864, Nathaniel P. Banks MSS, ISHL.
80 Sumner to Lieber, February 10, 1864, in Palmer, *The Selected Letters of Charles Sumner,* 2:225.

3

Facing Freedom

After Senator Lyman Trumbull reported the antislavery amendment out of the Judiciary Committee on February 10, 1864, debate on the measure began – but not in Congress. The Senate took more than six weeks to get around to its discussion of Trumbull's resolution. By then, initial deliberation of the issue already had begun in the conversations and correspondence of politicians, legal theorists, political observers, and ordinary Americans. The time between the introduction of the amendment to the Senate and the congressional debates was truly a formative period for the measure and for African American rights in general.

During this period an amendment fever swept across the North. Local political meetings began issuing resolutions calling for constitutional revision on every issue from the abolition of slavery to the establishment of a national religion. Republicans in particular tried to puzzle out not only the meaning of the abolition amendment but the nature of the Constitution itself. Specifically, some began to consider whether one amendment alone would be enough to adjust the Constitution to fit the new state of the nation and the new status of African Americans. Perhaps the time had come to add a slate of amendments – in effect, to rewrite the Constitution. Meanwhile, some within the Democratic party began to take seriously the idea of endorsing the amendment, thereby changing the party's course on emancipation and stealing some wind from Republican sails. Oddly, the people who seemed least interested in the movement to abolish slavery by constitutional amendment were African Americans. Their lack of interest was not a sign of political apathy – the activism of African Americans during the last years of the war was as strong as ever – but instead was a reflection of their belief that the surest guarantee of equality lay in tangible economic and political power instead of a parchment promise of legal freedom.

What emerges from the study of these groups during this period is a sense of the complete diversity in American attitudes toward the Constitution and constitutional amendments. No single wartime doctrine regarding constitutional change, not even a set of competing doctrines, dominated the intellectual landscape. Instead, people's prewar attitudes toward the founding document and its revision constantly shifted in relation to changing political and social objectives. The immediate circumstances of

To the Honorable Senate and House of Representatives of the United States, in Congress Assembled.

The undersigned, citizens of Western Pennsylvania, would most respectfully pray your honorable bodies to take steps to amend the Constitution of the United States so as to contain,

1st. A clear and distinct acknowledgement of the being and authority of Almighty God.—(Ps. 47, 7; Zach. 14, 9.)

2d. An acknowledgement of Jesus Christ as the Governor of the nations, and Prince of the Kings of the earth.—(Rev. 1, 5.)

3d. An acknowledgement of the priesthood of Christ, whereby the pardon of national sin is obtained.

4th. An acknowledgment of the excellence of the Holy Scriptures as the doctrine of the Christian religion, and the supremacy of God's law as the basis of all civil legislation.

5th. That slavery or involuntary servitude, except for crime, shall not exist within the limits of the United States.

And your petitioners, as in duty bound, will ever pray, &c.

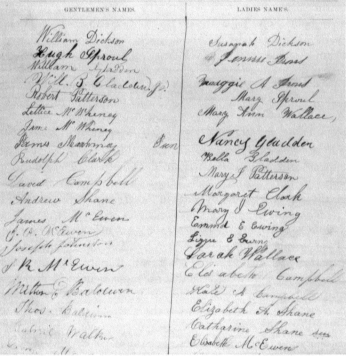

GENTLEMEN'S NAMES.	LADIES NAMES.

Figure 3. During the 1863–64 session, Congress received an increasing number of petitions that called specifically for constitutional amendments on various issues. This 1864 petition from western Pennsylvania called for four amendments establishing Christianity as a national religion and the basis of all civil law; almost as an afterthought, it called for a fifth amendment abolishing slavery. Like many emancipation initiatives, the petition was born out of a Christian sense of slavery's immorality. Also, like most nineteenth-century petition drives, this one followed the convention of segregating male and female signatures. (Courtesy National Archives)

the Civil War, rather than established principles concerning slavery and the Constitution, shaped people's understanding and appreciation of the antislavery amendment.

Legal Theory and Practical Politics

Senator Trumbull's announcement that he would bring the antislavery amendment up for debate set constitutional theorists to thinking anew about the founding charter and its mutability. One scholar in particular, Francis Lieber, who in December 1863 had advised his friend Charles Sumner not to propose an amendment granting all Americans equality before the law, now recognized the likelihood that Congress would soon propose revisions to the Constitution. Quickly he cobbled together a series of possible amendments and a general theory to justify the amending process. These pieces would become the core components of a draft of a pamphlet provisionally titled *Amendments of the Constitution, Submitted to the American People.*

As he wrote the document, Lieber struggled with his conception of American constitutionalism and engaged in an illuminating private dialogue on constitutional doctrine with some of the leading legal thinkers of the day. Although the pamphlet was not published until early 1865, just after Congress finally passed the Thirteenth Amendment, the document actually reflected the intellectual climate of early 1864, a time before the highly politicized congressional debates on the antislavery amendment had begun.[1] An examination of Lieber's amendments and the reaction to them reveals an early and enduring division within the Republican party about the benefits of any constitutional amendment, particularly one abolishing slavery. This internal conflict belies the dominant consensus among historians that the antislavery amendment was a foregone conclusion of Republican ideology.

A month after Trumbull reported the amendment out of committee, Lieber wrote to his friend Henry W. Halleck, the general-in-chief of the Union armies, that "for more than 15 years I have been convinced that the Const[itution] required to be amended."[2] Although Lieber was reading

1 Lieber's pamphlet is usually treated as a postwar document. See, for example, Philip S. Paludan, *A Covenant with Death: The Constitution, Law, and Equality in the Civil War Era* (Urbana: University of Illinois Press, 1975), 98; and Harold M. Hyman and William M. Wiecek, *Equal Justice under Law: Constitutional Development, 1835–1875* (New York: Harper and Row, 1982), 392–93. Two important exceptions to this trend are John R. Vile, "Francis Lieber and the Process of Constitutional Amendment," *Review of Politics,* 60 (Summer 1998), 525–43; and Frank Freidel, *Francis Lieber: Nineteenth-Century Liberal* (Baton Rouge: Louisiana State University Press, 1947), 378.
2 Lieber to Henry W. Halleck, March 10, 1864, Francis, Lieber MSS, HEH.

the present back into the past – he had not embraced the amending process prior to the outbreak of war – he had indeed argued before the war that the original Constitution was insufficient to the needs of the nation. As a budding political philosopher in the 1830s and 1840s, he had gained prominence, North and South, by attacking the idea of a fixed Constitution. He believed that federal power should expand slowly and organically – and thus constitutionally – as the nation grew. Yet there were limits to his assault on formalism: Lieber criticized northern "natural law" theorists who looked beyond written law to justify the centralization of power. His moderate constitutionalism carried over to his attitude toward slavery. Though a self-proclaimed "abolitionist," Lieber rejected the immediatism of William Lloyd Garrison and Frederick Douglass in favor of a belief that slavery would die a natural death so long as the nation and Constitution evolved organically, with no interference from states' rights or antislavery extremists.[3]

The war presented vast opportunities to Lieber, both personal and ideological. He believed that the war would solidify the Union and thus fulfill his dream, nurtured during his school years in Germany, of living in a modern nation-state. Because of the war, he now had a platform to popularize his distinctive brand of nationalism. As an expert on constitutional issues and as a respected leader of thousands of German Americans, he was sought after to write pamphlets, deliver speeches, and advise politicians on the civil and military policy of the Union. His many public statements used the South's insurrection to justify an expansion of federal power beyond what the Constitution expressly sanctioned. Yet this position was reminiscent of the "natural law" theories he had formerly criticized, and he sought for a way to give the new nation-state a more formal basis.

The answer lay in the amending process. Sometime in mid-1863 Lieber began thinking of a revised Constitution as the perfect "prize of victory" for the Union, and he began to draft a pamphlet to promote constitutional amendments.[4] As the planned publication took shape, Lieber devised a novel justification for tampering with the document so deeply revered by the nation. In the past, most Republican politicians and jurists had reconciled the Constitution's proslavery features with their own agenda by arguing that the framers desired an end to slavery but had granted temporary concessions to the institution. In contrast, Lieber directly challenged the framers and the document they had drafted. He believed that the authors of the Constitution were not exemplary egalitarians but flawed

3   Paludan, *A Covenant with Death*, 61–84; Freidel, *Francis Lieber*, 223–58.
4   Lieber, memorandum, June 12, 1863, folder LI 168, Francis Lieber MSS, HEH.

compromisers. That the founders had been willing to supplement the original Constitution with twelve amendments was proof enough for Lieber that "they had forgotten very important things" and that, contrary to common wisdom, "the framers were *not* inspired."[5]

Lieber's criticism of the framers was reminiscent of Garrison's assault on the proslavery Constitution in the 1850s. But there was an important difference. Whereas the Garrisonians had responded to constitutional imperfection by rejecting constitutional solutions to the problem of slavery, Lieber was quick to see the potential of the amending apparatus for achieving reform. Perhaps Lieber was more likely to take this approach because he had witnessed firsthand the frequent constitutional changes in Europe during the early nineteenth century.

Two of the seven amendments drafted by Lieber involved the abolition of slavery. The first proclaimed slavery "forever abolished," and the second enforced emancipation by prescribing the death penalty to those who continued to own or trade slaves.[6] Lieber declared: "We who know that the framers of our Constitution considered slavery an evil which . . . they felt ashamed to mention in the Constitution claim it as a right to mention now, for the first time, the word slavery in the Constitution, in order to abolish it."[7]

For Lieber, however, the abolition of slavery was not the same as a positive guarantee of equality. So he drafted a separate constitutional amendment providing that "no human being shall be excluded from the courts of justice as parties to actions, as indicted for offences or crimes, or as witnesses, on account of race or colour."[8] Without such a measure, Lieber feared, the legal system that had supported slavery might simply be replaced with one that "would require a *scale* of rights accommodated to diff. races."[9] As events during Reconstruction would reveal, Lieber's solution to legal inequality was not enough: the elimination of the color line in the courts did not end discrimination. Yet, even if he lacked the vision to construct the ideal equal rights amendment, Lieber understood that some such amendment had to accompany or soon follow one granting freedom. Even before the congressional debates on the Thirteenth Amendment began, he saw that an amendment like Senator Trumbull's, which abol-

5 Lieber, memorandum, undated, folder LI 168, Francis Lieber MSS, HEH.
6 Lieber, unpublished draft of *Proposed Amendments to the Constitution*, in Lieber to Charles Sumner, March 5, 1864, Francis Lieber MSS, HEH. The published pamphlet is reprinted in Francis Lieber, *Miscellaneous Writings*, vol. 2, *Contributions to Political Science* (Philadelphia: J. B. Lippincott, 1881), 177–79.
7 Lieber, *Contributions to Political Science*, 171.
8 Lieber, first draft of *Proposed Amendments to the Constitution*.
9 Lieber, memorandum, undated, "Proposed Amendments," Lieber MSS, HEH.

ished slavery but said nothing explicitly about equality, was only one of a series of amendments needed to stitch together a nation from the tatters of the Civil War.

Few legal theorists were as ready as Lieber to embrace this new use of the amending power. Sidney George Fisher, a Philadelphia farmer and a dabbler in political philosophy, is well remembered by historians today for denouncing constitutional constraints on Congress and defending the right of the people and their elected representatives to change the Constitution to fit the needs of the present. But even Fisher shuddered at the prospect of major revisions. In his famous 1862 tract *The Trial of the Constitution,* he had warned: "New forms are not easily invented, even when necessary, to serve a growing and advancing people. We should therefore retain the old that have been tested by experience, as long as we can, modify them with caution to suit new conditions, and in interests so momentous as those that depend on the organic laws of Government, 'Prove all things; hold fast to that which is good.' "[10] At the time he wrote this, Fisher opposed emancipation, and though he eventually came to accept emancipation as a wartime necessity, he probably would have recoiled at Lieber's antislavery amendment and certainly would have rejected his equal rights amendment. Fisher was a firm believer in white superiority, and even as he grew to see that emancipation would weaken the Confederacy, he never abandoned his assumption that blacks were better off enslaved than free.[11]

When Lieber sought comments on the first draft of his pamphlet, he turned not to the reclusive Fisher but to another Pennsylvanian, Horace Binney, one of Lieber's oldest friends and one of the nation's most renowned jurists. Now eighty-four, the Philadelphian had lived through the Constitutional Convention and the framing of the first twelve amendments. With his downturned, thin-lipped mouth, his thick, shiny white hair, and his penetrating, clear eyes, he had worn at least as well as the Constitution. But for his occasional nostalgic wanderings back to the days of the old Federalists and his hero, Alexander Hamilton, his mind was still sharp. From the beginning of the war, he had supported the Union effort and held to the Hamiltonian doctrine that the Constitution was supposed to extend rather than limit federal power. He conceded, however, that the document had not kept up with the nation's rapid growth.[12]

10 Sidney George Fisher, *The Trial of the Constitution* (Philadelphia: J. B. Lippincott, 1862), 360.

11 Paludan, *A Covenant with Death,* 170–218; John R. Vile, *The Constitutional Amending Process in American Political Thought* (New York: Praeger, 1992), 95–102.

12 Charles Chauncey Binney, *The Life of Horace Binney* (Philadelphia: J. B. Lippincott, 1903), 325–69.

Binney liked much of what he read in his friend's amendments, but he objected to Lieber's approach to enforcement. Unlike the antislavery amendment pending in the Senate, which simply authorized Congress to act as it deemed necessary to uphold abolition, Lieber's proposal specified that slaveholding would be punished by death. Binney believed that an amendment should not limit congressional discretion by specifying a penalty. To Lieber he wrote that the proposed enforcement clause was "unnecessary – Congress may act."[13] Binney also found superfluous Lieber's amendment granting black Americans equal access to the courts. "If slaves are made free," Binney told Lieber, "nothing more be necessary to qualify them to be witnesses, prosecutors before grand juries, etc."[14]

The private dialogue between Binney and Lieber rehearsed a public discussion among all Americans that would take place in the months and years ahead. At issue was the nature of the rights that inhere in freedom and the method of writing those rights into law. Binney shared Lieber's belief that freedom encompassed basic civil rights such as the right to sue, but, unlike Lieber, he resisted enumerating these rights lest other, unenumerated rights be denied. In a sense, Binney and Lieber were replaying the seventy-five-year-old debate that started among the framers about the wisdom of enumerating rights.[15] Although Binney and Lieber probably did not realize it, the congressmen who drafted the antislavery amendment had steered a middle course on this issue: they enumerated freed people's rights not in the amendment but in the reconstruction legislation meant to enforce the amendment.

In Binney's opinion, the problem of defining all the rights that inhere in freedom could be easily avoided by adopting a separate amendment that established African Americans as equal citizens. For Binney, the Constitution's ambiguity on citizenship, along with its ambiguity on slavery, had always been at the heart of the nation's troubles. "The word *citizen* or *citizens* is found ten times at least in the Constitution of the United States," he groused, "and no definition of it is given anywhere." This obscurity, Binney wrote, had allowed Chief Justice Roger B. Taney in the *Dred Scott* decision to deny citizenship to all African Americans. Without an amendment clarifying citizenship, "it might happen that after slavery was abolished and men of colour every where in the land made free, *Taney* would say again, that the offspring of an African slave, tho' free was not a citizen."[16] Despite the wishes of reformers like Binney, the government

13   Binney to Lieber, March 11, 1864, Francis Lieber MSS, HEH.
14   Binney to Lieber, March 14, 1864, Francis Lieber MSS, HEH.
15   Jack N. Rakove, *Original Meanings: Politics and Ideas in the Making of the Constitution* (New York: Alfred A. Knopf, 1996), 288–338.
16   Binney to Lieber, March 14, 1864, Francis Lieber MSS, HEH.

had so far done nothing to reverse the principle set down by Taney. Attorney General Edward Bates, for example, had written in late 1862 a long, unwieldy opinion arguing that native-born blacks were citizens of the United States, but that opinion had done nothing to change actual policy.[17] By 1864 the legal status of free African Americans was still unresolved.

In place of Lieber's measure barring discrimination in the courts, Binney offered an amendment that prefigured the Fourteenth Amendment and predated it by two years: "The free inhabitants of each of the states, territories, districts or other places, within the limits of the United States, either born free within the same, or born in slavery within the same, and since made or declared free, and all other free inhabitants as aforesaid, who are duly naturalized according to the laws of the United States, shall be deemed citizens of the United States, and without any exception of color, race, or origin, shall be entitled to all the privileges of citizens, as well in courts of judicature as elsewhere."[18] The amendment would have completely reversed the *Dred Scott* decision. In *Dred Scott*, Taney had drawn distinctions between state and national citizenship, whereas dissenting Justice Benjamin R. Curtis had argued that one type of citizenship guaranteed the other. Binney's amendment adopted Curtis's position, but it went even further, for it declared that national citizenship belonged to all free inhabitants of the states, not only state citizens. By guaranteeing national citizenship to all native-born Americans, Binney revived the principle of birthright citizenship that the *Dred Scott* decision had undercut.[19]

Binney's amendment was far-seeing in its approach to black citizenship, but it came up short on the issue of black suffrage. "The qualification of voters is a matter of State Regulation," wrote Binney, adding pointedly, "very wrong this, I think in principle, without much harm in fact."[20] Because the original Constitution clearly denied the federal government's power to regulate suffrage, Binney saw no reason to draft an amendment granting voting rights to blacks. He wished that the Constitution read otherwise on suffrage, not for the sake of blacks, whose disfranchisement he believed had caused little "harm in fact," but for the sake of national authority, which, in his opinion, should never have given way to states' rights. Lieber also felt constrained by the Constitution's clear statement on

17   Bates, "Citizenship" (letter of November 29, 1862, to Salmon P. Chase), in *Official Opinions of the Attorneys General of the United States*, 10:382–413.

18   Lieber to Binney, March 14, 1864, Francis Lieber MSS, HEH. A slightly revised version of Binney's amendment appeared in Lieber's published pamphlet; see Lieber, *Contributions to Political Science*, 179.

19   James H. Kettner, *The Development of American Citizenship, 1608–1870* (Chapel Hill: University of North Carolina Press, 1978), 287–333.

20   Binney to Lieber, March 14, 1864, Francis Lieber MSS, HEH.

state regulation of suffrage, and thus he omitted any discussion of voting rights from his pamphlet.

By the middle of March 1864 Lieber had completed a final draft of his pamphlet. He had incorporated all of Binney's stylistic revisions and added the Philadelphian's citizenship amendment, but he had retained, against Binney's advice, the clause prescribing punishment for slave owners and slave traders.[21]

Now Lieber's thoughts turned to publishing the document. In February he had become head of the Loyal Publication Society, which was in charge of bolstering sentiment for the Union cause and for Lincoln's reelection, and he toyed with the idea of having the society issue it. One of the officers of the society, John A. Stevens, Jr., who also served as treasurer of the Republican party, had received from Lieber an early draft of the pamphlet and now encouraged him to go ahead with publication. "It is high time," wrote Stevens, "to familiarize our people with the idea that the Constitution *may* be changed; that it is not a divine book; that its authors did not believe it would be permanent; that it was made flexible to allow of changes as the necessity for them should arise."[22]

But Lieber's other advisors seemed to share Lieber's own suspicion that the pamphlet was not yet "fit" for publication.[23] Representative Martin Russell Thayer of Pennsylvania told Lieber that the amendment process would take too long: "What are we to do in the mean time before we can amend the Constitution? . . . Slavery is wounded probably to the death but how shall we exterminate it *by due course of law?*" Thayer believed that Republicans should concentrate their efforts on reconstruction statutes that immediately gave emancipation the "force of law" rather than on a sluggish abolition amendment.[24] Lieber found no support either from Charles Sumner, who read the pamphlet but offered no response, even though the proposals were similar to the one Sumner had submitted to the Senate. At the moment that Lieber sent the senator the amendments, Sumner was readying himself for an assault on all of the fugitive slave laws. Lieber gently suggested to the senator that universal emancipation should take a higher priority than the protection of fugitive slaves, most of whom were no longer being tracked down: "let us abolish Slavery and no discussion about Fugitives will be necessary; in the mean time I suppose no fugitive could now be recaptured."[25] As single-minded as

21 Lieber to Charles Sumner, March 1, 4, and 12, 1864, all in Francis Lieber MSS, HEH.
22 John A. Stevens, Jr., to Lieber, March 28, 1864 (wrongly filed under 1863), John A. Stevens MSS, NYH.
23 Lieber to Martin Russell Thayer, February 3, 1864, Francis Lieber MSS, HEH.
24 Thayer to Lieber, February 6, 1864, Francis Lieber MSS, HEH.
25 Lieber to Sumner, March 12, 1864, Francis Lieber MSS, HEH.

ever, Sumner ignored the amendment – for the moment – and kept his sights on the fugitive slave laws. Even Lieber's most trusted advisor, Horace Binney, was discouraging. Lieber's proposed amendments, Binney said, were "a very *hot* string, which you may simmer and dip into water, a hundred times and still burn your fingers with."[26] "At present we have divisions between the disloyal and the loyal," Binney explained. "The paper may make them between different sections of the loyal, and give the disloyal an advantage."[27]

Faced with such criticism, Lieber decided to postpone publication. He did not publish the pamphlet until February 1865. By then, the Republicans had won overwhelming electoral victories, the Union armies were on the verge of final triumph, and Congress had already passed the Thirteenth Amendment abolishing slavery. But in early 1864, when the future of the Republican party and the nation was uncertain, Lieber and leading Republicans thought better of submitting to the country any far-reaching constitutional changes.

That pattern of inaction carried over to Congress, which did not debate the amendment for more than a month after the measure had been reported out by Trumbull's Senate Judiciary Committee. Perhaps the delay was the result of the parliamentary convention that Trumbull, as sponsor of the bill, should speak first. Since the Illinois senator was at home in Chicago mourning the death of his son during the last weeks of February and most of March, little was likely to happen with the bill.[28] Yet the amendment was also stalled in the House. There, James Wilson's Judiciary Committee had yet to report out an amendment. Only a few Republican congressmen seemed interested in pursuing the legislation. One of these, Isaac Arnold, a steadfast Republican from Chicago and a friend of Lincoln, proposed his own antislavery amendment and conducted an immediate test vote on the measure. The result, 78 to 62 in favor of the resolution, fell far short of the two-thirds majority that an amendment required (see Appendix Table 2).[29]

Hoping that the president might be able to rally the necessary votes for an amendment, Congressman Arnold pressed Lincoln to issue a special message to Congress endorsing the measure, but the president balked at the request.[30] When it came to revising the Constitution for any reason, he still advised caution. To the repeated delegations of clergymen who

26 Binney to Lieber, March 11, 1864, Franics Lieber MSS, HEH.
27 Binney to Lieber, March 14, 1864, Francis Lieber MSS, HEH.
28 Ralph Roske, *His Own Counsel: The Life and Times of Lyman Trumbull* (Reno: University of Nevada Press, 1979), 106–7.
29 *CG* (February 15, 1864), 659–60.
30 I. N. Arnold to George Schneider, February 25, 1864, George Schneider MSS, CHS. For a similar chilly response by the president to the same request, see Lincoln to John D. Defrees, February 7, 1864, *CW*, 7:172.

implored him to back an amendment declaring the existence of God, Lincoln flatly replied that "the work of amending the Constitution should not be done hastily."[31] As Arnold discovered, Lincoln was equally reluctant to rush toward an amendment abolishing slavery.

The Republican press also was lukewarm toward the measure. "We do not believe in the wisdom of amending the Constitution at all *now*," reported Henry J. Raymond's *New York Times*, which most considered an organ of the Lincoln administration.[32] By backing the amendment, warned the *Times*, Republicans would give the advantage to their political enemies, who would use the measure to bolster the charge that the war was being fought strictly for abolition. The time for changing the Constitution was at the war's end: "Slavery cannot be resolved to death, nor constitutionalized to death; fighting only can reach it, and through victory alone will it perish."[33] Even the more radical *Chicago Tribune*, which clearly supported the measure, feared that the amendment represented a congressional challenge to Lincoln that might ultimately divide the party. In an election year, reported the *Tribune*'s Washington correspondent, "there should above all things be unity in the party."[34] Only those Republican papers that were critical of Lincoln were ready to back the amendment. One of these, the *Cincinnati Gazette*, which promoted Salmon P. Chase for the presidency, announced that "the issue of direct abolition of slavery is already . . . in the seething cauldron of public discussion, and they who fear double trouble from its boil and bubble had better keep away from the kettle."[35]

As the amendment prohibiting slavery received wider notice in the early months of 1864, Republicans were slow to endorse it. Some feared that it would force the party to take a stand on the sensitive issue of black equality. Others saw no reason to press the measure until the party commanded the necessary two-thirds majority in Congress. In the midst of a highly turbulent political climate, Republicans thought it safer to let the amendment lie.

The Democracy Divided

As Republicans fumbled the amendment, some Democrats thought about seizing the measure for themselves. In the early months of 1864, before it had become clear what course congressional Democrats would take on the amendment, some party members began to consider the advantages of

31 Washington *Daily National Intelligencer,* February 24, 1864, p. 3.
32 *New York Times,* February 11, 1864, p. 4.
33 Ibid., February 13, 1864, p. 6.
34 *Chicago Tribune,* February 17, 1864, p. 2.
35 *Cincinnati Gazette,* February 20, 1864, p. 2.

endorsing the measure and reversing the party's course on slavery. Thus arose one of the most peculiar phenomena in northern public life during the war: Democrats became the leading backers of the antislavery amendment.

It might seem odd that the same Democrats who had opposed the Emancipation Proclamation would accept the antislavery amendment, which went further than the proclamation toward establishing freedom for the enslaved. The change was, in part, a result of the fluidity of politics and popular attitudes. Democrats did not know where to stand on emancipation. The more that northerners seemed to approve of converting white southerners' human property into Union regiments, the more that Democrats questioned the wisdom of supporting slavery. Democrats were also attracted to the amendment because, in providing an explicitly constitutional end to slavery, the measure took the sort of formalist approach to reform that the party had always favored. Party members could invoke the amendment to reinforce their claim that the Emancipation Proclamation was unconstitutional: if the proclamation had been constitutional, they said, no amendment would have been necessary. Because Lincoln had not yet endorsed the amendment, some Democrats saw the proposal as an alternative rather than a supplement to the Emancipation Proclamation.

Perhaps the earliest evidence of opposition support for the amendment came from the *New York Herald,* which had the highest circulation of any northern paper and which, though hardly a party organ, had traditionally allied with the Democrats. The paper's editor, James Gordon Bennett, was a political chameleon who, since the war's onset, had identified himself as an independent but had consistently criticized Lincoln's policies, especially those aimed at emancipation. In mid-February 1864, right after Senator Trumbull reported the antislavery amendment out of committee, Bennett endorsed the amendment as "a constitutional platform for the absolute extinction of slavery against the unconstitutional, incongruous, mischievous and impracticable emancipation scheme of President Lincoln and his party." It was time, Bennett declared, for the Democrats to drop their proslavery position and "to take a new departure – to strike out boldly for an amendment of the constitution which will forever settle this troublesome question of slavery by removing the institution from the country."[36]

Bennett, who was no friend to African Americans, made his assault on slavery strictly for the sake of political expediency. For almost a year he had been recommending a union of War Democrats and conservative

36 *New York Herald,* February 8, 1864, p. 4. See also, February 6, 1864, p. 4, and February 7, 1864, p. 4.

Republicans to oppose Peace Democrats on one side and radical Republicans on the other. That the amendment assured the end of slavery was for Bennett incidental; the measure's real value lay in its power to attract disaffected elements of the two competing parties. With these fragments Bennett would form a new party, and at its head he would place his champion, General Ulysses S. Grant. Although the esteemed Union general had shown no political aspirations, Bennett was certain that he could be swayed to run for the presidency.[37]

As the independent *New York Herald* took up the cause of the emancipation amendment, the *New York World,* generally accepted as the party organ, or at least the voice of the War Democrats, began to make distinctly antislavery noises. In reply to recent charges by Republicans that the Democrats were proslavery, the *World* asked, Had not the Democrats consistently supported the free-state constitutions in the North? "What then can be more absurd, or more calumnious, than to pretend that the northern Democrats are in favor of slavery?" On the question of the antislavery amendment, the *World* complimented congressional Republicans for framing a measure that offered a constitutional solution to slavery and thus admitted that Lincoln's Emancipation Proclamation and Reconstruction Proclamation were unconstitutional.[38] Without explicitly saying so, the editors of the *World* appeared ready to endorse the measure.

As democrats at the *World* approached but stopped short of promoting universal emancipation, other Democrats decided to cross the line. The first notable convert was Representative James Brooks of New York, who, on the floor of Congress on February 18, 1864, declared that slavery was dying, if not already dead, and that his party should stop defending the institution.[39] Although the speech was deleted from the pages of the *Congressional Globe,* news of it spread through the country and stunned the public, for the New Yorker was known as an extreme Peace Democrat, or "Copperhead." As Brooks's about-face gained publicity, he began sharpening his position in the pages of the *New York Evening Express,* which he and his brother Erastus edited. One of Brooks's editorials announced "that there are but ten Democratic members of the House who do not in principle and substance agree with what Mr. Brooks

37 Douglas Fermer, *James Gordon Bennett and the New York Herald: A Study of Editorial Opinion in the Civil War Era, 1854–1867* (New York: St. Martin's Press, 1986), 244–247, 254–61; Brooks D. Simpson, *Let Us Have Peace: Ulysses S. Grant and the Politics of War and Reconstruction, 1861–1868* (Chapel Hill: University of North Carolina Press, 1991), 52.
38 *New York Daily World,* February 11, 1864, p. 4.
39 There is no verbatim record of Brooks's speech because the Indiana Democrat Daniel Voorhees demanded that it be expunged from the record. See *New York Tribune,* February 23, 1864, p. 4.

said, viz: That as a FACT, be it right or wrong, and as a FACT to be recognized and accepted, as much as daylight or darkness, the slavery institution is dead."[40] An unsteady convert to abolition, Brooks was careful not to commit himself explicitly to the antislavery amendment. He seemed ready to endorse the measure, but he also had created an escape hatch: if necessary, he could argue that because slavery was now dead, it need not be outlawed by constitutional amendment.

A more assertive endorsement of the amendment came from Senator Reverdy Johnson, a War Democrat and one of the most respected legal minds in the country. Johnson had enjoyed an extraordinary career of public service. He had been a Whig in the U.S. Senate in the late 1840s, the attorney general under President Zachary Taylor, an attorney for Dred Scott's owner before the Supreme Court, and a member of the Washington Peace Convention in the secession winter of 1861. A good friend to both Roger B. Taney and Abraham Lincoln, Johnson at times seemed to exist outside of political parties. He opposed the Republican party and in 1860 ran for the Maryland state assembly as a supporter of the Democrat Stephen A. Douglas. At the outbreak of war, he and other Maryland Douglas Democrats joined in a bipartisan state Union party. But he opposed many of Lincoln's actions, and in 1863 he ran successfully as a Democrat to the Thirty-eighth Congress. Over the course of his career he had come to hate slavery and had freed his own slaves, but he had consistently opposed all legislation interfering with the slave-owning rights of others. Reluctantly he supported the Emancipation Proclamation as a wartime measure aimed at the disloyal, but he refused to endorse any legislation affecting the slaves of loyal citizens. The antislavery amendment had caught Johnson's eye, however, because it offered an indisputably constitutional solution to the problem of slavery. In a widely noted address to the Metropolitan Club of Washington, D.C., in early February 1864 he pledged his support for the amendment.[41]

After Johnson's speech, it seemed that the whole Democratic party was on the verge of a reversal on slavery. New York's Tammany Hall organization, still the linchpin of the party and the center of War Democrat strength, appeared ready to follow the lead of Brooks and Johnson. In

---

40 *New York Evening Express,* reprinted in *Chicago Tribune,* March 4, 1864, p. 2.
41 Letter of "Agate," *Cincinnati Gazette,* February 8, 1864, p. 3, February 12, 1864, p. 1; John Conness to Charles Halpine, February 27, 1864, Charles G. Halpine MSS, HEH. On Johnson, see Jean H. Baker, *The Politics of Continuity: Maryland Political Parties from 1858 to 1870* (Baltimore: Johns Hopkins University Press, 1973), 42, 65, 110; Charles Lewis Wagandt, *The Mighty Revolution: Negro Emancipation in Maryland, 1862–1864* (Baltimore: Johns Hopkins Press, 1964), 39–40, 47; Christopher Dell, *Lincoln and the War Democrats: The Grand Erosion of Conservative Tradition* (Rutherford, N.J.: Fairleigh Dickinson University Press, 1975), 273.

March 1864, Tammany's general election committee issued an address announcing that "slavery, as a subject of political agitation, has passed from the politics of this country."[42] Although the address fell short of endorsing an antislavery amendment, it did suggest that the party would not oppose such a measure. Then Carolan O'Brien Bryant, one of Tammany's known operatives in the state legislature, introduced a resolution in the New York Assembly asking the state's congressmen to support the antislavery amendment. Bryant had been elected as an Independent, but his affiliation with Tammany was sufficiently well known to create a stir throughout New York and the rest of the Union.[43]

Some advocates of emancipation were ready to believe that a glorious bipartisan attack against slavery was at hand. Lydia Maria Child, the well-known reformer and author, looked favorably on the new antislavery ground taken by her longtime rivals. No stranger to politics, Child saw that swallowing emancipation was the only way Democrats could again rise to power, and she wrote to a friend that "it would be curious if they should eat the oyster, the hard shell of which has been opened by the Republicans."[44] The abolitionist tone of Democratic rhetoric had even lightened the normally grim demeanor of John Nicolay, one of the president's private secretaries, who wrote: "when the Herald endorses Sumner's plan for amending the Constitution of the United States to abolish slavery – When Brooks in the House makes a speech declaring it dead – When Bryant in the N.Y. Legislature offers a series of resolves declaring it should be extinguished . . . the people may take courage that the country is progressing."[45] The secretary had wrongly identified the amendment as Sumner's instead of Trumbull's, but his sentiment nonetheless captured the feeling of many northerners.

Anxious Republicans speculated that the recent demonstrations in favor of emancipation by Democrats signified not a bipartisan effort against slavery but a ploy by Democrats to take a back road to victory over Republicans. A Republican in Boston predicted that the Democrats would hold an early convention, endorse the abolition amendment, and then drop the amendment after winning the election: "they would do anything to get back into power and if they should secure power on that

---

42 *New York Tribune,* March 14, 1864, p. 4.
43 *Journal of the Assembly of the State of New York,* 87th sess., 1864, p. 737. See ibid., pp. 496, 1418; *New York Tribune,* March 15, 1864, p. 4; and Phyllis F. Field, *The Politics of Race in New York: The Struggle for Black Suffrage in the Civil War Era* (Ithaca: Cornell University Press, 1982), 156.
44 Lydia Maria Child to George W. Julian, March 27, 1864, Joshua R. Giddings and George W. Julian MSS, LC. For similar abolitionist sentiment, see the *National Anti-Slavery Standard,* February 27, 1864, p. 3, and March 12, 1864, p. 3.
45 John G. Nicolay, memorandum, March 9, 1864, John G. Nicolay MSS, LC.

idea, I should have no confidence that such an amendment would be made for they are not to be trusted."[46] A newspaper correspondent in Washington suspected "that this new movement is part of plan to throw the Union party off its guard, to divide and distract it, . . . *and get out a third candidate for the Presidency,* or, at least, raise such dissensions in our ranks . . . to distract us on the subject of our Presidential candidate."[47] Because of the threat of a preemptive move on the amendment by the Democrats, John D. Defrees, the superintendent of public printing and one of Lincoln's political aides, advised the president to recommend the amendment to Congress. "If not done very soon," Defrees wrote, "the proposition *will* be presented by the Democracy and claimed by them as *their* proposition." The president brushed aside his informant's advice, writing curtly that "our own friends have this [amendment] under consideration now, and will do as much without a Message as with it."[48]

Some Democrats were indeed pondering the possibility of backing a candidate who would endorse the antislavery amendment and divide the Republicans. One Washington insider heard of a "movement, way down deep, to get Tammany to toss the carcass of Slavery into the potter's field, and to grab Ben Butler and run for President on an antislavery platform!"[49] In the end, Butler, a former Democrat renowned for refusing to return slaves to rebel masters, did not emerge as the candidate of a pro-amendment party. Instead, the third-party ploy of the Democrats took form some months later in the candidacy of General John C. Frémont, who would run as a "Radical Democrat" on a platform endorsing an abolition amendment.

If Democratic leaders early in 1864 had made a concerted effort to seize the popular initiative for an antislavery amendment, they might well have found themselves with an effective weapon to wield against the Republicans. But uniting the party behind any new policy at this time was no easy feat. Still split between advocates and opponents of further war, the party faced serious trouble in the coming election. The state elections of 1863 had made clear that charges against Republicans for "arbitrary" arrests and rampant abolitionism had lost their effectiveness in political campaigns. No new issue had surfaced to unite the party. Nor had any one leader emerged who could satisfy the interests of all and fill the vacuum at the head of the party created by the death of Douglas early in the war. Despite General George B. McClellan's shortcomings on the battlefield,

46 J. F. Goodwin to Elihu B. Washburne, March 24, 1864, Elihu B. Washburne MSS, LC. See letter of "Agate," *Cincinnati Gazette,* February 12, 1864, p. 1.
47 *Chicago Tribune,* February 16, 1864, p. 2.
48 *CW,* 7:172–73.
49 Samuel Wilkeson to Sydney Howard Gay, "early March," Sydney Howard Gay MSS, ColU.

he still enjoyed the popularity of a war hero, but he lacked the political know-how and rhetorical flair needed to heal the breach in the party. With no dominant issue to serve as a rallying point, and with no forceful leader to rein in political rogues like James Gordon Bennett, the party had become temporarily disoriented. This state of affairs enabled some Democrats to toy with measures like reversing the party's stance on slavery, but the instability also made it difficult for any new doctrine to gain currency with all of the party's factions.

Even if the party had enjoyed the cohesion necessary for its leaders to unite behind a new issue such as constitutional emancipation, party leaders might have a difficult time selling rank-and-file Democrats on a measure like the antislavery amendment, which so abruptly reversed the party's traditional allegiance to "the Constitution as it is." "The Constitution is the one sheet anchor of our hopes," a War Democratic paper in upstate New York warned in response to the *New York Herald*'s endorsement of the antislavery amendment. "One change will tempt to another, and two will beget the habit of change." It was no love of slavery that kept the editor from supporting the measure; he applauded the "march of freedom" in the border states and thought that an amendment outlawing slavery would indeed "end all pretexts and quibbles." But he also believed that only victory *and* the preservation of the Constitution "as our fathers wrote it" would give "evidence of the ability of our people to govern themselves." To alter the Constitution was to defame the dream of the founders, to concede the defeat of constitutional government even in the midst of military victory.[50] The Ohio Democrat W. M. Corry agreed that the Constitution must not be changed. Corry was particularly enraged by James Brooks's "Yankee cant about the abolition of slavery," and he denounced "all N.Y. politicians destitute of any scientific knowledge of the Const[itution]."[51] "The Constitution as it is" remained for many Democrats the shining idol.

Besides the insistence by some within their ranks on an unchanged Constitution, the Democrats' persistent racism made it unlikely that the party would take the lead in the fight for black freedom.[52] The notion that African Americans were better suited to be slaves than free people was still

---

50   *Utica* (New York) *Morning Herald,* February 10, 1864, clipping in Horatio Seymour scrapbooks, NYS.
51   W. M. Corry to John A. Trimble, February 26, 1864, John Allen Trimble MSS, OHS.
52   See Jean H. Baker, *Affairs of Party: The Political Culture of Northern Democrats in the Mid-Nineteenth Century* (Ithaca: Cornell University Press, 1983), 177–258; Edward L. Gambill, *Conservative Ordeal: Northern Democrats and Reconstruction, 1865–1868* (Ames: Iowa State University Press, 1981), 3–19; Joel H. Silbey, *A Respectable Minority: The Democratic Party in the Civil War Era, 1860–1868* (New York: W. W. Norton, 1977), 80–83; and Forrest G. Wood, *Black Scare: The Racist Response to Emancipation and Reconstruction* (Berkeley: University of California Press, 1968), 1–39.

alive in the northern Democracy, even as such racist paternalism waned in the South. In early 1864 northerners were still requesting proslavery literature from the Society for the Diffusion of Political Knowledge, the Democratic party's propaganda organ in New York City. The most requested pamphlet was the hackneyed defense of slavery written by Samuel F. B. Morse, the head of the society.[53] As the society distributed proslavery literature, Democratic papers tried to reinforce the idea that slaves were unfit for freedom by relating stories of the evils that had befallen the freed people. "The freedom of the liberated slaves along the Mississippi," reported the *Cincinnati Enquirer,* "would seem to consist now solely in that of starving, dying and rotting by thousands."[54] The Democrats' message was clear: in Republicans' misguided attempt to help African Americans, they had destroyed the only institution that could preserve the African race from extinction.

This racism, even more than devotion to states' rights and an unchanged Constitution, kept the Democratic manager Samuel L. M. Barlow from taking seriously the idea that his party should embrace an antislavery amendment. Ever since late 1863, Barlow, the part owner of the *World* and the political lieutenant of General McClellan, had received flurries of letters from Democrats who thought that the party should renounce its former position on slavery. Two of the most prominent of these correspondents were Congressman Henry G. Stebbins of New York and Senator Reverdy Johnson of Maryland.[55] Barlow told Stebbins and Johnson that emancipation would burden whites with endless, needless squabbling about how best to care for the freed people. Much worse, it would lead to the annihilation of black Americans – one of "the inevitable consequences of inferiority of race." It was best, therefore, if the Democrats ignored blacks, free or slave. "I have 'the White man on the brain,'" Barlow admitted.[56] Barlow offered a similar response to Montgomery Blair, a former Democrat and Lincoln's postmaster general, when Blair tried to persuade Barlow that emancipation would bring political advantages to the Democrats. "By giving up the past, [and] considering slavery to be extinct," Blair wrote to Barlow in December 1863, "you can make an issue upon which not only the Democracy of the North and South may unite ag[ain]st the abolitionists, but on which the larger portion of the

53 See Samuel F. B. Morse, *An Argument on the Ethical Position of Slavery in the Social System, and its Relation to the Politics of the Day* (Society for the Diffusion of Political Knowledge no. 12, 1863). For an example of a request for the pamphlet, see C. E. Fahrnstock to Samuel F. B. Morse, March 28, 1864, Samuel F. B. Morse MSS, LC.
54 *Cincinnati Enquirer,* February 12, 1864, p. 2.
55 See Stebbins to Barlow, January 20, 1864, and Johnson to Barlow, January 23, 1864, both in Samuel L. M. Barlow MSS, HEH.
56 Barlow to Stebbins, February 1, 1864, and Barlow to Johnson, January 19, 1864, Samuel L. M. Barlow letter books, HEH.

Republicans will join in sustaining the exclusive right of Govt of the white race."[57] Barlow rejected Blair's strategy: "to free [the slaves] would be an act of cruelty to the race compared with which their actual extermination would be a blessing."[58]

Regardless of their political affiliation or the label that history has affixed to them – Barlow, Stebbins, and Johnson the War Democrats, Blair the conservative Republican – all of these men thought blacks inferior to whites. Yet there was a significant shade of difference in their racial attitudes. Although Blair was the most devoted opponent of slavery in the group, he was able to reconcile his antislavery sentiments with a belief that blacks were inferior and deserved no special treatment from the federal government. Although Stebbins and Johnson were not Republicans, they shared Blair's view that slaves should be emancipated and then left to fend for themselves. Barlow, however, could not abandon his notion that social status should reflect a people's natural status, that racially inferior humans were better off as slaves. His pseudohumanitarian justification for slavery was growing as obsolete in the North as in the South, but, like many Democrats, he clung to the idea of a fixed racial hierarchy with the same tenacity that he held to the idea of an unchanging Constitution. Perhaps a shrewder political manager than Barlow, one conscious of the popular currents running in favor of constitutional emancipation, might have seen the wisdom of suspending his racial beliefs and backing a constitutional amendment that abolished slavery.

Although the disorganized political situation gave rise to Democrats ready to endorse an abolition amendment, the party was not yet ready to unite behind the measure. But even if the prospect of a complete Democratic reversal on slavery was unlikely, Republicans faced the danger that antislavery Democrats might join with dissatisfied Republicans to form a third party, an antislavery coalition that would rob support from Lincoln and give the election to the Democrats. By the spring of 1864 no such party had emerged, although political observers suspected that more partisan jockeying on the slavery issue was still to come. For the moment, however, it seemed that neither of the two main parties was ready to embrace an abolition amendment.

African Americans and the Inadequacy of Constitutional Emancipation

If neither the Republicans nor the Democrats united behind the amendment early on, who, then, were the real champions of the measure? The slaves who had sought their own freedom certainly deserved much of the

57 Blair to Barlow, December 25, 1863, Samuel L. M. Barlow MSS, HEH.
58 Barlow to Blair, December 23, 1863, Samuel L. M. Barlow letter books, HEH.

credit for the Union's emancipation policy so far.[59] Perhaps then, as one
legal scholar has suggested, the slaves were the real "authors" of the
amendment.[60]

There is much to commend this approach to the Thirteenth Amendment. Free and enslaved blacks played no small part in forcing Congress
and Lincoln to construct an emancipation policy that culminated in the
Emancipation Proclamation. And once Lincoln issued the proclamation,
African Americans continued to be aware – often in the most personal
ways – of the need for even firmer emancipation legislation. Annie Davis,
a slave living in northern Maryland, spoke for many African Americans
frustrated by their ambiguous legal status when she wrote in 1864 to
President Lincoln, "you will please let me know if we are free. [A]nd what
I can do."[61] Blacks well understood that there was much work still to do if
emancipation was to become a fact and not simply a stated policy, and
they swarmed across Union lines in unprecedented numbers during the
last years of the war. These African Americans were engaged not only in a
project of self-emancipation but in a joint operation with the Union government and army to free all the slaves. As one former slave of South
Carolina testified after the war, "I wanted the Union army to succeed over
the rebels so I and all colored men would be free, I knew we could never be
free if the Confederates were victorious."[62]

In addition to leaving their masters and joining Union armies, African
Americans often acted in ways that were more overtly political. Many free
blacks, for example, took part in the petition drive of the Women's Loyal
National League for a universal act of emancipation. Originally, the
league's petitions had purposely avoided specifying how slavery should be
abolished, but after Trumbull reported the antislavery amendment out of

59   On the controversial question of whether slaves were the primary agents of their own
     freedom, see Ira Berlin, "Who Freed the Slaves? Emancipation and Its Meaning," in
     David W. Blight and Brooks D. Simpson, eds., *Union and Emancipation: Essays on
     Politics and Race in the Civil War Era* (Kent, Ohio: Kent State University Press, 1997),
     105–21, which presents a convincing argument as well as citations to the relevant
     literature.
60   Guyora Binder, "Did the Slaves Author the Thirteenth Amendment? An Essay in Re-
     demptive History," *Yale Journal of Law and the Humanities*, 5 (Summer 1993), 474.
     For a similar view, one that presents African Americans as the "best interpreters" of the
     reconstruction amendments, see David A. J. Richards, *Conscience and the Constitu-
     tion: History, Theory, and Law of the Reconstruction Amendments* (Princeton: Prince-
     ton University Press, 1993), 257.
61   Annie Davis to "Mr president," August 25, 1864, in Ira Berlin et al., eds, *Freedom: A
     Documentary History of Emancipation, 1861–1867* (Cambridge: Cambridge Univer-
     sity Press, 1985), ser. 1, vol. 1, *The Destruction of Slavery*, 384.
62   Testimony of Mack. Duff. Williams, August 24, 1872, in Berlin et al., *Freedom*, ser. 1,
     vol. 1, *The Destruction of Slavery*, 812. See Mary Frances Berry, *Military Necessity and
     Civil Rights Policy: Black Citizenship and the Constitution, 1861–1868* (Port Wash-
     ington, N.Y.: Kennikat Press, 1977), 61–74.

committee, the petitions began to call specifically for a constitutional amendment.[63] At the same time, editors of black abolitionist newspapers started to include the amendment in their demands. One paper heralded the amendment as a sign that "the freedom of every slave must result at a day not far distant," while another touted the measure as a preferred alternative to federal colonization efforts.[64] If abolitionists' self-appointed role as spokespersons for the slaves was legitimate, then perhaps they and the slaves they represented should indeed be credited as the "authors" of the antislavery amendment.

This interpretation has its problems, however. Most abolitionists in 1864 did not think that the amendment was, by itself, the surest path to black freedom. The white abolitionist Gerrit Smith, for example, feared that the amendment jeopardized abolitionist unity. "The proposition to amend the Constitution tends to produce divisions amongst ourselves," Smith warned. "It will be time enough to amend the Constitution after we shall have ended the Rebellion."[65] Smith was worried that the amendment would stir up the old feud between radical constitutionalists like himself, who believed that the Constitution was antislavery and thus needed no amendment, and Garrisonians, who saw the Constitution as proslavery.

Black abolitionists were even less likely than their white allies to throw their weight behind the amendment. By early 1864 they had begun to shift their attention away from slavery and toward the fate of the freed people. An anonymous black correspondent captured the spirit of much black abolitionist thought when, in January 1864, he complained about two recent antislavery speeches: "We have had enough of politics and slavery – of the latter we are nearly tired to death. We read it, we sing it, we pray it, we talk it, we speak it, we lecture it, and the whole United States is in arms against it. You come to tell us it is dead. Well, if that is so, I thank God. Don't bother its carcass. Let us improve the living who have been under slavery. . . . Don't come anymore riding that old weather beaten horse, anti-slavery."[66]

63 See Susan B. Anthony to Charles Sumner, March 1, 1864, Charles Sumner MSS, HL; Wendy Hamand Venet, *Neither Ballots nor Bullets: Women Abolitionists and the Civil War* (Charlottesville: University Press of Virginia, 1991), 119–20; and James M. McPherson, *The Struggle for Equality: Abolitionists and the Negro in the Civil War and Reconstruction* (Princeton: Princeton University Press, 1964), 125–26.

64 *Pacific Appeal,* February 20, 1864; letter of Thomas H. C. Hinton, *Christian Recorder,* April 16, 1864.

65 Gerrit Smith, "To My Neighbors," February 24, 1864, in Smith, *Speeches and Letters of Gerrit Smith* (New York: American News Company, 1865), 2:5.

66 Anonymous, Washington, D.C., to Robert Hamilton, January 17, 1864, *Weekly Anglo-African,* in C. Peter Ripley et al., eds., *The Black Abolitionist Papers* (Chapel Hill: University of North Carolina Press, 1992), 5:270.

African Americans well understood that a constitutional amendment that emancipated the slaves might do little to prevent economic and legal inequality. For evidence of the potential shortcomings of emancipation, black activists had only to look at free African Americans in the North, most of whom were the victims of disfranchisement and discrimination.[67] An anonymous black writer derided those who agitated for emancipation, arguing that freedom for the slaves would do little to change the degraded condition of African Americans in general: "The slave bears the irons of slavery; the other [the free black] has been relieved from them, but, enclosed in the same dark dungeon with the former, they are both prisoners."[68] Nor had the military service of African Americans improved their legal status. In April 1863 Douglass had promised free blacks that "to fight for the Government in this tremendous war is . . . to fight for nationality and for a place with all other classes of our fellow-citizens." But by the spring of 1864, black soldiers still did not receive the same pay as white soldiers, and Congress had yet to pass an act assuring the freedom of enslaved wives and children of black recruits.[69] Far from making the antislavery amendment their primary political objective, black Americans sought empowerment in forms more immediate and tangible.[70]

At the very time that Congress was poised to debate the emancipation amendment, African Americans tended to look at three other objectives as more likely to secure permanent freedom and equality. The first of these was equality before the law – not merely equal pay and equal treatment in the military, but equal access to civilian institutions such as courts and public conveyances. "We at the North are contending for and shall not be satisfied until we get equal rights for all," the prominent attorney John S. Rock told a black artillery regiment in May 1864.[71] By 1864 black lobbyists already had persuaded Congress to pass laws allowing African Americans the right to carry the U.S. mail and to serve as witnesses in District of Columbia courts. African Americans now took aim at the all-white streetcars in the district. While black newspapers remained relatively silent on

---

67　See Field, *The Politics of Race in New York;* V. Jacque Voegeli, *Free but Not Equal: The Midwest and the Negro during the Civil War* (Chicago: University of Chicago Press, 1967); McPherson, *The Struggle for Equality,* 221–37; Leon Litwack, *North of Slavery: The Negro in the Free States, 1790–1860* (Chicago: University of Chicago Press, 1961).

68　"A Negro" to the *Pacific Appeal,* reprinted in *Christian Recorder,* January 9, 1864, p. 1.

69　*Douglass' Monthly,* April 1863, in Philip S. Foner, ed., *The Life and Writings of Frederick Douglass* (New York: International Publishers, 1952), 3:345.

70　Eric Foner, "The Meaning of Freedom in the Age of Emancipation," *Journal of American History,* 81 (September 1994), 451–54.

71　Ripley et al., *The Black Abolitionist Papers,* 5:274.

the amendment in the early months of 1864, they gave much publicity to the initiative of Major A. T. Augusta, a black army surgeon who tried to ride in a streetcar but was forcibly removed. Augusta's efforts spurred Charles Sumner to introduce a bill in the Senate to desegregate the streetcars.[72] But Frederick Douglass still feared for the future of African Americans, because he saw "looming up in the legislation at Washington in almost every bill where rights are to be guaranteed and privileges secured, that the word white is carefully inserted."[73] Douglass's apprehension was justified: most of the black initiatives for civil rights legislation met with success only after the war was over.

Along with civil rights, blacks held dear the goal of economic self-sufficiency. From their experience as free but economically oppressed laborers in the North and South, those African Americans free before the war knew that emancipation did not necessarily lead to unimpeded economic opportunity. The abolition amendment might still leave African Americans as something other than free agents in the labor market. As the veteran abolitionist James McCune Smith predicted, "the word *slavery* will, of course, be wiped from the statute book, but the 'ancient relation' can be just as well maintained by cunningly devised laws."[74] Thus African American reformers focused their efforts less on the antislavery amendment than on measures promising more palpable forms of economic security. The editors of the *New Orleans Tribune,* for example, suggested the formation of labor courts, modeled on the French *counseils de prud'hommes,* composed of government-appointed officials and representatives of employers and employees.[75] In their plea for courts of arbitration, the editors revealed the great extent to which African Americans, while embracing much of free-labor ideology, rejected that strain of it that envisioned labor and capital working out equitable arrangements organically, without government intervention. Eventually, the movement for an institution regulating relations between freed people and former slave holders was fulfilled – but only partly – by congressional legislation

72 David Donald, *Charles Sumner and the Rights of Man* (New York: Alfred A. Knopf, 1970), 152–61; James M. McPherson, ed., *The Negro's Civil War: How American Negroes Felt and Acted during the War for the Union* (1965; repr., Urbana: University of Illinois Press, 1982), 261–62.

73 Douglass, "Representatives of the Future South," in John W. Blassingame et al., eds., *The Frederick Douglass Papers* (New Haven: Yale University Press, 1991), ser. 1, 4:27.

74 Smith to Robert Hamilton, in *Weekly Anglo-African,* August 27, 1864, in Ripley et al., *Black Abolitionist Papers,* 5:300–301.

75 James D. Schmidt, *Free to Work: Labor Law, Emancipation, and Reconstruction, 1815–1880* (Athens: University of Georgia Press, 1998), 172. See Eric Foner, *Reconstruction: America's Unfinished Revolution, 1863–1877* (New York: Harper and Row, 1988), 62–65.

creating the Freedmen's Bureau, which was proposed in early 1864 but not passed until 1865. By concentrating their efforts on that legislation rather than on the antislavery amendment, African Americans revealed their preference for explicit rights *for* free labor over a constitutional decree *against* slavery.

A sophisticated system of labor regulation such as the editors of the *New Orleans Tribune* envisioned certainly had its appeal to African Americans, but even more popular was the method most commonly asserted by blacks as the truest path to economic self-sufficiency: land owning. "When the plantations of the South shall be parcelled out to the hardy sons of toil who have made them, under the system of slavery, what they are," exhorted one African American writer, ". . . war shall cease in our fair land; prejudice shall die by the force of a just moral sentiment; the descendants of Africa shall no longer be despised because God has been pleased to make them black, but . . . they will be received on the broad principles of their manhood."[76] The plea for land for the freed people arose everywhere – from the freeborn editors of the *New Orleans Tribune*, from the former slaves in the South Carolina Sea Islands working under new, northern planters, and from northern legislators like George Julian and Thaddeus Stevens.[77] For many blacks as well as whites, land redistribution was a solution to a problem of class more than race. Reformers of all colors carried on the antebellum tradition of promoting land distribution as the key to what Lydia Maria Child termed the "individualizing of the masses."[78] The absence of any explicit promise of land for the freed people within the antislavery amendment gave black Americans another reason to regard the measure as insufficient.

Of all the reasons African Americans had for concentrating their efforts elsewhere than on the antislavery amendment, the most important was the absence of voting rights within the measure. Whereas the notion of an antislavery amendment captured the attention of northern white editors, jurists, and politicians, the question of black suffrage, even more than the issues of civil rights and land and labor reform, dominated the rhetoric of African Americans.[79] "Emancipation without affranchisement," wrote

76   "Junius" to the *Christian Recorder,* February 13, 1864.
77   LaWanda Cox, "The Promise of Land for the Freedmen," *Mississippi Valley Historical Review,* 45 (December 1958), 413–40.
78   Child to George W. Julian, March 27, 1864, Joshua R. Giddings and George W. Julian MSS, LC.
79   See Xi Wang, *The Trial of Democracy: Black Suffrage and Northern Republicans, 1860–1910* (Athens: University of Georgia Press, 1997), 1–48; Brooks D. Simpson, "Land and the Ballot: Securing the Fruits of Emancipation?" *Pennsylvania History,* 60 (April 1993), 176–88; Herman Belz, "Origins of Negro Suffrage during the Civil War,"

the black editor Robert Hamilton, was "a partial emancipation unworthy of the name."[80] Frederick Douglass all but ignored the proposed amendment during late 1863 and early 1864 because he believed that only suffrage would provide African Americans with the power necessary to make themselves truly free. As Americans began considering the merits of the proposed antislavery amendment, Douglass advised them to strive "not so much for the abolition of slavery . . . but for the complete, absolute, unqualified enfranchisement of the colored people of the South."[81] The amendment was for Douglass an abstraction, a promise of freedom with no teeth, whereas the right to vote translated into real equality.

The loudest calls for black suffrage came from free black communities in the South, most notably from the African Americans of New Orleans. In February 1864 white voters in Louisiana elected a slate of Unionist candidates pledged to statewide emancipation. The constitutional convention scheduled to meet in April would definitely outlaw slavery, but many of the state's African Americans demanded as well an extension of voting rights to people of color. Northerners watched and debated among themselves as New Orleans residents took up the issue of voting rights. Leading the movement for an expanded franchise were two prominent free men of color from the Crescent City, Jean-Baptiste Roudanez and Arnold Bertonneau, who toured the North in the spring of 1864 to stir up support for their cause. They came to Washington and presented Lincoln with a petition demanding black suffrage signed by over one thousand African Americans.[82] Lincoln was impressed. The day after the meeting, he wrote to the newly elected Louisiana governor Michael Hahn suggesting that intelligent African Americans and black veterans be allowed to vote.[83]

The struggle for equal suffrage, which yielded little in the way of actual legislation until the last months of the war, revealed the extent to which African Americans initially – and perhaps correctly – mistrusted the antislavery amendment. They were not interested in "authoring" the amendment, for the amendment lacked the explicit political rights that they

Southern Studies, 17 (Summer 1978), 115–30; and McPherson, *The Negro's Civil War,* 271–91.

80 *Weekly Anglo-African,* September 26, 1863, reprinted in Ripley et al., *Black Abolitionist Papers,* 5:256.

81 Blassingame et al., *The Frederick Douglass Papers,* 4:28.

82 McPherson, *The Negro's Civil War,* 277–80; Belz, "Origins of Negro Suffrage during the Civil War," 121–24. The petition, it should be noted, initially restricted black suffrage to those African Americans "born free before the rebellion."

83 *CW,* 7:243. Lincoln may have told the delegation that he would support black suffrage – or at least given them that impression. See the Indianapolis *State Sentinel,* March 5, 1864, p. 3; and the Springfield *Illinois State Register,* March 11, 1864, p. 2.

thought necessary to end slavery. White politicians might contend that slavery was abolished once the Constitution said so, but African Americans tended to follow Frederick Douglass's decree that "slavery is not abolished until the black man has the ballot."[84]

Any suggestion that African Americans were responsible for the creation of the Thirteenth Amendment is a distortion that threatens to neglect their separate, more farsighted legal, economic, and political goals. The struggle to write abolition into the Constitution was not a grass-roots movement initiated by African Americans. Rather, it was a legislative solution to the problem of how to make emancipation legal and permanent. Moreover, it was a peculiarly moderate solution, because many who backed the measure – Montgomery Blair and James Gordon Bennett, for example – believed that ex-slaves would have no positive rights beyond the right not to be owned. In the disparaging words of one of the editors of the *New Orleans Tribune,* too many white politicians looked coldly at the slaves and said, "it is enough to free them . . . let them be free as the beasts in the fields."[85]

Over time, an increasing number of Washington lawmakers would come to share with African Americans a sharper sense of the positive rights that should be attached to freedom. But in 1864 lawmakers' understanding of the meaning of freedom was still inchoate, and many still believed that the mere absence of slavery was enough to guarantee equal opportunity and equal rights. In 1864 the antislavery amendment was still incomplete and would remain so until lawmakers understood all that constitutional emancipation should accomplish. For the time being, African Americans would concentrate their efforts elsewhere.

African American reformers may have had a clear sense of the sort of legislation needed to secure their version of freedom, but they did not help their cause by being so inattentive to the antislavery amendment. In their haste to look past the legal mechanics of emancipation toward the fulfillment of equal rights, they threatened to undermine the lesser goal of abolishing chattel slavery. African Americans were right to assume that the war had dealt slavery a deathblow, but they were too neglectful of the possibility that the institution might linger on longer than they expected. Had blacks early on embraced the constitutional amending process as a potential avenue of reform, they might have strengthened the popular momentum for the antislavery amendment. Moreover, had blacks at this

---

84 Douglass, "In What New Skin Will the Old Snake Come Forth?" in Blassingame et al., *The Frederick Douglass Papers,* 4:83.

85 Jean-Charles Houzeau, *My Passage at the New Orleans Tribune: A Memoir of the Civil War Era,* ed. David C. Rankin, trans. Gerald F. Denault (Baton Rouge: Louisiana State University Press, 1984), 92.

early stage looked more favorably on the idea of amendments, more of them might have seen, as Charles Sumner, Horace Binney, and Francis Lieber had seen, that the amending process was an ideal way not only to abolish slavery but to establish equal rights.

Only after Congress passed the Thirteenth Amendment in early 1865 did large numbers of African Americans come to embrace the amending process as a superior method of securing legal equality. In early 1864, many African Americans still regarded the Constitution with suspicion. It was, after all, a document that had authorized the reenslavement of runaways and the exclusion of blacks from citizenship. How could this same charter now be used to secure emancipation or equality? Other African Americans like Frederick Douglass stood at the opposite extreme. Like many of the old radical constitutionalists, Douglass overly trusted the unamended Constitution as an instrument for securing individual rights. "Abolish slavery tomorrow," Douglass said, "and not a sentence or syllable of the Constitution need be altered."[86] The orator failed to take full stock of northern whites' acceptance of the Constitution as a safeguard for the slave-owning rights of loyal southerners. Most northerners did not see in the original Constitution the power to abolish slavery universally, and most agreed that the wartime emancipation legislation of the federal government would be legally precarious once the war was over. Only by changing the document, and not by simply reading it in a favorable light, would the Constitution become an aid rather than an obstacle to social and institutional change.

In the early months of 1864, as the proposal for an antislavery amendment awaited debate in Congress, the measure received praise from people of diverse backgrounds and varying political affiliations. But the measure had yet to find its champion. Republican constitutional theorists like Francis Lieber and Horace Binney liked the idea of amending the Constitution, but they also believed amendments needed to do more than simply prohibit slavery. Fearing that the more expansive amendments they envisioned would hinder the war effort, they kept their opinions private. Meanwhile, and with only a few exceptions, Republicans seemed indifferent toward the amendment. They did not yet see how the measure put the slaves' freedom – as well as their own political future – on a surer footing. Some Democrats, however, did see political capital in the amendment: endorsing it meant renouncing the party's vulnerable stand on slavery. But Democratic attitudes toward race and the Constitution kept the

---

86 Douglass, "Address for the Promotion of Colored Enlistments," in Foner, *Life and Writings of Douglass*, 3:365.

party leadership from incorporating the amendment into party policy. Not even African Americans appeared particularly interested in the amendment. Although they approved of any assault on slavery, they assumed that the amendment would do less than other measures to secure legal, economic, and political equality. As Congress prepared to debate the antislavery amendment, the fate of the measure was uncertain, and its popularity unclear.

4

Debating Freedom

The winter of 1864 had been long and dreary for Noah Brooks. By February 1864 the esteemed Washington correspondent of the *Sacramento Daily Union* was downright surly. Military news, political rumor, society gossip – all had been in short supply these past few months. In desperation for something to share with his readers, Brooks turned to one of his least favorite venues: the halls of Congress.

"I have already said that 'gab' is the word for the present Congress, and 'gab' it is from morning until night," the reporter complained. There had been a time when he was enthralled by the momentous, often entertaining oratory that rang through the chambers of the Capitol. But the days of engaging debate were gone:

> Now when a member rises to speak it is usually with a formidable pile of manuscripts before him, the sight of which dismays the members, who will read it in the *Globe* if worth reading, otherwise it is worth nothing. So the member goes on, audible or inaudible, loud or low-voiced, graceful or loutish, it is all the same to the scattered few who remain in their seats – some writing letters, some reading newspapers, munching apples, or dozing in their comfortable chairs. Only the members of the same political faith with the party speaking profess to pay any attention, those of the opposite party generally lounging in the cloak rooms, enjoying a social smoke and chat. . . . Of course all this breath and labor is wasted, for the speech is not intended for any special effect in the House or Senate, but upon the country, or as used for a campaign document; printed and circulated by members, it flies all over the country, and has its small sum of influence upon the masses of the people.[1]

The disdain Brooks felt for congressional speeches has not been shared by historians and legal scholars who have pored through them to understand the dynamics of legislation during the Civil War and Reconstruction. History has tended to treat congressional proceedings as records of the weighty process of law making instead of the more lowly regarded business of politicking. In examining the Reconstruction amendments in particular, historians using the rich debates have too often assumed that

---

1   Letter of "Castine," *Sacramento Daily Union*, March 14, 1864, p. 1.

the participants were more concerned with making meaningful law than with persuading their constituents to vote the right ticket.

The congressional debates on the Thirteenth Amendment must be viewed in their proper context. Congressional speeches then, as now, articulated significant ideological strains and legal doctrines, but they simultaneously performed the more immediate function of marking political territory. This was particularly true of the debate on the Thirteenth Amendment in early 1864. While the debate served as a forum for legislators to consider the merits and meaning of constitutional freedom, it also served as an arena for politicians to sharpen their partisan weapons in anticipation of the great political battles in the near future.

That the debate took place in the midst of a national political campaign affected all parties involved. The effect was especially pronounced on the Republicans. Republicans sincerely wanted to see the amendment adopted, and they knew that securing the requisite two-thirds majority in Congress required Democratic votes. Yet they also saw in the amendment an issue that they could use to define themselves *against* the Democrats in the upcoming election. Because Republicans did not yet appreciate the strength of Democratic support for the amendment, and because they felt an immediate need for defining issues, they opted for party combat over cooperation. Most Democrats also gave into partisanship and threw themselves against the amendment. But a small and significant number of Democrats opted to back the measure. In doing so, they not only helped to generate public excitement about the measure but also provided crucial intellectual justification for constitutional amendments as potential instruments of reform.

The Antislavery Amendment and Republican Unity

Prior to the first round of debates on the amendment, Republicans had not united behind a single, clear policy on emancipation. They had not yet rallied behind the antislavery amendment as the best method of achieving abolition. In fact, the constitutional amendment that would have preserved slavery forever, which Congress had passed in 1861, was still rattling around northern state legislatures. In February 1864 a proposal by Senator Henry B. Anthony of Rhode Island to rescind that amendment had died in the Senate Judiciary Committee, which found no constitutional authority to recall an amendment already submitted to the states.[2]

---

2   CG, 38th Cong., 1st sess. (February 8, 1864), 522. See Herman Ames, *The Proposed Amendments to the Constitution of the United States during the First Century of Its History* (1896; repr., New York: Burt Franklin, 1970), 197.

Nor had Republicans united behind a single presidential candidate. Lincoln was likely to be renominated, but he hardly had the unanimous support of his party. In the first months of 1864, a group of Republicans led by Senator Samuel C. Pomeroy of Kansas attempted to secure the party's presidential nomination for Salmon P. Chase, the secretary of the treasury. The Chase boom seemed to be over by March, when Chase issued a public letter withdrawing his name from contention, but Lincoln still faced the prospect of further challenges from within his own party or from some third party.[3]

One of the main functions of the congressional debate of the antislavery amendment, therefore, was to unite Republicans behind the measure and to link it to their likeliest presidential candidate, Abraham Lincoln. The president himself had said nothing publicly about the amendment – perhaps he hoped to win the nomination without saying anything more about slavery – but he may have worked privately with congressional Republicans on behalf of the measure.

Perhaps the hidden hand of the president was at work on March 19, 1864, when representatives Isaac Arnold of Illinois and James Wilson of Iowa delivered the first congressional speeches in favor of the amendment and connected the measure directly to Lincoln's candidacy. It was also possible that these congressmen were acting on their own, hoping to press the president into endorsing a new policy on abolition. Arnold's address was an unabashed stump speech that celebrated Lincoln as the party's best candidate and touted the abolition amendment as the party's best policy. The amendment, Arnold declared, would define the Republicans in the coming campaign against the Democrats, those northern minions of the southern "slave kings."[4] Like Arnold, Wilson wrote his speech as both a statement of legislative policy and as a campaign document.[5] Wilson joined Arnold in asking his listeners not to let Democratic orators sway them into thinking that the opposition's commitment to slavery was in

3   John Niven, *Salmon P. Chase: A Biography* (New York: Oxford University Press, 1995), 357–64; Frederick J. Blue, *Salmon P. Chase: A Life in Politics* (Kent, Ohio: Kent State University Press, 1987), 212–27; William Frank Zornow, *Lincoln and the Party Divided* (Norman: University of Oklahoma Press, 1954), 23–54.

4   *CG*, 38th Cong., 1st sess. (March 19, 1864), 1196–99. That this speech was intended as a campaign speech is indicated by the careful paragraphing – complete with section titles – that Arnold gave to the speech in the *Congressional Globe* and the fact that he immediately distributed it to various Republican organs. See, for example, the *Ohio State Journal*, March 22, 1864, p. 2.

5   The Union Congressional Committee, the campaign organization composed of Republican congressmen, eventually distributed Wilson's speech as a pamphlet titled "A Free Constitution." See E. D. Morgan et al. to Elihu B. Washburne, June 29, 1864, Elihu B. Washburne MSS, LC.

any degree diminished. The Iowa congressman echoed Arnold in declaring that the Democrats were working solely "in the interests of slavery."[6]

The speeches of Arnold and Wilson suggested that Republicans had begun to identify the antislavery amendment as a campaign issue with wide appeal. Of course, Republicans also maintained a moral commitment against slavery. Arnold, for example, confided to a friend a few days after his speech: "If I could remain in Congress until this bill passes, I would be content."[7] But the immediate purpose of promoting this particular measure at this particular time was clearly to stake out ground against the Democrats. Yet Arnold and Wilson failed to engage the Democrats in debate on the amendment in the House of Representatives. Not one Democrat there responded to their speeches, probably because many Democrats still felt unsure about where to stand on the measure. Republicans in the House postponed further discussion of the amendment, in part because Democrats seemed uninterested in discussing the measure, but also because they suspected, perhaps wrongly, that they could not secure the two-thirds majority necessary to pass the amendment.

The amendment stood a much better chance in the Senate, where Republicans, with the help of unionist congressmen from the border states, might muster the necessary supermajority. On March 28, 1864, only nine days after the speeches of Arnold and Wilson in the House, the Republican senators Lyman Trumbull and Henry Wilson delivered speeches that seemed to confirm the amendment as the defining policy of the party.

Neither of these speeches showed much passion for the measure, however. Trumbull mostly rehashed old Republican attacks against the Slave Power. Although he praised the abolition amendment because it would "relieve us of all difficulty in the restoration of the Union" and would "restore to a whole race that freedom which is theirs by the gift of God," he candidly admitted that the Union needed military victories more than it needed antislavery legislation.[8] So lukewarm was the address that James Gordon Bennett, the editor of the *New York Herald*, unjustly accused Trumbull of making "the emancipation of the slaves . . . not even a secondary consideration in prosecuting the war."[9] Henry Wilson's speech was equally uninspired. He failed to say why the amendment was preferable to other emancipation measures, and he gave no clue as to the rights and powers it encompassed.[10] Hardly an impassioned plea, the speech's

6 CG, 38th Cong., 1st sess. (March 19, 1864), 1199, 1203.
7 Arnold to George Schneider, March 24, 1864, George Schneider MSS, CHS.
8 CG, 38th Cong., 1st sess. (March 28, 1864), 1313–14.
9 *New York Herald*, March 31, 1864, p. 4.
10 CG, 38th Cong., 1st sess. (March 28, 1864), 1319–24.

delivery was flat – and it was read to "empty benches," one correspondent noted.[11]

With time, Republicans like Trumbull and Wilson would better appreciate the amendment's potential for bringing justice to African Americans, but in early 1864 party members were less interested in the amendment's long-term legal effects than its immediate role in the coming election. Wilson in particular saw the amendment mainly as a vehicle for expressing his antislavery views. One reporter accurately surmised that Wilson had delivered the address "not for the sake of influencing any vote in the Senate, but to be printed and circulated as a campaign document."[12] That year's campaign was especially important to the senator, who was running for reelection. A restatement of his long-held antislavery views provided a much more attractive campaign document than did a legalistic explication of the amendment. In the midst of a highly fluid political situation, Wilson and Trumbull had not yet worked out a precise understanding of the amendment's scope and meaning. They were interested in the measure mainly because of its potential for keeping the party united on the slavery issue instead of divided over more controversial matters such as equal rights.

Trumbull made this function of the amendment clear when a number of radical senators tried to shift debate from the amendment to the question of black suffrage in the Montana territory. The Illinois senator quickly cut short the radicals. He moved for a vote on the Montana question and a return to the antislavery amendment.[13] Trumbull undoubtedly supported voting rights for African Americans – he joined with the majority that ultimately passed the Montana bill – but he wanted to keep antislavery, and not black suffrage, the central issue of the party. He later called the Montana bill "evil" because it gave "men who are really opposed to the Government something to go to the people upon, and get up divisions and distractions, when we want no divisions."[14] In contrast, he hoped that the amendment would find favor among all Republicans and even some Democrats, and that it would force the main body of Democrats into the increasingly unpopular position of defending a defunct institution.

11 *Rochester Democrat and American*, April 13, 1864, p. 2.
12 Correspondent of the *Boston Courier*, reprinted in the Springfield *Illinois State Register*, April 10, 1864, p. 2.
13 *CG*, 38th Cong., 1st sess. (March 30, 1864), 1346; (March 31, 1864), 1364. See Allan G. Bogue, *The Earnest Men: Republicans of the Civil War Senate* (Ithaca: Cornell University Press, 1981), 205–9; and Michael Les Benedict, *A Compromise of Principle: Congressional Republicans and Reconstruction, 1863–1869* (New York: W. W. Norton, 1974), 77–79.
14 *CG*, 38th Cong., 1st sess. (April 19, 1864), 1706.

Trumbull's strategy worked well. In the Senate amendment debate, Republicans united behind the amendment, while Democrats, with a few notable exceptions, opposed it. But neither Trumbull nor anyone else fully anticipated the wide-ranging debate that the amendment triggered. The senators did more than merely pass judgment on one piece of legislation. In effect, they offered a retrospective of the war that defined for themselves and their parties the crucial issues in the coming election.

Slavery, Union, and the Meaning of the War

The question that most dominated the Senate debate was whether the Civil War was about slavery. For the Republicans, who had long believed that slavery was at the root of the sectional conflict, the debate on the amendment provided yet another opportunity to repeat their diatribes against the Slave Power. Typical was the charge of Daniel Clark of New Hampshire: "She [the Slave Power] sent assassins to murder the Chief-Magistrate. . . . She shot down Union soldiers in the streets of Baltimore; she has set armies in the field, and she now seeks the nation's life and the destruction of the Government." Investing the Slave Power with a female persona – a rhetorical technique new to the Civil War – only strengthened Republican rhetoric. Feminizing the southern conspiracy made it seem simultaneously cowardly and conniving. Simple emancipation legislation would not suffice to destroy the sinister Slave Power, Clark declared; only the abolition amendment could finish the job. Without it, the hands of the witch were left "unlopped, to clutch again such unfortunate creatures as it could lay hold upon."[15]

By making the Slave Power once again their main target, Republicans invited Democrats to offer their own account of slavery's role in precipitating the conflict. The Peace Democrats, those party members who

---

15 Ibid. (March 31, 1864), 1369. For a similar speech, see ibid. (April 4, 1864), appendix, 116–17 (Howe). On the rhetorical strategy of feminizing the cowardly villain, see Karen Halttunen, *Confidence Men and Painted Women: A Study of Middle-Class Culture in America, 1830–1870* (New Haven: Yale University Press, 1982), 56–59; Mary P. Ryan, *Cradle of the Middle Class: The Family in Oneida County, New York, 1790–1865* (Cambridge: Cambridge University Press, 1981), 186–91, 218–29; and Nina Silber, *The Romance of Reunion: Northerners and the South, 1865–1900* (Chapel Hill: University of North Carolina Press, 1993), 13–38 (showing how northerners deployed the rhetoric of feminization against the defeated Confederates). For the centrality of the Slave Power in Republican rhetoric, see William E. Gienapp, "The Republican Party and the Slave Power," in Robert H. Abzug and Stephen E. Maizlish, eds., *New Perspectives on Race and Slavery in America: Essays in Honor of Kenneth M. Stampp* (Lexington: University of Kentucky Press, 1986), 51–78; and Eric Foner, *Free Soil, Free Labor, Free Men: The Ideology of the Republican Party before the Civil War* (New York: Oxford University Press, 1970).

favored an immediate armistice, conceded that slavery was somehow responsible for the war, but they also pointed out that this fact alone did not
lead logically to an abolition amendment. Senator Lazarus Powell of Kentucky reminded the Senate that wars had been fought over religion, yet no
one had proposed abolishing worship.[16] The junior senator from Kentucky, Garrett Davis, was much more direct: it was not the Slave Power
but New England abolitionist "Puritans" who had caused the war.[17]
Davis therefore offered an alternative constitutional amendment that proposed to diminish the power of the Northeast by reforming the six states
of New England into two. The Senate hastily dismissed the measure.[18]
Democratic tirades against "Puritans" were as common as Republican
attacks on the Slave Power. While anti–Slave Power rhetoric played on
northern animosities toward the archaic slave kings of the South, anti-
Puritanism exploited western and immigrant hostility toward the staid,
self-righteous Protestants of the Northeast.[19]

One of the reasons that the congressional debate on the amendment
would leave future scholars perplexed about the legislators' intentions was
that congressmen took the politically safer course of describing their opponents' transgressions instead of specifying the precise legal function of
the amendment. Yet, even if the debate did not explore all the dimensions
of the amendment's potential, it did reveal two distinct constellations of
beliefs about the meaning of the war and the proper condition of society.
On one side was the idea, espoused mainly by Republicans, that the Slave
Power had caused the war by perverting democracy and liberty. The war's
purpose, then, was to return the nation to its original order: the Slave
Power was to be demolished so that the federal government could again
regulate freedom among the people in a fair manner. On the other side
was the idea, propagated mainly by conservative Democrats, that Puritan
fanatics had started the war by attempting to legislate morality. In this

16 CG, 38th cong., 1st sess. (April 8, 1864), 1483. See also ibid. (March 28, 1864), 1314
    (Trumbull); (April 8, 1864), 1480 (Sumner).
17 Noah Brooks, *Washington, D.C. in Lincoln's Time*, ed. Herbert Mitgang (1895; rev. ed.
    1971; repr., Athens: University of Georgia Press, 1958), 100; CG, 38th Cong., 1st sess.
    (March 30, 1864), appendix, 104.
18 CG, 38th Cong., 1st sess. (March 31, 1864), 1364.
19 For examples of anti-Puritan rhetoric, see G. R. J. Bowdoin to Lewis B. Parsons, March
    2, 1861, Lewis B. Parsons MSS, ISHL; James A. Bayard, Jr., to Thomas F. Bayard,
    August 19, 1862, Thomas F. Bayard MSS, LC; Samuel S. Cox, *Puritanism in Politics*
    (New York: Van Evrie, Herton, 1863); New York *Journal of Commerce*, reprinted in
    Indianapolis *State Sentinel*, January 15, 1864, p. 2; *New York Evening Express*, Janu-
    ary 16, 1865, p. 2; Jean H. Baker, *Affairs of Party: The Political Culture of Northern
    Democrats in the Mid-Nineteenth Century* (Ithaca: Cornell University Press, 1983),
    143–76; and Joel Silbey, *A Respectable Minority: The Democratic Party in the Civil
    War Era, 1860–1868* (New York: W. W. Norton, 1977), 74–77.

version of events, the war's purpose again was to restore order – but order of a different sort. The Puritan impulse was to be restrained so that Americans could be left unperturbed by federal interference and fall into their natural place – some superior, some inferior; some righteous, some sinful.

While the amendment debate mapped out familiar ideological terrain, it simultaneously exposed some subtle new shifts in party doctrine. So far in the war, antislavery legislation had received support mostly from Republicans and a smattering of War Democrats who regarded emancipation as a necessary war measure. Meanwhile, most Democrats had contended that because the Constitution protected slavery, the destruction of slavery would destroy the Constitution and further divide the Union. In the debates on the Thirteenth Amendment, however, there were signs that the Democrats might deviate from their traditional position. Democrats whose obligation to the constitutional protection of slavery had so far outweighed any moral revulsion they felt toward the institution could now obey their conscience by supporting a measure that did not violate but simply augmented the Constitution. When two Democrats, both from slave states, took the Republican line that either the Union or slavery must perish, they exposed the changing sympathies of their party and delivered a powerful blow for black freedom.

Reverdy Johnson of Maryland was the first to turn against his party. Already the Democratic senator, a former Whig, had told an audience outside of Congress that the antislavery amendment, not the Emancipation Proclamation, was the proper, constitutional device to achieve abolition.[20] Now, in the Senate, he delivered the most persuasive, nonpartisan speech in favor of the amendment.[21] He did not join in the Republican tirades against the Slave Power, though he admitted that slavery was a "sin." Yet, even as he played down Republican ideology, he echoed Lincoln's "House Divided" speech from six years before. Lincoln, then a Republican candidate for senator, had predicted that the nation would not endure half slave and half free.[22] Now Johnson, elected as a Democrat, confirmed that "a prosperous and permanent peace can never be secured if the institution is permitted to survive." The only thing more dangerous than slavery, Johnson declared, was the belief that states' rights trumped federal power. "There never was a greater political heresy," Johnson told Senator Willard Saulsbury of Delaware, a fellow Democrat who had invoked John C. Calhoun's doctrine of state supremacy. Johnson even read an old speech he had made in the Senate against Calhoun. To Garrett

20 Letter of "Agate," *Cincinnati Gazette,* February 8, 1864, p. 3.
21 CG, 38th Cong., 1st sess. (April 5, 1864), 1419–24.
22 CW, 2:461.

Davis, who argued that abolition undercut the framers' guarantee of property rights, he pointed to the Preamble of the Constitution as evidence that the founders would not have sustained slavery had they anticipated how it would interfere with the nation's peace and tranquility. When he finished, many Democrats scowled at him while Union senators rushed to shake his hand.[23]

Johnson's address sent a jolt into national politics. Prior to the speech, few members of the press had followed the debate on the amendment. But this speech, coming from a respected member of a party consistently opposed to emancipation, could not be ignored. "We doubt if the rebel cause has got a harder blow since Vicksburg was taken," reported the *Chicago Tribune*, "than it got in the Senate when Reverdy Johnson laid his blows."[24] "Think of Reverdy Johnson sustaining and advocating [the amendment]!" wrote the New York diarist George Templeton Strong: "'John Brown's soul's a-marching on' – double quick."[25] Johnson's speech seemed to presage the end of sixty years of Democratic sanction of human bondage.

It also reflected the progress of proemancipation sentiment in the border states. Republican senators already had pointed to emancipation movements in the border states as evidence of popular support for the antislavery amendment; Johnson's speech now confirmed their position.[26] The day after Johnson delivered his speech, his home state of Maryland voted to hold a state convention to draft a new antislavery constitution. Even more remarkable, three of the counties that voted for the convention were on Maryland's eastern shore, an area normally controlled by slave owners.[27] When Johnson heard the news, he joyfully wrote a Baltimore editor, "a new era is now dawning on our State. . . . If it is done also in the whole country – as I think it will be – great as our prosperity has been in the past, and high as has been our name with the nations of the world, both will be almost immeasurably enhanced."[28] Border state emancipationists like the reverend Dr. Robert J. Breckinridge in turn praised Johnson's address on the amendment. Breckinridge had lived in Baltimore for thirteen years before moving to Kentucky and even-

23 *New York Times,* April 6, 1864, p. 1.
24 *Chicago Tribune,* April 10, 1864, p. 2.
25 Allan Nevins and Milton Halsey Thomas, eds., *The Diary of George Templeton Strong* (New York: Macmillan, 1952), 3:427.
26 See *CG,* 38th Cong., 1st sess. (March 28, 1864), 1323 (Wilson), and (April 4, 1864), appendix, 118 (Howe).
27 Charles Lewis Wagandt, *The Mighty Revolution: Negro Emancipation in Maryland* (Baltimore: Johns Hopkins Press, 1964), 197–220 (esp. table at 219).
28 Johnson to Charles C. Fulton, April 7, 1864, in *Baltimore American,* April 9, 1864, reprinted in Boston *Daily Evening Transcript,* April 11, 1864, p. 2.

tually leading the Union party there. "The Old War Horse of Kentucky" was a symbol of the divided border. He was uncle to the Confederate leader John C. Breckinridge and father to two sons in the Confederate army and one in the Union army. Senator Johnson's speech harmonized perfectly with Breckinridge's own antislavery views, and he told the senator that the amendment was fortunate to have "a leading advocate in a Senator from Maryland, and that Senator yourself." The reverend agreed with Johnson that slavery must not be left "in its present frightful condition – utterly demoralized in point of fact, full of doubt as to its legal status, and the fruitful source of intolerable mischiefs."[29]

For those who wondered if Johnson's stand on the amendment might be exceptional among border state senators, John B. Henderson's speech two days after Johnson's removed all doubts. The Missouri senator was a slaveholder and former Democrat who, as a brigadier general, had defended his state against secessionists in 1861 and been elected to the Senate by the state's Union party. Because Henderson had proposed the initial version of the antislavery amendment which Trumbull's Judiciary Committee had revised into its present form, his speech in its favor was anticipated. Like Johnson, he was a friend of Lincoln and a conservative caught between two state parties: the Democrats, who sought immediate peace with the Confederacy, and the Radical Unionists (called "Charcoals" in Missouri), who desired immediate emancipation and subjugation of the South. His address, like Johnson's, avoided extreme partisan rhetoric: it was no single party but slavery, through both its defenders and its detractors, that had caused the war. "Shall we then leave slavery to fester again in the public vitals?" Henderson asked.[30] The Missourian's speech bred yet more optimism among antislavery activists. "An argument in favor of freedom from the lips of Sumner, Wilson, Hale, Harlan, Trumbull, or any of the long-tried friends of the slave is not a novelty, nor is it a particular pleasure to hear," reported the *Anti-Slavery Standard*, an abolitionist organ. "But when Mr. Henderson of Missouri or Mr. Johnson of Maryland argues in favor of extinguishing slavery, root and branch, it is a strange luxury to listen."[31]

Henderson had been careful, however, to deny any alliance with radical antislavery activists or even more conservative Republicans. Instead, he pledged his loyalties to the Democrats and predicted the party's revitalization if it adopted an antislavery position. "The Democratic party in its better days was strong," Henderson reminded his audience. "It was irresistible, because the principles it professed were right," and "when it shall

29 Breckinridge to Johnson, May 3, 1864, Reverdy Johnson MSS, LC.
30 CG, 38th Cong., 1st sess. (April 7, 1864), 1461.
31 "Avon" to *National Anti-Slavery Standard*, April 16, 1864, p. 3.

cease to be the advocate of African slavery its zeal in behalf of the liberty of the white man and the true principles of Government will be properly appreciated." Once they abandoned slavery, the Democrats would rise above Republicans, whose natural tendency was "to centralize power, to destroy the powers of the States and to make a nation supreme in all things."[32]

Henderson's words sounded the death knell of a long-standing strain of Democratic policy toward slavery. For ten years, while Republicans had argued that leaving slavery to its own devices would imperil the Union, Democrats had contended that noninterference with slavery would preserve it. But now, with distinguished members of their own party imploring them to shed their proslavery image, Democrats found their previous position increasingly untenable. Opponents of the amendment would need a stronger case to unite Democrats against the amendment. If a plea to save the Union would not work, then perhaps an appeal to white supremacy would.

Constitutional Freedom and Racial Equality

"This Government was made by white men and for white men," Democratic Senator Lazarus Powell announced during his speech on the amendment, "and if it is ever preserved it must be preserved by white men."[33] Every Democrat in Congress who spoke on the amendment echoed Powell's contention that the measure threatened the racial order of the country. And as the opposition worked assiduously to keep visions of "negro equality" and "amalgamation" hanging over the congressional proceedings, the debate on the amendment became a discussion not simply about the future of slavery but about the fate of African Americans.

Democrats had always played on race prejudice to combat Republican antislavery policies. Their antiblack position was in part a political technique and in part a by-product of a popular culture that embraced images of black inferiority. Racism fused with Democrats' wish for public order and civic purity to generate a party doctrine claiming that newly freed African Americans represented the greatest threat to the nation's political and social integrity. In every new policy of their opponents, from a proposed national railroad to a national currency to, of course, emancipation, Democrats saw the specter of disorderly free blacks.[34] Not surprisingly, when Democrats came to the issue of the antislavery amendment, most of them wheeled out the old bugbear of racial upheaval.

32   CG, 38th Cong., 1st sess. (April 7, 1864), 1462.
33   Ibid. (April 8, 1864), 1484.
34   See Baker, *Affairs of Party*, 212–58.

All too familiar was the Democratic argument that because blacks were naturally suited for slavery, any measure freeing them would lead to the suffering and extinction of the race. Slavery, said Willard Saulsbury, was the will of God: "His providence is inequality and diversity."[35] Abolish slavery, added Thomas Hendricks of Indiana, and you remove the inferior blacks from the wardship of the superior whites. Once free, they would succumb to their natural "downward" tendency, becoming victims of white racism rather than beneficiaries of white protection.[36] They would go the way of the Indians, James McDougall of California argued, "destroyed by our own people, by our vices, our luxuries, and our violence."[37]

Everyone had heard this reasoning before. The antebellum proslavery argument had affected the same sort of sentimental concern for the welfare of blacks, and by the time of the Civil War, many Democrats still accepted some of the principles of proslavery. It is important to note, however, that the party had never been uniformly in support of slavery. A number of northern Democrats had deserted the party prior to the war because of their opposition to slavery or to slavery extension, and many of those who remained in the party found slavery morally repugnant but nonetheless constitutional.[38] Some of those antislavery Democrats who had stayed with the party, including John B. Henderson in the Senate and Henry G. Stebbins in the House, would give crucial support to the antislavery amendment. Yet a core of northern Democrats still took the line that nature protected blacks by making them slaves. That such a belief could still be maintained was understandable: it allowed northern Democrats to preserve their bond with southern members of the party, and it comported well with the party's vision of a society structured by the dictates of nature rather than the fiat of government.

For all that Democrats spoke of the amendment's evil effect on blacks, what they truly feared was its impact on whites. Universal emancipation, suggested Senator McDougall, would lead to racial cross-breeding and the eventual sterilization of both races. McDougall declared: "It may not be within the reading of some learned Senators, and yet belongs to demonstrated science, that the African race and the Europeans are different, and . . . the eighth generation of the mixed race formed by the union of the African and European cannot continue their species."[39] McDougall's reference to future sterilization among mulattoes carried an obvious insinua-

---

35 *CG*, 38th Cong., 1st sess. (April 6, 1864), 1442.
36 Ibid. (April 7, 1864), 1457.
37 Ibid. (April 8, 1864), 1490.
38 See Sean Wilentz, "Slavery, Antislavery, and Jacksonian Democracy," in Melvyn Stokes and Stephen Conway, eds., *The Market Revolution in America: Social, Political, and Religious Expressions* (Charlottesville: University Press of Virginia, 1996), 202–23.
39 *CG*, 38th Cong., 1st sess. (April 8, 1864), 1490.

tion about the immediate effect of the amendment: the measure would authorize, if not promote, sexual relations between whites and blacks. The charge that Republicans were amalgamationists was an old weapon in the Democrats' arsenal. Throughout the 1850s and into the early years of the war, Democrats exploited racial fears with accusations that Republicans meant to free all the slaves, declare them equal, distribute them to the northern states, and promote intermarriage.

Such charges were flying freely in the spring of 1864, just as Congress was considering the amendment. The furor was mostly the result of a pamphlet published in early 1864 titled *Miscegenation* – the first recorded use of that term. Written anonymously by two newsmen at the Democratic *New York World*, but purporting to be a legitimate Republican tract, the pamphlet pretended to extol the benefits of interbreeding between blacks and whites.[40] Notice of the booklet appeared in various papers, but it received its greatest boost when Congressman Samuel Sullivan "Sunset" Cox cited it in a speech in February 1864 that denounced the proposed Freedmen's Bureau bill.[41] By March, when the debate on the antislavery amendment began in the Senate, "miscegenation" had entered the political vocabulary. In newspapers and stump speeches, Democrats made the term synonymous with equal rights and labeled all Republicans miscegenationists.[42] Republicans in the meantime, using a tactic developed by abolitionists before the war, accused Democrats of being the real miscegenationists. It was the Democrats, Republicans charged, who lent tacit approval to male slave owners' ravishment of innocent slave women.[43] At times the word took on farcical dimensions. James Gordon Bennett, upon

40 [David Croly and George Wakeman], *Miscegenation: The Theory of the Blending of the Races, Applied to the American Man and Negro* (New York: H. Dexter, Hamilton, 1864). See David E. Long, *The Jewel of Liberty: Abraham Lincoln's Re-Election and the End of Slavery* (Mechanicsburg, Penn.: Stackpole Books, 1994), 153–78; Forrest G. Wood, *Black Scare: The Racist Response to Emancipation and Reconstruction* (Berkeley: University of California Press, 1968), 53–79; J. M. Bloch, *Miscegenation, Melaleukation, and Mr. Lincoln's Dog* (New York: Schaum Publishing, 1958); and Sidney Kaplan, "The Miscegenation Issue in the Election of 1864," *Journal of Negro History,* 34 (1949), 274–343.

41 CG, 38th Cong., 1st sess. (February 17, 1864), 708–13; Samuel S. Cox, *Eight Years in Congress, From 1857 to 1865* (New York: D. Appleton, 1865), 354.

42 See, for example, J. W. Sheahan to Elihu B. Washburne, March 17, 1864, Elihu B. Washburne MSS, LC; Springfield *Illinois State Register,* February 23, 1864, p. 2, March 6, 1864, p. 2; *Cincinnati Enquirer,* March 15, 1864, p. 2, March 25, 1864, p. 2.

43 See, for example, *Cleveland Leader,* March 19, 1864, p. 2; *Cincinnati Gazette,* April 15, 1864, p. 4; Indianapolis *Daily Journal,* April 5, 1864, p. 2, April 7, 1864, p. 2, April 25, 1864, p. 2; *New York Times,* March 30, 1864, p. 4, April 3, 1864, p. 4; *New York Tribune,* March 17, 1864, p. 4; *Chicago Tribune,* April 3, 1864, p. 2. On antebellum uses of antiamalgamation rhetoric by the antislavery movement, see Ronald G. Walters, *The Antislavery Appeal: American Abolitionism after 1830* (Baltimore: Johns Hopkins University Press, 1976), 70–87.

hearing that black suffrage might become legal in Montana, wondered if
the new territory should not be called "Miscegenia."[44] An Illinois paper
called the marriage between a fully grown woman and a male dwarf
"almost miscegenation."[45] Even Abraham Lincoln, joking with some War
Democrats, called miscegenation "a democratic mode of producing good
Union men."[46]

Yet, for all that, miscegenation would become commonplace in conversation by late 1864, the term rarely entered the Senate amendment debate
in the early part of that year. Senator McDougall's reference to race
mixing – and he did not use the term miscegenation – proved to be
exceptional. It seems that congressional Democrats during this period
were not yet sure how much weight to give the issue, especially because
most everyone knew that the purported Republican *Miscegenation* pamphlet was in fact a hoax. To press the issue was to risk charges such as the
one published by the *Chicago Tribune*, which rightly identified the miscegenation controversy as but another effort "to stir up the old bias
against the blacks, under the newly found term of 'miscegenation.' Years
ago it was 'amalgamation'; but new words create a new interest in old
things."[47] Democratic speeches against the amendment in the Senate did
reveal the old racist notion that, as Lazarus Powell put it, "the white man
is [the Negro's] superior, and will be so whether you call him a slave or an
equal."[48] But, for the moment, congressional Democrats chose to make
miscegenation only a minor theme of their speeches against the amendment. Two months later, when the amendment reached the House of
Representatives, the Democrats would make miscegenation their main
line of attack.

Although the race-baiting in the Senate by opponents of the amendment
was subdued, supporters of the measure already had constructed several
lines of defense. First, Republicans revived their old argument that hostility to slavery was not by itself an endorsement of racial equality. One
could admit of blacks, said Senator Timothy Howe of Wisconsin, that "as
a race they are inferior to the race of whites," but "is [that] a fact which
authorizes you or me to enslave them?"[49] The argument was common to
Republican rhetoric and had been made famous six years before by Lin-

44 James Gordon Bennett, undated memo in "articles" file, James Gordon Bennett MSS,
    LC.
45 Springfield *Illinois State Register,* March 6, 1864, p. 2.
46 *CW,* 7:508.
47 *Chicago Tribune,* April 1, 1864, p. 2. For examples of similar race-baiting strategies in
    the election of 1860, see Leon Litwack, *North of Slavery: The Negro in the Free States,*
    1790–1860 (Chicago: University of Chicago Press, 1961), 269–71.
48 *CG,* 38th Cong., 1st sess. (April 8, 1864), 1484.
49 Ibid. (April 4, 1864), appendix, 113.

coln, who repeatedly denied in his debates with Senator Stephen A. Douglas that his hatred for slavery reflected a wish to have a black man as his equal or a black woman as his wife.[50]

African American initiative during the war provided the amendment's defenders with a second defense against charges that the measure established "negro equality." Because blacks were making their way toward equality on their own, the proamendment side argued, the government would have to do nothing more for them beyond ending slavery. Supporters of the amendment cited blacks' achievement in battle and their success on the home front to give the lie to the Democrats' position that the race depended entirely on the beneficence of Republicans. Senator James Harlan of Iowa pointed to the thousands of newly freed blacks in the District of Columbia and Maryland who already were providing food, shelter, schools, and churches for themselves. Only a few of these people, Harlan claimed, were "in any way dependent on the support of the white race."[51] Ironically, blacks' efforts on behalf of their own freedom, their instinct for "self-emancipation," may have diminished antislavery congressmen's sense that government had to mandate egalitarian measures proactively. When Democrats foretold of insidious designs to bring equality to blacks, their adversaries simply shot back: what could we do for blacks that they are not already doing for themselves?

In refuting the prediction that the amendment established black equality, the measure's defenders occasionally offered an explicit denial. "I will not be intimidated by the fears of negro equality," said John Henderson; "in passing this amendment we do not confer upon the negro the right to vote. We give him no right except his freedom, and leave the rest to the states."[52] Henderson, a War Democrat from a slave state, was a newcomer to the antislavery movement but a predictable opponent of federal legislation granting political or civil rights. Yet, even senators with a stronger commitment to black equality denied that the federal government would have to legislate for the freed people. Harlan, for example, who often voted with the more radical members of his party, declared that enslaved African Americans would need no further attention from the federal government once they were free. The senator believed that state laws should protect both races equally, but he never suggested that the federal government would take action in instances where state laws discriminated against blacks.[53]

---

50 See, for example, *CW*, 3:16.
51 *CG*, 38th Cong., 1st sess. (April 6, 1864), 1438.
52 Ibid. (April 7, 1864), 1465.
53 Ibid. (April 6, 1864), 1438.

Among the amendment's supporters, War Democrats like Henderson and Republicans like Harlan agreed that states would oversee the rights of the freed people, but these two groups clearly had different assumptions about the rights that states should uphold. Like most Democrats, Henderson believed that the legal order of a society should reflect its natural order. He had broken from his party by denying that slavery was a natural condition – "This thing of slavery is a heresy" – even though he himself was a slaveholder.[54] But Henderson still thought that laws should not tamper with people's natural status, and he assumed that once slavery was abolished, nature would keep whites in a superior position to blacks. Government should then follow nature's law by lending its "zeal in behalf of the liberty of the white man."[55] Henderson seemed to believe that, under the amendment, the states could pass discriminatory laws against free blacks, for such measures merely extended nature's law of white superiority.

In contrast, Harlan, Henry Wilson, and other Republican senators assumed that blacks and whites would generally receive equal treatment before the laws. This notion of equal treatment, however, rested on a more narrow vision of equality than we are used to today. The Republican notion of "equal before the law" during this period flowed from free-labor ideology and thus was usually restricted to laws regulating labor. If ex-slaves failed to become industrious free laborers, then they would be subject to the same vagrancy and pauper laws that had long applied to all free people. Like white vagrants and paupers, unemployed free blacks might well be forced to work.[56] By the same token, if they did find employment, they would be entitled to the same working conditions and contracts as white laborers.[57] Republican senators said nothing about other types of rights, such as the right to sue and testify in court or the right to own land. Their belief in the equal rights of labor would suggest that they expected free blacks to be able to sue if an employer violated a labor contract, but they did not mention such use of the courts during the debate. Similarly, their adherence to free labor would suggest that they expected free blacks to be able to use their wages to buy land, just as white

---

54 Ibid. (April 7, 1864), 1461.
55 Ibid., 1462.
56 Ibid. (April 6, 1864), 1438 (Harlan). James D. Schmidt, *Free to Work: Labor Law, Emancipation, and Reconstruction, 1815–1880* (Athens: University of Georgia Press, 1998), 118–20; Schmidt, "'Nor Involuntary Servitude': Antebellum Labor Law and the Meaning of the Thirteenth Amendment," paper presented at the meeting of the American Society for Legal History, 1994; Amy Dru Stanley, "'Beggars Can't Be Choosers': Compulsion and Contract in Postbellum America," *Journal of American History*, 78 (March 1992), 1265–93.
57 Lea S. VanderVelde, "The Labor Vision of the Thirteenth Amendment," *University of Pennsylvania Law Review*, 138 (December 1989), 437–504.

laborers could, but they said nothing about landowning rights during the debate. Moreover, all of the debate seemed to be about free blacks in the South. Republicans failed to address the effect of the amendment on discriminatory legislation in the North. A few states in the Midwest, for example, still restricted black immigration. Republican legislators had only begun to wrestle with the many questions concerning African American rights in post emancipation society. By debating abolition in the midst of a war that might end in a Confederate, proslavery victory, they could look into the future only so far. They saw only a rough outline of the contours of freedom in a nation without slavery.

In the same way that Republicans could not yet fathom and articulate all the rights that inhered in freedom, they were unable to express with clarity the related issue of citizenship. In private, Republicans like Francis Lieber and Horace Binney already had begun to puzzle out the amendment's potential impact on citizenship, but many party members had deemed the citizenship issue too divisive to discuss in the midst of a war and a national election. A number of Republicans therefore willfully postponed consideration of some of the amendment's potential effects on state and national citizenship. Not all Republicans put off the citizenship question on purpose. Some simply did not yet see that an amendment granting equal labor rights necessitated further legislation clarifying citizenship. Or, to put it differently, some Republicans saw labor and citizenship as synonymous. That was a view simultaneously expansive and limited: it envisioned all free laborers as citizens, but it saw citizenship exclusively in terms of labor rights.[58] Whether willfully or not, Republicans during the early debates on the amendment postponed a thorough exploration of citizenship and instead focused narrowly on the amendment's elimination of a regressive form of labor. Only as emancipation became more of a reality would Republicans openly confront the changing dimensions of citizenship.

Because Republicans' understanding of the meaning of freedom was still embryonic, their vision of postemancipation society did not yet seem radically different from that of the War Democrats who supported the antislavery amendment. The difference between the visions would grow more pronounced over time, but in early 1864 the difference still seemed slight enough that both groups could take common ground on the issue of equality. For the moment, both groups could agree that the fate of the freed people would be left to the states and that no revolution in race relations would follow emancipation.

58 David Montgomery, *Citizen Worker: The Experience of Workers in the United States with Democracy and the Free Market during the Nineteenth Century* (Cambridge: Cambridge University Press, 1993), 13–51.

Significantly, none of the advocates of the amendment responded to the charge of "negro equality" by promising to colonize the freed people. Once a popular proposal among more conservative opponents of slavery, colonization had only a few disciples in Congress by the spring of 1864. Congressmen could not with good conscience ask African Americans to leave the country that they had so bravely defended. Nor did it make sense strategically to send abroad potential Union soldiers. Just weeks after the Senate debated the antislavery amendment, Congress passed and Lincoln signed an act revoking all funds appropriated for colonization.[59] Yet even with colonization defunct, some proponents of the amendment still entertained dreams of racial separation. During the debate on the amendment, Republican Senator James Lane of Kansas delivered a speech in New York predicting that universal emancipation would lead naturally to racial segregation. Once the threat of enslavement was removed, northern blacks would join others of their race in the more favorable climate of the South. The amendment, said Lane, would not "invalidate the future peace of the nation or the dominancy of our race; it means a gradual and voluntary drifting of the black man into the semi-tropical belt of our country."[60]

For most of the amendment's backers, deflection rather than direct refutation was the preferred method of response to the fearful cry of "negro equality." To keep the amendment from becoming known as an equal rights measure and thus losing the much-needed support of the Democrats, Republican senators stifled the question of equal rights at every turn. Twice when Garrett Davis tried to add to the amendment a clause proscribing blacks from citizenship and officeholding, Republicans voted against the addition and then suppressed further discussion on civil rights by adjourning the Senate for the day.[61] A similar fate awaited Davis's proposal to distribute African Americans among all the states of the Union in proportion to each state's white population.[62] These were not serious proposals by Davis but rather attempts to link the amendment to racial integration. Republicans could see what Davis was up to, and they easily fended off his jabs.

Republicans dodged not only the proposed revisions of the Democrats but the renewed effort by the Republican Charles Sumner to replace the

59 *CG*, 38th Cong., 1st sess. (March 15, 1864), 1108; *Statutes at Large*, 13 (1863–65), 352 (chap. 210, sec. 7). See Michael Vorenberg, "Abraham Lincoln and the Politics of Black Colonization," *Journal of the Abraham Lincoln Association*, 14 (Summer 1993), 23–46.

60 James H. Lane, *The People's Choice. Speech of Hon. James H. Lane, Before the Union Lincoln Campaign Club, at the Cooper Institute, New York, March 30, 1864* (Washington, D.C.: William H. Moore, 1864), 13.

61 See *CG*, 38th Cong., 1st sess. (March 31, 1864), 1370; (April 5, 1864), 1424–25.

62 Ibid. (April 5, 1864), 1425.

amendment abolishing slavery with one declaring all persons "equal before the law."[63] The measure had the undeniable appearance of endorsing racial equality, and Republicans quickly moved to squelch it. Trumbull pointed out that the Judiciary Committee had already rejected Sumner's amendment. Even Jacob Howard of Michigan, a member of the Judiciary Committee and a steadfast radical, told Sumner that enough was enough. "In a legal and technical sense," said Howard, "that language is utterly insignificant and meaningless."[64] Seeing that even an ally like Howard was against him, Sumner backed down and withdrew his amendment. The amendment's sponsors had parried the bogey of amalgamation.

The Unconstitutional Constitutional Amendment

Trimmed of any trace of racial equality, the amendment still faced the objection that it violated the Constitution. Of all the arguments made against the amendment, the charge of unconstitutionality seemed the strangest. The amendment, after all, was supposed to provide a constitutional foundation to an emancipation policy resting on flimsy legal supports. But opponents were steadfast in their claim that, by overthrowing slavery, an institution accepted by the framers, the amendment was inherently unconstitutional. If the amendment were adopted, the opposition charged, the amending power might be used to effect even more radical changes against the wishes of the framers. As Senator Garrett Davis put it, "The power of amendment as now proposed . . . would invest the amending power with a faculty of destroying and revolutionizing the whole Government."[65]

This was no trifling argument. The Constitution – not only the constitutional system but the very text of the document – had become sacred in American culture. It had been amended only twice since the ratification of the Bill of Rights, and had stood untouched for the past sixty years. For the American people, revising the document was a momentous act, especially when a revision flouted the wishes of some of the framers. Because the amendment overturned an explicit agreement of the framers, the measure forced congressmen and their constituents to question the scope of the amending power, to ask whether the framers themselves would have approved such a change.

That question yielded no easy answer. Backers of the amendment took the traditional free-soil position that the Constitution's authors sanctioned slavery only reluctantly and hoped that the institution would soon

---

63 Ibid. (April 8, 1864), 1482–83.
64 Ibid., 1488. For Sumner's earlier effort to introduce his amendment, see Chapter 2.
65 CG, 38th Cong., 1st sess. (April 8, 1864), 1489.

expire. Antislavery congressmen hauled out the writings of Patrick Henry, John Adams, and James Madison to prove that the natural sentiments of the founding generation were against slavery. The real expression of the framers' opinion of slavery, ran this familiar argument, could be found in the Declaration of Independence's assertion that all men were created equal. The amendment, then, was not a departure from the framers' wishes; instead, as Charles Sumner said, it simply brought "the Constitution into avowed harmony with the Declaration of Independence."[66]

Opponents of the amendment responded that the Declaration of Independence was intended for whites, not blacks, and that the framers obviously approved of slavery wholeheartedly. When the founding fathers "stood around the baptismal font and proclaimed the birth of the Constitution," declared Kentucky Democrat Lazarus Powell, "every minister at that altar, save those from one State, was a representative of a slave State, and four fifths of them were slaveholders."[67]

Most Republicans conceded that the Constitution was at least partly proslavery. During a recent debate on Sumner's bill to repeal all fugitive slave laws, a faction of Republican senators led by Ohioan John Sherman argued that, while the Fugitive Slave Law of 1850 should be abolished, the law of 1793 should stand because it was authored by the same men who had drafted the Constitution.[68] Sherman's stance, which "deeply mortified and greatly astounded" at least a few of his constituents, revealed the widespread, bipartisan desire to remain faithful to laws created by the framers.[69]

In assessing the founders' approval of slavery, senators in the amendment debates tried to resolve the related issue of whether the framers conceived of slaves as property. This question was crucial to the issue of whether slave owners should be compensated for their emancipated slaves. In previous emancipation legislation, Republicans had divided over the principle of compensation. Although they had refused to compensate disloyal slave owners, and some Republicans argued against compensating *any* slave owners, most Republicans seemed to think that loyal masters should be compensated in some way. But the policy of compensation, which continued to receive Lincoln's endorsement, had stalled in Congress. Republicans in 1863 voted down a bill compensating slave

66 Ibid., 1482.
67 Ibid., 1486.
68 Bogue, *Earnest Men,* 188–94.
69 Joseph Emery to John Sherman, April 23, 1864; see F. D. Parish to John Sherman, June 16, 1864, and Simeon Nash to John Sherman, June 17, 1864, all in John Sherman MSS, LC.

owners in the loyal state of Missouri, and now they backed a constitutional amendment that said nothing about compensation.[70] War-weariness had heightened Republicans' desire for vengeance against slave owners. Despite the Fifth Amendment's requirement of "just compensation" for public taking of private property, Republicans increasingly believed that it was the slave owners who should pay – in lost property as well as in blood – for the war they had started. If compensation was to be paid, said Sumner, it should be paid to the slave who had been robbed of his labor, not to the slaveholder who had stolen it.[71] Against such pronouncements, opponents of the amendment recited the framers' claims that slaves were property to make the case that the amendment should include a compensation clause.[72] The majority voted down compensation, but they also refused to deny explicitly that loyal slave owners should be reimbursed for their loss, thus leaving open the possibility of future legislation granting compensation.

The most divisive debate over the framers' intentions, however, arose over the issue of federalism. The senators asked, Would the Founding Fathers have endorsed a measure that granted to the federal government powers initially reserved for the states? Since the outbreak of war, this question had dominated every congressional debate on emancipation. Now, as they had done before, Democrats read from Madison's writings on the necessity of a "mixed" government to make the case that any federal usurpation of the states' power over slavery would lead to the complete destruction of constitutional democracy. Upset the delicate balance between state and federal power, claimed the amendment's opponents, and the federal government would assume all powers over religion, local election laws, and the marital rights of husbands.[73] Such reasoning was based on a false premise, the amendment's supporters responded, because Madison never meant "mixed" to suggest a dual sovereignty between states and nation. Instead, he had used the term to apply both to the form of the new government – its division into three branches – and to the diversity of views represented in Congress. Both sides in the amendment debate had valid claims to reading Madison correctly.[74] The oppo-

70 Bogue, *Earnest Men*, 184–88.
71 *CG*, 38th Cong., 1st sess. (April 8, 1864), 1480–81.
72 Ibid. (April 5, 1864), 1425 (Powell) (April 8, 1864), 1489–90 (Saulsbury); (April 8, 1864), 1489 (Davis).
73 Ibid. (March 30, 1864), appendix, 104–5 (Davis); (March 31, 1864), 1366 (Saulsbury); (April 7, 1864), 1458 (Hendricks); (April 8, 1864), 1485 (Powell). See Amy Dru Stanley, "Conjugal Bonds and Wage Labor: Rights of Contract in the Age of Emancipation," *Journal of American History*, 75 (September 1988), 471–500.
74 For Madison's views on the amending process and federalism, see John R. Vile, *The*

nents of the measure were on far more treacherous ground, however, because by making the same states' rights argument used by the secessionists, they seemed to sympathize with the Confederacy.

Yet, although Republicans could accuse Democrats of treasonable utterances, most acknowledged that the framers had conferred little authority over slavery to the federal government. Only a few Republican senators, including Sumner, Benjamin F. Wade of Ohio, and Zachariah Chandler of Michigan, adopted the old radical constitutionalist doctrine that the Constitution empowered Congress to abolish slavery by statute. Most Republicans and all Democrats still took issue with this position. Indeed, the movement for an antislavery amendment was born as much in reaction to radical constitutionalism as to a basic repugnance for human bondage. In the opinion of Reverdy Johnson, the amendment's most renowned Democratic supporter, the measure would help silence the "few wild men carried away by some loose and undefined notions of human liberty with which the Constitution does not deal."[75]

Although the amendment's supporters tended to share their opponents' belief in limited federal power over slavery under the *existing* Constitution, they added a new wrinkle to the debate by arguing that the framers themselves had envisioned federal power expanding under an *amended* Constitution. The clause providing for the Constitution's amendment, asserted Reverdy Johnson, was inserted by the framers "from a conviction that the time would come when justice would call so loudly for the extinction of [slavery] that her call could not be disobeyed."[76]

The framers' opinion of the amending power, unlike their sentiment on slavery, was a new topic of discussion for the country and for Congress. Garrett Davis led the opposition in denying that those who drafted the Constitution would have approved of an amendment affecting an institution so ingrained in the nation. "The power of amendment," said Davis, "can only be made to embrace the forms and the provisions and principles of secondary importance."[77] A limited amending power became the crux of the Democrats' opposition.[78]

Republicans in the Senate offered no response to the Democrats' argument for a limited amending power. Perhaps the argument was, in their

Constitutional Amending Process in American Political Thought (Westport, Conn.: Praeger Publishers, 1992), 26–46; and Michael Zuckert, "Completing the Constitution: The Thirteenth Amendment," *Constitutional Commentary*, 4 (Summer 1987), 259–62.

75 *CG*, 38th Cong., 1st sess. (April 5, 1864), 1422.

76 Ibid., 1423. Republican Representative James Wilson of Iowa had made a similar argument in the House two weeks before; see ibid. (March 19, 1864), 1200.

77 Ibid. (March 30, 1864), appendix, 106.

78 See ibid. (April 7, 1864), 1458 (Hendricks); (April 8, 1864), 1489 (Davis).

view, so preposterous as to be unworthy of a response. After all, there were no explicit limits to the amending power besides the restriction, explicitly described in Article 5 of the Constitution, against depriving a state of equal suffrage in the Senate. Yet it is clear from later debates on the amendment that at least some Republicans did believe that there were implicit restrictions of the amending process.[79] Probably most Republicans at this point had not yet grappled with the meaning of the amendment clause. Francis Lieber was well ahead of the rest of the party in that respect. Because Republicans had always favored legislative discretion over rigid formalism, it is no surprise that few of them had dwelt upon the issue of formal constitutional change.

In contrast, Democrats who supported the amendment identified with the formalist constitutionalism of the Democrats who opposed the measure, and so they believed that the opposition's case merited a response. With typical legal precision, Reverdy Johnson denied that the framers' decision to leave slavery intact precluded future amendments abolishing the institution. Instead, said Johnson, the authors of the Constitution knew that a future generation might abolish slavery even though the framers had chosen not to do so.[80] As Democrat John Henderson put it, "the power to amend was inserted to enable us to utilize the experience of the future and correct error. It was designed to let deliberate and matured convictions of public policy take a place in organic law. It was to be the safety-valve of our institutions."[81] The War Democrats successfully challenged the interpretation of the amending power offered by the rival wing of their party. They offered a justification of the amending process that would serve well not only the defenders of the antislavery amendment, but the advocates of all future constitutional revision. The fate of the nation, ran the argument, rested on the stability and longevity of the Constitution, but the Constitution could survive only if its interpreters, in adherence to the wishes of the framers, revised the document in response to the logic of events.

For years historians have credited the Republican party with carrying the Thirteenth Amendment through Congress. Obviously, Republicans were more committed than Democrats to the measure. Yet it was the proamendment Democrats, not the Republicans, who first publicly articulated a defense of an unlimited amending power. The faith of these Democrats in the amending power was perfectly consistent with the party's traditional preference for formal over informal methods of constitutional development. This formalist tendency of the Democrats has

79 CG, 38th Cong., 2d sess. (January 11, 1865), 222 (George S. Boutwell).
80 Ibid. (April 5, 1864), 1423.
81 Ibid. (April 7, 1864), 1460.

often earned them scorn from historians, but it was precisely this ideological strain that provided crucial support to the antislavery amendment. It is time for historians to recognize that, while a majority of Democrats may have opposed this particular amendment, the party's commitment to formalism added much-needed legitimacy to the measure and helped lay a foundation for future constitutional revision.

Dubious Victory

On April 8, 1864, the Senate held its final vote on the amendment. That two of the most celebrated speeches in favor of the antislavery amendment were delivered by border state Democrats suggested that the final vote might not divide strictly along party lines. Certainly, the debate contained the intensified partisan scuffling one expects during a major election year, yet the debate had revealed clear bipartisanship. Those speaking on behalf of the amendment comprised a broad coalition of Republicans and border state War Democrats, whereas those opposed to the measure were mainly Peace Democrats from Kentucky and Delaware, the only two Union slave states where proemancipation movements had been thwarted. For the amendment's supporters, there was reason to hope that the vote on the amendment would not only secure the measure's adoption, but would reveal a major party realignment on the issue of slavery.

The Senate galleries were more crowded than usual during the final vote. Although there were seats available in the men's gallery, the ladies' gallery was packed.[82] Many of the women who watched had worked tirelessly in circulating the "mammoth petition" for universal abolition that Sumner had presented to the Senate two months before. Congress had failed to act on the petition then, but now it stood ready to take the first step in making emancipation final. When the vote was called, the senators adopted the amendment 38 to 6, giving the measure 8 votes more than it needed to secure two-thirds approval.[83] As the senators retired for dinner, the Peace Democrat Willard Saulsbury bellowed sorrowfully, "I now bid farewell to any hope of the reconstruction of the American Union."[84]

---

82 Letter of "Castine," *Sacramento Daily Union,* May 9, 1864, p. 1.

83 Five senators were absent from the voting, making the total number of senators voting 44, and the minimum number required to carry the amendment 30. Two of those absent, it should be noted, were Democrats: Charles Buckalew, who reportedly opposed the amendment, and William Richardson. Their absence was almost certainly due to unforeseen circumstances rather than a bargain to secure the amendment. See *Rochester Democrat and American,* April 13, 1864, p. 2.

84 CG, 38th Cong., 1st sess. (April 8, 1864), 1490.

At first glance, the vote seemed strictly partisan: no Republican voted against the measure, and every vote cast against it came from a Democrat (see Appendix Table 1).[85] But on closer examination the vote confirmed what political insiders had begun to suspect, that the antislavery coalition had made further inroads into the Democrats and border state unionists. As expected, Reverdy Johnson and John Henderson voted for the amendment, as did three members of border state Union parties and three free-state Democrats. The only free-state Democrats who had spoken against the amendment, Hendricks and McDougall, proved to be the only free-state senators to vote against it. All the other negative votes came from the Kentucky and Delaware senators.

The diverse support for the amendment had a stifling effect on the principal party newspapers. The leading organ of the Republican administration, the *New York Times,* had run a series of editorials two months before calling the amendment an unnecessary distraction. The paper's editor, Henry Raymond, could not possibly continue to berate an antislavery measure that drew such bipartisan support, but neither could he reverse his position without appearing hypocritical. Meanwhile, the editors at the *New York World,* the leading sheet of the Democrats, faced a similar dilemma. They also had refused to endorse the antislavery amendment, but they could hardly continue to do so when only two northern Democrats in the Senate had opposed the measure. Both of these leading party papers gave notice of the vote on the amendment in the Senate, but neither offered any commentary.

The apparent indifference of the press perhaps stemmed from Lincoln's silence on the amendment. In the midst of a presidential campaign, political strategists thought it better to await the opinion of the president on the measure before taking their positions. During the Senate debates on the amendment, however, and even after the final vote, Lincoln said nothing publicly about the amendment. He may have privately supported the amendment, but he had decided to let Congress take the lead on the measure. Maybe he was uncertain whether the amendment would make a good political issue in the coming election. Or perhaps his silence reflected the fatalistic posture toward slavery he seems to have adopted at this time. In the midst of the Senate debate on the amendment, he had written to Albert G. Hodges, a Kentucky unionist, that he had acted against slavery in the past only because "events have controlled me." He would do noth-

---

85 Garrett Davis, who was elected as a Union party member in 1861 and voted against the amendment, might be considered an exception. Although not technically a Democrat in 1861, Davis voted consistently with the Democrats during the war and was reelected as a Democrat in 1867.

ing now to assure the death of slavery – that goal could be secured only by "the justice and goodness of God."[86]

Trusting in God had not been enough for antislavery senators, who had taken a crucial step toward making emancipation both universal and constitutional. But in helping to settle the ultimate fate of slavery, the senators left unresolved some significant issues. They had not explained, for example, the precise way that slavery would be eradicated by the amendment. Would state legislation providing for gradual emancipation satisfy the amendment's demand that "neither slavery nor involuntary servitude . . . shall exist"? And what would happen to persons or states defying the amendment? The meaning of the enforcement clause of the amendment was an issue strangely missing from the Senate debate; even in the first House debate two months later, the subject would receive only meager consideration. Also, the Senate had not begun to resolve the ultimate legal status of the freed people. The amendment's advocates avoided any sustained consideration of the amendment's long-term legal consequences, preferring instead to treat it only as an immediate remedy to the problem of the present war.

Perhaps antislavery congressmen were too shortsighted, but they had good reason to be. If Union armies were defeated on the battlefields – or, for that matter, if Republicans were defeated in the polls – the amendment would certainly be lost. There would be time later to work out the details of the amendment. First, the measure had to be secured by military and electoral victory.

86　CW, 7:281.

5

The Key Note of Freedom

In the months after the Senate debate on the amendment, partisan lines on slavery, which already had begun to totter, seemed ready to crumble completely. In the New York legislature, for example, it was not a Republican but a Democrat, Carolan O'Brien Bryant, who sponsored a resolution instructing New York congressmen to back the antislavery amendment. Although many other state legislatures already had adopted similar resolutions, some Democrats in the New York Assembly, especially those belonging to Fernando Wood's "Mozart Hall" organization, refused to budge on slavery. One of Wood's men jabbed at Bryant by asking him what party he belonged to.[1] Bryant shouted back, "Not to the rumhole, Copperhead party, at any rate." The assembly broke into tumultuous applause. It was strange enough that a Democrat sponsored the amendment, and stranger still that he called his fellow Democrats by the derisive "Copperhead" label created by Republicans.[2]

The incident revealed the unsteady state of politics, slavery, and the constitutional amendment. The Democratic party was badly split, and the Republicans were becoming increasingly so. The Republicans in the Senate had all voted for the measure, but some radical members of the party preferred an antislavery measure that explicitly granted equal rights to African Americans. Democrats in the meantime still struggled with the party's traditional stance against emancipation. As the reaction to Bryant's proposal in the New York Assembly had demonstrated, many Democrats still refused to back down on slavery. The president's continued silence on the amendment made it particularly difficult for people to understand the measure's place in the political landscape. Did Lincoln see the amendment as a threat to his reconstruction program? Or had he initiated the measure without showing his hand? With politics saturated by uncertainty, it was impossible to predict the future of the antislavery amendment or any other initiative concerning African Americans.

1   For a report on the state legislatures that had adopted such resolutions, see the *New York Herald,* May 3, 1864, p. 4.
2   *New York Tribune,* April 26, 1864, p. 4. See also ibid., March 15, 1864, p. 4, April 25, 1864, p. 4; *Journal of the Assembly of the State of New York,* 87th sess., 1864, pp. 496, 737, 1418; Phyllis F. Field, *The Politics of Race in New York: The Struggle for Black Suffrage in the Civil War Era* (Ithaca: Cornell University Press, 1982), 156; and Sidney David Brummer, *Political History of New York State during the Period of the Civil War* (New York: Columbia University, 1911), 368.

Only one thing was certain: the fate of the amendment, and of all similar legislation, was intricately linked to the struggle over the upcoming presidential election. In the months to come, not only was the House scheduled to debate the amendment, but both parties would hold national conventions to nominate presidential candidates. Debate on the amendment, inside and outside of the Capitol, would shape the terrain of party politics. In turn, everyday political circumstances would shape the way that lawmakers, politicians, and ordinary Americans came to understand the amendment.

A New Party, a New Amendment: The Radical Democrats

Lincoln's silence on the antislavery amendment left the door open for some other presidential candidate to take up the measure. Indeed, some political observers still saw the amendment as part of a movement to form a third party that would run a candidate on a platform of immediate, universal emancipation. Such was the opinion of James Gordon Bennett, the political independent and editor of the *New York Herald*. Bennett declared that the Senate's passage of the amendment was in effect a censure of Lincoln's reconstruction program: "in contempt of his preposterous projects of emancipation and reconstruction the Senate . . . warns Mr. Lincoln that his petty tinkering devices of emancipation will not answer, and that if he desires the abolition of slavery in the reconstruction of the Union there is but one course to pursue – the course of action ordained in the supreme law of the land."[3] In the coming election, Bennett warned, if the Republicans embraced Lincoln "in preference to the constitution touching the abolition of slavery, they will surely go by the board."[4] The Washington correspondent of the Republican *Chicago Tribune*, J. K. C. Forrest, also interpreted the Senate vote as part of a movement to unseat Lincoln. But, unlike Bennett, he did not regard the third-party movement for universal emancipation as legitimate. Instead, Forrest suspected that all the bluster was a Democratic ruse to drive a wedge into the Republicans.[5]

Forrest's doubts were well founded. The Democratic press consistently played up third-party movements that threatened to split the Republican party. The editors of the Democratic *New York World*, while issuing no clear opinion on the amendment, indirectly touted it as part of a bipartisan movement against Lincoln by printing Democrat Reverdy Johnson's speech in favor of the amendment next to an excerpt from an Iowa paper

3 *New York Herald*, April 9, 1864, p. 4.
4 Ibid., April 8, 1864, p. 4.
5 *Chicago Tribune*, April 12, 1864, p. 2.

promoting a "People's Party" composed of "undivided Democrats" and Republican "outs."[6] Republican strategists like Forrest who saw what the Democrats were up to advised Lincoln "to take such radical grounds as will satisfy all but a few evil spirits."[7] But Lincoln remained mute on slavery.

The president's silence opened the way for a radical third-party candidate ready to embrace the amendment. Some still thought Salmon P. Chase was a strong contender, though the treasury secretary had issued a public statement declining to run. Chase himself had long envisioned a new antislavery party on the foundation of the old Democracy, and on such a platform he would attempt to secure the Democratic presidential nomination in 1868. But for now, he had suspended such aspirations. The "boom" for his nomination had collapsed during the early months of the year, and he was not yet ready to abandon the Republicans.[8]

Ulysses S. Grant was another possible third-party challenger, and the favorite of James G. Bennett. Yet the general still denied any interest in the presidency. Grant was certainly the most popular American in the Union. Victories at Vicksburg and Chattanooga in 1863 had secured his reputation; then, in February 1864, Lincoln appointed him commander of all Union armies, with the rank of Lieutenant General. He was the first to wear that rank since George Washington. Although Grant had said nothing about the antislavery amendment, Bennett fused his pet cause of the amendment to Grant's name. The editor hoped that by convincing Americans that the candidate and the cause would carry the day, he could build a groundswell that would force Grant to run as an independent.[9] Meanwhile, some Democratic strategists considered making the general the standard bearer of the regular Democratic party. They saw that if the military campaign that Grant was to launch in the spring resulted in the capture of Richmond, then the presidency would be his – if he wanted it.[10] But Grant was to be no party's candidate. He had little love of politics and thought he could serve the Union best in the field. Fearing that any public statement denying presidential aspirations would be misconstrued, Grant maintained his silence, but privately he made sure the president knew that

6 *New York Daily World*, April 11, 1864, p. 2.

7 *Chicago Tribune*, April 12, 1864, p. 2.

8 John Niven, *Salmon P. Chase: A Biography* (New York: Oxford University Press, 1995), 131, 426–32; and Frederick J. Blue, *Salmon P. Chase: A Life in Politics* (Kent, Ohio: Kent State University Press, 1987), 73, 288–91.

9 *New York Herald*, February 13, 1864, p. 4, June 2, 1864, p. 4; John Cochrane to Elihu B. Washburne, December 17, 1863, Elihu B. Washburne MSS, LC.

10 John M. Berry to Samuel L. M. Barlow, January 24, [1864]; Samuel Ward to Barlow, February 13, 1864; John Thomas Doyle to Barlow, June 30, 1864, all in Samuel L. M. Barlow MSS, HEH; Joseph Medill to Elihu B. Washburne, May 30, 1864, Elihu B. Washburne MSS, LC.

he would not run. A powerful advocate of emancipation, Grant tended to the destruction of slavery on the battlefield rather than in the political arena.[11]

Benjamin F. Butler, on the other hand, stood as ever with ears pricked, waiting for the opportunity either to replace Lincoln on the Republican ticket or to challenge him at the head of a third party. Even more than Grant, Butler had earned a reputation as a friend of black freedom. Early in the war, he had been one of the first generals to refuse to return escaped slaves to their former masters. But he was not nearly as popular as Grant, especially after his failed assault on Richmond in late 1863. John A. Stevens, Jr., of New York, a financier of the Republican party who spent most of 1864 trying to bump Lincoln from the Republican ticket, saw little hope in Butler. "A year ago," the New York banker wrote in January 1864, "Genl Butler could have carried a convention. Now I think not."[12] Nor was Butler, who had been a proslavery Democrat before the war, as convincing a radical as Chase or Grant. Rarely was Butler the first to be named as an alternative to Lincoln.[13]

By the time that the Senate passed the antislavery amendment in April 1864, the role of spoiler to Lincoln was left to John C. Frémont alone. Frémont had earned his fame and his nickname, "the Pathfinder," as a western explorer in the 1840s. In 1856 he became the first presidential candidate of the Republicans. As the commanding general in the West in 1861, he tried to force Lincoln's hand on slavery by issuing an order imposing martial law in Missouri and freeing the slaves of rebels. When Frémont refused to modify his order, the president reassigned him to the Mountain Department of western Virginia. From then on, the general distrusted Lincoln and suspected him of being under the spell of the Blair family, whose members included Francis P. Blair, Jr., a leader of the conservative "Claybank" faction in Missouri that opposed Frémont's policies, and Montgomery Blair, Lincoln's postmaster general and the leading conservative in the cabinet. Frémont's constituency was an odd mix of disaffected Missouri "Charcoals," the radical Missouri faction that opposed the "Claybanks," German Americans opposed to Lincoln, old-line

11 David Herbert Donald, *Lincoln* (New York: Simon and Schuster, 1995), 490–92; Brooks D. Simpson, *Let Us Have Peace: Ulysses S. Grant and the Politics of War and Reconstruction, 1861–1868* (Chapel Hill: University of North Carolina Press, 1991), 50–54; Simpson, "'The Doom of Slavery': Ulysses S. Grant, War Aims, and Emancipation, 1861–1863," *Civil War History,* 36 (March 1990), 36–54; and William S. McFeely, *Grant: A Biography* (New York: W. W. Norton, 1981), 162–64.

12 John A. Stevens, Jr., to L. E. Chittenden, Washington, January 5, 1864, John A. Stevens MSS, NYH.

13 Hans L. Trefousse, *Ben Butler: The South Called Him Beast!* (New York: Twayne Publishers, 1957), 158–63; William Frank Zornow, *Lincoln and the Party Divided* (Norman: University of Oklahoma Press, 1954), 65–71.

abolitionists, and a small, largely unknown group of New York War Democrats. This last group issued the earliest call for a national third-party convention in Cleveland. Besides hoping to nominate Frémont as an independent candidate, the convention's organizers meant to steal the limelight from the Republican convention scheduled for the very next week.[14]

Frémont's disciples at first demanded no distinct program of emancipation, only a more resolute war leader. But, by coincidence, at the moment that the call went out for a third-party convention, the Senate passed the antislavery amendment. Lincoln's detractors now saw a way to distinguish themselves from the president: they hitched the amendment to their candidate. They revised their calls to the Cleveland convention to include an appeal for "an amendment of the Federal Constitution for the exclusion of slavery."[15] The more radical abolitionists saw an opportunity to advance the new party's platform even further. Just before the convention met, Wendell Phillips, Elizabeth Cady Stanton, Frederick Douglass, and a host of other well-known abolitionists claimed the coming meeting as an opportunity to write into Frémont's platform an amendment explicitly granting legal equality and suffrage to African Americans.[16] The abolitionists thus tried to transform an unstable antislavery coalition into a radical party. Although some antislavery Democrats kept a blind eye to the abolitionists' radical program, many were put off by it. Meanwhile, those Democrats who had backed the original movement simply to divide the Republicans now doubted the splinter group's destructive power. New York Democrat Max Langenschwartz, for one, feared that the Pathfinder would soon drop out of the race – especially if Lincoln recalled him to the army – "thus preventing the splitting of our opponents (our best hope) and we would have a very, *very* bad stand!"[17]

The gathering at Cleveland on May 31 proved indeed to be little more than a paper convention.[18] Only about three hundred people attended, a

---

14   Zornow, *Lincoln and the Party Divided*, 72–78; Allan Nevins, *Fremont: Pathmarker of the West* (1939; repr., New York: Longmans, Green, 1955), 570–74. Not all abolitionists joined the movement; William Lloyd Garrison, for example, refused to join for fear of splitting the Republican party and giving the election to the Democrats. James M. McPherson, *The Struggle for Equality: Abolitionists and the Negro in the Civil War and Reconstruction* (Princeton: Princeton University Press, 1964), 260–62.

15   Edward McPherson, *The Political History of the United States of America during the Great Rebellion* (1865; repr., New York: Da Capo Press, 1972), 411.

16   Ibid., 411. Some abolitionists, especially a German American contingent led by Karl Heinzen, had pressed for such an amendment since 1863. McPherson, *The Struggle for Equality*, 260–62.

17   Max Langenschwartz to Samuel L. M. Barlow, March 10, 1864, Barlow MSS, HEH.

18   See William F. Zornow, "The Cleveland Convention, 1864, and the Radical Democrats," *Mid-America*, 36 (January 1954), 39–53.

mishmash of Lincoln dissenters of every stripe. They called themselves the "Radical Democracy," an odd name joining the two poles of the political spectrum. Likewise, they linked Frémont, the westerner who had been the first Republican presidential candidate, to vice-presidential nominee John Cochrane, the easterner who had been a leader of the New York Democratic party before the war. Most Republicans, including Lincoln, mocked the poor showing at the convention. The antislavery activists who controlled the meeting were more upbeat: Frémont was their longtime champion and Cochrane, though a Democrat, was the nephew of a prominent abolitionist, Gerrit Smith.[19] Most Democrats also played up the convention, mainly in the hope of nurturing divisions among Republicans.[20] But privately, party members like T. J. Barnett, one of the *New York World*'s Washington insiders, ridiculed the Frémont-Cochrane combination: "What! an apostate from democracy [Cochrane] – and then a rebel abolitionist – like Frémont, between the upper and lower mill-stone of these pressing and great inconsistencies, each of which has a fierce, large, determined political opposite? . . . There is nothing in the Frémont movement but folly and absurdity."[21]

Despite its lack of cohesion and prominence, the Cleveland meeting did play a crucial role in bringing constitutional amendments into the wide-open arena of the presidential campaign. The platform contained no fewer than three proposed amendments, one limiting the presidency to one term, one providing for the popular election of president and vice-president, and, finally, one resolving "That the Rebellion has destroyed slavery, and the Federal Constitution should be amended to prohibit its re-establishment, and to secure to all men absolute equality before the law."[22] Now thrust into open view was an explicit amendment for equality like the one Charles Sumner had proposed to the Senate. Also radical was the platform's doctrine of confiscation and redistribution of rebel lands to ex-slaves. The success of the abolitionists at Cleveland in writing their program into the platform – an effort that one abolitionist described as the "hardest agony" – helped politicize many among their ranks for the coming election.[23] The Democrats in attendance complied with the radi-

---

19   Ralph Volney Harlow, *Gerrit Smith: Philanthropist and Reformer* (New York: Henry Holt, 1939), 440.

20   See *New York Daily World*, June 2, 1864, p. 4; Francis Lieber to Henry W. Halleck, June 4, 1864, Francis Lieber MSS, HEH.

21   T. J. Barnett to Samuel L. M. Barlow, June 11, 1864, Samuel L. M. Barlow MSS, HEH. Some Democrats retained their faith in the staying power of the new movement; see, for example, James Asheton Bayard to Samuel L. M. Barlow, June 2, 1864, Barlow MSS, HEH.

22   McPherson, *Political History*, 413.

23   Parker Pillsbury to Wendell Phillips, June 1, 1864, Wendell Phillips MSS, HL.

cal platform only because they feared that too much dissent would dissolve the third party and thwart the larger strategy of splitting the Republicans.

Because of the Democrats' strategic silence, the abolitionists were able to frame a platform that was too radical even for the nominees. In their letters accepting the nomination, both Frémont and Cochrane denied any wish to distribute confiscated land to free African Americans, and both said nothing about legal equality for African Americans.[24] The only measure that they explicitly embraced was the antislavery amendment. The candidates knew that the only prospect of success for the "Radical Democracy" lay in keeping the focus limited to emancipation in order not to alienate conservative Republicans and War Democrats. In the proposed amendment, Lincoln's adversaries had found a potentially effective campaign issue. However, the new movement would stall if Democrats turned against the antislavery amendment, and it would crumble altogether if Lincoln adopted the amendment into his own platform.

The "National Union Party" and the Amendment

The president so far had kept his thoughts on the amendment private. He neither addressed Frémont's radical program nor sent word to the House of Representatives urging passage of the amendment adopted by the Senate. When the House of Representatives began debate on the amendment on May 31, the same day as the Cleveland convention, congressmen still did not know whether the amendment met with Lincoln's approval or whether the Republican party would endorse it in the national convention scheduled to meet on June 7. Perhaps in anticipation that the Baltimore meeting would make some statement on the amendment, or perhaps because many Republicans had to prepare for the trip to Baltimore, the representatives, after only one day of debate on the amendment, agreed to suspend consideration of the measure until after the convention.[25]

By the standards of nineteenth-century national conventions, the Baltimore meeting was singularly undramatic. Lincoln's nomination was certain. During the weeks leading up to the convention, state party conventions in Ohio, Illinois, and New York all had passed resolutions in support of the president and sent delegates favorable to him. John G. Nicolay, Lincoln's personal secretary, reported the good news to his fiancée: "a similar unanimity has not occurred during the whole history of our coun-

---

24 McPherson, *Political History*, 413–14.
25 *CG*, 38th Cong., 1st sess. (June 3, 1864), 2722–23. See also John V. S. L. Pruyn to Manton Marble, June 3, 1864, Manton M. Marble MSS, LC.

try."[26] David Davis, who managed Lincoln's candidacy in 1860, was so certain of Lincoln's nomination that he stayed at home in Illinois. "If there had been a speck of opposition," Davis explained to the president, "I would have gone to Baltimore."[27]

Because Lincoln's renomination was so secure, the convention spent most of its energy reshaping the party's image. One of the major efforts in that direction was the Republicans' christening of themselves as the "National Union Party." Union parties had formed at the county and state level since the beginning of the war. Generally conceived of as provisional organizations, they combined people of any political background willing to support the war. Lincoln had endorsed and nurtured these organizations, knowing that they would widen his administration's constituency in the years to come. Few people expected these loose coalitions to last beyond the war, however, so when the Republicans at Baltimore presented themselves as the "National Union Party," most observers likewise doubted the staying power of the alliance between regular Republicans and pro-Lincoln War Democrats.[28] Yet for many Republicans, the new name reflected a genuine desire to restyle the party that had been created in the 1850s. So many of the goals that Republicans had articulated in the party platform of 1860 had been realized – the Homestead Act, the Pacific Railroad, the prohibition of slavery in the territories – that the time had come to design a new program. Whatever new positions it might take, the party would do well to shed the Republican name, which still carried connotations of radical abolitionism. "It is very clear to me that no one can be elected if he be styled the Republican candidate and if the distinctive Republican name and organization be kept up," a low-level political operative in New Jersey had written a year before. A successful political organization, the writer explained, needed the support of at least some of the Democrats, and since Democrats had been "taught to stigmatize and hate ... 'Abolitionism' and 'Black Republicanism,'" Lincoln's party should adopt the "Union" label for its national organization.[29] The correspondent's arguments made good sense and no doubt matched the reasoning of the Baltimore convention's organizers. The selection of Maryland as

---

26 John G. Nicolay to Therena Bates, May 29, 1864, John G. Nicolay MSS, LC.
27 David Davis to Abraham Lincoln, June 2, 1864, David Davis MSS, CHS.
28 James G. Randall with Richard N. Current, *Lincoln the President* (New York: Dodd, Mead, 1945), 2:214–16. Historians remain puzzled about when and how the party took on its new name. Although many historians credit Lincoln for the change, no one has discovered the origins. See Michael Holt, "Abraham Lincoln and the Politics of Union," in John L. Thomas, ed., *Abraham Lincoln and the American Political Tradition* (Amherst: University of Massachusetts Press, 1986), 124–25.
29 Martin Ryerson to William H. Seward, Washington, October 20, 1863, William Henry Seward MSS, UR.

the meeting place put an extra shine on the party's "Union" label. A hotbed of secessionism three years before, Maryland was now the showcase of border state unionism. In the 1863 elections, the people had elected a proemancipation ticket, and in April 1864 they had voted for a state constitutional convention that was expected to enact statewide abolition.[30]

Aside from affirming the party's new image, the convention also hoped to effect some personnel changes within the party leadership. For many delegates, the ejection of the conservative Montgomery Blair from the cabinet was the first priority. The removal of Blair, a longtime advocate of gradual emancipation and colonization, would signal vindication for the cause of immediate emancipation throughout the Union but particularly in Maryland, Blair's home state. "President Lincoln must shake off the *Blair coil* or he is politically dead and d[amne]d," one Ohio man advised.[31] The president listened to such suggestions but did nothing to affect Blair's position. Nor did he involve himself in the deliberations that led to Andrew Johnson's nomination as vice-president in place of Hannibal Hamlin. It was natural that an organization billing itself as the National Union Party would replace Hamlin, a steadfast Republican from Maine, with Johnson, a southern War Democrat. Lincoln may have approved of the decision, but he took no part in it.[32]

When it came to the party platform, however, the president did get involved. A number of party members on their way to Baltimore stopped at the White House to ask the president whether he expected the platform to retract or modify his Emancipation Proclamation. Repeating the pledge that he had made in his annual message to Congress of 1863, Lincoln refused to revoke a word of the proclamation.[33] Yet Lincoln went even further. To at least one Republican confidante, he expressed his hope that the convention would endorse the antislavery amendment "as one of the articles of the party faith."[34] And to Edwin D. Morgan, the chairman of the party and a senator from New York, the president proposed that the amendment serve as the "key note" of the opening address.[35]

30 Charles L. Wagandt, *The Mighty Revolution: Negro Emancipation in Maryland, 1862–1864* (Baltimore: Johns Hopkins Press, 1964), 155–220.
31 C. H. Spahr to John Sherman, Washington, May 6, 1864, John Sherman MSS, LC.
32 *CW*, 7:376–77; Donald, *Lincoln*, 505–6; Don E. Fehrenbacher, "The Making of a Myth: Lincoln and the Vice-Presidential Nomination in 1864," *Civil War History*, 41 (December 1995), 273–90.
33 Thompson Campbell to Elihu B. Washburne, December 9, 1864, Elihu B. Washburne MSS, LC.
34 Noah Brooks, *Washington in Lincoln's Time*, ed. Herbert Mitgang (1895; rev. ed. 1971; repr., Athens: University of Georgia Press, 1989), 141–42.
35 Isaac N. Arnold, *The Life of Abraham Lincoln* (Chicago: Jansen, McClurg, 1885), 357–58.

Morgan followed Lincoln's instructions by endorsing the amendment in his speech to the convention. The resolutions committee then drafted a platform recommending that slavery be immediately abolished by constitutional amendment, although no explicit reference was made to the amendment then pending in Congress. A further resolution affirmed the constitutionality and wisdom of the president's wartime measures, including the Emancipation Proclamation, and another promised the government's wartime protection of soldiers of any color who had served in the war.[36] These were the only resolutions dealing with African Americans, and they stood in sharp, conservative contrast to the proequality resolves from Cleveland a week before. Lincoln and his managers thus plucked from the Cleveland platform the plank calling for an emancipation amendment and pruned from it the explicit promise of equal rights for blacks.

This slap at black equality accompanied a public emasculation of African American power at the convention. A delegation of sixteen men from South Carolina, four of whom were black, had tried to gain admission. One of the black delegates, Robert Smalls, was known throughout the Union for stealing a Confederate gunboat and escaping from slavery. Smalls's heroism, however, failed to sway the chairman of the convention, William Dennison, who allowed the South Carolinians into the meeting but refused to recognize them officially.[37] The *New York Herald* was quick to notice the connection between the final platform and the treatment of the delegation: "Negro suffrage, negro equality, miscegenation, free love and woman's rights, and c., are among the reforms which the Convention turned out of doors with the mixed delegation of army sutlers and contrabands, whites and blacks, from South Carolina. What Wendell Phillips and his radical faction will say to this we think it will not be difficult to conjecture."[38] As the *Herald* suspected, Phillips and his radical colleagues, including William Wells Brown and Frederick Douglass, were indignant at the convention's treatment of African Americans. The convention managers may have sympathized with the cause of Phillips, Brown, and Douglass, but they undoubtedly feared that overt egalitarian actions or policies might be unpopular with the northern electorate. Certainly the Democratic opposition was ready to pounce on the Republicans if they recognized the delegation. Just before the convention met, a mid-

36 Donald B. Johnson, *National Party Platforms* (Urbana: University of Illinois Press, 1978), 1:35–36.
37 Okon Edet Uya, *From Slavery to Public Service: Robert Smalls, 1839–1915* (New York: Oxford University Press, 1971), 38–39; Larry E. Nelson, "Black Leaders and the Presidential Election of 1864," *Journal of Negro History,* 63 (January 1978), 48–52.
38 *New York Herald,* June 9, 1864, p. 4.

western Democratic paper told its readers that the admission of the South Carolina men would show that "Republicans not only favor negro equality with the white race, but are determined to force it upon the country."[39]

Even though the results of the "National Union" party convention might not have satisfied more radical abolitionists, the platform managed to measure up to some of the abolitionists' moderate goals without alienating northern conservatives.[40] William Lloyd Garrison, who attended the Baltimore convention with his ally Theodore Tilton, editor of the New York *Independent,* was much pleased with the antislavery resolution. He and Tilton traveled afterward to Washington and met with the president, who said nothing of the radical Cleveland platform but instead declared the amendment plank as his own. This claim was valid yet somewhat misleading because, prior to his party's convention, Lincoln had done nothing, despite the urging of his advisors, to promote the amendment publicly. But Garrison for one was convinced that the president stood by the measure. After meeting with the nominee, the abolitionist believed in his "desire to do all that he can . . . to uproot slavery, and give fair-play to the emancipated."[41] Wendell Phillips, on the other hand, saw in the Baltimore platform nothing but duplicity. Lincoln's party, said Phillips, had co-opted the radicals' emancipation program while jettisoning their endorsement of universal equality and suffrage. Through the early weeks of the summer he and Tilton debated on the pages of the *Independent* the merits of the two party platforms, and eventually the debate ripped into the ranks of the American Anti-Slavery Society.[42] Republicans may have caused divisions among abolitionists by moving only part way toward an explicit endorsement of equality, but at least the party went far enough to hold onto its alliance with some abolitionist leaders while purposefully distancing itself from others.

In Lincoln's acceptance of the nomination, he kept his language general, saying nothing about the platform's resolutions save one: the emancipation amendment. "The unconditional Union men, North and South, perceive [the amendment's] importance, and embrace it," Lincoln announced. "In the joint names of Liberty and Union, let us give it legal form, and practical effect."[43]

---

39 Indianapolis *State Sentinel,* June 3, 1864, p. 2.
40 Phillip Shaw Paludan, *"A People's Contest": The Union and Civil War, 1861–1865* (New York: Harper and Row, 1988), 250–52.
41 Cited in McPherson, *Struggle for Equality,* 272.
42 Theodore Tilton to Wendell Phillips, May 31, 1864 (with enclosure from the *Independent*), and July 17, 1864, as well as James Miller McKim to Wendell Phillips, July 12 and 20, 1864, all in Wendell Phillips MSS, HL. See McPherson, *Struggle for Equality,* 275–79.
43 CW, 7:380.

Seven months after the amendment had been introduced in Congress, Lincoln was finally giving the measure his public approval. His support was genuine, but why had he waited so long to bring his opinion to the public? Perhaps he had wanted Congress to consider the measure on its own merits rather than as a Lincoln-sponsored program of reconstruction, or perhaps he had wanted to see how people took to the amendment before giving it his blessing. By the time of the convention, he knew that the measure was favored by a majority of Republicans and a growing minority of Democrats.[44] If he did not announce his support for the amendment, some rival faction or party might use the measure against him. Radical Republicans in particular meant to use the measure not only to ensure universal, unconditional emancipation, but also to criticize a presidential reconstruction policy that could have kept some African Americans enslaved after the war. Just before the convention, one of the constituents of the radical congressman Thaddeus Stevens wrote, "I think you and the radical men in and out of Congress should make some demonstration which will free Mr. L. up to some *higher point* and then go to Baltimore and put it in the platform."[45] Had Frémont not been nominated on a platform endorsing an abolition amendment, other radical pressures might have prompted Lincoln to make sure that the amendment appeared in the Republican platform. But it was the Frémont candidacy that forced him to act. By grafting an antislavery amendment onto Republican policy and claiming the plank as his own, Lincoln derailed the efforts of his rivals to use the amendment to rebuke his administration.

It is tempting to regard Lincoln's handling of the amendment as one more instance of political calculation trumping principle. Yet it is more accurate to see his behavior as the product of his growing realization that he could do more for the cause of emancipation through private actions than public pronouncements. Between the Reconstruction Proclamation of December 1863 and the party convention of June 1864, the president had been careful not to issue statements that might substantiate the opposition's charge that the war was being fought solely to end slavery. A public endorsement of the antislavery amendment, a measure that some thought had little bearing on the immediate military conflict, might turn northern public opinion more resolutely against all emancipation measures. Instead of making new announcements in favor of abolition in general or the amendment in particular, Lincoln worked vigorously behind the scenes to promote the drafting of antislavery constitutions in Louisiana, Arkansas, and other southern states undergoing reconstruc-

---

44 See, for example, the resolutions of the Ohio Union party just prior to the national convention; *Ohio State Journal,* May 26, 1864, p. 1.
45 John A. Hiertand to Thaddeus Stevens, May 29, 1864, Thaddeus Stevens MSS, LC.

tion.[46] At the time of his party's convention, when the absence of a public gesture against slavery might do more harm than good to his candidacy – and thus to the cause of black freedom – he finally spoke out. In making the amendment the "key note" of Union Party policy, Lincoln allowed the party to coalesce around a measure that kept most abolitionists in tow without broaching the thorny question of the scope of African American rights under reconstruction.

At the start of the war, Republicans and northern Democrats had pledged with equal earnestness to abide by the principle of federal noninterference with slavery in the states. Now Republicans were taking new ground, nudged along on one side by more radical party members and, on the other side, by Democrats demanding a formal, unequivocally constitutional approach to emancipation. The endorsement of the antislavery amendment by Lincoln and the National Union party helped bring emancipation to the forefront of the presidential campaign, and it made everyone attentive to the fate of the amendment in Congress. As congressmen prepared to resume debate of the amendment in the House of Representatives, they recognized the measure as more than a piece of antislavery legislation. It was now a Republican symbol and a test of party loyalty, representing not merely the issue of black freedom but the candidacy of Abraham Lincoln.

Race, Reconstruction, and the Constitution: The Changing Context

As a result of the amendment's new role in Lincoln's candidacy, congressmen in the House amendment debate spent as much time evaluating the president's administration as they did arguing the specific merits of the amendment. Like the amendment debate in the Senate two months before, the House debate revolved around the measure's effect on reunion, race relations, and the Constitution. But in the House debate, partisan rhetoric became particularly blistering, and legislators increasingly substituted campaign speeches for well-reasoned arguments.

On the question of the amendment's effect on reunion, representatives' speeches often sounded like those made by their counterparts in the Senate. Republicans like Thomas B. Shannon of California argued that the amendment would ensure permanent peace by destroying slavery, which he called the cause of the war, the "root of the accursed tree."[47] Demo-

---

46 William C. Harris, *With Charity for All: Lincoln and the Restoration of the Union* (Lexington: University Press of Kentucky, 1997), 123–228.
47 *CG*, 38th Cong., 1st sess. (June 14, 1864), 2949. See also ibid., 2944–45 (Higby), 2984 (Kelley), 2889–90 (Ingersoll).

crats countered with the familiar warning that the amendment, in the words of Samuel J. Randall of Pennsylvania, "throws away every hope of reconciliation."[48]

But the issue of reconstruction took on new meaning in the House debate, because that body already had passed a bill outlining the method by which rebel states were to be readmitted to the Union. Early in the session of Congress, Congressman James M. Ashley of Ohio, one of the first lawmakers to propose an antislavery constitutional amendment, also introduced a bill reconstructing the southern states. His bill conformed largely to Lincoln's Reconstruction Proclamation, with the significant difference of granting African Americans the vote. But Ashley had been unsuccessful in bringing his bill to debate. Instead, the measure had been supplanted by a reconstruction bill drafted by Henry Winter Davis, a radical congressman from Maryland. Although the Davis bill was more conservative than Ashley's in its restriction of suffrage to whites, it nonetheless represented an effort to repudiate Lincoln's program of reconstruction. Whereas Lincoln's plan restored full civil and political rights to most of those who took a mild oath to uphold the Union and Constitution, Davis's proscribed all those who had held any civil or military office in the Confederacy or who had "voluntarily borne arms against the United States." Moreover, unlike the president's program, which required only 10 percent of a state's loyal citizens to vote for a new state constitutional convention, Davis's bill demanded the approval of 50 percent. That provision would effectively keep any state from being readmitted to the Union before the end of the war. Finally, in contrast to Lincoln's Reconstruction Proclamation, which left open the possibility of some blacks in the Confederacy still being enslaved at the end of the war, Davis's bill declared slaves in *all* rebellious areas forever free; moreover, the bill granted federal habeas corpus rights to ex-slaves so they could sue for their freedom in federal courts.[49]

House Democrats, almost all of whom had opposed Davis's bill, naturally assumed that the antislavery amendment and the reconstruction measure were part of the same program for overthrowing state governments and preventing easy reunion. The two measures together, said Anson Herrick of New York, were parallel outgrowths of "the avowed object

---

48 Ibid. (June 15, 1864), 2991. For a similar view held privately by John Stiles, Randall's Democratic colleague from Pennsylvania, see Arnold M. Shankman, *The Pennsylvania Antiwar Movement, 1861–1865* (Rutherford, N.J.: Fairleigh Dickinson University Press, 1980), 170.

49 See Michael Les Benedict, *A Compromise of Principle: Congressional Republicans and Reconstruction, 1863–1869* (New York: W. W. Norton, 1974), 70–83; Herman Belz, *Reconstructing the Union: Theory and Practice during the Civil War* (Ithaca: Cornell University Press, 1969), 198–243.

of the party in power to prevent the restoration of a solitary State with any of its independent rights."[50]

The constitutional amendment and the reconstruction bill were indeed close cousins. Representative Ashley, who had introduced both pieces of legislation to the House, regarded his version of the reconstruction bill as an enforcement device for the constitutional amendment. By contrast, Davis saw his version, which had replaced Ashley's, as an *alternative* to the amendment. Thus Davis's version, unlike Ashley's, contained a general emancipation provision. The Maryland representative saw his bill as the only means of ensuring black freedom if the abolition amendment were voted down. Also, he meant his bill as a rebuke to Lincoln's more conservative program on emancipation and reconstruction. Davis despised Lincoln, in large part because the president had always favored the Blair family over Davis's faction in Maryland politics. Once Lincoln had endorsed the antislavery amendment, Davis saw his bill as the only emancipation policy left that could rally Republicans against the president.[51]

Regardless of whether other Republican congressmen shared Davis's animosity for Lincoln, or whether they preferred the reconstruction bill to the constitutional amendment, they had an important tactical reason for keeping the debate on the amendment from becoming a replay of the discussion of the reconstruction bill. If the amendment's advocates tied the measure to reconstruction, they would invite the question of whether former Confederate states would be allowed to vote on ratifying the amendment before being reconstructed. In other words, supporters of the amendment would have to take a uniform position on whether rebel states, prior to reconstruction, were still technically states within the Union. Yet Republicans had reached no consensus on the issue. During debates on reconstruction, radical Republicans had argued that rebel states should be treated as territories outside the Union, whereas conservative Republicans and War Democrats contended that their status was unchanged. These factions had to stand united for the amendment to receive the necessary two-thirds majority, so those who spoke for the measure steered clear, where possible, of the status of southern states – and thus their role in ratification.

---

50 *CG*, 38th Cong., 1st sess. (May 31, 1864), 2616. See also comments of William S. Holman, ibid. (June 14, 1864), 2976.
51 During the debates on the antislavery amendment in 1864, Davis was silent, and he left Washington before the House took its final vote on the measure. According to a colleague, Davis missed the vote because he was ill; see *CG*, 38th Cong., 1st sess. (June 15, 1864), 2995 (Edwin Webster). But a private letter by Davis reveals that he had never planned on being in Washington at the time of the vote; see Davis to Samuel F. DuPont, May 17 or 18, 1864, Samuel Francis DuPont MSS, EM.

When pressed by opponents of the amendment to make a statement on the ratification issue, Republicans fudged a middle position. Daniel Morris of New York, for example, claimed that "the revolting States are still in the Union. . . . But these States can have no voice in the enactment of law or in amending the Constitution until they are pardoned and re-stored to their forfeited rights."[52] William D. Kelley of Pennsylvania tried to render the question moot by predicting that the war would be over and the rebel states reconstructed before the state legislatures began to con-sider the amendment.[53] The deliberation over reconstruction had injected new issues into the amendment debate, and rather than confront these questions directly, advocates of the amendment put them off to draw the broadest possible support for the measure. Because Republicans wanted the amendment ratified as quickly as possible, it made sense for them to disconnect ratification from the potentially long process of reconstruc-tion. Therefore, in a move that would frustrate later lawmakers and scholars, Republicans stayed quiet on the question of the South and ratification.

Shifting currents on the issue of race, like those on the issue of recon-struction, gave new direction to the debate in the House. In some ways, House Democrats simply followed the lead of their colleagues in the Senate. Congressman Randall, for example, made the all-too-familiar claim that Republicans meant "to make the African that which God did not intend – the physical, mental, and social equal of the white man."[54] William S. Holman, another Democrat, made the most persuasive case for Republicans' ulterior, radical motives. "Mere exemption from servitude is a miserable idea of freedom," Holman argued, demonstrating a good understanding of free-labor ideology.[55] But the conclusion that Holman drew from this premise – that Republicans would grant African Ameri-cans citizenship and the vote – was less than accurate. In fact, Republicans had not begun to resolve the citizenship of ex-slaves, and they were not uniformly in favor of black voting rights. There was a new ring to Demo-cratic rhetoric, however. Whereas Senate Democrats refrained from call-ing their opponents "miscegenationists," House Democrats applied the new label liberally. When the Republicans were defeated in the coming election, said Daniel Marcy, a New Hampshire Democrat, they would travel "into the heart of Africa, or be content with the four years of miscegenetic beatitude they have so hugely enjoyed."[56]

52   CG, 38th Cong., 1st sess. (May 31, 1864), 2614; see ibid., 2618 (Orlando Kellogg).
53   Ibid. (June 15, 1864), 2984.
54   Ibid., 2991.
55   Ibid. (June 14, 1864), 2962.
56   Ibid., 2951.

Defenders of the amendment deflected such invective as they had in the Senate, not with a clear exposition of the degree of equality embodied in the amendment, but rather with counterattacks upon the Democrats as the real miscegenationists. The House debate at times turned into a contest over which party believed more deeply in white supremacy. Against charges that his party advocated black equality and racial mixing, Republican John Farnsworth of Illinois retorted that the Democrats were the real miscegenationists, because by condoning slavery, they implicitly approved of the interracial sex that took place between masters and slaves. "We do not practice miscegenation," Farnsworth proudly announced; "we do not belong to that school; that is a Democratic institution; that goes hand in hand with slavery."[57]

Yet, at the same time as they joined the alarm against miscegenation, Republicans revealed an ever growing egalitarianism. They heaped praise on African American soldiers in particular. Farnsworth, for example, coupled his blast against miscegenation with a paean to a black Union spy who had helped him during his days as a brigadier general. "Was he not better entitled to respect," Farnsworth asked, ". . . than any man now in the rebel ranks, or who sympathizes with them?"[58] Equally powerful was Congressman Kelley's reference to the recent massacre at Fort Pillow, Tennessee, where Confederates under Nathan Bedford Forrest had slaughtered more than two hundred Union soldiers, most of whom were black.[59] The self-sacrifice and martyrdom of African Americans, ran the Republican argument, demanded the nation's restitution. Like occasional modern proposals by whites to "apologize" for slavery, the amendment represented, at least for some whites, a chance to wipe the debt clean. But for some Republicans, the amendment represented much more than mere restitution. It was a sign, in Isaac Arnold's words, of "a new nation," one in which "Liberty, *equality before the law* is to be the great cornerstone."[60]

Despite Arnold's promise of "equality before the law," the phrase was construed as narrowly by House Republicans as by the Senate Republicans, who already had debated the amendment. Equality before the law did not mean that state and national governments had to adopt positive laws ensuring that different sorts of people enjoyed freedom equally. Rather, the phrase indicated an expectation that state and national gov-

---

57 Ibid. (June 15, 1864), 2979.
58 Ibid., 2980.
59 Ibid., 2984–85. See John Cimprich and Robert C. Mainfort, Jr., "The Fort Pillow Massacre: A Statistical Note," *Journal of American History,* 76 (December 1989), 830–37.
60 CG, 38th Cong., 1st sess. (June 15, 1864), 2989 (emphasis in original).

ernments would *not* adopt positive laws that protected rights for some but not others. Also, equality before the law generally referred to civil rights alone, not to political rights such as voting or social rights such as marriage (or, more precisely, racial intermarriage). Finally, with a few notable exceptions, Republicans read equal rights through the lens of free labor. The Illinois Republican Ebon C. Ingersoll said that the amendment provided precisely those rights that were denied to unfree laborers: "a right to till the soil, to earn his bread by the sweat of his brow, and enjoy the rewards of his own labor . . . [and] a right to the endearments and enjoyment of family ties."[61] He might have added the right of geographic mobility, the right to be free from arbitrary violence, and the right to own property. Senate Republicans held a similar vision of equality before the law, and thus they had seen little difference between the antislavery amendment and Charles Sumner's amendment declaring all persons equal before the law.[62] Yet, while our hearts may jump when we hear "equality before the law" in the amendment debate, we must remind ourselves again that Republicans never meant to define for future generations the exact rights guaranteed by the amendment. They were interested mainly in eliminating the institution of slavery that had caused the war. And because few of them were able to envision a time without war, they saw no urgency in codifying the rights of freedom for the postwar Union.

The constraints that the war imposed on Republicans' foresight also kept them from resolving what the federal government would do if a state *did* adopt a law abridging the civil rights of ex-slaves or anyone else. The revolutionary potential of the amendment's enforcement clause, which after the war would be used by Congress to override state laws denying civil rights, seemed to be lost on congressional Republicans in 1864. House Democrats, however, spoke freely about the implications of the clause – something that Senate Democrats had failed to do. With the power to enforce emancipation, explained William Holman, Republicans would "invade the States" to effect the "elevation of the African to the August rights of citizenship."[63] Republicans chose not to respond to Holman's charge and instead maintained their silence on the meaning of enforcement. Even in their private conversations and writings, they seemed oblivious to potential enforcement legislation beyond the reconstruction bill then pending in Congress. If some Republicans did have the intentions ascribed to them by the Democrats – and most probably did not – they had good reason to be silent, for conservative Republicans and War Democrats would never endorse the amendment if they believed that

61 Ibid., 2990.
62 See my discussion in Chapter 2.
63 CG, 38th Cong., 1st sess. (June 15, 1864), 2962.

it gave the federal government the power to enact civil rights laws against state opposition. Many conservatives, in fact, supported the amendment precisely because they believed it preempted a more radical program. War Democrat Ezra Wheeler pleaded with his allies among the Democrats to end the agitation over slavery by passing the amendment, "so as to take from the radicals all motives and excuses for the violation of and breaking up the foundations of our Government."[64]

Despite Wheeler's dire prediction, most Republicans, even the radicals among them, did not foresee a time when the clause would be invoked to increase federal power over the states. Instead, they assumed that the states would apply the laws of freedom equally. Republicans who assumed that the states would act responsibly may have been naive, but their assumption was nonetheless genuine. William D. Kelley, a steadfast advocate of equality for African Americans, sincerely believed that no legislation beyond the amendment was needed to achieve his egalitarian goals. To Democrats who predicted that the amendment would lead to further federal legislation on behalf of blacks, Kelley replied: "I will trust the freed negroes to the care of God, under our beneficent republican institutions."[65] Kelley expected the amendment to lead to a future in which whites and blacks mingled as equals. In contrast, the War Democrat Wheeler hoped the amendment would lead to an influx of European immigrants who would drive out the country's black population.[66] Yet both congressmen supported the amendment with equal passion. They could do so because the specific rights provided by the amendment, along with the meaning of enforcement, remained largely unarticulated.

Although opponents of the amendment found new ways to raise the specter of black equality, most of their criticism of the measure continued to be on constitutional rather than racial grounds. House Democrats replayed the Senate Democrats' argument that the amendment represented a dangerous, unconstitutional use of the amending power. "The alteration once commenced," Martin Kalbfleisch declared, ". . . may cause other and more radical changes, until in the end, of the now solid and perfect structure which has stood the test of years, scarce a vestige will remain."[67]

The debate about constitutionality, like the debate about all other matters, took on new dimensions because of recent events outside the Capitol. Just before the House debate began, Lincoln ordered the arrest of a num-

---

64 Ibid. (June 14, 1864), appendix, 125.
65 Ibid. (June 15, 1864), 2985.
66 Ibid. (June 14, 1864), appendix, 126.
67 Ibid., 2945–46. See also ibid., 2940 (Fernando Wood), 2981 (Robert Mallory), 2991 (Samuel J. Randall).

ber of Union men who had published a "bogus proclamation" purporting to be a presidential order calling for a day of thanksgiving and the drafting of four hundred thousand men. (Two newspapermen had issued the document to make a fortune by driving up gold prices.) The president had the forgers imprisoned and the editors and owners of the two New York papers that had published the proclamation, the *World* and the *Journal of Commerce,* arrested. Lincoln even had the operators of the Independent Telegraph Company imprisoned because administration officials suspected them of transmitting the false order on their lines.[68] During the House amendment debate, Democrats referred specifically to the arrests. Congressman Kalbfleisch, for example, spent about a third of his speech telling of the "sad page the recital of these wrongs will fill in the history of our country."[69] Administration opponents had already made the topic of civil liberties a staple of political discourse; now they used recent events to combat the constitutional amendment.

But the Democrats' objection to the amendment as unconstitutional was more than mere rhetoric. When Congressman John V. S. L. Pruyn of New York warned that "if one right can be taken away, several can be – all can be," his concern was genuine.[70] As he explained to a visitor from England, the authors of the Constitution intended the states to have authority on "domestic matters," whereas the federal government was to be supreme "in that which concerns the outer world."[71] To those like Francis Lieber, who despised states' rights doctrine, Pruyn's view was "hyper-Calhounistic."[72] But, unlike the followers of Calhoun, Pruyn and his congressional allies denounced nullification and secession as firmly as they opposed federal intrusion into the states.[73] Determined to rise above partisan bickering, Pruyn gave the amendment careful consideration. He recorded his opinions in his diary and discussed the amendment at least twice with Jeremiah S. Black, the attorney general and secretary of state under President Buchanan.[74] Pruyn's final opinion, that "the right to amend is not a right to *extend and enlarge* the powers granted under the

68 See Mark E. Neely, Jr., *The Fate of Liberty: Abraham Lincoln and Civil Liberties* (New York: Oxford University Press, 1991), 104–5; and Robert S. Harper, *Lincoln and the Press* (New York: McGraw-Hill, 1951), 289–303.
69 *CG,* 38th Cong., 1st sess. (June 14, 1864), 2947. See also ibid. (May 31, 1864), 2617 (Anson Herrick).
70 Ibid. (June 14, 1864), 2940.
71 John V. S. L. Pruyn, Personal Journal no. 4, September 12, 1864, NYS.
72 Francis Lieber to Charles Sumner, June 8, 1864, Francis Lieber MSS, HEH.
73 See John V. S. L. Pruyn et al., *Reply to President Lincoln's Letter, of 12th June, 1863* (Society for the Diffusion of Political Knowledge no. 10); and Pruyn to Hamilton Fish, March 4, 1864, Hamilton Fish MSS, ColU.
74 John V. S. L. Pruyn, Washington Journal, June 14, 1864, NYS; and Pruyn to Manton Marble, June 15, 1864, Manton M. Marble MSS, LC.

Constitution," was the product of heartfelt ideology.[75] War Democrats like Pruyn joined Peace Democrats like Fernando Wood to oppose the amendment, not simply because both groups had a common rival in the Republicans, but because both thought that they were being true to the framers' vision of the amending power.

Faced with the charge that the amendment went beyond the scope of the amending power, most of the measure's advocates adopted the strategy deployed by their counterparts in the Senate: instead of defending an expansion of the amending power, they argued that the scope of that power was not, in fact, being enlarged. Republican Martin Russell Thayer made a novel move in this direction. Because state legislatures would make the final vote on the amendment during ratification, said Thayer, and because the legislatures more genuinely represented the people than did Congress, the people, and not Congress, would be acting as revisers of the Constitution; Congress, therefore, seized no new power and left intact the original constitutional framework.[76] As in the Senate debate, the most persuasive speech upholding the amendment as a conservative form of constitutional change came from a War Democrat, in this case Ezra Wheeler. The amendment, Wheeler argued, did not violate the framers' wishes but, quite the opposite, made the Constitution "conform to the original intention of the framers."[77]

Although most of the amendment's supporters joined the detractors in arguing that Congress should be guided by the framers' intentions, others began to take a new tack. Specifically, some lawmakers began a direct assault on originalist jurisprudence by contending that the framers were flawed, that lawmakers of the present, not the past, knew what was best for the country. William Kelley declared that the Founding Fathers "were good men and were wise in their day and generation, but all wisdom did not die with them, and we are expiating in blood and agony and death and bereavement one of their errors . . . the toleration and perpetuation of human slavery."[78] Such criticism of the Constitution's authors was a remarkable departure for members of a generation that grew up revering the framers. Already such sentiments had been expressed in private; Francis Lieber, for example, had drafted his pamphlet, as yet unpublished, which called the framers "uninspired." But now, in the House debate, these feelings became public.

The antislavery amendment forced many Americans to confront the Constitution's imperfections for the first time. And now an increasing

75 CG, 38th Cong., 1st sess. (June 14, 1864), 2940.
76 Ibid. (June 15, 1864), 2980.
77 Ibid. (June 14, 1864), appendix, 125.
78 Ibid. (June 15, 1864), 2983.

number of lawmakers were willing to challenge publicly the work of the framers. The war had caused the crucial shift. In recent weeks, the fighting had been particularly horrific. During General Grant's campaign into the Wilderness of Virginia, which began a few weeks before the House debate, Union forces suffered more than forty-five thousand casualties. At Cold Harbor on only one day, June 3, seven thousand Union men were killed or injured. The scale of destruction had sent Americans searching for the deepest roots of the struggle. Inevitably, some pointed their fingers at the framers. More overt challenges to the Constitution's authors lay in the future, but the debate over the Thirteenth Amendment delivered an early, powerful blow to the confining edifice of Americans' sometimes blind reverence for the founding generation.

Party Unity and Presidential Politics

In all of their deliberations, House members were influenced as much by circumstances outside of Congress as by the ideas circulating within. And by far the most significant event shaping the House debates was the nomination of Abraham Lincoln on a platform of emancipation by constitutional amendment. During the Senate debates, Lincoln's nomination was fairly certain, but no one knew whether he or his party would embrace the amendment as an election issue. By the time of the House debate, however, the Republicans had written the measure into their platform and Lincoln had endorsed it. As a result, the House debate centered as much on Lincoln as it did on the amendment.

Because it was sponsored by the administration during a presidential election year, the amendment could not possibly receive objective, nonpartisan consideration. Rather than defining the amendment's meaning and scope, its backers in the House tended to take the more partisan course of denouncing the Democrats or praising Lincoln. Republican Francis W. Kellogg of Michigan contrasted the typical Democrat – "the half-way traitor, the sympathizer with treason, who will do all he can in behalf of the enemies of the Union" – with "our worthy President," who would be reelected "by an overwhelming majority."[79] Democrats were no better. They only occasionally described what the amendment meant for constitutional law, choosing instead to use the opportunity to condemn Lincoln and his party. Instead of reflecting on the merits or weaknesses of the amendment, the Indiana Democrat Joseph Edgerton focused instead on the Baltimore platform, reading portions of that document to demonstrate the "lack of all political integrity" of the Republicans.[80] Such par-

79 Ibid. (June 14, 1864), 2956.
80 Ibid. (June 15, 1864), 2986.

tisan grappling was, of course, nothing new in legislative debates. But party rivalry was so intensified by Lincoln's nomination that any measured, enlightened deliberation of the amendment seems to have been suspended in favor of outright electioneering.

Heightened partisanship jeopardized the amendment. About ten Democratic votes were needed to secure the measure, but Democrats were unlikely to turn against their party by voting for an amendment written into their opponents' national platform. The Republican Ebon Ingersoll, a former Democrat, tried in vain to draw his old friends into bipartisan action: "Why cannot we . . . forget that we ever have been partisans, and unite, with heart and hand?"[81] Although the speech won Ingersoll many friends in his home state of Illinois – at least his brother told him it did – it did him no good in Congress.[82] There, prominent Democrats like Fernando Wood demanded perfect party discipline. Wood reminded would-be converts to the amendment that party members who had left the fold "are now erased from the memorials of the Democratic party, and are expunged and blotted out from the respect of those who still hold fast to its time-honored principles."[83] In the Senate debate, the speeches in support of the amendment from War Democrats like Reverdy Johnson had electrified the debate and aroused speculations that Democrats inclined against slavery were ready to bolt the party. But in the House, only one Democrat, Ezra Wheeler of Wisconsin, spoke on behalf of the measure, and his endorsement carried none of the weight of Johnson's. As retribution for his support of the amendment, Wheeler, a little-known, one-term congressman, was denied the nomination for reelection by his state's Democratic party.[84]

Republicans were equally hesitant to jostle party ranks. Although all party members supported the amendment, many may have preferred a more explicitly radical amendment such as Sumner's measure declaring all persons "equal before the law." Certainly the idea of writing more radical language into the measure was circulating at the time of the House debates. Newspaper articles frequently contrasted the proposed amendment with the amendment endorsed by the recent Frémont convention, which secured to all men "absolute equality before the law." One correspondent of the Washington *Daily National Intelligencer* suggested a constitutional amendment that granted citizenship to blacks who were

81 Ibid., 2991.
82 Robert G. Ingersoll to Ebon Ingersoll, June 17, 1864, Robert G. Ingersoll MSS, ISHL.
83 *CG*, 38th Cong., 1st sess. (June 14, 1864), 2942.
84 Christopher Dell, *Lincoln and the War Democrats: The Grand Erosion of Conservative Tradition* (Rutherford, N.J.: Fairleigh Dickinson University Press, 1975), 305.

literate or had served in the military for three years.[85] Some of the more radical members of the House may also have been unsatisfied with the amendment's language, though they still would have assumed that it implicitly offered equality before the law. House Republicans who consistently championed the cause of African American rights, men like Thaddeus Stevens and George W. Julian, were not among those who spoke on the amendment's behalf. Their silence perhaps suggests guarded dissatisfaction.[86] In the Senate, Sumner had been able to propose his explicitly egalitarian amendment partly because Republicans had yet to write the more narrowly phrased measure into the party platform. But in the House, the recent addition of the amendment to the platform made any suggested revision a rebuke to the party.

The result of this powerful tug of party discipline was a nearly perfect partisan division in the final vote on the amendment on June 15, 1864. The amendment failed to secure the necessary two-thirds majority, falling short by thirteen votes (see Appendix Table 2). Every Republican voted for the measure, and all but four Democrats voted against it. The vote signaled the failure of designs to draw antislavery Democrats away from their party and toward Republicans or Frémont's "Radical Democracy." Some Democrats were certainly disposed toward the measure but refused to abandon their party. Democratic congressman Henry Stebbins had advised party members to reverse their position on slavery, but in the final vote, he decided to absent himself rather than vote against his party.[87] "It was hoped that a sufficient number of War Democrats would have come over to the Union side on this question," the Washington correspondent of the *Chicago Tribune* reported, "but it has proved a delusion. The party lash has been unsparingly applied, and all disposed to bolt have been relentlessly lashed back."[88] The dream of a new antislavery coalition was dashed – at least for the moment.

Once the House voted down the constitutional amendment, Republicans quickly declared the measure the central issue in the coming political

---

85 "G. M.," "The War and Its Issues," Washington *Daily National Intelligencer,* June 18, 1864, p. 2. Although it was mostly egalitarian, the proposal denied the vote to African Americans and barred them from federal office holding.

86 Of the fifteen Republicans classified as "extreme radical" by Michael Les Benedict, an authority on Congress during the Civil War and Reconstruction, not one spoke for the amendment during the House debates in the first session of the Thirty-eighth Congress. Of the thirty Republicans classified as "radical," only one, William D. Kelley, spoke in favor of the measure. For these classifications, see Benedict, *A Compromise of Principle,* 339–42.

87 Henry George Stebbins to Samuel L. M. Barlow, January 20, 1864, Samuel L. M. Barlow MSS, HEH.

88 *Chicago Tribune,* June 18, 1864, p. 2.

campaign. The *New York Tribune* announced, "the Democratic party in the House to-day deliberately strapped the burden of Slavery on its shoulders for the coming Presidential election."[89] An Iowa man, saddened by the amendment's defeat, moaned that "Congress has failed to meet the expectations of the people," but he predicted that the coming election would make "our rulers . . . hasten to learn wisdom."[90] The *New York Times,* which, a few months before, had recommended postponing consideration of the amendment until after the war, now backed the measure and said that its fate hinged on the reelection of the president.[91] In the House, Congressman James M. Ashley of Ohio made the same declaration: "When the verdict of the people is rendered next November, I trust this Congress will return determined to ingraft that verdict into the national Constitution."[92] Ashley also changed his vote on the amendment so that, under the terms of congressional procedure, he could bring it up for reconsideration in the next session.[93]

The emergence of the amendment as a campaign issue had a powerful effect on public perceptions of the measure. In an effort to make the amendment politically attractive, congressional Republicans purposefully kept it vague on the status of rebellious states and the future rights of African Americans. Before the many understandings of the measure could be reconciled, politics forced people to accept or reject it based largely on their partisan affiliation. Democrats who otherwise would have supported the amendment as a constitutional method of emancipation (and only emancipation, not "equality before the law") were compelled by the party whip to join with the majority of the Democrats opposing the amendment. Meanwhile, Republicans who wished for a more explicit guarantee of African American rights nestled in the same camp with those who possessed a more narrow understanding of the rights attached to freedom.

The evolution of the amendment from a proposed law to a campaign issue may have sent the measure to the people in the coming election, but it prevented, for the moment, any further clarification of the amendment's meaning. The premature transformation of a proposed law into a political platform is a familiar story, one with important consequences for law and history. In one sense, the transformation had a positive effect. Because the

---

89 *New York Tribune,* June 16, 1864, p. 4. For similar attacks on the Democrats, see *Philadelphia Inquirer,* June 17, 1864, p. 4; and *Cincinnati Gazette,* June 23, 1864, p. 1.
90 D. A. Lough to James Lough, June 28, 1864, William Lough MSS, CiHS.
91 *New York Times,* June 17, 1864, p. 4.
92 *CG,* 38th Cong., 1st sess. (June 28, 1864), 3357.
93 Ibid. (June 15, 1864), 2995, 3000.

amendment emerged as a party measure before its precise meaning was clear, Americans could rally behind the measure regardless of their diverging views on race, reconstruction, or the Constitution. But, in another sense, the transformation was tragic. The making of the amendment into an election issue before Americans fully deliberated its legal meaning led to a future in which the struggle over that meaning would divide the country.

6

The War within a War:
Emancipation and the Election of
1864

With the high season of electioneering in front of them, Republicans in mid-1864 were ready to tie their fortunes to the antislavery amendment. James M. Ashley, the sponsor of the measure in the House of Representatives, believed that the coming political campaign would turn on the question of constitutional abolition. "We must go to the country on this issue," he told his colleagues.[1] Yet, for reasons that no one could have predicted, the election of 1864 became both something more and something less than a referendum on emancipation and the amendment. The election did in fact help to decide the fate of black freedom – even the fate of the Union – but the issue of emancipation was nonetheless muted in the campaign.

No matter how much Republicans might have wished to make the election about emancipation, they knew that the most important issue to the northern people was the success of Union forces. These were pivotal times in military affairs. In northern Virginia, General Ulysses S. Grant gave up his first line of attack on Richmond, moved his army across the James River, and set his sights on Petersburg. Meanwhile, in Georgia, General William T. Sherman's troops were stalled by Confederate defenses at Kennesaw Mountain, only twenty miles northwest of their objective: Atlanta. Military events did more than overshadow the abolition amendment during the political campaign. They shaped the entire issue of emancipation. If Union arms were successful, the northern people would be inclined to support the administration and its policies, including emancipation. But if Union arms were unsuccessful, northerners were likely to take seriously the Democratic alternative: a negotiated settlement of the war with the Union – and slavery – intact. In the struggle over whether a peace could be negotiated or had to be won, the specific issue of the antislavery amendment sometimes faded from sight, even as the larger question of the relationship between the war and slavery loomed over all.

---

1   CG, 38th Cong., 1st sess. (June 28, 1864), 3357.

The centrality of racial issues, in particular the subject of miscegenation, also kept the amendment at the periphery of the campaign. Democrats were finding that the preservation of white purity was a much more effective political program than the defense of southern slave-owning rights. The escalation in antiblack and antimiscegenation rhetoric, however, did not simply reflect white anxieties over the ongoing process of emancipation. Rather, racial declension became a metaphor for deeper concerns about wartime changes. Ultimately, the racialized language of the campaign would have a powerful impact on political style in general and the antislavery amendment in particular.

Also driving the amendment from center stage was the normal machinery of state politics. As was typical in nineteenth-century politics, state political parties focused on those national issues that were most likely to energize local constituencies or to have a powerful impact on state affairs. Because the House had voted the amendment down in the summer of 1864, ratification of the measure seemed a distant prospect, and state-level parties tended to play up other, more immediate issues.

With such a complex constellation of issues before the people, it was no surprise that by the fall the abolitionist Theodore Tilton would complain that "the Constitutional amendment is not awarded its due share in the canvass." Tilton insisted that "the November vote must be made to mean, not only a settlement of the War question, but of the Slavery question."[2] In the struggle to assign a meaning to the election – a sort of war within the war – those like Tilton who expected the vote to be a referendum on constitutional freedom were destined for disappointment.

The Parties Dividing

During the House of Representatives debate on the antislavery amendment, Republicans and Democrats had come to see the measure as the defining issue in the coming campaign. Republicans could unite behind an amendment that was firm on emancipation yet vague on equal rights. The Democrats could rally against the measure as a symbol of Republican willingness to fight the war for the wrong reasons. Immediately after the debate in the House, however, unforeseen events created internal party divisions that could not be healed simply by appeals for or against the amendment.

Problems arose first for the Democrats. At the upcoming national convention, scheduled for July 4 in Chicago, party managers hoped to unite the prowar and propeace factions of the party. But before the convention

2   *New York Tribune,* October 12, 1864, p. 2.

met, the unexpected return to Ohio of Clement Vallandigham, the Peace Democrat whose exile Lincoln had ordered almost a year before, ignited an explosion of antiwar sentiment in the Midwest. Bolstered by the Peace Democrat's magical reappearance, the *Cincinnati Enquirer,* the leading Democratic paper of Ohio, instructed newly elected delegates to the national convention not to nominate any candidate pledged to further prosecution of the war.[3] To avoid a disastrous split at the convention, the Democratic national committee decided to put off the meeting to the end of August. The *New York World* tried to put the best face on the embarrassing postponement, predicting that "events may transpire [before the convention] . . . which will sweep away [Lincoln's] prospects as with a whirlwind of fire."[4] In private, Dean Richmond, the chair of the New York Democrats, was more specific: "There is quite a difficulty in [Republican] ranks that will widen until we have a man in the field."[5]

Richmond's prediction was on target. Soon after the Democrats postponed their convention, Lincoln obliged them with two actions that aggravated existing divisions within his party. First, on June 30, he accepted the resignation of Secretary of the Treasury Salmon P. Chase. Chase had offered to resign before, and he had expected Lincoln to reject the gesture again, particularly since the incident provoking the resignation involved a relatively minor dispute over a New York City customshouse appointment. But Lincoln had grown tired of Chase's attempts to turn the Treasury Department into his personal campaign office. The president's decision infuriated Chase's allies, one of whom proposed calling a new Republican convention.[6]

Then, eight days after accepting Chase's resignation, Lincoln pocketvetoed the bill for reconstruction sponsored by Benjamin Wade and Henry Winter Davis. Unlike Lincoln's Reconstruction Proclamation, which recommended that 10 percent of a state's citizens take a lenient oath for a state to draft a new constitution and submit it to Congress, the Wade-Davis bill provided a far stricter oath and demanded that 50 percent of the state's voters take it before the state could be considered for readmission. The Wade-Davis bill also was more severe than Lincoln's plan on emancipation. In Lincoln's plan, emancipation was enacted through new state constitutions; in the Wade-Davis bill, emancipation took the form of a

---

3 George H. Porter, *Ohio Politics during the Civil War Period* (1911; repr., New York: AMS Press, 1968), 193–96; *Cincinnati Enquirer,* June 16, 1864, p. 2.
4 *New York Daily World,* June 23, 1864, p. 4.
5 Dean Richmond to Manton M. Marble, June 16, 1864, Manton M. Marble MSS, LC.
6 Charles D. Cleveland to Chase, July 1, 1864, Salmon P. Chase MSS, HSPa. See John Niven, *Salmon P. Chase: A Biography* (New York: Oxford University Press, 1995), 362–66; Frederick J. Blue, *Salmon P. Chase: A Life in Politics* (Kent, Ohio: Kent State University Press, 1987), 234–36.

federal statute. In Lincoln's plan, the freed people had only those rights granted to them by each state; in the Wade-Davis bill, former slaves were granted federal habeas corpus rights, and former masters who denied freedom to the enslaved were subject to federal fines and imprisonment. If the bill passed, the federal government would be able to intrude into any state by emancipating slaves immediately and transferring legal authority over ex-slaves from state to federal courts.[7]

The bill's emancipation provisions had given congressmen a special sense of urgency in pressing for its passage. With Congress set to adjourn on July 4, the defeat of the antislavery constitutional amendment on June 15 left the Wade-Davis bill as the last opportunity to outlaw slavery before the session closed. As Henry Winter Davis told his counterpart Wade, because the "constitutional amendment is dead – as I always knew and said it was," the bill on reconstruction was "the *only* practical measure of emancipation *proposed* in this Congress."[8]

The president saw the bill for what it was: an attempt to undermine his reconstruction program. If he signed it, he would sabotage the reconstruction movements in states like Louisiana, Arkansas, and Tennessee, all of which had seceded but were under the control of a loyal minority.[9] The bill might also jeopardize state-level emancipation movements in loyal states like Missouri and, especially, Maryland, where a convention was being held to draft a new, proemancipation constitution. Most of all, the bill's passage threatened to destroy the delicate political coalitions that Lincoln had begun to construct between northern and southern moderates.[10]

Instead of vetoing the bill outright, the president took the more conciliatory course of pocket-vetoing the measure and issuing an explanation. He restated his wish not "to be inflexibly committed to any single plan of restoration," especially one that disrupted free-state governments newly in place in some of the southern states. He also denied a "constitutional competency in Congress to abolish slavery in States, but . . . [was] at the same time sincerely hoping and expecting that a constitutional amendment, abolishing slavery throughout the nation, may be adopted."[11]

7   See Herman Belz, *Reconstructing the Union: Theory and Policy during the Civil War* (Ithaca: Cornell University Press, 1969), 176–87, 237–43.

8   Davis to Wade, June 21, 1864, Benjamin F. Wade MSS, LC.

9   William C. Harris, *With Charity for All: Lincoln and the Restoration of the Union* (Lexington: University Press of Kentucky, 1997), 123–70.

10 See Michael Les Benedict, *A Compromise of Principle: Congressional Republicans and Reconstruction, 1863–1869* (New York: W. W. Norton, 1974), 80–83.

11 *CW*, 7:433–34.

What Lincoln accomplished here was a neat bit of legislative distortion. Congress had framed a two-tiered plan of reconstruction: first, a simple, irrevocable commitment to emancipation, now in the form of a constitutional amendment; and, second, a specific procedure for reconstructing the Union, now in the form of the Wade-Davis bill. When legislators proposed both types of measures, they assumed that both, in some form and at some time, would pass. An abolition amendment was meaningless without practical legislation to enforce it, and reconstruction legislation alone could be overturned by the Supreme Court or a later Congress. Lincoln had simply plucked from the whole package the most politically attractive piece, the amendment. And rather than acknowledge the amendment for what it was – a *counterpart* to congressional reconstruction – he treated it as an *alternative* to a congressional program. By renewing his commitment to the constitutional amendment without committing himself to a single plan of reconstruction, the President hoped to keep the party united on emancipation rather than divided on reunion.

Lincoln may have hoped to preserve party unity, but his rejection of the Wade-Davis bill, like his acceptance of Chase's resignation, played right into the hands of the Democrats, who always amplified any quarrel among Republicans. The editors of the *Cincinnati Enquirer,* for example, dutifully informed its readers of every Republican who denounced the pocket veto. "Repudiated at the same time by the conservative masses of the country and by the honest among the Abolition radicals," the *Enquirer* announced, "Lincoln's case appears to be a hopeless one."[12]

In fact, Lincoln's action had touched off only a slight squall among Republicans. Had Congress still been in session, things might have been different; in the words of Representative James G. Blaine, "a very rancorous hostility would have developed against the President."[13] But Congress had adjourned, and most of the members had returned to campaign in their home districts, where Republicans running for reelection could hardly hope to improve their prospects by turning against Lincoln. The president upset mainly those who already opposed him. Foremost among these enemies was Henry Winter Davis, whom the journalist Noah Brooks described as "insatiate in his hates, mischievous in his schemes and hollow hearted and cold blooded."[14] The Maryland congressman had backed every effort to derail Lincoln's renomination, and after the pocket veto, he

12 *Cincinnati Enquirer,* July 15, 1864, p. 2.
13 James G. Blaine, *Twenty Years of Congress: From Lincoln to Garfield* (Norwich, Conn.: Henry Bill Publishing Company, 1884–86), 2:43.
14 Letter of "Castine," *Sacramento Daily Union,* July 26, 1864, p. 1.

joined Wade and others in planning a protest against the president.[15] The
dissenters would not complete their efforts for another month.

Peace Feelers and Peace Fiascoes

Opposition from congressional radicals like Wade and Davis turned out to
be the least of Lincoln's problems during the summer of 1864. By far the
greatest of his troubles was the absence of Union military victories. On
June 18 Grant's attempt to take Petersburg by assault failed, forcing the
general to begin a long siege of the city. General Sherman did no better in
the Atlanta campaign. In late June, Confederates easily repelled Sherman's troops at Kennesaw Mountain, inflicting the worst losses seen so
far in the western theater. Even more humiliating for the Union was
Confederate General Jubal Early's raid into Maryland in early July. Meeting almost no resistance from Union armies, Early's small force reached
the outskirts of Washington on July 11 after terrorizing a number of
surrounding communities. The next day, Union reinforcements arrived
and Early began his retreat, but the Confederate general had scored an
impressive blow against Union morale. In the North, the faint cries for
peace now became howls.

Even Lincoln, who so far had been skeptical of settling a peace, began to
take seriously some proposed peace missions. Yet, if Lincoln was now
open to negotiation, it was not because he thought an acceptable peace
could be settled. Instead, he saw peace negotiations as opportunities to
dispel the popular misconception, fueled by Confederate and Democratic
propaganda, that southerners would surrender if the Union backed off
from emancipation. Lincoln knew the truth: only independence would
satisfy the Confederates. If, in the course of peace talks, Jefferson Davis or
some other Confederate official admitted the Confederacy's true aims,
then the fuss over emancipation as a war aim would be silenced, for only a
small minority in the North would agree to disunion. In the absence of
Union military victories, the president needed such a statement from the
Confederates in order to justify the war.

Lincoln was sure to have a hard time exposing the true war aims of the
Confederacy, because Confederate leaders had much to lose if they admitted their actual goals. Unless the Confederacy could achieve some stunning military victories, its best chance at independence lay in a Democratic
victory in the North. A Democratic president might accept a separate
Confederacy or at least a temporary cease-fire. So Confederates needed

---

15 Henry Winter Davis to Samuel F. DuPont, July 7, and July 7 or 8, 1864, Samuel F.
    DuPont MSS, EM. See Gerald S. Henig, *Henry Winter Davis: Antebellum and Civil
    War Congressman from Maryland* (New York: Twayne Publishers, 1973), 208–13.

northerners to believe that peace and reunion required the defeat of Lincoln and his emancipation policy.[16] Lincoln could have undermined this strategy by asking Davis to state Confederate peace terms, but he could not do this without acknowledging Davis as the authentic president of an authentic nation – a move that would undermine the Union president's claim that secession was illegitimate. Also, Lincoln could not solicit peace terms with no precondition of emancipation. He was firmly committed to reunion with emancipation, and he refused even to give the appearance of going back on his promise to the enslaved.

Because normal diplomatic maneuvers were unavailable to the president, he had to rely on unofficial agents to draw Davis out into the open about his true war aims. Lincoln approved two such missions. In mid-July he dispatched John R. Gilmore, an antislavery author, and Colonel James Jaquess, a member of Union general William Rosecrans's staff, to Richmond with an informal offer of amnesty for all rebels and financial compensation to slave owners if Confederates abolished slavery and returned to the Union.[17] On July 17 the messengers spoke directly with Jefferson Davis, who promptly rejected the offer. A few days later the men returned to Washington, where Gilmore tried to please a president eager for good news by reporting that Davis had said precisely what Lincoln had hoped he would, that regardless of the Union's policy on slavery, the Confederacy would fight until it was either independent or annihilated. In fact, the Confederate president had probably said nothing so strong. But Lincoln felt increasingly desperate for political ammunition, so he encouraged the author to publish his account immediately. In the *Boston Evening Transcript* of July 22, under his pseudonym of Edmund Kirke, Gilmore relayed Davis's message: "We are not fighting for slavery. We are fighting for INDEPENDENCE, and that, or extermination, we *will* have."[18] But, as the editor James Gordon Bennett observed, Gilmore's account "did not amount to much," for it was merely the dubious hearsay of an inexperienced and unofficial envoy.[19] Northerners failed to take Gilmore's story seriously. The first peace mission had fallen well short of the president's goals.

16 See Larry E. Nelson, *Bullets, Ballots, and Rhetoric: Confederate Policy for the United States Presidential Contest of 1864* (University: University of Alabama Press, 1980).

17 James G. Randall and Richard N. Current, *Lincoln the President: Last Full Measure* (1955; repr., Urbana: University of Illinois Press, 1991), 165–66; Edward C. Kirkland, *The Peacemakers of 1864* (New York: Macmillan, 1927), 85–96; James R. Gilmore, *Personal Recollections of Abraham Lincoln and the Civil War* (Boston: L. C. Page, 1898), 230–93.

18 *Boston Evening Transcript*, July 22, 1864. A fuller account of the mission appears in the *Atlantic Monthly*, 14 (1864), 372–83, 715–26.

19 *CW*, 7:461.

The second mission proved to be even more disastrous. On July 7
Horace Greeley, the editor of the *New York Tribune,* advised the president
that so-called Confederate "ambassadors" at Niagara Falls, Canada,
should be granted safe passage into the United States to negotiate for
peace.[20] The southerners were Clement C. Clay of Alabama, a senator in
the Confederate Congress, Jacob Thompson of Mississippi, a former secretary of interior, and J. P. Holcombe of Virginia, a representative in the
Confederate Congress. But they were hardly ambassadors. Rather, they
were Confederate agents hoping to ruin Lincoln's reelection prospects by
fomenting propeace sentiment in the North. Greeley doubted that the
southerners were genuine envoys, but he thought negotiations might rally
unionist sympathies in Confederate states. (In North Carolina, for example, voters were about to hold an election to determine whether to remain
in the Confederacy.) The editor also hoped to use the peace talks to
promote his own plan of reconstruction, which looked like Lincoln's and
took the now common form of amendments to the Constitution.[21]

Lincoln had initially hoped that Greeley's efforts might lead to an official statement of the Confederacy's true war aims, but he soon realized
that the southerners had neither the authority to speak for Jefferson Davis
nor a genuine interest in peace. Greeley was still optimistic about the
benefits of a peace conference, and he traveled to Niagara Falls to meet the
"ambassadors." To put an end to the bogus peace effort – and perhaps to
embarrass Greeley, who had been nettlesome since the onset of secession –
Lincoln sent the southerners a letter addressed "TO WHOM IT MAY CON-
CERN." The letter declared: "any proposition which embraces the restoration of peace, the integrity of the whole Union, and the abandonment of
slavery, and which comes by and with an authority that can control the
armies now at war against the United States will be received."[22] When the
letter arrived, Greeley saw that he had been played by the southerners –
and by Lincoln. He delivered the president's message and sulked back to
New York.

Although Lincoln must have suspected that his letter would become
public, he never anticipated the full furor it would cause. As soon as the
Niagara conference dissolved, one of the northern allies of the southern
agents sent a copy of the letter to the Associated Press. Almost instantly, it
appeared in every major northern newspaper, and northern Democrats

---

20   Greeley to Lincoln, July 7, 1864, RTL. For a review of the Greeley effort, see Randall
     and Current, *Lincoln the President: Last Full Measure,* 158–65, and Kirkland, *The
     Peacemakers,* 51–85. The full texts of the relevant letters are published in Harlan Hoyt
     Horner, *Lincoln and Greeley* (Urbana: University of Illinois Press, 1953), 296–324.
21   Greeley to Lincoln, July 7, 1864, RTL.
22   *CW,* 7:451.

joined with Confederates in attacking it as proof that Lincoln was sacrificing the prospect of peaceful reunion for the sake of an abolition war. The *Cincinnati Enquirer* declared the letter "a *finality*, which . . . will preclude any conference for a settlement. Every soldier . . . that is killed, will lose his life not for the Union, the Stars and Stripes, but for the negro."[23] The president had nothing to counter the opposition's battering. The unreliable testimony of Jaquess and Gilmore about Jefferson Davis's true war aims could not stand up against the written proof of Lincoln's intransigence on emancipation. To make matters worse, the president's ultimatum was made public just as he called for five hundred thousand more volunteers. The *New York World* asked, "shall men be continued in power who may call for five hundred thousand more men . . . to make the 'abandonment of slavery' *a fact?*"[24] As if the fates were aligned against Lincoln, news simultaneously arrived of a disgraceful Union disaster outside of Petersburg. A failed effort to take the city by exploding a mine under the Confederates' defensive works resulted in almost four thousand Union casualties, many of whom were African American soldiers. The misfortunes of the Union army, the call for troops, and the Niagara letter all seemed to confirm Democratic claims that the administration was badly fighting a needless war.

As the opposition played up the "To Whom It May Concern" letter, the proposed antislavery amendment was all but forgotten. Had the president not sent the letter, perhaps the amendment would have become a more potent issue in the election, as Lincoln and other Republicans intended it to be. Democrats were sure to attack any proemancipation policy, but the Niagara letter was much less defensible than the amendment. Whereas the amendment could be put off until peace and sectional harmony had been restored, the "To Whom It May Concern" letter made emancipation a prerequisite to peace. Moreover, it was easier to accept a constitutional amendment than an executive ultimatum as a constitutional approach to emancipation.

One of the most damaging effects of the Niagara letter, then, was the wedge it drove between Republicans and those Democrats who supported the antislavery amendment. Only a few such Democrats were willing to ignore the president's peace terms and stay focused on the amendment. Joseph Wright, a War Democrat from Indiana, was a rare example. During the campaign, Wright told audiences that "every voter is either voting to amend the Constitution in such a way that slavery shall never exist . . . or that slavery shall remain in all those States where it now legally ex-

23 Letter of "Cleveland," July 21, 1864, in *Cincinnati Enquirer*, July 25, 1864, p. 2.
24 *New York Daily World*, July 29, 1864, p. 4.

ists."[25] More common was the stance of Maryland senator Reverdy Johnson. Johnson had been the most prominent Democrat to speak for the amendment in Congress, but after the Niagara incident, he turned against the administration. While he "would have slavery abolished by constitutional amendment, or by State action," he refused to make emancipation a condition of reunion. As for Lincoln's rejection of the Niagara peace overtures, Johnson asked, "could there be a refusal so insane, so reckless, so inhuman, so barbarous?"[26] The tenuous coalition between Republicans and antislavery War Democrats facilitated by the amendment and crucial to the creation of a genuine, lasting National Union Party had been jeopardized by Lincoln's peace terms.

By the end of August, Lincoln's position was more precarious than ever. Early in the month, Henry Winter Davis and Benjamin Wade published their blistering "manifesto" against the president for his rejection of their reconstruction bill. Composed chiefly by Davis, the protest accused the president of using reconstruction to secure electors in the South who would "be at the dictation of his personal ambition," it condemned his efforts to usurp power from Congress, and it implicitly recommended dumping him from the Republican ticket.[27]

Historians who read the manifesto only as a censure of presidential power overlook the document's more explicit criticism: that Lincoln meant to leave slavery "exactly where it was by law at the outbreak of the Rebellion." Restating what had been said all too often – that the Emancipation Proclamation was ineffectual because it "merely professed to free certain slaves while it recognized the institution" – the writers speculated that "every Constitution of the Rebel States at the outbreak of the Rebellion may be adopted without the change of a letter." Amending the federal Constitution to abolish slavery, Wade and Davis believed, was an effective way to outlaw slavery, but they saw no way of adopting the amendment anytime soon. They therefore regarded the president's expectation that the amendment could be adopted as nothing more than rhetoric, and they asked him "on what his expectation rests, after the vote of the House of Representatives at the recent session, and in the face of the political complexion of more than enough of the States to prevent the possibility of its adoption within any reasonable time." Unable to chal-

25 Indianapolis *Daily Journal*, September 6, 1864, p. 2.
26 *Speech of Hon. Reverdy Johnson, of Maryland, delivered before the Brooklyn Mc-Clellan Central Association, October 21, 1864* (Brooklyn, N.Y.: Brooklyn McClellan Association, 1864), 7.
27 "To the Supporters of the Government," *New York Tribune*, August 5, 1864, p. 4. All quotations from the "manifesto" are from this source.

lenge the constitutionality of Lincoln's solution to slavery, they questioned instead the genuineness of his commitment, not only to the amendment but to emancipation in general. In the wake of the president's recently published ultimatum against slavery to the Niagara agents, such a challenge appeared absurd.

Although the manifesto met with much scorn – one Ohioan claimed that Wade was "universally denounced" at home – many northerners agreed with the two authors that Lincoln should be removed from the presidential ticket.[28] During the last three weeks of August, dissenters considered many strategies for securing a new candidate, but the only plan with any promise was the one initiated by Davis to hold a new convention in September. Backers of the convention did not agree on a replacement candidate, though General Grant, who still insisted he would not run, seemed to be their favorite. It was an odd coalition that propelled the movement. Included was the ever disgruntled radical Salmon P. Chase, the conservative Vermont Republican senator Jacob Collamer, and the New York Democrat Amasa J. Parker, who had been recommending a fusion with disaffected Republicans since June.[29] Some of the dissenters genuinely wanted to secure a new candidate for the upcoming election. But others were looking beyond the immediate contest. James Ashley, for example, supported Lincoln in 1864 but saw the new coalition as the beginning of a *"permanent organization* of the war Democrats into a great National Party, which properly managed could take possession of the Great Government in 1868 – even if *they fail now."*[30] Ashley intended to make Chase, a fellow former Democrat, the presidential candidate of 1868, and he expected the abolition amendment, which he had sponsored, to be the cornerstone policy of the new party.[31] The jockeying to build an alternative party for the future, even among those committed to Lincoln, added momentum to the Wade-Davis protest movement.

---

28 R. M. Corwine to John Sherman, August 12, 1864, John Sherman MSS, LC.

29 The call for this convention and the responses to it may be found in the John A. Stevens MSS, NYH. The most relevant documents were printed in the *New York Sun,* June 30, 1889. See Randall and Current, *Lincoln the President: Last Full Measure,* 210–13; William Frank Zornow, *Lincoln and the Party Divided* (Norman: University of Oklahoma Press, 1954), 110–12. For Parker's wish for a Democrat-Republican alliance, see Parker to Samuel J. Tilden, July 7, 1864, Samuel J. Tilden MSS, NYP.

30 James M. Ashley to Salmon P. Chase, August 5, 1864, Salmon P. Chase MSS, LC. See Robert F. Horowitz, *The Great Impeacher: A Political Biography of James M. Ashley* (Brooklyn: Brooklyn College Press, 1979), 100–101.

31 Jessie Marshall Ames, *Private and Official Correspondence of Gen. Benjamin Butler during the Period of the Civil War* (Norwood, Mass: privately published, 1917), 4:534–36.

By late August, the political insiders that Lincoln trusted most all predicted defeat. Leonard Swett, Lincoln's old friend from Illinois, advised him to withdraw from the race after the Democratic convention.[32] Thurlow Weed, the veteran political "wizard," told the president that he knew of no one "who authorizes the slightest hope of success."[33] Henry Raymond, the chairman of the National Union party and the editor of the *New York Times*, identified for Lincoln the two sources of his unpopularity: "the want of military successes" and the perception "that we are not to have peace *in any event* under this administration until Slavery is abandoned."[34] Demoralized by these reports, the president prepared a memorandum in anticipation of defeat. "It seems exceedingly probable that this Administration will not be re-elected," he began. He then promised to cooperate with the president-elect after the election to "save the Union . . . as he will have secured his election on such ground that he can not possibly save it afterwards." He brought the memorandum to the cabinet meeting, folded it so his secretaries could not read the text, and asked each of them to sign it.[35] Now Lincoln had a document that would serve forever as evidence that, while his opponents had misled the people into thinking that peace could be settled with the Union intact, he had always understood that the price of peace was disunion.

The Retreat from Niagara

Not ready to abandon all hope, the president did consider two desperate schemes to save his campaign – and the Union. Both strategies represented a retreat from the hard-line position on emancipation that he had taken with the Niagara peace agents. First, he drafted a message that qualified the "To Whom It May Concern Letter." The new letter, addressed to Charles D. Robinson, a Wisconsin Democrat who complained about the Niagara letter, threw down a challenge to his Confederate counterpart: "If Jefferson Davis wishes . . . to know what I would do if he were to offer peace and re-union, saying nothing about slavery, let him try me."[36] It was an empty dare. Lincoln knew that Davis would not seek peace on the basis of reunion, just as he knew that he himself would not back down from emancipation. The president worried that the new letter would be criticized by northern abolitionists. Frederick Douglass, whose opinion he had come to trust, confirmed his anxieties. In a private meeting in the

32 Ibid., 5:68.
33 Thurlow Weed to William H. Seward, August 22, 1864, RTL.
34 Henry J. Raymond to Abraham Lincoln, August 22, 1864, RTL.
35 *CW*, 7:514.
36 *CW*, 7:499–501.

White House, Douglass told the president that the letter would "be taken as a complete surrender of your anti-slavery policy, and do you serious damage."[37] Lincoln then shelved the letter. But he did not let go entirely of the strategy. Immediately after his talk with Douglass, he told two of Robinson's friends, "my enemies condemn my emancipation policy. . . . Let them prove . . . that we can restore the Union without it."[38]

The second strategy that Lincoln considered to undo the damage of the Niagara letter was another peace mission to Richmond. The idea for the mission came from Henry Raymond, who believed that if Jefferson Davis were offered peace on the "sole condition of acknowledging the supremacy of the Constitution," he would refuse the offer, and thus dispel the illusion that Lincoln's demand for emancipation was the only obstacle to reunion.[39] It was a sign of how desperate the president had become that he immediately drafted a letter empowering Raymond to negotiate with Jefferson Davis for the "restoration of the Union and the national authority, . . . all remaining questions to be left for adjustment by peaceful modes."[40] But then Lincoln came to his senses. He realized that the effort would lead only to "utter ruination."[41] It would earn him further condemnation from his fellow Republicans, and worse, as his critic Henry Winter Davis understood, it would allow Jefferson Davis to force the issue back on Lincoln by asking, "What terms are you willing to accept – speak first?"[42] In the end, the president aborted the Raymond mission.

From the draft of Lincoln's response to the Wisconsin Democrat Robinson, and from the proposed Raymond mission, also never sent, some historians have concluded that the president was ready to renounce emancipation. In fact, he was no more willing to retreat now than he had been in July; however, he was more prepared to take the risk of *appearing* to consider a retreat in order to secure his election. In taking this risk, or at least in considering it, he did no disservice to the slaves, for he understood that the election of his opponent would do far more harm to the prospect

---

37 Douglass to Theodore Tilton, October 15, 1864, in Philip S. Foner, ed., *The Life and Writings of Frederick Douglass* (New York: International Publishers, 1952), 3:423. The conversation almost certainly occurred on August 19, although Douglass remembered it taking place only "six weeks" before October 15. It was also during this interview that Lincoln predicted to Douglass that the new president would settle a peace with slavery intact; he therefore asked Douglass to devise a plan to bring as many slaves as possible within Union lines.

38 *CW*, 7:507.

39 Henry Raymond to Abraham Lincoln, August 22, 1864, RTL.

40 *CW*, 7:517.

41 John G. Nicolay to John Hay, August 25, 1864, John G. Nicolay MSS, LC.

42 Henry Winter Davis to Samuel F. DuPont, August 25, 1864, in John D. Hayes, ed., *Samuel Francis DuPont: A Selection from His Civil War Letters* (Ithaca: Cornell University Press, 1969), 3:372–75.

of black freedom than would his own empty gesture toward peace. As the historian Larry Nelson has argued, the Confederate president could have put Lincoln in a difficult position had he offered Union with slavery preserved, but, as Lincoln understood, Davis could not afford politically to advocate anything less than Confederate independence.[43] Too often historians, like many of Lincoln's contemporaries, wrongly assume that the Confederates were prepared to accept a peace based on something less than independence, and they compound this fallacy by thinking that Lincoln was equally ready to negotiate on slavery.

The failure of Lincoln to dispel false hopes for a peaceful reunion, combined with the absence of Union military victories, led Democrats at their national convention at Chicago to call for an immediate armistice. The peace plank was not the first choice of the War Democrats, who were forced to accept the language of Clement Vallandigham and the other Peace Democrats to keep the peace men from bolting the convention and splitting the party. The War Democrats also conceded to the nomination of the Peace Democrat George Pendleton, an ally of Vallandigham, as the vice-presidential nominee. But, as everyone had anticipated, the presidential nomination went to a War Democrat, George B. McClellan.

In an effort to put McClellan on a more secure footing, War Democrats advised the candidate to announce that he supported continued war, but that he would not make emancipation a condition of reunion.[44] McClellan complied. His acceptance letter pledged to fight until reunion was assured, and it removed emancipation as a peace term by promising any state "willing to return to the Union" that it would be "received at once, with a full guaranty of all its constitutional rights."[45] Democratic strategy continued to rest on depicting Lincoln's armies as ineffectual and his emancipation policy as obstructionist.

The strategy might have worked had it not been for a sudden turn in military events. On September 2, General Sherman took Atlanta. Sherman's "very effective stump speeches in Georgia," as one Ohioan described the victory, reversed the fortunes of the Republican party.[46] The capture of Atlanta also heightened the significance of Union admiral David Farragut's victories in Mobile Bay during the previous four weeks. Secretary of State William Henry Seward gloated that "Sherman and

---

43   Nelson, *Bullets, Ballots, and Rhetoric,* 173–75.
44   See, for example, Amasa J. Parker to Samuel L. M. Barlow, September 5, 1864, and William Cassidy to Samuel L. M. Barlow, September 5, 1864, both in Samuel L. M. Barlow MSS, HEH.
45   McPherson, *Political History,* 421.
46   Joseph B. McCullogh to John Sherman, September 6, 1864, John Sherman MSS, LC.

Farragut have knocked the bottom out of the Chicago Platform."[47] The military victories not only damaged the Democrats but effectively ended all movements to remove Lincoln from the ticket or to use a third party against him. Many of those who had taken the cue of the Wade-Davis manifesto and campaigned for a new convention now retreated into line behind the President.[48] Meanwhile, John C. Frémont, the candidate of the Radical Democracy, also pledged his support for Lincoln and withdrew from the race. Those dismayed by Frémont's withdrawal may have been consoled by the President's removal of the conservative Montgomery Blair from the Cabinet, a move which some mistakenly interpreted as payment for Frémont's exit.[49]

Although military success and a brief cease-fire in factionalism instilled the Republicans with optimism, they still struggled against the un-popularity of Lincoln's "To Whom It May Concern" letter. The Demo-crats continued to keep the letter before the public, especially since their own platform had proved an embarrassment after the Atlanta victory. Almost every pamphlet the Democrats distributed included a section ti-tled "The Republican Platform," which reproduced not the eleven planks framed at Baltimore but simply the one sentence written by the President to the peace agents at Niagara.[50]

In response, the Republicans tried to keep the campaign focused away from Lincoln's peace terms. The clearest sign of Republican retreat from the Niagara position came in the party's distribution of "Union Campaign Document no. 1," a reprint of Seward's September 3 speech at Auburn, New York, in which he denied that universal emancipation was a condi-tion of reunion. Instead, said Seward, the issue of slavery would at the end of the war "pass over to the arbitrament of courts of law, and to the

47 Cited in James M. McPherson, *Battle Cry of Freedom: The Civil War Era* (New York: Oxford University Press, 1988), 775.
48 See, for example, John A. Andrew to Richard Yates, September 7, 1864, "Letters Official," John A. Andrew MSS, MaA; James W. Sheffey to Thurlow Weed, September 14, 1864, Thurlow Weed MSS, UR; Henry Winter Davis to Samuel F. DuPont, Septem-ber 23 or 24, 1864, DuPont MSS, EM.
49 Even before Frémont's withdrawal, Lincoln had decided to let Blair go. See Phillip Shaw Paludan, *The Presidency of Abraham Lincoln* (Lawrence: University Press of Kansas, 1994), 288–89; H. L. Trefousse, "Zachariah Chandler and the Withdrawal of Frémont in 1864; New Answers to an Old Riddle," *Lincoln Herald*, 70 (Winter 1968), 181–88; Francis P. Blair, Sr., to Montgomery Blair, "Monday," box 2, Folder 1860–65, Blair family MSS, LC; Elizabeth Lee to Samuel Phillips Lee, September 24, 1864, in Virginia Jeans Laas, ed., *Wartime Washington: The Civil War Letters of Elizabeth Blair Lee* (Urbana: University of Illinois Pres, 1991), 432–34.
50 See *Democratic Campaign Document no. 1* and the other campaign documents com-piled in the *Handbook of the Democracy* [1864].

councils of legislation."[51] Only ten days after Seward's speech, another cabinet member, Secretary of the Interior John P. Usher, took the same line in a speech at Indianapolis: "whenever the Southern people lay down their arms and submit to the Government, there will be no conditions whatever insisted upon by the Government in regard to the subject of slavery. The entire question of slavery will be left to the decisions of the Courts."[52]

Neither Seward nor Usher claimed to speak for the president – Seward, in fact, explicitly denied doing so – but both men, by nature of their positions in the Lincoln administration, gave the impression that the president had changed his mind on emancipation as a condition of reunion. In fact, Lincoln was still steadfast in his commitment to black freedom. But the president was equally determined to make no further public statement on slavery as a peace term until after the election, and he had said as much in private.[53] As the president held his tongue on emancipation, he allowed his lieutenants to speak freely. Lincoln did not authorize and certainly did not engineer the addresses of Seward and Usher, but neither did he denounce them. Lincoln could easily have qualified what his cabinet members said about slavery. Indeed, he did make a statement clarifying Seward's Auburn speech on a point unrelated to emancipation.[54] But the president chose not to deny Seward's suggestion that slavery might last beyond the war. Lincoln was committed to the policy that he had taken with the Niagara agents, but he was also willing to let his underlings act on their own to make the administration *seem* more flexible on slavery. This was a delicate maneuver, for it might make the president seem to be speaking out of both sides of his mouth. Yet the peculiar and well-known detachment between Lincoln and his cabinet officers made the strategy

---

51 William H. Seward, *Issues of the Conflict. Terms of Peace*, reprinted in George E. Baker, ed., *The Works of William H. Seward* (Boston: Houghton Mifflin, 1884), 5:503–4.

52 "Speech of Hon. John P. Usher, Delivered in the Circle, Indianapolis, on Wednesday Evening, Sept. 14, 1864," in Indianapolis *Daily Journal*, September 16, 1864, pp. 1–2 (quotation at 2).

53 "Peck" to James W. Singleton, October 14, 1864, Orville Hickman Browning MSS, ISHL. On one occasion during the period between the publication of the Niagara letter and the final election, Lincoln did consider issuing a public letter reaffirming his commitment to emancipation, but he never sent the letter. See *CW*, 8:2.

54 Seward reported that if Lincoln were defeated, he might face a coup from Democrats, Confederate sympathizers, or some combination of both in the months before McClellan took office (Seward, *Issues of the Conflict*, 3). Many people, including New Jersey governor Joel Parker, read Seward's speech as evidence of a determination by Lincoln to "perpetuate his reign by the force of the bayonet" (excerpt of Parker's speech may be found in clipping from unidentified newspaper in letter from "A New Yorker" to William Henry Seward, September 19, 1864, Seward MSS, UR; for a similar reaction, see *New York Daily World*, October 15, 1864, p. 1). In response, the president publicly denied that he intended to "ruin the government" if defeated (*CW*, 8:52).

workable.[55] Because none of the cabinet officers was thought to speak for the president, different members could take a different line from Lincoln without making their chief seem hypocritical.

It became much less necessary for Republicans to dodge the emancipation issue after early October, when Jefferson Davis, in an attempt to lift lagging Confederate spirits, announced that a northern pledge to leave slavery alone would not end the war because the South refused to consider peace "on any other basis than independence."[56] Lincoln now had the evidence of Confederate intransigence that he had sought all summer. Davis's message, which Republicans circulated throughout the North, provided an effective corrective to Democratic propaganda that identified emancipation as the only obstacle to peace.

However effective Republicans may have been at reversing the harm done by the Niagara letter, their strategy had the inevitable effect of stifling the subject of the antislavery amendment. Under different circumstances, people might have regarded an amendment requiring approval by Congress and the state legislatures as less obstructionist than a nonnegotiable peace demand of the president. But the mounting fatalities of the summer made any move toward abolition seem like a certain obstacle to peace. Republican leaders allowed their fear of reopening the wounds of Niagara to get the better of them. The Union Congressional Committee, which in June had distributed at least six speeches in favor of the amendment as campaign documents, by the fall listed no addresses or writings on the measure in its list of publications.[57] Not until after the November election would the amendment again find its way before the public eye.

The Republicans' silence on slavery was unacceptable to the people who cared most about black freedom: African Americans. Some African Americans saw the retreat from Niagara as a sign that Republicans were embarrassed by their former pledge against slavery. Or, as Frederick Douglass put it, Republican orators treated "the Negro" as "the deformed child, which is put out of the room when company comes."[58]

---

55 See Paludan, *Presidency of Abraham Lincoln*, 170–77.
56 Davis, speech at Augusta, Georgia, October 10, 1864, in Dunbar Rowland, ed., *Jefferson Davis, Constitutionalist: His Letters, Papers and Speeches* (Jackson: Mississippi Department of Archives and History, 1923), 6:358–59 (quotation at 359).
57 Contrast the titles of speeches listed on the flyer from E. D. Morgan et al., June 29, 1864, Elihu B. Washburne MSS, LC, with the title list dated September 2, 1864, on the back of James Harlan, *The Constitution Upheld and Maintained* (Union Congressional Committee no. 11).
58 Foner, *The Life and Writings of Frederick Douglass*, 3:422–24. Douglass had used the same metaphor to describe the disappearance of the black suffrage issue in the 1860 election; see Leon Litwack, *North of Slavery: The Negro in the Free States, 1790–1860* (Chicago: University of Chicago Press, 1961), 91.

Other African Americans were even more cynical and believed that Republicans meant to abandon emancipation at the first sign of peace. From the time of the Emancipation Proclamation, abolitionists had feared that once peace came, Republicans would drop their promise to the enslaved. Such anxieties had led the abolitionist Wendell Phillips to declare in May 1864: "If I were a negro, I should pray God that this war might last twenty years."[59] If these fears were put to rest by Lincoln's Niagara letter, they were reawakened by Seward's speech at Auburn. After all, if the issue of emancipation were left to the courts, a possibility suggested by Seward, and if the war were to end in the fall of 1864, a prospect made likely by the Atlanta victory, then the administration might well leave in bondage more than two million African Americans, one-half of the slave population of 1860.[60]

Unwilling to stand by idly as Republican leaders kept quiet on emancipation, African Americans in October called for a national convention of "colored men" to meet in Syracuse, New York – the first national meeting of African Americans in nine years. About 150 men attended, including Frederick Douglass, who was elected president of the convention.[61] In his opening speech, Douglass denounced Seward for suggesting in his Auburn speech "that if peace by any means be secured the status of the colored people should remain as it is to-day."[62] Although those assembled agreed that the administration could show more backbone on emancipation, they reluctantly conceded that Lincoln was the only candidate who could represent their interests. Frémont had dropped out of the race,

---

59 *The Liberator,* May 20, 1864, cited in George H. Hoemann, *What God Hath Wrought: The Embodiment of Freedom in the Thirteenth Amendment* (New York: Garland, 1987), 120.

60 This is a conservative estimate calculated by subtracting from the total number of slaves in 1860 the number of slaves whose freedom was likely to be secured if the war ended before the Thirteenth Amendment was adopted. Lincoln estimated in 1864 that there were 200,000 ex-slaves fighting in Union armies, all of whom I assumed would remain free. Assuming Lincoln's number to be low, I doubled it and added an estimate of the number of soldiers' wives and children (freed by various congressional militia acts), arriving at a rough estimate of 600,000 freed slaves. To this number I added all the slaves living in areas that passed emancipation legislation during the war (Louisiana, Missouri, Maryland, Arkansas, Tennessee, Washington, D.C., West Virginia). By this calculation, of course, I would be counting twice the slaves from these states who joined Union armies. For this and other reasons, the number I arrived at – 1.5 million slaves freed by 1864 – should not be taken as hard fact.

61 Larry E. Nelson, "Black Leaders and the Presidential Election of 1864," *Journal of Negro History,* 63 (January 1978), 52–55.

62 *Proceedings of the National Convention of Colored Men* (Boston: J. S. Rock and George L. Ruffin, 1864), reprinted in Howard Holman Bell, *Minutes of the Proceedings of the National Negro Conventions, 1830–1864* (New York: Arno Press and the New York Times, 1969), 14.

and McClellan, as the esteemed lawyer John S. Rock put it, was "for despotism and slavery."[63] One purpose of the convention, then, was to lend support to Lincoln while sending him a message: "You are sure of the enmity of the masters, – make sure of the friendship of the slaves; for, depend upon it, your Government cannot afford to encounter the enmity of both."[64] Another purpose was to drive the final stake into the idea of colonizing blacks abroad. Former proponents of colonization, including Henry Highland Garnet, now joined with old rivals in a pledge to improve the lives of the freed people at home rather than sending them away.[65]

The African Americans at Syracuse also moved beyond their old disputes about the nature of the Constitution. In the antebellum era, many black reformers had accepted William Lloyd Garrison's proslavery reading of the Constitution, while others had taken the radical constitutionalist position that the Constitution guaranteed not only freedom but some measure of legal equality. At the Syracuse convention, however, all the attendees gave the Constitution an egalitarian reading. By using the old radical constitutionalist method of incorporating the Declaration of Independence into the Constitution, they declared that blacks had a right to "equality before the law" in addition to freedom. And in contrast to most Republicans, who generally understood "equality before the law" to mean only the absence of state laws impinging on blacks' economic rights, black reformers in 1864 envisioned "equality before the law" to mean equal voting rights as well. "Are we good enough to use bullets, and not good enough to use ballots?" the convention asked.[66] Such egalitarian constitutionalism would characterize black legal thought during Reconstruction.[67] But, by promoting the original Constitution as an instrument for equality, African Americans unwittingly undermined the cause of the antislavery amendment. By the radical constitutionalist logic of the African Americans at Syracuse, further amendment of the Constitution was unnecessary. Ironically, then, African Americans' egalitarian constitutionalism was one more factor working against the appearance of the antislavery amendment in the political campaign of 1864.

63 Ibid., 25.
64 Ibid., 60–61.
65 Ibid., 25–28.
66 Ibid., 58–61.
67 Donald G. Nieman, "The Language of Liberation: African Americans and Equalitarian Constitutionalism, 1830–1950," in Nieman, ed., *The Constitution, Law, and American Life: Critical Aspects of the Nineteenth-Century Experience* (Athens: University of Georgia Press, 1992), 67–90.

Miscegenation and Abolition

Frederick Douglass may have complained that African Americans had been "put out of the room" during the 1864 political campaign, but, in fact, they were the subject of much debate. Unfortunately, the debate took the shape of a vicious, race-baiting contest about miscegenation rather than a rational discussion about emancipation or equal rights – or the antislavery amendment.

Race mixing had already become a heated issue during the amendment debates in the spring, when antiemancipationists published the *Miscegenation* pamphlet. But during the summer electioneering, miscegenation drew so much attention that it eclipsed the antislavery amendment as a campaign issue. Typical was the speech in Philadelphia of the prominent Democrat Jeremiah Black, who denounced the Republicans' "theories of miscegenation" as "too disgusting to be mentioned." Then, of course, he mentioned them. While God had made the darker race "lower in the scale of creation," Black declared, the Republicans believed in "the natural right of the negro to political, legal and social equality."[68] Throughout the nation, pamphlets and party songs, the tools of party warfare, carried warnings of the race mixing to come if "Abraham Africanus I" were voted back into office. The election of Lincoln, announced a Democratic circular out of Illinois, "will usher in that new era of our country's glory, . . . when the North and the South, the lion and the lamb, the black and the white, shall lie down together."[69] "*All* the painful woes that wreck our lovely land," ran a Democratic ditty, "Are due the Abolitionists, the Miscegenation band."[70] If Democrats were to be believed, there was no difference between radical abolitionists and the main body of Republicans. In *Miscegenation Indorsed by the Republican Party*, the authors listed abolitionists' positive responses to the first *Miscegenation* pamphlet alongside speeches by Lincoln and other administration officials, though these speakers had said nothing about race mixing.[71]

The antimiscegenation campaign played on fears of gender disorder as well as those of racial impurity. The widely circulated caricature "Mis-

68 Speech of Jeremiah S. Black to the Keystone Club in Philadelphia, October 24, 1864, cited in Sidney Kaplan, "The Miscegenation Issue in the Election of 1864," *Journal of Negro History*, 34 (1949), 321n.

69 "Copperskin" to *Sangamon* (Illinois) *Tribune*, September 27, 1864, reprinted as *An Argument against the Abolition of the Constitution of the United States* (1864) (quotation at 12).

70 William D. Potts, *Campaign Songs for Christian Patriots and True Democrats* (New York: privately published, 1864).

71 *Miscegenation Indorsed by the Republican Party*, Campaign Document no. 11 (New York, 1864).

cegenation: Or the Millennium of Abolitionism" featured pairings of black females with prominent white male Republicans such as Horace Greeley and Thaddeus Stevens. Two white women on one side of the caricature clutched two African American males, and one of the white woman asked her consort: "now you'll be sure to come to my lecture tomorrow night, won't you?" This last scene in particular was meant to arouse the whole gamut of white male fear, from interracial sex to female empowerment to free love.[72]

An equally provocative caricature was "The Miscegenation Ball," which showed black women dancing gaily with white men in a long hall. The print was released in tandem with a bogus story printed in the *New York World* about a "negro ball" held at the Central Lincoln Club for "colored belles" and white Republican men. The story contained two of the classic elements of political race-baiting: the hypersexuality of young black women and the debased morality of Republican men, as shown in their "love sick glances" for the "octoroons."[73]

On those rare occasions when Republicans replied to the charge of miscegenation, they usually resorted to the familiar strategy, employed most recently in the amendment debate in Congress, of denouncing the Democrats as the true advocates of race mixing. A popular Republican pamphlet identified miscegenation as one of many horrors that would follow McClellan's election. Under a Democratic administration, warned the tract, suffrage would be limited to the rich, free schools would be abolished, universal taxation would be established, and, worst of all, "the poor whites would be amalgamated with the negroes, and both would be reduced to slavery."[74]

There was much that was familiar in this dialogue. For example, the Republicans had labeled their opponents amalgamationists ever since the formation of their party. "It is the institution of slavery which is the great parent of amalgamation," Horace Greeley had written in 1854. "Gentlemen need not fear it from those opposed to that institution."[75] In the same way, when Democrats in 1864 accused Lincoln, "the original ourangoutang," of having African American forbearers, they simply were repeating an anthem that had been played every year since 1860, when Lincoln

72 Martha Hodes, *White Women, Black Men: Illicit Sex in the Nineteenth-Century South* (New Haven: Yale University Press, 1997), 144–46; Forrest Wood, *Black Scare: The Racist Response to Emancipation and Reconstruction* (Berkeley: University of California Press, 1968), 71–74.

73 *New York Daily World*, September 23, 1864, p. 1.

74 *Proofs for Workingmen of The Monarchic and Aristocratic Designs of the Southern Conspirators and Their Northern Allies* (1864), 1.

75 Cited in Eric Foner, *Free Soil, Free Labor, Free Men: The Ideology of the Republican Party before the Civil War* (New York: Oxford University Press, 1970), 266.

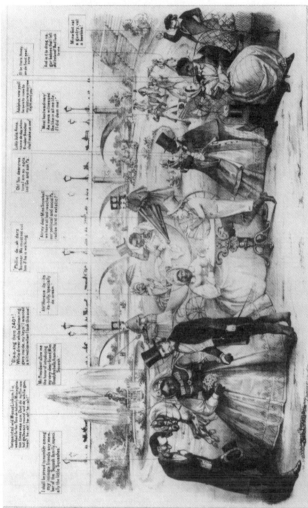

Figure 4. "Miscegenation, Or the Millennium of Abolitionism," a caricature circulated during the campaign of 1864, was part of the Democrats' attempt to shift attention away from the constitutional amendment abolishing slavery and toward the issue of race mixing. In the foreground, Republicans and antislavery activists including Abraham Lincoln, Thaddeus Stevens, Horace Greeley, and Anna E. Dickinson step across the color line, flouting conventions of race and gender; in the background, African Americans in elite garb ride in a carriage and white immigrants, a core group in the Democrats' constituency, decry the scene before them. (Courtesy Brown University Library)

was first accused of having a mother of mixed race.[76] Even the infamous "miscegenation ball," a staple of the nineteenth-century minstrel show, was merely a reworked version of integrated dances reported in earlier antiblack political rhetoric.[77]

Yet, there was much about the race issue in the campaign of 1864 that was unusual – besides, of course, the word "miscegenation," which would henceforth become the preferred term for race mixing. One distinguishing characteristic of the campaign was the frequency of white women appearing as willing rather than reluctant miscegenationists. In prior political campaigns, antiabolitionists and anti-Republicans had often attacked antislavery groups as promoters of "free love" and "free women," and such accusations occasionally included images of white women aggressively embracing black men. But just as often, antiemancipation imagery had featured lustful black men pursuing innocent, fearful white women.[78] In 1864, however, white women appeared in antiemancipation rhetoric and caricature almost exclusively as the consensual partners of black men. The image merged old anxieties about the dangerous sexual allure of African Americans, a common theme in antebellum culture, with new suspicions toward the white women who had left the domestic hearth during the war to take an active, visible role in national politics. Women had generally received praise when taking on traditional feminine roles in the war – sewing uniforms, nursing soldiers, aiding the impoverished – and they continued to be depicted, as before the war, as the most reliable receptacles of patriotic virtue.[79] The antimiscegenation campaign, how-

76 For an example of the charge against Lincoln, see *Cincinnati Enquirer,* September 19, 1864, p. 3. Similarly, the old smear against Thaddeus Stevens as having an affair with a mulatto woman was wheeled out. See, for example, "The Lincoln Catechism," in Frank Freidel, ed., *Union Pamphlets of the Civil War, 1861–1865* (Cambridge, Mass.: Harvard University Press, 1967), 2:997. For varying accounts of the reality of this relationship, see Hans L. Trefousse, *Thaddeus Stevens: Nineteenth-Century Egalitarian* (Chapel Hill: University of North Carolina Press, 1997), 69–70, and Fawn M. Brodie, *Thaddeus Stevens: Scourge of the South* (New York: W. W. Norton, 1959), 86–93.

77 See, for example, Thomas Brown, "The Miscegenation of Richard Mentor Johnson as an Issue in the National Election Campaign of 1835–1836," *Civil War History,* 39 (March 1993), 17; Jean H. Baker, *Affairs of Party: The Political Culture of Northern Democrats in the Mid-Nineteenth Century* (Ithaca: Cornell University Press, 1983), 227–28; and George Rable, "'Missing in Action': Women of the Confederacy," in Catherine Clinton and Nina Silber, eds., *Divided Houses: Gender and the Civil War* (New York: Oxford University Press, 1992), 143.

78 For examples of both types of images of white women in antebellum racial rhetoric, see Litwack, *North of Slavery,* 269, and William Gillette, *Jersey Blue: Civil War Politics in New Jersey, 1854–1865* (New Brunswick, N.J.: Rutgers University Press, 1995), 93.

79 Jeannie Attie, *Patriotic Toil: Northern Women and the American Civil War* (Ithaca: Cornell University Press, 1998), 19–49; Mary P. Ryan, *Women in Public: Between Banners and Ballots, 1825–1880* (Baltimore: Johns Hopkins University Press, 1990), 141–55.

ever, revealed a dark underside to society's endorsement of women's public role. In contrast to women who took on domestic-style duties, women who were aggressively involved in politics could represent a real threat.[80]

No female politician was better known in 1864 than Anna E. Dickinson, and it was no coincidence that she appeared as one of the women sitting on the lap of an African American man in the "Miscegenation" caricature. Dickinson rose to prominence in the 1850s as a youthful, sharp-tongued sensation on the abolitionist circuit. At the age of twenty-two, in January 1864, she delivered the first address ever given by a woman in the halls of Congress.[81] James A. Garfield, a former Union general now serving as a congressman from Ohio, was one of many in attendance who noted the odd effect of the speaker's gender on her proemancipation message. "She is really a wonderful woman, and has a great power over her audience," Garfield wrote to his wife of Dickinson. "How much of that power is because she is a woman and has a beautiful face I cannot tell."[82] An opposition editor was also swayed by Dickinson's influence, but, unable to reconcile her gender with her political dynamism, he concluded that she was an "unsexed political Don Quixote."[83] The charge was typical, for most critics of female activists found it necessary to denounce not only their cause but their womanhood.

Dickinson was a perfect target for Democratic gibes because she epitomized the increasing power of northern women, and she raised anxieties about the transformation of traditional political roles. Democrats tried to capitalize on these anxieties by asserting that the Republican agenda transformed white women from sexual innocents to complicit miscegenationists. Almost immediately after Lincoln's victory, a white woman appeared kissing a black man on the cover of the pamphlet, *What Miscegenation is! and What we are to Expect Now that Mr. Lincoln is Reelected.* The kiss was clearly consensual. Largely ignored by the press, the pamphlet proved to be one of the final bursts of race-baiting in the campaign and one of the last characterizations during the Civil War era of

---

80 Rebecca Edwards, *Angels in the Machinery: Gender in American Party Politics from the Civil War to the Progressive Era* (New York: Oxford University Press, 1997), 21–35.

81 *National Anti-Slavery Standard,* January 23, 1864, p. 2. See Wendy Hamand Venet, *Neither Ballots nor Bullets: Women Abolitionists and the Civil War* (Charlottesville: University Press of Virginia, 1991), 124–27; James M. McPherson, *The Struggle for Equality: Abolitionists and the Negro in the Civil War and Reconstruction* (Princeton: Princeton University Press, 1964), 128–31.

82 James A. Garfield to "Crete" (Lucretia) Garfield, January 17, 1864, James A. Garfield MSS, LC.

83 Springfield *Illinois State Register,* February 4, 1864, p. 2.

white women and black men as equal sexual partners.[84] By the late nineteenth century, such depictions subsided in favor of imagery that sought to reinforce traditional gender and racial hierarchies by emphasizing the theme of innocent white women victimized by black male rapists.[85]

Also new to the dialogue of race in 1864 was the way that Democrats abandoned their traditional strategy of promoting white supremacy and southern slavery as mutually beneficial programs. Now, with their assault on miscegenation, they made white supremacy the only issue, substituting it for any further defense of slavery. In the early years of the war, the Democracy had scored important political victories because of the party's opposition to emancipation, but by 1864 party members could see that slavery was dying and that the proslavery position meant political suicide. Thus the Democrats chose to omit their traditional defense of slaveowning rights from the 1864 national platform. Governor John Brough, a War Democrat campaigning for Lincoln, scoffed that it was the first time "where the irrepressible negro was smothered in the room of the Committee on Resolutions."[86] Occasionally the party still did defend slavery. In Rye, New York, for example, a pro-McClellan rally attacked the antislavery amendment because it stripped the South "of the only available labor from which it derives its value."[87] But usually, Democrats neither mentioned the amendment nor offered explicit endorsements of slavery. The Society for the Diffusion of Political Knowledge, the Democrat-sponsored organization that had distributed proslavery material in the early years of the war, finally folded in 1864.[88] Democrats had turned their backs on slavery and embraced only the campaign for white purity.

Despite the inflamed rhetoric about race mixing, northern whites seemed little shaken from their belief in the immutability of racial hierarchy and the unlikelihood of widespread miscegenation. During the political campaign of 1864, there was no antiblack violence of the sort that

---

84 L. Seaman, *What Miscegenation is! and What we are to Expect Now that Mr. Lincoln is Re-elected* (New York: Waller and Willetts, 1864). See Wood, *Black Scare,* 75–76, and pl. 5.
85 The postwar theme of white women (especially elite white women) needing white men's protection against dangerous black men is discussed in many works, including Hodes, *White Women, Black Men,* 165–73; Laura Edwards, *Gendered Strife and Confusion: The Political Culture of Reconstruction* (Urbana: University of Illinois Press, 1997), 184–217; Gail Bederman, *Manliness and Civilization: A Cultural History of Gender and Race in the United States* (Chicago: University of Chicago Press, 1995), 45–57; and Joel Williamson, *The Crucible of Race: Black-White Relations in the American South since Emancipation* (New York: Oxford University Press, 1984), esp. 306–10.
86 *Cincinnati Gazette,* September 5, 1864, p. 1.
87 Portchester (New York) *Monitor,* October 22, 1864, clipping in Horatio Seymour scrapbooks, NYS.
88 A. G. Jennings to Samuel F. B. Morse, July 28, 1864, and Charles O'Conor to Samuel F. B. Morse, September 9, 1864, both in Samuel F. B. Morse MSS, LC.

had followed the Emancipation Proclamation and conscription acts in 1862 and 1863. Nor did white lawmakers offer much opposition to the efforts underway in 1864 to repeal state laws in the Midwest barring African American immigration; within a year of the election of 1864, all of the states but Indiana had repealed these and other "black laws."[89] Even those whites who backed legal equality between the races usually assumed that the tenaciousness of white racism would inhibit any impulse toward miscegenation. Republican congressman William D. Kelley of Pennsylvania, one of the most vocal defenders of emancipation and equal rights, characterized racism as a permanent fixture on the American landscape. In a speech during his 1864 reelection campaign, Kelley declared, "if the Almighty had told [the Negro] in advance what sort of a place America was, and advised him of the prejudice its people have against dark colors . . . I have no doubt that the negro would have chosen to be of the white race.[90] Democrats also were capable of doubting their own party's rhetoric about the impending doom of the white race under the Republicans. In the late stages of the campaign, Democrats lauded Dr. John Van Evrie's *Subgenation,* a tract that refuted *Miscegenation* point by point and affirmed the permanence of whites' superior status and incorruptible bloodline.[91]

The clamor over miscegenation was only partly the product of genuine fears about racial declension. It was just as much a reflection of traditional party concerns. Democrats invoked miscegenation to signify both the immediate danger of wartime abolition as well as a set of older fears: centralization of power, government imposition of new social values, and female emancipation. Republicans in the meantime continued to represent miscegenation as a natural consequence of bowing to the Slave Power. By doing so, they used racism in the service of freedom. If slavery led to race mixing, ran Republican logic, freedom assured same-race marriages. As always, cultural conventions shaped political language. But the uncertainty of the war's outcome added even more force to the rhetoric: the precariousness of every facet of life during the war led people to cling more desperately than ever to the idea of social stability. Miscegenation, a

89   V. Jacque Voegeli, *Free but Not Equal: The Midwest and the Negro during the Civil War* (Chicago: University of Chicago Press, 1967), 170; James M. McPherson, ed., *The Negro's Civil War* (1965; repr., Urbana: University of Illinois Press, 1982), 252–54. Indiana retained its black laws well into Reconstruction.

90   William D. Kelley, *Replies of the Hon. William D. Kelley to George Northrop, Esq., in the Joint Debate in the Fourth Congressional District* (Philadelphia: Collins, 1864), 52.

91   John Van Evrie, *Subgenation (The Theory of the Normal Relations of the Races; An Answer to 'Miscegenation')* (New York: Bradburn, 1864). See David E. Long, *The Jewel of Liberty: Abraham Lincoln's Re-Election and the End of Slavery* (Mechanicsburg, Penn.: Stackpole Books, 1994), 172–73; Wood, *Black Scare*, 58–59.

classic symbol of social disorder, thus became an even more powerful political weapon. While the assault on miscegenation tells us much about underlying racial attitudes in the North, it tells us even more about northerners' profound yearning for order at a time of unprecedented chaos. Instead of a clear contest about emancipation in general or the antislavery amendment in particular, the political campaign seemed at times a united war against miscegenation, a term representing not so much the actual practice of interracial sex as the disruption of the Union and all social relations.

State Politics and Abolition

Besides being neglected in the midst of talk of peace and miscegenation, the antislavery amendment was also dwarfed by issues that people thought might have a greater impact at the local level. Had northerners in 1864 known that Congress would pass the amendment in early 1865, and that the newly elected state legislatures would vote on ratification, they might have made the amendment more of an issue in the state-level campaigns. But, because northerners had no reason to suspect that the amendment would be adopted in the next session of Congress, they allowed issues generating more immediate and local concern to drive the amendment to the periphery of state-level campaigns in 1864.

For Democrats in many states, the actual intervention by the federal government in state affairs was much easier to campaign against than an antislavery amendment that Congress had yet to adopt. Democrats in Delaware, for example, would have made more of the amendment issue in 1864 had they anticipated that its adoption a year later would abolish slavery in that state. Because the amendment was not yet a pressing issue, Democrats focused instead on the more immediate issue of federal interference at the polls. That was a subject sure to produce a powerful reaction from residents who remembered how the Union army had openly interfered in the state elections two years before. Thomas F. Bayard, from the most famous Democratic family in the state, used the free-elections issue with particular effectiveness by fusing it to the race issue. He warned white Delawareans that free blacks in the Union army would now be "their guard at the polls – and their jailers in Bastilles!"[92]

Illinois Democrats had a different reason to harp on federal interference. In June 1864 federal authorities shut down the *Chicago Times* and the *Jonesboro Gazette* for "disloyal" and "incendiary" editorials.

---

92 Patience Essah, *A House Divided: Slavery and Emancipation in Delaware, 1638–1865* (Charlottesville: University Press of Virginia, 1996), 180. See Thomas F. Bayard to Rodmon Gibbons, March 7, 1864, Gibbons family MSS, HSD.

Even after Lincoln allowed the press to resume publication, Illinois Democrats, led by the *Times* editor Wilbur Storey, pounded the Republican candidates much more on civil liberties than on emancipation.[93] Yet here, as in other states, Democrats could push the civil liberties issue only so far. As Republicans liked to remind their opponents, it was the *Democratic* presidential candidate, George B. McClellan, who had ordered the arrest of disloyal members of the Maryland legislature in the first month of the war.[94]

For other Democrats, especially those in Indiana, the most pressing issue was the impending draft. Because enlistments in Indiana had fallen short of the quota, conscription was scheduled to begin there just before the state election in October (Indiana, Pennsylvania, and Ohio held their state elections a month before the national election). Democrats pointed to the "gross inconsistency," as one editor put it, of Republicans who "are zealous against African slavery, but who can see nothing wrong in conscripting and reducing white men in the North . . . to a far worse form of slavery than domestic servitude."[95] Republicans in the state begged Lincoln and Secretary of War Edwin M. Stanton to postpone the draft until after the election, but their pleas went unfulfilled. The Lincoln administration chose instead to back General William T. Sherman, who furloughed Indiana troops so that they could go home to vote but refused to put off the draft out of fear that postponement would lead to a revolt by troops already conscripted.

In Indiana, conscription eclipsed emancipation, but in the border states, the two issues were fused because federal commanders enlisted – and thus emancipated – enslaved African Americans. Black recruitment was a divisive topic in all the border states, but it was particularly explosive in Kentucky. Federal commanders previously had turned away potential black recruits in order to avoid antagonizing white Kentuckians. In early 1864, however, the state fell short of its military quota, and the new commander, Stephen Burbridge, acting on Lincoln's authority, began accepting about one hundred blacks per day into Union ranks. The policy of paying bounties to loyal masters whose slaves enlisted made matters no better. Kentuckians saw the policy for what it was: a system of compensated emancipation that left the initiative for emancipation in the hands of

93 Arthur Charles Cole, *The Era of the Civil War, 1848–1870* (1918; repr., Springfield: Illinois Centennial Commission, 1987), 303–5 (quotation at 304).
94 Mark E. Neely, Jr., *The Fate of Liberty: Abraham Lincoln and Civil Liberties* (New York: Oxford University Press, 1991), 14–18, 207–9.
95 Indianapolis *State Sentinel*, August 2, 1864, p. 2. Equating conscription with slavery was a familiar tactic; see David M. Osher, "Soldier Citizens for a Disciplined Nation: Union Conscription and the Construction of the Modern American Army" (Ph.D. diss., Columbia University, 1992), 91–225, 449–85.

the slaves rather than their masters.[96] Resistance from Kentucky whites finally forced the president to declare martial law in the state on July 5. For the rest of the war, military commanders in Kentucky had the power to suspend the writ of habeas corpus, to close down antiadministration newspapers, and to block the distribution of opposition literature.[97] Yet even martial law could not prevent the Democrats from electoral triumph. They held onto the state legislature and carried Kentucky for McClellan.

As Democrats heaped abuse on Republicans for usurping state authority, Republicans fired back a much worse charge: collusion with rebel southerners. The accusation carried much weight in Ohio, where Clement Vallandigham, recently banned from the Union for sympathizing with the Confederacy, now campaigned for the Democrats. But the charge of disloyalty was even more potent in Indiana, where a few secret societies were in fact plotting with Confederates. Probably only a small minority of Indiana Democrats belonged to such societies, but Republicans nonetheless labeled all Democrats as traitors. To lend credibility to the charge, Oliver P. Morton, the Republican governor, and Henry C. Carrington, the Union army commander in Indiana, staged a well-publicized trial of members of the most prominent secret society, the "Sons of Liberty." The prosecution of the society's grand commander commenced strategically only three weeks before the state election. Despite the lack of hard evidence against the society, Republicans turned the proceedings into a political sensation.[98]

In most Union states, the loyalty issue aggravated the existing divisions between the Peace and War Democrats. The Ohio Democracy was so badly split that both Vallandigham and Samuel Medary, the editor of the propeace Columbus *Crisis*, refused to endorse Samuel "Sunset" Cox, the War Democrat running for reelection to Congress from the Columbus district. Cox lost the election, and he blamed the peace men for the defeat

---

96　See *Louisville Journal*, cited in *Sacramento Daily Union*, November 20, 1863, p. 2; and James G. Randall, *Constitutional Problems under Lincoln* (1926; rev. ed., 1951; repr., Gloucester, Mass.: Peter Smith, 1963), 363–65.

97　On martial law in Kentucky in 1864, see *CW*, 7:425–27, and Neely, *Fate of Liberty*, 91–92. On the battle over slavery in Kentucky, see Ira Berlin et al., eds., *Freedom: A Documentary History of Emancipation, 1861–1867*, ser. 1, vol. 2, *The Wartime Genesis of Free Labor: The Upper South* (Cambridge: Cambridge University Press, 1993), 625–38, esp. 678–79; William E. Gienapp, "Abraham Lincoln and the Border States," *Journal of the Abraham Lincoln Association*, 13 (1992), 22–27, 37–38; and Victor B. Howard, *Black Liberation in Kentucky: Emancipation and Freedom, 1862–1884* (Lexington: University Press of Kentucky, 1983), 56–76.

98　G. R. Tredway, *Democratic Opposition to the Lincoln Administration in Indiana* (Indianapolis: Indiana Historical Bureau, 1973), 224–48; Kenneth Stampp, *Indiana Politics during the Civil War* (Indianapolis: Indiana Historical Bureau, 1949), 230–49.

of Democrats throughout the state.[99] Democrats had held fourteen of the state's nineteen seats in the House of Representatives. They lost all but two in the 1864 election. Factionalism had the same effect in New York. In northern Manhattan's ninth district, for example, two Democratic candidates for Congress, the propeace Fernando Wood and the prowar Anson Herrick, divided Democratic voters and gave the election to the Republican, William Darling.[100]

Republicans well understood how Democratic factionalism helped their cause, so they amplified the loyalty issue while trying to muffle emancipation and equal rights, topics that Democrats usually united against. In the wake of the damaging "To Whom It May Concern" letter, Sydney Howard Gay, the managing editor of the *New York Tribune*, finally took to heart the advice of a Washington correspondent who had written earlier that year: "How would it do to suspend for a while antislavery writing in the paper and attack the Copperhead foe for their treasonable votes and treasonable writing?"[101] Gay now advised his readers to put aside questions concerning emancipation and reconstruction in favor of the question "A COUNTRY OR NO COUNTRY?"[102] The same strategy appealed to Republicans in Illinois, who attributed their stunning defeats in 1862 to initiatives abolishing the state's black laws and importing newly freed blacks to the state.[103] Leading Illinois Republicans now shied away from issues involving African Americans. A month before the election, the abolitionist Josephine S. Griffing asked the Republican governor Richard Yates to establish a policy for freed people emigrating to Illinois, but Yates insisted that such a plan should be made only after the elections.[104] The Republican press in Illinois preferred damning the opposition to making a positive case for emancipation and equal rights.[105] In Ohio, Republicans adopted the same strategy. A Republican editor there explained privately that it was best to "dodge" positive endorse-

---

 99 S. S. Cox to Manton Marble, October 12, 1864, Manton M. Marble MSS, LC. See David Lindsey, *"Sunset" Cox: Irrepressible Democrat* (Detroit: Wayne State University Press, 1959), 84–87.
100 Jerome Mushkat, *Fernando Wood: A Political Biography* (Kent, Ohio: Kent State University Press, 1990), 150–51.
101 Samuel Wilkeson to Sydney Howard Gay, April 1864, Sydney Howard Gay MSS, ColU.
102 *New York Tribune*, September 13, 1864, p. 4.
103 Bruce Tap, "Race, Rhetoric, and Emancipation: The Election of 1862 in Illinois," *Civil War History*, 39 (June 1993), 101–25.
104 Josephine S. Griffing to William P. Fessenden, October 1, 1864, William P. Fessenden MSS, WRH.
105 See, for example, *Canton Weekly Register*, September 12, 1864, p. 2; *Chicago Tribune*, October 14, 1864, p. 2; and *Aurora Beacon*, November 3, 1864, p. 2, all in Arthur C. Cole notes, Illinois Historical Survey, University of Illinois, Champaign-Urbana.

ments of candidates and policies and instead to "assail the principles of the opposition."[106] That same editor had endorsed the antislavery amendment in the spring, but now he told his readers that only after the war would it be time "to canvass amendments to the Constitution."[107] The Republican effort to shift the focus from emancipation to loyalty was most heavy-handed in Indiana, where Republicans responded to criticism of Lincoln's Niagara letter by telling of a much worse "To Whom It May Concern" letter, a message allegedly circulated by the Sons of Liberty that called for disunion.[108]

Rare was the Republican candidate who, in a close race, made black freedom the keynote of his political campaign. James M. Ashley, the Ohio congressman who would help steer the antislavery amendment through Congress during the next session, was an exception. On the campaign trail, Ashley repeatedly affirmed "man's equality before the law" and even boasted – inaccurately – that he had written the antislavery amendment.[109] Ashley nearly lost his race, perhaps because of his forthrightness on emancipation, but more likely because the Democrats in his district were able to unite behind one candidate, a one-legged war hero named A. V. Rice.[110]

Republicans may have kept quiet on the issue of federally enforced emancipation, but they remained as vocal as ever in favor of emancipation enacted by individual states. In Missouri, Republicans encouraged voters to use their ballots as the final blow to an institution already ground down by guerrilla conflict. The new constitution drafted by the state convention in 1863 called for gradual emancipation to begin in 1870, but that was not good enough for the radical "Charcoals," who by the fall of 1864 had replaced their conservative rivals the "Claybanks" as the dominant Republican faction in the state. By calling for a new state constitution abolishing slavery immediately, the Charcoals made emancipation the leading issue in the campaign. They won overwhelming victories in all the districts but St. Louis.[111] Although the Missouri vote was an important blow for

---

106　Richard Smith to Joseph H. Barrett, August 14, 1864, William Henry Smith MSS, OHS.

107　*Cincinnati Gazette*, August 18, 1864, p. 2.

108　Indianapolis *Daily Journal*, September 20, 1864, p. 2.

109　James M. Ashley, speech before the Republican Congressional Convention at Toledo, May 24, 1864, in Benjamin W. Arnett, ed., *Orations and Speeches: Duplicate Copy of the Souvenir of the Afro-American League* (Philadelphia: A.M.E. Church, 1896), 300 (quotation). S. A. Raymond to John Sherman, May 17, 1864, John Sherman MSS, LC; *Cincinnati Enquirer*, October 17, 1864, p. 1.

110　Horowitz, *The Great Impeacher*, 101.

111　On Missouri emancipation, see Berlin et al., eds., *Freedom*, ser. 1, vol. 2, *The Wartime Genesis of Free Labor: The Upper South*, 556–62; Gienapp, "Lincoln and the Border States," 27–32, 36–37; Michael Fellman, *Inside War: The Guerrilla Conflict in Mis-*

black freedom, it was not necessarily an endorsement of federally enforced, universal abolition. At best, it was a call for statewide emancipation. And, if some Union military authorities in the area were to be
believed, the election was actually less an endorsement of *any* sort of
emancipation than a vote of confidence in the Union army, which successfully repelled a Confederate invasion of Missouri during the final
week of the political campaign.[112]

Statewide emancipation also took center stage in Maryland, where
citizens were scheduled to vote in October on a newly drafted constitution
outlawing slavery.[113] The abolition of slavery in Maryland was something
of a formality because, by 1864, the federal army and the slaves themselves had nearly destroyed the institution in the state. One of the delegates to the recent constitutional convention explained: "If one of your
servants saw fit to approach you tomorrow morning and say: 'I intend to
leave your service forever,' . . . you would not think it worth your while to
take any steps to prevent his absconding."[114] Nonetheless, the movement
for official emancipation faced stiff opposition. Much of the resistance
came from whites who still believed that blacks were better off as slaves.
Although a free black community continued to thrive in Baltimore and
blacks everywhere had proved themselves equal to whites in battle, a
Democratic delegate at the recent constitutional convention had wheeled
out old proslavery dogma about "the negro's condition" having been only
"bettered and improved in a state of slavery."[115] Even one of the proe-

souri during the American Civil War (New York: Oxford University Press, 1989), 65–
72; John W. Blassingame, "The Recruitment of Negro Troops in Missouri during the
Civil War," *Missouri Historical Review,* 58 (1964), 326–38; and William E. Parrish,
Turbulent Partnership: Missouri and the Union, 1861–1865 (Columbia: University of
Missouri Press, 1963), 178–96. In St. Louis in 1864, a Claybank counterrevolt led by
Frank Blair, Jr., split the proadministration electorate and assured victory for the
district's Democrats. See J. G. Nicolay to Abraham Lincoln, October 10 and 18, 1864,
RTL; and William Ernest Smith, *The Francis Preston Blair Family in Politics* (New
York: Macmillan, 1933), 2:294–95.

112 S. R. Curtis, "Report of Campaign against Major-General Sterling Price in October–
November, 1864," Provost Marshal's Report, NA.

113 See Jean H. Baker, *The Politics of Continuity: Maryland Political Parties from 1858 to
1870* (Baltimore: Johns Hopkins University Press, 1973), 102–11, 130–33; Charles
Lewis Wagandt, *The Mighty Revolution: Negro Emancipation in Maryland, 1862–
1864* (Baltimore: Johns Hopkins Press, 1964), 221–45.

114 Speech of Mr. Valliant, June 17, 1864, *The Debates of the Constitutional Convention
of the State of Maryland, Assembled at the City of Annapolis* (Annapolis: Richard P.
Bayly, 1864), 2:547. See Berlin et al., eds., *The Wartime Genesis of Free Labor: The
Upper South,* 481–99; Barbara Jeanne Fields, *Slavery and Freedom on the Middle
Ground: Maryland during the Nineteenth Century* (New Haven: Yale University
Press, 1985), 90–130; Wagandt, *The Mighty Revolution;* John W. Blassingame, "The
Recruitment of Negro Troops in Maryland," *Maryland Historical Magazine,* 58
(1963), 20–29.

115 Speech of Mr. Peter, June 17, 1864, *Debates of the Constitutional Convention,* 2:551.

mancipation delegates privately admitted that he thought "the Slave . . . is unfit for freedom *as yet.*"[116] Despite persistent racism and complaints that emancipation was not coupled with colonization or compensation, Maryland carried the new constitution, but only by a tiny majority provided by the soldier vote.[117] As if by divine calculation, Maryland's most prominent defender of slavery, Chief Justice Roger B. Taney, who had denied Dred Scott his freedom in 1857, died on the day of the vote. As the New York diarist George Templeton Strong put it, "two ancient abuses and evils were perishing together."[118]

The Maryland election was a victory for statewide emancipation, but, as in Missouri, the vote was not a clear call for *federal* emancipation. Indeed, debate over state-level abolition in Maryland crowded out any discussion of the antislavery amendment or any other proposal of national emancipation. The declining emphasis on federal emancipation was, in part, a result of a power shift in state politics. Many members of Congressman Henry Winter Davis's Unconditional Unionist faction, the group that supported federally mandated emancipation and had controlled the state Republican party for the past two years, lost their nomination bids to members of Montgomery Blair's Union party, a coalition of conservative Republicans and War Democrats. Blair had forged the Union party on the principle that state-level emancipation would actually preempt further federal interference in Maryland. He told one Democrat that the new constitution would create "neither an oligarchy of slave holders or of abolitionists, but [would] . . . leave the political power where it belongs to the white people of all sections of the country." And if Davis had his way, Blair explained, radicals would defeat the new antislavery constitution in order to give Congress an excuse to "suppress stability in the State and show the necessity of putting an extinguisher upon state rights."[119] Many of the Marylanders who voted in favor of emancipation may have done so not because of their attitudes toward slavery or black Americans, but because they hoped to immunize their state from further federal intrusion. Such people understandably felt betrayed when, only days after the adoption of the new constitution, federal commander Lew Wallace, acting on his own authority, declared void the state laws allowing

---

116 William Meade Addison to Hiram Barney, July 6, 1864, Hiram Barney MSS, HEH.
117 Donald Scott Barton, "Divided Houses: The Civil War Party System in the Border States" (Ph.D. diss., Texas A&M University, 1991), 132–35; Wagandt, *Mighty Revolution*, 260–63.
118 Allan Nevins and Milton Halsey Thomas, eds., *The Diary of George Templeton Strong* (New York: Macmillan, 1952), 3:501.
119 Montgomery Blair to Thomas G. Pratt, March 27, 1864, Blair family MSS, LC. The strategy of the Maryland unionists is also described in Archibald Stirling to A. J. Creswell, "Wednesday," vol. 6, James A. J. Creswell MSS, LC.

former owners to hold the children of freed people as apprentices.[120] The triumph of black freedom in Maryland thus masked a continued resistance to federal programs of emancipation and equal rights. Or, to put it more precisely, Maryland's vote for statewide emancipation fell short of being a mandate for the *national* abolition amendment.

When the election was over, the results showed a clear victory for the National Union party. Lincoln won 55 percent of the popular vote and the electoral votes of all but three states – New Jersey, Kentucky, and Delaware. A month after the election, the president told Congress that the results represented a popular mandate for the antislavery amendment: "It is the voice of the people now, for the first time, heard upon the question."[121] The interpretation seemed reasonable enough. The Republican national platform called explicitly for an antislavery amendment. Moreover, voters in 1864 knew that a Democratic victory meant no abolition amendment and an end to federal emancipation commitments, whereas a Republican victory meant a continued war for freedom.

Still, one of the most remarkable aspects of the 1864 political campaign was the disappearance rather than the dominance of the antislavery amendment. Throughout the campaign, the amendment was overshadowed by Lincoln's Niagara letter, the miscegenation "scare," and a slate of other issues more likely to arouse local concern. The results of the election would long be remembered, but the neglect of the amendment would soon be forgotten.

Much more than a popular decision for emancipation, the vote of 1864 was a call for the return of stability under the Union. Certainly, many who voted in 1864 hoped that their ballots would help free the slaves, but even some of the fiercest enemies of slavery understood that black freedom could only be built on the foundation of a restored Union. In explaining the meaning of the coming election, a Massachusetts antislavery man wrote that he only wanted "safety for free institutions, and a true peace; . . . [and was] willing to trust to the negro's getting his rights, if we can only establish a true democracy; for the greater involves the lesser."[122] Meanwhile, others less committed to emancipation were equally convinced that only a Union victory would assure "safety for free institutions." The Albany, New York minister W. B. Sprague, for example, was a

120   Andrew S. Ridgely to A. W. Bradford, November 10, 1864; and W. Viers Bouie to Bradford, November 16, 1864, both in A. W. Bradford MSS, MdA. See Fields, *Slavery and Freedom on the Middle Ground*, 148–49.

121   *CW*, 8:149.

122   J. M. Forbes to G. V. Fox, September 6, 1864, in Sarah F. Hughes, *Letters and Recollections of John Murray Forbes* (Boston: Houghton Mifflin, 1900), 2:104.

lifelong Democrat who had never hesitated "to bear testimony against Abolitionism," but in 1864, he voted the Union ticket. Sprague had been turned by a speech in which the famous orator Edward Everett warned that Democratic victory would lead to disunion and a massive uprising of black Americans.[123] Antiabolitionists like Sprague must have been surprised after the election to hear their votes being interpreted as a mandate for the emancipation amendment.

To a certain extent, Republicans who read the election results as a call for black freedom were deceiving themselves. Although it was true that many who voted the Union ticket supported the administration's emancipation policy, many others who voted the same way were determined to resist any further agitation by the federal government on behalf of African Americans. One conservative Republican even predicted, "unless the administration is . . . surrounded by men who will look at *other* questions as well as that of the *negro,* the great Union organization, strong as it is, will go to the Devil in a year."[124] That forecast turned out to be on target, but at least the cement of the Union party held long enough for Congress to adopt the Thirteenth Amendment.

123   W. B. Sprague to Erastus Corning, November 8, 1864, Erastus Corning MSS, Albany Institute of History and Art. For Everett's speech, see Everett, *The Duty of Supporting the Government in the Present Crisis of Affairs. Address Delivered in Faneuil Hall, October 19, 1864,* esp. pp. 4, 6–7, 14.
124   Lewis D. Campbell to Thurlow Weed, November 12, 1864, Thurlow Weed MSS, UR.

7

A King's Cure

With the impassioned and frenetic political campaign of 1864 at an end, Frederick Douglass reflected: "We have been living at an immense rate, and have hardly had time to take breath and review the ground over which we have travelled. . . . Only after-generations will be able to contemplate intelligently the events of to-day, and appreciate their grand significance."[1] Douglass was right – to a degree. With the conflict still raging, it was too soon to render final judgments, but Americans were nonetheless determined to make sense of the war, to understand its origins and survey its results. The renewed debate on the antislavery amendment, which followed soon after the election, became a forum for northerners to express for themselves and each other the way the war had transformed their world.

Over the course of the renewed debate, it became clear that the coalition in favor of the amendment was growing. Many came to support the measure out of newfound principle, others out of political opportunism. As before, the amendment's backers held diverse, sometimes competing notions about the measure's scope and meaning. Yet, even more striking than this division of opinion was the shared realization among the amendment's supporters – and even some of its opponents – that the amending process was a means not only of social reform but of making history. Americans of all stripes now came to appreciate the amending method as a way of announcing a new national identity, of defining the present for the "after-generations" described by Douglass.

The New Campaign for Constitutional Emancipation

In the first few weeks after his election, Lincoln made two bold strokes to secure black freedom. First, he replaced Chief Justice Roger Taney, who had died in October, with Salmon P. Chase, a renowned champion of African American freedom and equality. Second, he urged Congress to adopt the abolition amendment immediately.

The appointment of Chase was an obvious but painful choice for Lincoln. The former treasury secretary had angled to take Lincoln's place in

---

1 "The Final Test of Self-Government: An Address Delivered in Rochester, New York, on 13 November 1864," in John W. Blassingame et al., eds., *The Frederick Douglass Papers* (New Haven: Yale University Press, 1991), ser. 1, 4:32–33.

the White House for years. As the president put it, Chase had "the Presidential maggot in his head and it will wriggle there as long as it is warm."[2] But, while Lincoln may have frowned on Chase's scheming, he approved of his stand in favor of universal emancipation. If the antislavery amendment were not adopted soon, an antislavery chief justice like Chase could take the alternative route of having the Supreme Court issue a judicial decision that affirmed all wartime acts of emancipation, a method that one editor described as "a short cut to freedom."[3]

Yet even with Chase in place, the possibility still loomed of slavery's defenders someday retaking the Court and ruling against wartime emancipation. To assure the permanence of black freedom, Chase's appointment had to be supplemented by the antislavery amendment. The measure was sure to be adopted by the recently elected House of Representatives, which would have a two-thirds Republican majority. But that body was not scheduled to meet until December 1865, a full year after the meeting of the current, lame-duck session. If the president did not want to wait that long, he could call a special session of the new Congress as soon as his second term began in March. For some people, however, even this four-month delay was too long.[4]

The president was one of those who wanted to see the amendment adopted by this Congress rather than the next. If Congress quickly adopted the amendment and submitted it to the states, Lincoln could say that slavery was out of his hands. No longer could his opponents spread the false word that only his demand for emancipation stood in the way of peace. Also, the adoption of the amendment sooner rather than later might heal divisions among Republicans about reconstruction. In mid-1864 Lincoln had clashed with party radicals over whether Congress had the power to abolish slavery by statute. With slavery outlawed by constitutional amendment, at least part of the squabble over reconstruction would be silenced. As one Ohio Republican predicted, "with the Constitutional Amendment the war of faction ends – the troubles of reconstruction disappear."[5] Others less naive saw that ideological differences over race and federal power would fuel factionalism even after slavery was gone, but no one could deny that the process of rallying Republicans behind the amendment would achieve at least a moment of

---

2 Michael Burlingame, ed., *An Oral History of Abraham Lincoln: John G. Nicolay's Interviews and Essays* (Carbondale: Southern Illinois University Press, 1996), 85.
3 *Rochester Democrat and American*, December 29, 1864, p. 2.
4 See, for example, John Jay to Charles Sumner, November 15, 1864, Charles Sumner MSS, HL.
5 Warner M. Bateman to Salmon P. Chase, December 10, 1864, Warner M. Bateman MSS, WRH. For a similar view, see Henry Everett Russell, "The Constitutional Amendment," *Continental Monthly*, 6 (September 1864), 323–24.

party unity. The president also saw in a hasty adoption of the amendment an opportunity to narrow the breach between Republicans and Democrats. The abolition of slavery, the most divisive issue between Republicans and Democrats, might open the way to an expanded Union party that would last beyond the war. In attempting to secure the amendment's adoption in the coming session of Congress, Lincoln and others – most notably Secretary of State William H. Seward – would test the waters to see if a new coalition party was viable, for the measure could pass only if a significant number of its former opponents switched their positions. The adoption of the amendment, then, would be both a rehearsal and a catalyst for the establishment of a permanent Union party.

Of all Lincoln's reasons for wanting a speedy adoption of the amendment, by far the most influential was the public's demand for the measure. Although the amendment was generally neglected during the campaign of 1864, people proclaimed the election results an endorsement of abolition. From Kentucky as well as from Maine, Congressman Elihu B. Washburne received word that "the sun of freedom has arisen upon us" and that "the administration will have no cause to hold back now for the want of endorsement by the people."[6] According to Frederick Douglass, African Americans also read the election results as a mandate that "the Constitution of the United States shall be so changed that slavery can never again exist in any part of the United States."[7] Even a delegation of former slaveholders from Louisiana joined in the call against "the institution to which habit had alone wedded them."[8]

Lincoln had good reason, then, to ask for the amendment's immediate adoption. "The next Congress will pass the measure if this does not," he declared in his annual message to Congress. "Hence there is only a question of *time* as to when the proposed amendment will go to the States for their action. And as it is to so go, at all events, may we not agree that the sooner the better?"[9]

Although the tone of the president's message was optimistic, the fate of slavery – and of the Union – was still uncertain. Confidence in the Union armies, although invigorated by victories in recent months, remained unsteady. Richmond and Petersburg stood strong against General Ulysses S. Grant's siege; Confederate forces in Tennessee pressed northward without resistance; and General William Tecumseh Sherman's Army of the West

6 James H. Bristow to Elihu B. Washburne, December 9, 1864, and Charles L. Stephenson to Washburne, November 21, 1864, both in Elihu B. Washburne MSS, LC.
7 "The Final Test of Self-Government," in Blassingame et al., *Frederick Douglass Papers*, ser. 1, 4:36.
8 A. P. Field, Charles Smith, I. M. Wells, R. King Cutler, R. R. Taliafero, M. F. Bonzano to Nathaniel P. Banks, December 12, 1864, Nathaniel P. Banks MSS, LC.
9 *CW,* 8:149.

was nowhere to be found, having disappeared into eastern Georgia after taking Atlanta. If the Union failed to press the military advantage it had gained during the fall, Lincoln and his party might not have the popularity to enact its policies, including the antislavery amendment.

Things were equally unpredictable in party politics. Edward Bates, who would soon resign as attorney general, mused that "there are now, no parties, properly so called." Although Bates overstated matters when he wrote that the Republican party was decomposing "into its original elements," the party did still suffer from feuds among the various factions.[10] The Democrats were even more divisive. The party manager Samuel L. M. Barlow reported that many who had called themselves Democrats prior to the recent election were "today, practically, members of no party."[11] Haunted by old animosities between the prowar and propeace wings, the Democracy now faced the additional threat of a bolt by recently defeated congressional Democrats, who were torn between remaining loyal to their debilitated organization and making alliances with the party in power.

Fluidity in politics worked both for and against the antislavery amendment, which was now sponsored by James M. Ashley in the House of Representatives. Factional strife within the Democracy was surely a benefit: fifteen or so Democrats who had voted against the measure back in June might now switch their vote, or so some Washington insiders predicted.[12] But factionalism within the Republicans was still a problem: radical members of the party might turn against the amendment in favor of some version that established legal equality for African Americans more explicitly. Ashley himself wanted more radical wording but was careful not to press his case lest he "hazard the passage" of *any* antislavery amendment.[13] Because the amendment required a supermajority for adoption, Ashley wisely kept the wording as it was and used other legislation, such as his own reconstruction bill, to press for explicitly radical measures like black male suffrage and land for ex-slaves.[14]

Ashley needed harmony within his own party and cooperation between the two parties, but, early in the session, it seemed that he would get neither. James Brooks, a Democrat who, a year before, had urged his party to retreat from the defense of slavery, now called on Democrats to stand

10 Edward Bates to Anna Ella Carroll, November 5, 1864, Anna Ella Carroll MSS, HSMd.
11 Samuel L. M. Barlow to Montgomery Blair, January 4, 1865, Samuel L. M. Barlow letter books, HEH.
12 Letter of "Castine," *Sacramento Daily Union,* January 11, 1865, p. 1.
13 *CG,* 38th Cong., 2d sess. (January 31, 1865), 531.
14 Robert F. Horowitz, *The Great Impeacher: A Political Biography of James M. Ashley* (Brooklyn: Brooklyn College Press, 1979), 106–9; Herman Belz, *Reconstructing the Union: Theory and Policy during the Civil War* (Ithaca: Cornell University Press, 1969), 251–68.

against the antislavery amendment. When Brooks sat down, the Iowa Republican Hiram Price rose and ripped into the Democracy as a treasonous body in league with the Confederacy and "endeavoring to tear down the best Government ever given to mankind."[15] The next day, the radical Republican Henry Winter Davis, still determined to stir his party against Lincoln, introduced a resolution that condemned the president's foreign policy and in effect denounced his presidency.[16] Harmony in the halls of Congress eluded Ashley.

The Ohio congressman could see that he had not prepared the political ground well. He announced that the debate on the amendment would be postponed until January.[17] Then, over the Christmas holiday, he wrote notes to Republican congressmen who had returned home, imploring them to lobby for the amendment. By his calculation, 108 members were pledged to the amendment – 14 short of adoption – but 19 current opponents might change their positions or at least sit out the vote. He therefore urged Republicans to sing the praises of the measure in their home states. At the very least, wrote Ashley, Republicans should convince their opponents that the amendment would "dispose of the slavery agitation." "Is there not one sinner among the opposition from your State who is on praying ground," he asked one Pennsylvania congressman.[18] But as the date of the final vote approached, converts seemed in short supply.

Lame Ducks, Lobbyists, and Lincoln

Ashley was not alone in the search for disciples among the damned. Members of the Lincoln administration joined him in the effort to persuade Democrats to change their position. Foremost among the amendment's allies was Lincoln himself. No piece of legislation during Lincoln's presidency received more of his attention than the Thirteenth Amendment.

The president, who had seemed rather indifferent to the amendment during the previous session of Congress, began lobbying for the measure as soon as the new session met.[19] On December 7, he talked strategy with

---

15   CG, 38th Cong., 2d sess. (December 14, 1864), 38–44 (quotation at 38).
16   Ibid. (December 15, 1864), 52–53; Glyndon G. Van Deusen, *William Henry Seward* (New York: Oxford University Press, 1967), 399.
17   CG, 38th Cong., 2d sess. (December 15, 1864), 53–54.
18   J. M. Ashley to "Dear Sir," December 25, 1864 (form letter with annotation), Edward McPherson MSS, LC.
19   Some historians contend that Lincoln tried to secure votes for the amendment even before Congress convened in December 1864. Such accounts rely on the testimony of Charles A. Dana, the assistant secretary of war, whose 1898 memoir claimed that Lincoln told Dana in March 1864 to offer patronage deals to three congressmen in exchange for their votes for the amendment. In the same meeting, according to Dana, Lincoln also urged the hasty admission of the solidly Republican state of Nevada in

Abel Rathbone Corbin. Once a congressional clerk, Corbin was now a wealthy New York City financier with powerful friends in city politics.[20] He promised to secure a few votes for the amendment in exchange for Lincoln's gratitude – and, implicitly, the favors gratitude might bring. The president told Corbin of his wish to see the amendment adopted prior to his second inauguration in March; he did not want to call a special session of Congress. The New Yorker thought he could change the votes of some Democratic congressmen from his state, or at least guarantee their absence for the final vote. Uncertain about the rules for adopting an amendment, Lincoln had to be assured by Corbin that absences would indeed be helpful, that passage required only two-thirds approval of the members in attendance rather than two-thirds of the whole House.

Corbin already had a plan to win the votes of Austin A. King and James S. Rollins, two Missouri congressmen who had voted against the amendment in June. Lincoln was scheduled to appoint a new federal judge in Missouri. Corbin asked him to leave the place vacant so that King and Rollins might earn some say in the appointment by voting for the amendment. In this way, the president would not commit himself to anyone but would use the vacant judgeship – "a serpent hanging up on a pole," Corbin called it – to manipulate votes.[21] Although there is no positive evidence that Lincoln took Corbin's plan seriously, the president never did appoint anyone to the Missouri post. Also, according to Rollins, the president called him into the White House some weeks before the final vote and told him of his "anxiety to have the measure pass." Lincoln may have been putting Corbin's strategy into play. The Missouri congressman delighted the president by telling him that he already planned to back the

order to secure one more state for ratification. But Dana's account, written more than thirty years after the war, confuses Lincoln's involvement in the Nevada statehood act with his sponsorship of the Thirteenth Amendment later that winter. Certainly, some people recognized early on that Nevada's admission would aid the amendment (see, for example, D. L. Gregg to Elihu B. Washburne, March 25, 1864, Elihu B. Washburne MSS, LC; and George Rothwell Brown, ed., *Reminiscences of Senator William M. Stewart* [New York: Neale Publishing Company, 1908], 166). But there is no evidence that Lincoln had this motive when he helped Nevada become a state. In general, Lincoln did not seem to care about Nevada, and he probably did not realize that, in signing Nevada into the Union, he was helping the cause of the amendment. See Charles A. Dana, *Recollections of the Civil War* (New York: D. Appleton, 1898), 174–77; Earl S. Pomeroy, "Lincoln, the Thirteenth Amendment, and the Admission of Nevada," *Pacific Historical Review*, 12 (December 1943), 362–68.

20 Mark Wahlgren Summers, *The Era of Good Stealings* (New York: Oxford University Press, 1993), 184–85; Summers, *The Plundering Generation: Corruption and the Crisis of the Union, 1849–1861* (New York: Oxford University Press, 1987), 102–3; William S. McFeely, *Grant: A Biography* (New York: W. W. Norton, 1981), 319–29.

21 Abel Rathbone Corbin to Lincoln, December 8, 1864, RTL.

amendment and that he could probably secure King's support as well.[22] Presidential arm twisting may not have been wholly responsible for the Missourians' change of heart, but Lincoln's pressure surely played a part.

Less willing to reverse their positions on slavery were Samuel "Sunset" Cox of Ohio and John Todd Stuart of Illinois, two other lame-duck congressmen who talked with Lincoln about the amendment. Both thought that peace should take priority over abolition, although Cox already had suggested privately that Democrats might "vote to '*eliminate*' the 'Slavery question' out of our politics, for the purpose of future success."[23] During the Christmas recess of Congress, Cox joined Stuart, Lincoln's former law partner and Mrs. Lincoln's cousin, in promising to support the amendment if a "sincere effort" toward peace were attempted but failed.[24] Perhaps the offer made Lincoln more sympathetic to the plan of Francis P. Blair, Sr., who had asked to go to Richmond to negotiate with Jefferson Davis. If the president let the old man go, and Davis rejected all terms short of Confederate independence, as Lincoln knew he would, Democrats like Cox and Stuart might vote for the amendment. If Lincoln conceived of such a strategy, he kept it to himself. But it may have been partly for the cause of the amendment that the president allowed Blair to visit Richmond unofficially in late December.

Besides Ashley and Lincoln, the most diligent manager of the amendment was Secretary of State William Henry Seward. Perhaps on Lincoln's advice, but just as likely on his own initiative, Seward decided to take a leading role in steering the amendment through Congress. The lobby he organized became renowned, not only for its dogged pursuit of opposition votes but also for its use of questionable, even corrupt methods. Even before sustained debate on the amendment began, lame-duck Democrats told of Republican agents using "temptations" and "the usual appliances of power" to swing the opposition to the amendment.[25] It was Seward's men that one newspaper correspondent probably had in mind when he complained of "rascality" within the so-called third house of lobbyists.[26] The lobby included William N. Bilbo, a Tennessee native and former Confederate who knew Seward from their days in the Whig party; Robert W. Latham, a New Yorker who had been a liaison between speculators

---

22 Isaac N. Arnold, *The Life of Abraham Lincoln* (Chicago: Jansen, McClurg, 1885), 358–59.
23 S. S. Cox to Manton Marble, December 7, 1864, Manton M. Marble MSS, LC.
24 Samuel S. Cox, *Union – Disunion – Reunion: Three Decades of Federal Legislation* (1885; repr., Freeport, N.Y.: Books for Libraries Press, 1970), 310–11.
25 S. S. Cox to Manton Marble, December 21, 1864, Marble MSS, LC; Samuel L. M. Barlow to William H. Wadsworth, December 28, 1864, Samuel L. M. Barlow letter books, HEH.
26 *Cleveland Plain Dealer*, January 7, 1865, p. 2.

and politicians during the Buchanan administration; George O. Jones, an agent of the powerful New York Central Railroad; and Richard Schell, a member of Tammany Hall, the leading Democratic organization of New York City. Their motives were obscure. Perhaps they acted out of friendship with Seward, or perhaps they simply owed or sought favors from him. Or, as seems to have been the case with Bilbo, they genuinely believed they were acting for the Union cause.[27]

During the first few weeks of December, the Seward lobby set to work. Bilbo sought allies among Democratic congressmen, and found a valuable one in Homer A. Nelson, a one-term representative from Poughkeepsie, New York, who had raised a regiment of volunteers at the start of the war. For help on the House floor, Bilbo relied also on Augustus Frank, a representative from western New York and the nephew of George W. Patterson, one of Seward's oldest friends. Nelson and Frank did not speak publicly in favor of the amendment, but both demonstrated their allegiance to the measure – and to Seward – by pressuring New York Democrats to lend their support.[28] While Bilbo worked directly with congressmen in Washington, George O. Jones operated in Albany, where, in December, he met with Governor Horatio Seymour, the most prominent Democrat in the Union besides George McClellan, and Dean Richmond, the head of the Albany Regency, one of the oldest Democratic organizations in New York. Seymour and Richmond were ambivalent about the amendment. They wanted the Democrats to shed their proslavery image, but they also worried that the amendment would disturb the balance between federal and state power. By the end of the meeting, and apparently without offering any enticements, Jones had secured a halfway commitment from the Democrats: although they refused to endorse the amendment, they would also "not advise against voting for it."[29]

As Seward wheeled his lobby into action, Montgomery Blair made independent efforts along a similar line. The former postmaster general wished to use the amendment to build a coalition of Democrats and conservative Republicans. "Having settled by the Constitution that Slavery can be no more," Blair explained to his friend Samuel L. M. Barlow,

---

27 LaWanda Cox and John H. Cox, *Politics, Principle, and Prejudice, 1865–1866: Dilemma of Reconstruction America* (New York: Free Press, 1963), 1–30. On Bilbo's early support of the Confederacy, see William N. Bilbo, "The Past, Present, and Future of the Southern Confederacy . . . ," cited in Drew Gilpin Faust, *The Creation of Confederate Nationalism: Ideology and Identity in the Civil War South* (Baton Rouge: Louisiana State University, 1988), 7, 15.

28 At least two Washington correspondents credited Frank with the change of four votes in the New York delegation. See *New York Tribune*, February 1, 1865, p. 1; and *New York Herald*, February 2, 1865, p. 5.

29 William N. Bilbo to William Henry Seward, December 20, 1864, Seward MSS, UR.

the Democratic kingpin, radical Republicans would be brought "face to face with the question which is next in order and which they dread to broach but will be forced to meet when the Slave question is disposed of – that is the Negro equality question." And when the radicals took their inevitable stand in defense of black equality, they would be scorned by the public and left powerless against the conservatives and Democrats. Did it not then make sense, asked Blair, for Barlow to persuade his friends in Congress to vote for the amendment and to print an endorsement of the measure in the *New York World,* the party organ that Barlow partly owned?[30] Barlow had rejected this scheme the previous May, when Blair had first proposed it, but in the wake of Democratic defeat, and with the ultimate passage of the amendment assured, the plan now seemed more reasonable. Although Barlow refused to support the amendment and doubted Blair's promise of a rosy future for the Democrats if they turned against slavery, he conceded to his friend a pledge of neutrality and a promise to circulate Blair's ideas to leading Democrats.[31] During the holiday recess of Congress, Blair continued to pester Barlow and other Democrats. By Christmas, Blair's sister, Elizabeth Blair Lee, could report to her husband that Montgomery was hard at work for the amendment and that "a large number of Democrats are willing to vote for it now."[32]

In lobbying for the amendment, Blair had different motives from those of Lincoln and Seward. The president and secretary of state wanted to settle the constitutionality of emancipation while keeping within the Republican fold those party members in favor of African American rights. Blair simply wanted to read the radicals out of the party. Disparity in political standing and racial sympathies explained the difference in approach. Blair blamed his alienation from the Lincoln administration on the radicals, and he wanted revenge. He also despised the radicals for their hostile posture toward the South, and he thought they overestimated the ability of blacks to thrive as free people in a country without slavery. Seward and Lincoln, in the meantime, had survived challenges from the radicals and had come to sympathize with their racial attitudes, though, like Blair, they wished the radicals were less vindictive toward the South. Unlike Blair, the president and his secretary of state had no need or desire

30 Blair to Barlow, December 20, 1864, Samuel L. M. Barlow MSS, HEH. Also see Blair to Barlow, January 7 and 12, 1865, Barlow MSS, HEH.
31 Barlow to Blair, December 22, 1864, Samuel L. M. Barlow letter books, HEH. See Barlow to William H. Wadswoth, December 28, 1864, and Barlow to Samuel S. Cox, February 9, 1865, Barlow MSS, HEH.
32 Lee to Samuel Phillips Lee, December 26, 1864, in Virginia Jeans Laas, ed., *Wartime Washington: The Civil War Letters of Elizabeth Blair Lee* (Urbana: University of Illinois Press, 1991), 453.

to cut the radicals loose. Complicating the different motivations even further was the long-standing personal hatred between Seward, the veteran Whig, and Blair, the onetime Jacksonian Democrat. Independent of each other, and with different designs, these two bitter enemies took common ground in the effort to secure the Thirteenth Amendment.

Confronting Constitutional Failure

When debate on the amendment began in earnest on January 5, 1865, it was clear that, in the six months since the representatives last took up the issue, circumstances outside of Congress had reshaped the opinions of those within.[33] Although the speeches often repeated familiar themes, it was clear that changing circumstances had altered people's views of the amendment and that time had allowed people's attitudes to mature. For example, circumstances in the Confederacy had begun to change some congressmen's opinion of whether the Union's emancipation policy would prolong the Civil War. Most significantly, the Confederacy was on the verge of emancipating its slaves. In November, Jefferson Davis had asked the Confederate Congress to buy the freedom of forty thousand bondsmen and enlist them in the army. (Davis was careful to specify that the ex-slaves should serve only as unarmed laborers.) Who in the North could defend slavery, asked supporters of the amendment, now that the South was abolishing it?[34] Three more months would elapse before the Confederacy began emancipating and enlisting southern African Americans, but Davis's message, along with similar pleas already made by southern governors and military commanders, revealed that Confederate hopes of preserving slavery were secondary to the goal of independence. Davis already had made that point explicitly in speeches delivered during the last months of 1864.[35] For the Democratic representative James S. Rollins, Lincoln's ally from Missouri, Davis's recent speeches proved that the only way to obtain permanent peace was to crush the Confederacy and to dispose of the "disturbing element," slavery.[36]

33 Official debate began on January 9, 1865; the speeches on January 5 were unofficial because the House lacked the quorum necessary to consider the amendment formally. See *CG*, 38th Cong., 2d sess. (January 5, 1865), 120–26; and letter of "Castine," January 7, 1865, in *Sacramento Daily Union*, February 21, 1865, p. 1.
34 See, for example, *CG*, 38th Cong., 2d sess. (January 9, 1865), 170 (Yeaman), 173 (Morrill), 175 (Odell); and (January 12, 1865), 236 (Smith).
35 Dunbar Rowland, *Jefferson Davis, Constitutionalist: His Letters, Papers and Speeches* (Jackson: Mississippi Department of Archives and History, 1923), 6:394–97; Robert F. Durden, *The Gray and the Black: The Confederate Debate on Emancipation* (Baton Rouge: Louisiana State University Press, 1972), 110.
36 *CG*, 38th Cong., 2d sess. (January 13, 1865), 260.

Yet others could use recent events as evidence that peace was already at hand and should not be jeopardized by further legislation against slavery. By the time of the debate, northerners knew of two unofficial peace missions to Richmond, the one led by Francis P. Blair, Sr., and another by the Illinois Peace Democrat James Singleton (Singleton's real motive was to speculate in southern cotton).[37] Lincoln hoped that the missions, by their certain failure, would shatter northern dreams of an easy peace while simultaneously nurturing southern dissatisfaction with Confederate leaders. Conservative Democrats, however, took the missions seriously and insisted that the abolition amendment might stand in the way of final negotiations. William Cornell Jewett, an inveterate lobbyist for peace and a confidant of Singleton, petitioned Congress to suspend action on the amendment until the completion of the "wise policy of negotiations . . . inaugurated by the President of the United States."[38] Meanwhile, in the debate, Sunset Cox also asked how Republicans could condone peace initiatives while defending a constitutional amendment that might obstruct reconciliation.[39] Cox's point exposed the Republicans' hypocrisy. The party had denounced the Democrats for their peace platform in 1864, yet Union men, with Lincoln's permission, now traveled to talk peace with Confederates. All Republicans could do was deflect the peace talk, perhaps with humor. When Cox asked Congressman Thaddeus Stevens whether he also would like to go to Richmond, the distinguished radical and nemesis of the South retorted, "oh no; I do not think I would get back."[40] But as much as Republicans tried to avoid the subject of peace, the issue would continue to lurk in the shadows, threatening to undercut potential support for the amendment among the opposition.

Just as changing circumstances forced congressmen to rethink the amendment's effect on peace, so did new developments reshape the discussion of the amendment's effect on race relations. New evidence appeared daily that white unionists everywhere were prepared to accept all African Americans as free people. Appeals for the emancipation

37 Ludwell H. Johnson, "Lincoln's Solution to the Problem of Peace Terms, 1864–1865," *Journal of Southern History*, 34 (November 1968), 579–80; James G. Randall, ed., *The Diary of Orville Hickman Browning* (Springfield: Illinois State Historical Library, 1933), 2:1–2; Elbert B. Smith, *Francis Preston Blair* (New York: Free Press, 1980), 363–65; Edward C. Kirkland, *The Peacemakers of 1864* (New York: Macmillan, 1927), 197–99.
38 Petition of William Cornell Jewett, January 13, 1865, RG 233, HR38A-H1.2, NA. On the connection between Jewett and Singleton, see letter of Jewett, in *New York Tribune*, February 6, 1865, p. 8, in which he reveals his knowledge of Singleton's mission.
39 CG, 38th Cong., 2d sess. (January 5, 1865), 125.
40 Ibid.; letter of "Castine," *Sacramento Daily Union*, February 21, 1865, p. 1.

amendment poured into Congress from constituents, state legislatures, and popular conventions throughout the North and the border states.[41]

But the clearest sign of the people's voice against slavery, argued amendment supporters, was the recent election. Following Lincoln's lead, Republican representatives like Godlove S. Orth of Indiana claimed that the vote represented a "popular verdict . . . in unmistakable language" in favor of the amendment.[42] Democrats countered vigorously – and correctly – that the amendment had been only a peripheral issue in the election. The question of constitutional emancipation had not been submitted to the voters of his state, New York congressman Martin Kalbfleisch argued; instead, "it was carefully kept out of view during the campaign."[43] Although one Democrat previously opposed to the amendment did admit that the Republican victory helped persuade him to change his vote, most opposition members were unimpressed by the election results.[44]

Former opponents of the amendment were more likely to be swayed by the evidence from Maryland and Missouri that whites in the border states were now amenable to emancipation. Before the House amendment debate began, Maryland adopted a new constitution that outlawed slavery. Then, during the debate on the amendment, Missouri's constitutional convention passed an ordinance abolishing slavery. Meanwhile, in Congress, border state representatives like Austin A. King and James Rollins delivered the most passionate and persuasive addresses in favor of the amendment.[45]

41 For examples, see R. E. Fenton to E. D. Morgan, January 18, 1865, Edwin D. Morgan MSS, NYS (New York legislature's endorsement); petition of W. W. Armstrong (with covering letter of John Brough), January 12, 1865, John Sherman MSS, LC (Ohio legislature's endorsement); *New York Daily News*, January 7, 1865, p. 3 (Kentucky antislavery convention's endorsement); *New York Daily News*, January 17, 1865, p. 1 (Missouri constitutional convention's endorsement); E. B. Chase to Thomas Allen Jenckes, January 6, 1865 (petition), and C. Bailey to Thomas A. Jenckes, January 18, 1865 (Rhode Island legislature's endorsement), both in Thomas A. Jenckes MSS, LC; *CG*, 38th Cong., 2d sess. (January 28, 1865), 481–82 (Illinois legislature's endorsement); (January 31, 1864), 522–23 (Maine legislature's endorsement).

42 *CG*, 38th Cong., 2d sess. (January 6, 1865), 142. See also, ibid. (January 7, 1865), 155 (Higby); (January 10, 1865), 189 (Kasson); (January 11, 1865), 220 (Broomall); (January 12, 1865), 244 (Woodbridge); (January 13, 1865), 258 (Rollins).

43 Ibid. (January 31, 1865), 529. For similar opinions, see ibid. (January 9, 1865), 178 (Ward); (January 11, 1865), 219 (Holman); (January 11, 1865), 220 (Cravens).

44 Ibid. (January 31, 1865), 524–25 (Herrick).

45 For evidence of Democrats persuaded to vote for the amendment by border state emancipation, see ibid., 523 (Coffroth) and 526 (Herrick). On the positive effect of King, Rollins, and other border state representatives, see Indianapolis *Daily Journal*, January 19, 1865, p. 2; *New York Evening Post*, January 14, 1865, p. 2; Martin Russell Thayer to Francis Lieber, January 14, 1865, Francis Lieber MSS, HEH; and James M. Ashley, "Address before the Ohio Society of New York, February 20, 1890," in Ben-

But the evidence from the border states cut both ways. Opponents of the amendment rightly pointed out that a vote for emancipation in a border state was not the same as an endorsement of abolition everywhere. Emancipation movements in Maryland and Missouri could actually fuel the arguments of those who preferred that slavery and abolition be left to the states. Opponents of the amendment asked, If the measure was not needed to achieve abolition in Maryland and Missouri, why was it needed for the other slave states? And why in particular should it be used against Kentucky and Delaware, both of which, like Maryland and Missouri, had remained loyal to the Union?[46]

Regardless of how congressmen read the news from the border states, they found it increasingly difficult to stand against emancipation when not only slavery but legal inequality was everywhere under attack. In Illinois, African Americans led by John Jones, a tailor born in North Carolina, organized a powerful movement against the state black laws that barred black testimony and black immigration. Impressed by the movement, as well as by some whites' opinion that "the Negro will make a better citizen than the Southern refugee," Governor Richard Yates and Republican state legislators repealed the state's black laws.[47] Meanwhile, African Americans continued their fight against segregation in the street-cars of Washington, D.C., and Philadelphia.[48] In almost every state in the Union, African Americans put their greatest efforts into securing the right to vote. As congressmen debated the amendment, African Americans in the Ohio Equal Rights League issued resolutions demanding an end to racial restrictions at the polls.[49] In Louisiana, the Convention of Colored Men petitioned the state legislature to give blacks the vote. Congress might pass the abolition amendment, declared the New Orleans *Daily True Delta,* one of the city's black newspapers, but only the state's guaran-

jamin W. Arnett, ed., *Orations and Speeches: Duplicate Copy of the Souvenir from the Afro-American League of Tennessee to Hon. James M. Ashley of Ohio* (Philadelphia: A.M.E. Church, 1894), 707–13.

46 *CG*, 38th Cong., 2d sess. (January 9, 1865), 182–83 (Clay); (January 11, 1865), 219 (Holman); (January 28, 1865), 481 (Finck) and 482 (Starr); (January 31, 1865), appendix, 54 (Harding).

47 J. G. Andrews to Richard Yates, Springfield, Ill., January 3, 1865, Yates family MSS, ISHL. See Springfield *Illinois State Register,* January 14, 1865, p. 1, 4; *Chicago Tribune,* January 5, 1865, p. 2; V. Jacque Voegeli, *Free but Not Equal: The Midwest and the Negro during the Civil War* (Chicago: University of Chicago Press, 1967), 166; James M. McPherson, ed., *The Negro's Civil War: How American Negroes Felt and Acted during the War for the Union* (1965; repr., Urbana: University of Illinois Press, 1982), 252–54.

48 William Dusinberre, *Civil War Issues in Philadelphia, 1856–1865* (Philadelphia: University of Pennsylvania Press, 1965), 176–77; McPherson, *The Negro's Civil War,* 255–64.

49 McPherson, *The Negro's Civil War,* 288–89.

tee of suffrage rights would assure a change in the actual condition of its black residents.[50] In New York City, members of the Cooper Institute joined Wendell Phillips and Frederick Douglass in declaring: "let no negro's hand drop the bayonet till you have armed it with the ballot."[51]

The recent reports of progress toward legal and political equality aroused old fears among white conservatives that the amendment represented the entering wedge of a federal equal rights program. "When the war is done for freeing the negroes," declared a Democratic editor, "the war is to go on to give him a vote, – a seat in the Jury Box, and c."[52]

The response to the charge that the amendment bestowed equal rights on African Americans revealed the diversity of attitudes held by the measure's defenders. So far, the various factions in favor of the amendment – War Democrats, border state unionists, Republican radicals, and Republican moderates – had been able to overlook their different attitudes toward black equality while agreeing that the amendment would help end sectional conflict and ensure the constitutionality of emancipation. But now that equality before the law was becoming more of a reality than an abstraction, the conflicting attitudes began to surface, exposing fault lines that, after the war, would divide the coalition that now propelled the amendment toward adoption.

Congressmen who supported constitutional emancipation tended to take one of two general positions on black equality. War Democrats and border state unionists usually held that the amendment abolished only the chattel dimension of slavery, the dimension that allowed masters to own, sell, and rent humans as property and to coerce labor from them by force. The freedom envisioned by these conservatives would not allow for old-fashioned slavery but might well allow for discriminatory legislation against free blacks. They also suspected that once blacks were no longer forced to work, their lack of discipline would condemn them to fail in wage-labor society. George Yeaman of Kentucky, for example, backed the amendment but predicted that emancipation would bring to blacks "a natural, but not painful and violent, diminution."[53]

A second sort of opinion, subscribed to mostly by Republicans, held that African Americans would in fact be successful free laborers, but only if they enjoyed equality before the law in addition to freedom from their

---

50 LaWanda Cox, *Lincoln and Black Freedom: A Study in Presidential Leadership* (1981; repr., Urbana: University of Illinois Press, 1985), 124–26.

51 J. K. H. Wilcox to Abraham Lincoln, January 5, 1865, RTL; *National Anti-Slavery Standard*, January 14, 1865, p. 3.

52 *New York Evening Express*, January 17, 1865, p. 2. See also CG, 38th Cong., 2d sess. (January 7, 1865), 154 (Rogers); (January 9, 1865), 179 (Mallory).

53 CG, 38th Cong., 2d sess. (January 9, 1865), 171. For similar views, see ibid. (January 31, 1865), 524 (Coffroth) and 526 (Herrick).

prior chattel status. Equality before the law did not mean that African Americans were to be regarded as equivalent to whites, but simply that they deserved a chance to compete on fair terms. Republicans still squabbled among themselves about how far to push equality – they were divided, for example, on whether to distribute confiscated land to freed people – but they generally agreed that blacks should be equal to whites in their right to compete fairly in the labor market, to be free from arbitrary abuse, to own property, and to have a family. As the New York Republican Thomas T. Davis put it, he "would make every race free and equal before the law, permitting to each the elevation to which its own capacity and culture should entitle it, and securing to each the fruits of its own progression."[54]

Despite their belief in equality before the law, Republicans in prior debates on the amendment had tried to avoid the subject of equality for fear of losing Democratic support for the measure. Now, in the midst of African American struggles for equality throughout the Union, that strategy was nearly unworkable, but they tried to follow it nevertheless. Republicans postponed debate on Ashley's reconstruction bill and the Washington, D.C., desegregation bill until after the vote on the amendment. Similarly, party members put off introducing a bill that gave freed people the chance to rent and buy land confiscated from southern whites. They also avoided all discussion of the citizenship status of newly freed African Americans, even though the creation of a constitutional amendment offered an excellent opportunity to overturn Justice Roger B. Taney's decree against black citizenship in the 1857 *Dred Scott* decision. The political scientist and Union pamphleteer Francis Lieber continued to put off publication of his proposed equal citizenship amendment, awaiting the outcome of the current amendment debate in Congress. Finally, Republicans continued to hold their tongues on the meaning of the amendment's second clause, which gave Congress the power to enforce abolition by "appropriate legislation."

In those few instances during the amendment debate that Republicans did discuss the specific rights and powers conferred by the amendment, they evasively mentioned only those that the measure did *not* grant. For example, when opponents of the amendment claimed that it would lead to voting rights for black men, the Republican John R. McBride of Oregon responded: "a recognition of natural rights is one thing, a grant of political franchises is quite another." Few would dispute the idea that political

54 Ibid. (January 7, 1865), 155. For the evolving meaning of freedom and equality during this period, with citations to the vast literature on the subject, see Eric Foner, "The Meaning of Freedom in the Age of Emancipation," *Journal of American History*, 81 (September 1994), 435–60.

rights such as suffrage and jury service were not "natural" rights but rather exclusive rights created by governments. As McBride explained, "if political rights must necessarily follow the possession of personal liberty, then all but male citizens in our country are slaves."[55] But McBride's point left ambiguous the "natural" rights that did flow from the amendment. Similarly, when Sunset Cox pressed the radical Republican Thaddeus Stevens to explain where he stood on the issue of "negro equality," Stevens responded, "I never held to that doctrine of negro equality. . . . not equality in all things – simply before the laws, nothing else."[56] Rather than specifying how people were to be treated equally by the law, Stevens offered the evasive response that all people were not absolutely equal. He purposefully kept his interpretation of equality vague – at least during the amendment debate. For example, he did not mention, as he did on other occasions, his progressive program of land redistribution.[57] Republicans knew that if they turned the amendment debate into a forum on the rights and powers that should exist in the wake of a federal emancipation amendment, they might alienate those War Democrats and conservative Union party members whose votes were needed to carry the measure.

The necessity of keeping support for the amendment broad enough to secure its passage created a strange situation. At the moment that Republicans were promoting new, far-reaching legislation for African Americans, they had to keep this legislation detached from the first constitutional amendment dealing exclusively with African American freedom. Republicans thus gave freedom under the antislavery amendment a vague construction: freedom was something more than the absence of chattel slavery but less than absolute equality. That hazy definition allowed for a wide variety of thinking about the rights and powers promised by the amendment. The Republicans' political strategy thus left a legal snarl. Lawmakers during Reconstruction and legal thinkers of later generations would add further tangles by recovering *one* of the original ideas about civil rights and federal powers and attaching it to the amendment as *the* original meaning of constitutional freedom.

Historians have long understood that the amendment debate transpired during a crucial, transitional moment in the evolution of ideas about

---

55 *CG*, 38th Cong., 2d sess. (January 10, 1865), 202. For Democratic charges that the amendment's backers meant to grant the vote to blacks, see ibid. (January 9, 1865), 179 (Mallory); (January 10, 1865), 194 (Fernando Wood); (January 11, 1865), 219 (Holman); (January 12, 1865), 242 (Cox).

56 Ibid. (January 5, 1865), 125.

57 Hans L. Trefousse, *Thaddeus Stevens: Nineteenth-Century Egalitarian* (Chapel Hill: University of North Carolina Press, 1997), 167–68; Eric Foner, "Thaddeus Stevens, Confiscation, and Reconstruction," in Foner, *Politics and Ideology in the Age of the Civil War* (New York: Oxford University Press, 1980), 128–49.

freedom, but they have been less attentive to an equally important intellectual transition taking place in and around the debate: the new, widespread
acceptance of using a constitutional amendment to achieve a major reform. When Congress debated the amendment in mid-1864, the opposition's most powerful argument had been that the amendment would never
have been adopted by the Constitution's authors. In the intervening
months before the House again took up the amendment, however, the
public had warmed to the idea that the Constitution was a pliable text,
that the founders' wishes should not always constrain later generations.
So declared an article titled "The Constitution and Its Defects," which the
North American Review published during the summer of 1864. The author, E. L. Godkin, was an Irish-born journalist who had written for the
London *Daily News* before arriving in the United States in 1856. Like
Francis Lieber, another foreign-born advocate of constitutional amendments, Godkin was not burdened by the typical native-born American's
aversion to meddling with the text of the Constitution. Accustomed to
criticizing British political procedures that existed solely by reason of
tradition, the writer saw Americans' devotion to an unchanging constitutional text as a form of irrational idolatry. Before the war, Godkin explained, the Constitution was "held up to the gaze of the world as a final
result, which required no modification, and to which coming generations
would have to adapt themselves, not it to them." This "Constitution-
worship" undermined the nation's morals and put a stop to "all vigorous
exploration in the field of legislative science." The outbreak of the war
had exposed the imperfection of the Constitution, and the people should
seize the moment to correct the founding charter. The spirit of the document would prevail, promised Godkin, even if its words were altered.[58]

As might be expected, such ideas were scorned by defenders of slavery,
but they also sat poorly with some of those abolitionists who believed that
the original Constitution was already an antislavery instrument. Some of
these "radical constitutionalists," like Charles Sumner, did not see the
amendment as correcting the Constitution but rather as declaring its implicit antislavery character. Other radical constitutionalists, however, did
see the amendment as a fundamental revision that mistakenly implied a
proslavery Constitution.[59] Gerrit Smith had thought as much back in
February 1864, when he advised abolitionists not to press for the amend-

---

58 E. L. Godkin, "The Constitution, and Its Defects," *North American Review,* 99 (July
    1864), 117–18, 121; see Godkin to Charles Eliot Norton, October 12, 1864, Charles
    Eliot Norton MSS, HL.
59 See Jacobus tenBroek, *Equal under Law* (1951; repr., New York: Collier Books, 1965),
    170–73.

ment.[60] But now Smith picked up on Godkin's theme and constructed an argument that would allow like-minded thinkers to back the amendment. Just before the final amendment debate began, Smith wrote a public letter that postulated the existence of two Constitutions, one "literal" and the other "historical." The reformer initially opposed the antislavery amendment because it suggested that the literal Constitution, the document created by the framers, was proslavery. But he had come to accept the amendment as the necessary corrective to the historical Constitution, the imagined charter fixed on the American mind by proslavery politicians and jurists as "the cunning and wicked substitution" for the original text.[61] Smith's argument represented more than merely an expedient solution to the radical constitutionalists' quandary over the abolition amendment. It was, in effect, a revolutionary new understanding of the meaning of constitutionalism. Beginning in the 1790s, and then throughout the antebellum era, lawmakers and ordinary Americans, regardless of their view of slavery, had tended to assume that original meanings of the Constitution trumped meanings inscribed by later generations.[62] Radical constitutionalists had been among the most devoted originalists. They acknowledged that postrevolutionary generations had grafted onto the Constitution a new, proslavery meaning, but they assumed that convincing the public of the original, antislavery meaning would win the day.[63] Smith now broke ranks with his fellow radical constitutionalists. He agreed with them that later, proslavery meanings inscribed into the Constitution were a form of historical fiction, but he argued that they were so powerful a fiction that they could be unwritten only by rewriting the "literal" text of the founding document. By taking seriously the role of historicism in constitutional development, Smith anticipated the arguments of later opponents of originalism, and he helped open the floodgates for future amendments that would seek to perfect the Constitution.[64]

Echoes of the idea expressed by Smith and Godkin sounded in every locale. In the Kentucky legislature, William P. Kinney, a former defender

---

60 Gerrit Smith, "To My Neighbors," February 24, 1864, in Smith, *Speeches and Letters of Gerrit Smith* (New York: American News Company, 1865), 2:5.

61 Gerrit Smith to Charles Sumner, December 5, 1864, in Smith, *Speeches and Letters,* 2:57.

62 Jack N. Rakove, *Original Meanings: Politics and Ideas in the Making of the Constitution* (New York: Alfred A. Knopf, 1996), 339–65.

63 For an example of this sort of argument, see the pamphlet of William Howard Day quoted in Donald G. Nieman, *Promises to Keep: African Americans and the Constitutional Order, 1776 to the Present* (New York: Oxford University Press, 1990), 32.

64 Smith seemed to anticipate modern arguments in favor of respectable legal fictions; see, for example, Aviam Soifer, "Reviewing Legal Fictions," *Georgia Law Review,* 20 (Summer 1986), 871–915.

of slavery, invoked the flexibility of the Constitution as the safety valve of the Union. Believing the "Union to be the immutable basis of the government, and the Constitution its mutable policy," Kinney recommended that the legislature endorse the emancipation amendment.[65] The principle of an amendable Constitution was perhaps best articulated by an anonymous Cincinnati writer who denounced the "Constitution-worship" of Americans and proclaimed that "the work of the fathers was done to little purpose if it has not made the children wiser than they. . . . *The Constitution was made so well that we can make it better.*"[66]

Such arguments found an increasingly receptive audience. Northerners' initial resistance to reshaping the country's cornerstone had weakened, in large part because of the war's heightened destructiveness. The summer of 1864 had been the bloodiest so far. The amendment's defenders brought the violence into Congress by placing photographs of skeletal Union prisoners on members' desks. As usual, northerners blamed the South for the carnage, but they also now channeled their anger toward the founders, who had allowed the cause of the war, slavery, to survive. Indeed, as the prospect of sectional reunion became more real, northerners found it easier to point their fingers at long-dead framers than at the southerners who would be their brethren in a reconstructed Union. The amendment was thus a swipe at the founders and a sign that, as Godkin put it, "the spell [of the Constitution] has been broken by the war."[67]

Another reason that northerners warmed to the amendment was their increasing sense that the measure was a conservative form of change, a directed blow against the past instead of revolutionary break from it. During the summer, Lincoln had helped to give the amendment an anti-radical flavor when he invoked the measure as the preferred alternative to the Wade-Davis bill, which many perceived as an attempt to reorder southern society. Now, in the final amendment debate, the Pennsylvania Democrat Alexander Coffroth, who had spoken against the measure six months before, added more conservative gloss. With the amendment's adoption, he announced, "fanaticism 'Writhes with pain, and dies among its worshipers.'"[68]

One of the most effective methods used by amendment supporters to convey the measure's conservative character was to proclaim the permanence of patriarchal power within the American family in the face of this or *any* textual change to the Constitution. In response to Democrats who charged that the antislavery amendment was but the first step in a Re-

65 *New York Daily News*, January 16, 1865, p. 1.
66 "Jomil," to *Cincinnati Gazette*, February 4, 1865, p. 1.
67 Godkin, "The Constitution, and Its Defects," 123.
68 CG, 38th Cong., 2d sess. (January 31, 1865), 524.

publican design to dissolve all of society's foundations, including the hierarchical structure of the family, the Iowa Republican John A. Kasson denied any desire to interfere with "the rights of a husband to a wife" or "the right of [a] father to his child."[69] Outside of Congress, Godkin echoed Kasson's wish to retain the legal subservience of women and children. Gerrit Smith suggested that an amendment outlawing polygamy might complement one abolishing slavery.[70] As historians have noted, this sort of rhetoric reflected a common practice of invoking traditional notions about the family to assuage anxieties arising out of emancipation and an emergent system of contractual relations in both the household and the workplace.[71] But there was a more immediate purpose behind the rhetoric as well. When amendment supporters – especially those on the floor of the House – championed the permanence of the family structure, they purposefully distanced themselves from the women's rights activists who had helped to initiate the antislavery amendment and who now crowded the galleries to oversee the final debate. These women must have bristled at such talk. But they could take comfort in the knowledge that the conservative line would help secure the measure and thus might open the way for an amendment that *did* establish legal equality between the sexes.

Not all were swayed by assurances about the amendment's conservative character. The most ardent Peace Democrats like George Pendleton of Ohio believed that certain textual changes of the Constitution were inher-

69 Ibid. (January 10, 1865), 193. For examples of such Democratic accusations, see ibid., 1st sess. (June 14, 1864), 2940 (Fernando Wood); ibid., 2d sess. (December 14, 1864), 38 (Brooks); (January 7, 1865), 151 (Rogers); (January 12, 1865), 242 (Cox).

70 Godkin, "The Constitution, and Its Defects," 143–44; Smith to Charles Sumner, December 5, 1864, in Smith, *Speeches and Letters,* 2:59. For antipolygamy proposals, see resolution of Mr. Tripp, January 23, 1865, *Journal of the House of Representatives of Ohio for 1865,* 90–91 (see also *Cincinnati Enquirer,* January 26, 1865, p. 2); "Jomil," to *Cincinnati Gazette,* February 4, 1865, p. 1. Even before the amendment debate – and certainly after it – there was much resonance between antislavery and antipolygamy rhetoric, especially in the idealization of traditional gender roles. See Sarah Barringer Gordon, " 'The Liberty of Self-Degradation': Polygamy, Woman Suffrage, and Consent in Nineteenth-Century America," *Journal of American History,* 83 (December 1996), 815–47; David Brion Davis, "Some Themes of Counter-Subversion: An Analysis of Anti-Masonic, Anti-Catholic, and Anti-Mormon Literature," in Davis, *From Homicide to Slavery: Studies in American Culture* (New York: Oxford University Press, 1986), 137–54.

71 Amy Dru Stanley, *From Bondage to Contract: Wage Labor, Marriage, and the Market in the Age of Slave Emancipation* (Cambridge: Cambridge University Press, 1998); Stanley, "Conjugal Bonds and Wage Labor: Rights of Contract in the Age of Emancipation," *Journal of American History,* 75 (September 1988), 471–500; Kathleen Diffley, *Where My Heart Is Turning Ever: Civil War Stories and Constitutional Reform, 1861–1876* (Athens: University of Georgia Press, 1992), 24–26; Elizabeth B. Clark, "Matrimonial Bonds: Slavery and Divorce in Nineteenth-Century America," *Law and History Review,* 8 (Spring 1990), 25–54.

ently radical if not illegal, that there were implicit limits to the amending power in addition to the explicit restriction against using an amendment to deprive a state of its vote in the Senate.[72] And at a crucial moment in the debate, a radical Republican, George S. Boutwell of Massachusetts, seemed to agree with this line. He stated that no amendment should violate the Constitution's Preamble, which promised domestic tranquility, general welfare, and the blessings of liberty.[73] Other Republicans saw that Boutwell had weakened their position and quickly denounced their colleague's argument.[74]

But it was a Democrat, not a Republican, who best defended the principle of an unlimited amending power. Sunset Cox, the Ohio War Democrat, contended that Congress could not place limits on the amending power. If the people thought an amendment too radical, then they could vote against ratification; Congress could not usurp that power by becoming a "judge of what is subversion and what is change." In one of the most poetic addresses ever delivered in defense of constitutional change – and against what today goes by originalism – Cox declared, "this power of unlimited amendment is an element of democracy. . . . Why should we of the nineteenth century tie up the hands of the twentieth?"[75] Cox had both ideological and personal reasons for challenging Pendleton. As he explained to Manton M. Marble, the editor of the *New York World,* Cox thought that Pendleton "was bending the States' right bow, so far that Hickory couldn't stand it."[76] Knowing that the Democracy's most eminent advocates of states' rights, from Andrew Jackson (the "Hickory" of Cox's metaphor) to John C. Calhoun had supported constitutional revision, Cox had to speak up. Also, Cox already bore a personal grudge against Pendleton, in part because Pendleton was a leader of the rival Peace Democrats in Ohio and in part because Pendleton had lampooned Cox for arguing that the people could amend the Constitution "to do anything; to erect a monarchy in this country; to make the king of Dahomey, if you please, the king of this country."[77] (Cox's reference to the King of Dahomey, a notorious figure in popular accounts of Africa, demonstrated that race was never far from the minds of congressmen, even when they debated abstractions like the amending power.)[78] Al-

72　*CG,* 38th Cong., 2d sess. (January 11, 1865), 221–25.
73　Ibid. (January 11, 1865), 222.
74　Ibid. (January 12, 1865), 245 (Thayer); and (January 13, 1865), 264 (Garfield).
75　Ibid. (January 12, 1865), 241, 239.
76　S. S. Cox to Manton M. Marble, January 13, 1865, Manton M. Marble MSS, LC. See Samuel S. Cox, *Eight Years in Congress, From 1857 to 1865* (New York: D. Appleton, 1865), 396–97.
77　*CG,* 38th Cong., 2d sess. (January 10, 1865), 192.
78　Ibid. "The King of Dahomey," an image conflating fears of African American empowerment and foreign tyranny, became an oft-used expression in the second House

though Cox still believed that this particular amendment was ill-timed, he was grateful for the opportunity to stand against Pendleton on the general principle of an expansive amending power, and he knew that his speech had helped secure the measure. As he told Marble, "some of our [Democratic] members are beginning to think of voting it, who thought otherwise."[79]

The unanticipated exchange among lawmakers like Cox, Pendleton, and Boutwell revealed both the persistent fluidity in party politics as well as the embryonic state of thinking about amendments in general. For the moment, however, it seemed that most of the amendment's defenders, and even some of its detractors, had reached a consensus about the unlimited nature of the amendment power. One of the monumental legacies of the Thirteenth Amendment, then, was its signal to later generations that the Constitution could be amended to enact social reforms rejected or unimagined by the framers.

The Final Vote

Despite all of the efforts of lobbyists and proamendment speakers, passage of the amendment seemed unlikely. By mid-January, Washington insiders agreed that the measure had reached an impasse. One Republican representative complained to his wife that he was "utterly disgusted with the debate," which had been "a continuous freshet of floodwood from the beginning – generally a rehearsal of campaign speeches."[80] William Bilbo, the leader of the Seward lobby, reported that "the discussions in Congress, are not aiding us – the most strenuous efforts are made by the Leaders of the Democracy, to unite every member in the House against the Amendment."[81] Schuyler Colfax, the speaker of the House, along with a number of reporters covering the debate, put the amendment about five votes

debate. See ibid. (January 12, 1865), 241 (Cox); (January 12, 1865), 245 (Dawes); (January 13, 1865), 266 (Baldwin); (January 28, 1865), 486 (Morris); and *Richmond Dispatch,* February 7, 1865, reprinted in *New York Tribune,* February 10, 1865, p. 8. The use of the expression in early 1865 probably stemmed from the recent publication of the travelogue by Sir Richard Burton, *A Mission to Gelele, King of Dahome,* 2 vols. (London: Tinsley Brothers, 1864). The image of the king of Dahomey, however, had long been in circulation; see Robin Law, "Dahomey and the Slave Trade: Reflections on the Historiography of the Rise of Dahomey," *Journal of African History,* 27 (1986), 237–67.

79 Cox to Marble, January 18, 1865, Manton M. Marble MSS, LC.
80 Henry Laurens Dawes to Electa Dawes, January 13, 1865, Henry L. Dawes MSS, LC. See also Henry L. Dawes to Electa Dawes, January 11, 1865, Dawes MSS, LC.
81 William N. Bilbo to William Henry Seward, January 10, 1865, William Henry Seward MSS, UR. See also Indianapolis *Daily Journal,* January 14, 1865, p. 2; *New York Tribune,* January 12, 1865, p. 4.

short of adoption.[82] Sensing defeat, James Ashley postponed the final vote to the end of the month.[83]

It was at this point that the president wheeled into action on behalf of the amendment. A month before, he had talked only informally about the measure to congressmen like James Rollins and Austin King of Missouri. Now he became more forceful. To one representative whose brother had died in the war, Lincoln said, "your brother died to save the Republic from death by the slaveholders' rebellion. I wish you could see it to be your duty to vote for the Constitutional amendment ending slavery."[84] According to John B. Alley, a Republican congressman from Massachusetts, the president called two members of the House to the White House and told them to find two votes for the measure (it is not clear in Alley's story whether they already supported the amendment). When the congressmen asked for more specific instructions, Lincoln supposedly responded, "I leave it to you to determine how it shall be done; but remember that I am President of the United States, clothed with immense power, and I expect you to procure those votes."[85]

Alley's recollection, published twenty-three years after the event, was one of many reminiscences that implicated the president in the unseemly political bargaining that occurred during the days before the final vote. Such tales became ammunition for those critics of Lincoln – both his contemporaries and later historians – who accused him of forsaking principle in pursuit of policy. But the evidence in this instance does not bear out the image. There is not one reliable source, nor even an unreliable one, that reports the president making any specific promise in exchange for a vote for the amendment.[86]

Still, Alley's account, while difficult to believe in its specifics – Lincoln was not the sort of executive to say, "I am President . . . clothed with great power" – does suggest the role the President took in the final drive for the amendment. By endorsing the measure in his annual message and by directly confronting specific congressmen, Lincoln sent a clear signal that

82 *Chicago Tribune,* January 12, 1865, p. 1, January 13, 1865, p. 1; *New York Evening Express,* January 14, 1865, p. 4; Cornelius Cole to Olive Cole, January 10, 1865, Cornelius Cole MSS, University of California at Los Angeles.

83 *CG,* 38th Cong., 2d sess. (January 13, 1865), 257.

84 Isaac N. Arnold, *The History of Abraham Lincoln and the Overthrow of Slavery* (Chicago: Clarke, 1866), 469. Arnold did not identify the representative in question.

85 Allen Thorndike Rice, ed., *Reminiscences of Abraham Lincoln by Distinguished Men of His Time* (New York: North American Review, 1886), 585–86.

86 For a review of the relevant sources, see Frank J. Williams, "The End of Slavery: Abraham Lincoln and the Thirteenth Amendment," in Linda Norbut Suits and George L. Painter, eds., *Abraham Lincoln and a Nation at War: Papers from the Ninth Annual Lincoln Colloquium* (Springfield, Ill.: Lincoln Home National Historic Site, 1996), 69–86.

he would look kindly on those opposition members who switched their vote. The message was certainly received in the House. "The wish or order of the President is very potent," said an opponent of the amendment during the debate. "He can punish and reward."[87] Yet, rather than offer specific promises to potential converts, Lincoln let his lieutenants make the bargains and use his name to seal the agreement. This arrangement kept the president uninvolved in shady negotiations while giving tremendous bargaining power to Ashley, Seward, and others working for the amendment.[88]

Probably a few deals were designed in this fashion, and at least one is well documented. Congressman Anson Herrick, a New York Democrat, already approved of the amendment in principle (his paper, the *New York Atlas*, had published editorials in its favor), but he was reluctant to break with the majority of his party by voting against it. From Ashley and others – but not from the president – Herrick received a promise of an appointment for his brother as a federal revenue assessor in exchange for his vote. After Congress adopted the amendment, Lincoln assured Herrick that "whatever Ashley had promised should be performed," and he sent the recommendation for Herrick's brother to the Senate.[89] (Unfortunately for the congressman, Lincoln died after recommending his brother, and when the Senate refused to confirm the appointment, neither Seward nor President Andrew Johnson was willing to assist Herrick further.)[90]

Although Ashley and his allies meant to wait until the amendment had been adopted before informing the president of the details of the promises they made, on at least one occasion before the final vote they went to Lincoln directly. One day in mid-January, Ashley called at the White House bearing an offer of assistance for the amendment from agents of the Camden and Amboy Railroad Company. By a state incorporation law, the New Jersey company enjoyed a monopoly over the only line running the length of the state. For years, New Jersey residents had protested against the monopoly, and eventually the fight was taken up at the national level by reform-minded politicians who looked upon the monopoly with the same disdain that they regarded another antidemocratic institution, slavery. At the moment, the leading crusader against the Camden and

87 *CG*, 38th Cong., 2d sess. (January 9, 1865), 180. Also see ibid. (January 10, 1865), 189 (Kasson), 200 (Grinnell), and (January 31, 1865), appendix, 53–54 (Harding).
88 George S. Boutwell gave a sense of the process in *Reminiscences of Sixty Years in Public Affairs* (New York: McClure, Phillips, 1902), 36.
89 Herrick to William H. Seward, August 8, 1865, Seward MSS, UR.
90 See Herrick to William H. Seward, July 3, 1865, August 8 and 29, 1865, February 5, 1867, and Homer Nelson to Seward, July 29, 1865, November 20, 1866, all in William Henry Seward MSS, UR. Also see Montgomery Blair to Andrew Johnson, June 16, 1865, Andrew Johnson MSS, LC.

Amboy was Senator Charles Sumner. The Massachusetts senator had
sponsored a bill establishing a competitive railroad in New Jersey, and the
measure was now in the hands of the Senate Commerce Committee.
Sumner, who was not a member of the committee, pressured the committee to report out the bill. To Ashley the railroad lobbyists suggested a
swap: they would procure votes for the amendment, and he would persuade Sumner to lay off his bill. Ashley had no influence with Sumner, so
he took the matter to Lincoln. According to John G. Nicolay, Lincoln's
personal secretary, the president rejected the offer, saying he could "do
nothing with Mr. Sumner in these matters."[91]

The matter probably did not end there, however. After the House voted
to adopt the antislavery amendment, rumors circulated that the influence
of the Camden and Amboy had helped secure some votes.[92] The failure of
the Senate Commerce Committee to report the antimonopoly bill before
the end of the session fueled accusations. Many years later, veteran politicians still gossiped about a possible deal. In 1898, James Scovel, a longtime opponent of the railroad monopoly, reported that Congressman
Thaddeus Stevens had told him that Lincoln secured votes against
Sumner's bill and "these same votes helped Mr. Lincoln's amendment for
permanent emancipation." The amendment, said Stevens, "was passed by
corruption, aided and abetted by the purest man in America."[93]

Stevens's account of Lincoln's involvement, reported secondhand more
than forty years after the fact, seems implausible, especially when considered next to Nicolay's firsthand report. But perhaps Ashley did give the
railroad lobbyists the false impression that Lincoln would comply with
their wishes. Or maybe Republican senators on the Commerce Committee were convinced by Camden and Amboy agents, not by Lincoln, that
postponing Sumner's bill would lead to some positive result, such as the
passage of the amendment in the House, the election of a Republican
senator in New Jersey, or the ratification of the amendment by the New
Jersey legislature. One lobbyist for the railroad wrote to Joseph P. Bradley,
a lawyer for the Camden and Amboy and a future Supreme Court justice,
that he had spoken to members of the committee and other senators, and
"with all, the *political* view of the question was the one in which they

---

91 John Nicolay and John Hay, *Abraham Lincoln: A History*, (New York: Century Co.,
    1890) 10: 84–85; Helen Nicolay, *Lincoln's Secretary: A Biography of John Nicolay*
    (New York: Longmans, Green, 1949), 220–21.
92 See, for example, Indianapolis *Daily Journal*, February 6, 1865, p. 2.
93 James M. Scovel, "Thaddeus Stevens," *Lippincott's Monthly Magazine*, 61 (1898),
    550. See also Albert Gallatin Riddle, *Recollections of War Times: Reminiscences of
    Men and Events in Washington, 1860–1865* (New York: G. P. Putnam's Sons, 1895),
    324–25. Riddle, it should be noted, did not report a direct involvement by Lincoln in
    the railroad negotiations.

seemed most interested." In other words, congressmen were interested less in the specifics of the antimonopoly bill than in effects of the legislation on other matters such as the amendment. After talking with various senators, the monopoly's agent was "well satisfied" that any antimonopoly bill could be defeated, and that the present proposal by Sumner would not be hastily reported out of the Commerce Committee.[94]

Either by James Ashley or by Senate Republicans, or simply by their own judgment, the lobbyists for the Camden and Amboy were persuaded that helping the antislavery amendment would postpone Republican action against the monopoly. Almost certainly, the railroad's influence was behind the decision of Representative Andrew J. Rogers to absent himself on the day of the final vote. The New Jersey Democrat's opposition to the amendment was widely known, as was his association with the railroad.[95] But on the day of the final vote, Rogers was reported by Congressman James S. Rollins to be "confined to his room several days by indisposition."[96] That the report of Rogers's alleged illness should come from Rollins, who, with Lincoln's encouragement, had become one of the amendment's agents, suggests that the absence was part of a prearranged strategy.[97]

Vote swapping and patronage deals were not the only methods used by the lobby in the final push for the amendment. According to Albert G. Riddle, a Republican congressman during the first two years of the war, agents for the amendment assured a Democrat whose election was contested that he would receive his seat in the House if he voted correctly on the amendment.[98] The congressman whom Riddle had in mind was almost certainly Alexander Coffroth of Pennsylvania, who, upon voting for the amendment, was reviled by Democrats in his home district as a "stool-pigeon . . . ready at any moment to take his anxious flight to the [Republi-

---

94 J. R. Freese to Joseph P. Bradley, January 16, 1865, Joseph P. Bradley MSS, NJH. See George Shea to Bradley, January 16 and 25, 1865, Bradley, MSS, NJH. William Gillette, *Jersey Blue: Civil War Politics in New Jersey, 1854–1865* (New Brunswick, N.J.: Rutgers University Press, 1995), 300–4; George L. A. Reilley, "The Camden and Amboy Railroad and New Jersey Politics" (Ph.D. diss., Columbia University, 1951), 197–208.

95 *CG*, 38th Cong., 2d sess. (January 7, 1865), 150–54; Indianapolis *Daily Journal* December 29, 1864, p. 2.

96 *CG*, 38th Cong., 2d sess. (January 31, 1865), 530.

97 On Rollins's role in the amendment's adoption, see *New York Evening Post,* January 14, 1865, p. 2; and Elizabeth Blair Lee to Samuel Phillips Lee, February 2, 1865, in Laas, *Wartime Washington,* 472. George Middleton, another Democratic congressman from New Jersey, also missed the final vote, but, as the historian William Gillette observes, his absence was probably due less to the Camden and Amboy influence than to "his anti-slavery views, his lame-duck status, and his tendency to avoid tough votes." Gillette, *Jersey Blue,* 300.

98 Riddle, *Recollections of War Times,* 324–25.

cans'] well filled feed-troughs."[99] Republicans in the next Congress awarded Coffroth the promised congressional seat, though they ultimately forced the Democrat out of the House when the election was contested again. Yet, even without the urging of the lobby, Coffroth might have supported the amendment out of loyalty to the president, a personal friend. (He would later serve as one of Lincoln's pallbearers.)[100] Also, any Democrat who faced the prospect of leaving Congress was likely to expect that, even without a specific promise, a vote for the amendment would result in future assistance from Republicans. For example, because Congressman James E. English, a lame-duck Democrat from Connecticut, voted for the amendment, he was rewarded by Horace Greeley's endorsement in the coming governor's race, which English lost.[101]

Although most of the amendment's agents relied on accepted if ignoble methods of persuasion, some lobbyists did offer outright bribes. Robert W. Latham, one of Seward's men, boasted that "money will certainly do it, if patriotism fails." And the secretary of state seemed ready to underwrite any expense.[102] According to the newspaper correspondent Whitelaw Reid, members of the New York lobby were authorized to offer up to $50,000 in bribes. But after the amendment had been adopted, and the lobbyists asked a member of Congress (perhaps Ashley) how much they owed for the payoffs, the congressman responded that he had promised no bribes and had incurred expenses totaling only $27.50. "Good lord," exclaimed the lobbyists, "that isn't the way they do things at Albany!"[103] Although the specifics of Reid's story are no doubt apocryphal, other Washington observers, including some congressmen, attested to the existence of a bribery fund. Alexander Long, a Democratic representative from Ohio who opposed the amendment, wrote after the final vote that "rascality and corruption carry off the *Green Backs* in large quantities."[104] Many years later, Long's rival within the Ohio Democratic party, Sunset Cox, told of an unidentified character who arranged to receive $10,000 from "New York parties" for persuading Cox to vote for the amendment. No money ever changed hands, however, because the

---

99   Harrisburg (Pennsylvania) *Patriot and Union,* reprinted in *New York Tribune,* February 3, 1865, p. 4. See William H. Koontz to Edward McPherson, February 8 and 14, 1865 (from Bedford, Penn.), Edward McPherson MSS, LC.

100 *Biographical Directory of the United States Congress, 1774–1989,* Bicentennial ed. (Washington, D.C.: Government Printing Office, 1989), 804.

101 Horace Greeley to Elihu B. Washburne, February 6, 1865, Elihu B. Washburne MSS, LC; *New York Tribune,* February 10, 1865, p. 1.

102 R. W. Latham to William Henry Seward, January 9, 1865, William Henry Seward MSS, UR; Cox and Cox, *Politics, Principle, and Prejudice,* 27–28.

103 *Cincinnati Gazette,* February 14, 1865, p. 1.

104 Alexander Long to Alexander S. Boys, February 13, 1865, Alexander S. Boys MSS, OHS.

Ohio representative ultimately voted against the measure.[105] Evidence of bribe taking by anyone voting for the amendment has yet to surface.

However much the covert methods of Republicans played a part in winning converts to the amendment, an even stronger influence came from Democrats and border state unionists who made their own decision, born from a combination of political calculation and moral imperative, that slavery should be abolished constitutionally. Some of these non-Republicans were veteran opponents of slavery. The eminent historian George Bancroft, for example, a Democrat who had long favored black freedom, wrote to at least two Democrats in the House, "for the sake of internal peace, justice, the success of the Democratic party, pass the Amendment."[106]

Many others making a last-minute appeal for the amendment were taking their first stand against slavery. Two weeks before the final vote on the amendment, a delegation from Tammany Hall, New York's premier Democratic organization, arrived on the House floor to ask congressmen from the Empire State to "relieve them from the pro-slavery burden that now ruins the party."[107] It had taken Tammany a long time to make an open break with southern slave owners, and now that it did so, the organization went so far as to claim that Democrats were responsible for the amendment. According to the Tammany delegation, the amendment was "a democratic measure, suggested by democrats, and it ought to be supported by democrats."[108] Tammany's claim was not as absurd as it might seem: Democratic Senator John B. Henderson had proposed the initial version of the amendment; Tammany's own Carolan Bryant had been among the first to endorse the measure; and the Democratic party had a long tradition, particularly at the state level, of favoring constitutional reform over legislative discretion. As Tammany took a new course, the Albany Regency, the New York Democratic clique led by Dean Richmond, also backed away from slavery. Richmond asked Manton Marble, editor of the Democracy's leading journal, the *New York World,* not to make the amendment "a party question" and to allow "each member of Congress . . . [to] vote according to his own disposition."[109] Although the

105 Cox, *Union – Disunion – Reunion,* 329. Cox's reliability is questionable; he did not mention this incident in his earlier reminiscence, *Eight Years in Congress.*

106 George Bancroft to John V. S. L. Pruyn, January 28, 1865 (quotation) and Bancroft to Samuel S. Cox, January 28, 1865, both in George Bancroft MSS, MHS. Also see John V. S. L. Pruyn, "Washington Journal," January 30, 1865, John V. S. L. Pruyn MSS, NYS.

107 *Cincinnati Gazette,* January 14, 1865, p. 3; and *Chicago Tribune,* January 14, 1865, p. 1. See *New York Evening Post,* January 10, 1865, p. 2.

108 *New York Leader,* reprinted in Charles Nordhoff, ed., *America for Free Working Men* (Loyal Publication Society no. 80) (New York, 1865), p. iv.

109 Richmond to Marble, January 23, 1865, Marble MSS, LC.

editor failed to make good on his promise to print a pledge of neutrality, he at least stayed silent and offered no criticism of the amendment.[110] It was Dean Richmond, Montgomery Blair reported some months later, who deserved the most credit for the amendment's adoption.[111]

Other unlikely advocates of the amendment also labored diligently. As the final vote neared, visitors from Kentucky circulated through the House, assuring ambivalent congressmen that the border states welcomed constitutional emancipation.[112] The Kentucky Democrat James Guthrie, who had recently been elected to the Senate, wrote a letter to his friend Sunset Cox asking him to back the amendment.[113] Against Guthrie's wishes, the Ohio congressman shared the letter with many of his Democratic colleagues, some of whom read it as a call from the party leadership to retreat from slavery.[114]

Without the change of heart of slavery's former defenders, Congress would not have passed the amendment at this moment. The crucial role played by the opposition did not sit well with some Republicans, especially the old-line abolitionists among them, because they wanted full credit for the end of slavery. The Republican congressman George Julian thus attributed the votes given by opposition members less to honest motives than to "certain negotiations, the result of which was not fully assured, and the particulars of which never reached the public."[115] Historians also have found it difficult to stomach the fact that the most powerful provision against slavery owes its existence in part to slavery's onetime defenders, and they have relied on the idea of an illicit bargain to make the votes of opposition members more palatable. It may be true that the motives of those newly pledged to the amendment were not entirely humanitarian: they cared more about sectional harmony and political success than they did about black Americans, free or enslaved. (One might say the same of many Republicans.) Nevertheless, the approval of the amendment by slavery's former defenders was in most cases not the result of corruption. Indeed, as the final vote approached, Ashley counted on the sincerity of the newly converted to carry the measure.

---

110 William N. Bilbo to William H. Seward, January 26, 1865, Seward MSS, UR.
111 Blair to Andrew Johnson, June 16, 1865, Andrew Johnson MSS, LC.
112 *New York Herald,* January 18, 1865, p. 8.
113 Guthrie to S. S. Cox, January 22, 1865, Samuel S. Cox MSS, John Hay Library, Brown University, Providence, Rhode Island.
114 S. S. Cox to Manton Marble, January 26, 1865, Manton M. Marble MSS, LC; *New York Tribune,* February 3, 1865, p. 4; *Chicago Tribune,* February 10, 1865, p. 2. Cox would ultimately vote against the amendment, but his work on behalf of the measure persuaded William H. Seward that the Ohioan deserved the most credit for its adoption. See David Lindsey, *"Sunset" Cox: Irrepressible Democrat* (Detroit: Wayne State University Press, 1959), 93–95.
115 George W. Julian, *Political Recollections, 1840 to 1872* (Chicago: Jansen, McClurg, 1884), 250.

The House of Representatives assembled on January 31 for the final vote. The floor was densely packed. Chief Justice Chase and four of the associate justices were in attendance, as were various senators, Secretary of the Treasury William Pitt Fessenden, former postmaster general Montgomery Blair, and his successor, William Dennison of Ohio. Secretary of State Seward almost certainly lurked nearby.[116]

In the galleries, reporters were forced to stand, their seats occupied by women who had helped to make the moment possible by launching the petition drive for universal emancipation two years before. One such reformer was Laura Julian, wife of Representative George Julian and daughter of antislavery activist Joshua Giddings. She was frustrated that all she could do now was watch. To her sister she had complained of the "miserable air" in the galleries and the ineptitude of Congressman Ashley on the floor: "such a pity that he should have the charge of such a matter."[117] Also following the proceedings, no doubt with even more interest, were African Americans, whose presence already had occasioned some remarks by congressmen.[118] Particularly attentive among the black observers was Frederick Douglass's son Charles, a former Union soldier now working at the Freedmen's Hospital in Washington.[119] A collective excitement swelled among the hundreds of men and women as the realization dawned on them that they were taking part in one of the most significant moments in American history.

Ashley was fairly certain that he had enough votes, but unanticipated events threatened the amendment at the last minute. During the last moments of the debate, a rumor spread that three Confederate peace commissioners were on their way to Washington. Opposition congressmen had warned that passage of the amendment might inhibit negotiations; if they believed that envoys were on the way, they would demand a postponement of the vote. Quickly, Ashley sent a messenger to the president for a note denying the rumor. But the president knew that the rumor was true. After two trips to Richmond, both on Lincoln's authority, Francis P. Blair, Sr., had persuaded Jefferson Davis that a Confederate diplomatic mission to Washington might be welcomed by the president. Lincoln knew that the envoys were on their way. He eventually would meet them in Hampton Roads, Virginia, south of Washington, but he never intended to receive them in the nation's capital. To do so would

---

116 P. J. Staudenraus, ed., *Mr. Lincoln's Washington: Selections from the Writings of Noah Brooks, Civil War Correspondent* (South Brunswick, N.J.: Thomas Yoseloff, 1967), 408.

117 Laura G. Julian to "My Dear Sister" [Mollie Giddings], January 13, 1865, George W. Julian MSS, ISL.

118 See, for example, *CG*, 38th Cong., 2d sess. (January 12, 1865), 243 (Woodbridge).

119 Charles R. Douglass to Frederick Douglass, February 9, 1865, Frederick Douglass MSS, LC.

contradict his position that the Confederacy was not a legitimate nation deserving official recognition. So Lincoln wrote a clever reply to Ashley to put the rumors to rest: "So far as I know, there are no peace commissioners in the city, or likely to be in it." Ashley showed the note to opposition members to silence the peace murmurs.[120]

With the peace rumors temporarily dispelled, Ashley tried to shore up wavering congressmen by marching out Democrats newly committed to the antislavery cause. First to testify was Archibald McAllister of Pennsylvania. The lame-duck congressman had voted against the amendment in June, but at a recent dinner given by prominent Philadelphians for proamendment Democrats, he had announced his intention to reverse his position.[121] Now, in a message read by the House clerk, McAllister explained that the failure of all the peace missions of the past year, including those by Francis P. Blair, Sr., had convinced him that only independence would satisfy the Confederates. Therefore, he would cast his vote "against the corner-stone of the Southern Confederacy, and declare eternal war against the enemies of my country."[122] Next came Alexander Coffroth, the Pennsylvania Democrat whose election had been contested. Speaking sheepishly, with his hands in his pockets, Coffroth made a poor picture of a Democrat boldly redeemed, but his inaudible speech met with cheers nonetheless. The crowd already knew that the congressman would offer what correspondent Noah Brooks called "a public recantation of his heresy."[123] Then, after a brief interruption by William Miller, a Pennsylvania Peace Democrat who opposed the amendment, Ashley nodded to Anson Herrick, the last of his newly converted Democrats. The New Yorker's brief and poignant endorsement was the finale of Ashley's presentation.

Opponents of the measure now demanded equal time. James S. Brown of Wisconsin offered a last-ditch suggestion of four amendments freeing the slaves gradually and compensating the owners. But House Republicans would no longer suffer gradualism; no one even suggested voting on the proposal. After two more steadfast opponents aired their views, and a third tried a delaying tactic, Speaker of the House Schuyler Colfax called for the vote. It was just after three o'clock. Never had the House been so crowded, the mood so charged with expectation.

The clerk went down the roll. He came quickly to Sunset Cox. The

---

120   *CW*, 8:248; S. S. Cox to Manton M. Marble, February 1, 1865, Manton M. Marble MSS, LC.

121   *New York Evening Express*, January 21, 1865, p. 2.

122   *CG*, 38th Cong., 2d sess. (January 31, 1865), 523. It is unclear why McAllister did not give the speech himself.

123   Staudenraus, *Mr. Lincoln's Washington*, 409.

Ohio War Democrat had planned to vote for the amendment and had even prepared a speech in its favor. But Cox now believed that, despite Lincoln's suggestion to the contrary, peace commissioners from Richmond were headed north, and that the adoption of the amendment might turn them back. To the surprise of many in the hall, the Ohioan voted nay. As the clerk continued to call off names, each yea vote from a Democrat or border state representative caused an eruption in the galleries. Eleven members who had opposed the amendment in June now voted for adoption. Finally, in a dramatic gesture, Colfax asked that his name be called so he could vote. A vote from the speaker was rare, but, as he later admitted, Colfax was determined to record his name with "that great measure, which hereafter will illuminate the highest page in our History." After Colfax voted aye, he announced the final tally: 119 to 56, with 8 members absent. Two-thirds of the House had voted in the affirmative, with two votes to spare. Congress had adopted the amendment.[124]

For a moment there was only a disbelieving, hollow silence. Then the House exploded in cheers. Members threw their hats to the roof, caught them, and smashed them against their desks. For the lawmakers, and for the white observers who dominated the galleries, this was the vicarious day of jubilee. The normally staid Victorian audience lost its emotional bearings. Witnesses to the great event roared their approval, wept, embraced. The women waved their handkerchiefs. A man seized his female companion and kissed her repeatedly, ignoring her protest – "Oh, *don't* Charley!" Blacks in the audience were equally moved, not only by the meaning of the event but by the reaction of the whites around them. Like most African Americans, Charles Douglass had taken part in freedom celebrations held regularly even before the Emancipation Proclamation and the outbreak of war. But most of the celebrants at those occasions were black; Douglass had never seen anything like this. "I wish that you could have been here," the young man wrote to his father, "such rejoicing I never before witnessed . . . (white people I mean)." One black observer in the galleries chose to preserve his sense of dignity by expressing his elation in private. He found an unused anteroom and danced alone in jubilation. For five minutes the rejoicing continued, until Congressman Ebon Ingersoll of Illinois shouted out for adjournment. Opposition mem-

124 See Appendix Table 2; *CG*, 38th Cong., 2d sess. (January 31, 1865), 530; S. S. Cox to Manton M. Marble, February 1, 13, 1865, Manton M. Marble MSS, LC; Cox, *Eight Years in Congress*, 397–98; Alexander Long to Alexander St. Clair Boys, February 13, 1865, Alexander S. Boys MSS, OHS; letter of "Agate," *Cincinnati Gazette*, February 14, 1865, p. 1; Schuyler Colfax to "Mrs. Endicott," February 5, 1865, Schuyler Colfax MSS, ISL; Colfax to Francis Lieber, February 11, 1865, Francis Lieber MSS, HEH; *New York Tribune*, February 1, 1865, p. 1; Staudenraus, *Mr. Lincoln's Washington*, 409–10.

bers tried to prevent adjournment, but the crowd ignored them and spilled out the doors, taking their celebration to the streets, and to the rest of the Union.[125]

For most Republican congressmen, it was the crowning moment of their careers. As the clerk called the vote, Representative Cornelius Cole of California wrote to his wife, "the one question of the age is *settled*. Glory enough for one session, yes, even for a life."[126] Thirty years later, George Julian still remembered the transforming quality of the moment: "It seemed to me I had been born into a new life, and that the world was overflowing with beauty and joy."[127] Martin Russell Thayer of Pennsylvania rushed home to write to his friend Francis Lieber, "We have wiped away the black spot from our bright shield and surely God will bless us for it. . . . He seemed to smile from Heaven upon a regenerated people for as the great throng poured out of the House immediately afterwards the Sun broke through the clouds which had all day concealed him and lit up everything with his effulgence."[128]

By the day after the vote, almost everyone had heard the news. From Maine to the Sea Islands of South Carolina, men and women of all races held spontaneous rallies. Even those once aligned against emancipation approved. In New York, Morgan Dix, the son of General John A. Dix and a rector in Trinity Parish, pledged in his journal "humble gratitude to Almighty God." "How strange the changes of time!" he exclaimed. "4 years ago I was an out and out ultra-Southern and pro-slavery [man]."[129] At a massive gathering in Boston, William Lloyd Garrison announced that the Constitution, which he once had called "a covenant with death," was superseded by "a covenant with life."[130] John C. Gray, a Boston Democrat who had opposed Lincoln's policy on slavery, did not attend Garrison's rally, but he conceded to a friend that the amendment was "better than a thousand of your juggling emancipation proclamations."[131]

The president agreed. To a crowd of celebrants outside the White House the day after the vote in Congress, Lincoln observed that the

---

125 Indianapolis *Daily Journal,* February 6, 1865, p. 2; Charles R. Douglass to Frederick Douglass, February 9, 1865, Frederick Douglass MSS, LC.

126 Cornelius Cole, *Memoirs of Cornelius Cole* (New York: McLoughlin Brothers, 1908), 220.

127 Julian, *Political Recollections,* 251.

128 Thayer to Lieber, January 31, 1865, Francis Lieber MSS, HEH.

129 Morgan Dix diary, February 1, 1865, cited in Ernest A. McKay, *The Civil War and New York City* (Syracuse, N.Y.: Syracuse University Press, 1990), 295.

130 *Liberator,* February 10, 1865, p. 2.

131 John Chipman Gray to John Codman Ropes, February 8, 1865, in John Chipman Gray, ed., *War Letters, 1862–1865, of John Chipman Gray . . . and John Codman Ropes* (Boston: Houghton Mifflin, 1927), 452.

SCENE IN THE HOUSE ON THE PASSAGE OF THE PROPOSITION TO AMEND THE CONSTITUTION, January 31, 1865.

Figure 5. The passage of the Thirteenth Amendment in the House of Representatives, as depicted in *Harper's Weekly*. Not only congressmen but cabinet officials and Supreme Court justices crowded the House floor at the time of the vote. When the resolution for the amendment passed, the chamber erupted in celebration. The artist captured the unprecedented exhuberance in the House of the white male lawmakers but did not picture the similar reaction among the African American and white female observers who also crowded into the galleries that day.

"proclamation falls far short of what the amendment will be when fully consummated." The amendment ended all questions about the future of slavery. It was "a King's cure for all the evils."[132] He was so pleased with the measure that he signed it, though the Constitution did not require the president's signature on a proposed amendment. Those congressmen already worried about the swelling of presidential power later scolded him for signing the measure. But Lincoln was determined to leave his mark for posterity. He may also have wanted to redress the wrong done by his predecessor, James Buchanan, who signed the "first" Thirteenth Amendment of 1861, the one that would have given slavery eternal life.[133]

With the passage of the amendment, a nation committed to freedom no longer had to face a Constitution that protected slavery. As Congressman Cole told his wife, "we can now look other nations in the face without shame."[134] Both inside and outside of Congress, various groups with diverse motives provided the final impetus for constitutional change. Some felt a moral obligation to end slavery and establish a nation of equals; others cared less about enslaved African Americans than about political fortunes and sectional harmony. The confluence of motivations defies any attempt to attribute the measure to any one cause, or any single group, or any single person. But despite the disparity in motives and attitudes, a remarkable new consensus had emerged about the unlimited nature of the amending power: Americans of any generation had the authority to challenge the framers' Constitution and to draft a document better suited to the present.

Beneath this consensus, however, ideological differences over federal power and race still remained. Those who supported the amendment had been able to overlook these differences to secure the measure's adoption, but now that the goal was reached, a new battle began, one that exposed the delicacy of the amendment coalition and set its members against one another. The struggle to adopt the amendment was nearly over, but the struggle to define constitutional freedom had just begun.

132 CW, 8:254.
133 CG, 38th Cong., 2d sess. (February 4, 1865), 588. See Richard B. Bernstein, with Jerome Agel, *Amending America: If We Love the Constitution So Much, Why Do We Keep Trying to Change It?* (New York: Times Books, 1993), 100; R. Gerald McMurtry, "Lincoln Need Not Have Signed the Resolution Submitting the Thirteenth Amendment to the States," *Lincoln Lore*, no. 1604 (October 1971), 1–4.
134 Cornelius Cole to Olive Cole, February 1, 1865, Cornelius Cole MSS, University of California at Los Angeles.

8

The Contested Legacy of
Constitutional Freedom

The Thirteenth Amendment was commemorated before it was even ratified. Requests for official copies of the amendment flooded into Congress right after the measure's adoption. Souvenir collectors asked those who voted for the amendment to sign the duplicates, and the most industrious autograph hunters procured as well the signatures of President Lincoln and Vice-President Hamlin.[1] State legislatures vied to be the first to ratify. Senator Lyman Trumbull and Governor Richard Oglesby of Illinois pressed their state's legislature to ratify at once, even before Secretary of State Seward's official notification arrived. The legislature complied, making Illinois the first state to vote for the amendment and assuring it a prominent place in the emancipation record.[2] Opponents of the amendment also wished to add their distinctive mark. An Ohio state assemblyman proposed that his fellow legislators wear a "badge of mourning" for thirty days to acknowledge this "first step towards a centralized despotism."[3] Two weeks after the momentous vote in the House of Representatives, in the very chamber where the measure had passed, the New York minister Henry Highland Garnet delivered a rousing address commemorating the amendment – the first speech delivered by an African American in Congress. Garnet, who was there by invitation of President Lincoln, used the occasion to demand equal rights beyond emancipation: "When and where will the demands of the reformers of this and coming ages end? . . . When emancipation shall be followed by enfranchisement . . . when there shall be no more class-legislation, and no more trouble concerning the black man and his rights."[4] All wanted their

---

1   John G. Rhodehamel and Seth Kaller, "A Census of Copies of the Thirteenth Amendment to the U.S. Constitution Signed by Abraham Lincoln," *Manuscripts*, 44 (1992), 93–114.
2   Richard J. Oglesby letter book, January to April, 1865, pp. 143, 154–55, 191–92, Illinois State Archives, Springfield; *Chicago Tribune*, February 1, 1865, p. 1.
3   *Cincinnati Enquirer*, February 3, 1865, p. 2.
4   Henry Highland Garnet, *A Memorial Discourse*, in James M. McPherson, ed., *The Negro's Civil War: How American Negroes Felt and Acted during the War for the Union* (1965; repr., Urbana: University of Illinois Press, 1982), 289–90. See David Quigley, "Reconstructing Democracy: Politics and Ideas in New York City, 1865–1880" (Ph.D. diss., New York University, 1997), 23–26.

positions on the amendment recorded, in part to lay claim to a piece of history, but even more, to seize control over the meaning of constitutional freedom.

Controlling the meaning of freedom was now more important than ever. Prior to ratification, those who had considered the amendment had left many issues open-ended, sometimes on purpose, but just as often out of understandable shortsightedness. Because of unforeseen events, Americans now had to clarify the scope of the amendment, and those with opposing agendas and political persuasions would compete to offer the dominant interpretation. Contests over the amendment were fought out on an ever changing terrain, shaped as much by shifting ideology as by the day-to-day unfolding of events.

The Meanings of Freedom: The Union States and Ratification

Once the amendment had been adopted by Congress, the effort to assess the measure's significance and resolve its meaning shifted to the ratification debates. Legislatures in the Union states were the first to take up the amendment. Discussions at the state level generally echoed those in Congress, with two significant differences. First, state-level debate was shaped as much by local as by national politics. Second, as might be expected, state legislators were more attentive than their national counterparts had been to the effect of the amendment on state laws and institutions. In particular, the amendment's second clause, which empowered Congress to enforce abolition by "appropriate legislation" and which had been all but ignored by lawmakers at the national level, now emerged as a dominant issue. The ratification debates in the Union states were the earliest instances of northerners confronting the question of how they would be affected by an amendment originally aimed only at the South.

Throughout the Union, the political situation at the state level shaped the course of ratification. In New England, where Union parties composed almost exclusively of Republicans had won dominant victories in the elections of 1864, the Republican majorities in the legislatures ratified the amendment with minimal conflict and much celebration. The frailty of the Democratic party in most of the states of New England, combined with that region's long opposition to slavery, kept the amendment from emerging there as a controversial issue.[5]

5   For the dates and votes for ratification, see "Ratification of the Constitution and Amendments by the States," [Senate] Misc. Doc. 240, 71st Cong., 3d sess., 1931; and *Documentary History of the Constitution of the United States of America* (Washington, D.C.: Department of State, 1894), 2:520–637.

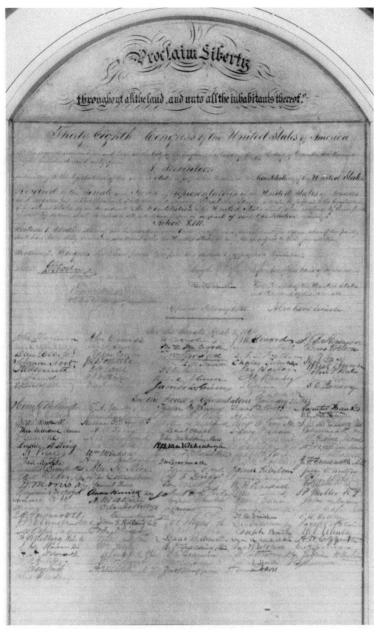

Figure 6. Signed copy of the Thirteenth Amendment. As soon as Congress voted to submit the amendment to the states for ratification, memorial copies of the measure were created and signed by congressmen who voted for it. A few copies, including this one, were signed also by Abraham Lincoln and Vice-President Hannibal Hamlin. The creation of these copies was one part of a larger process of commemorating and defining freedom. (Courtesy Cornell University Library)

In New York, by contrast, the Democratic minority in the legislature was powerful enough to stall ratification. A successful alliance between Republicans and War Democrats had helped the coalition Union party carry New York in 1864, but the Peace Democrats still had power in the legislature, and they were determined to use states' rights and antiblack rhetoric to draw War Democrats to the cause of blocking ratification. Typical was one Peace Democrat editorial that characterized the amendment as an instrument of "*mad, unthinking, unreasoning, wild Fanaticism*" because it granted three-fourths of the states the power "to deprive the people of the remaining fourth of the States of all their right of property in these persons [slaves], and to turn them loose upon them and the whole community, to plunder, steal and murder for a living."[6] Democratic legislators caucused soon after Congress approved the amendment and agreed to unite against ratification. New York Republicans carried ratification quickly through the senate, but Democratic opposition forced them to postpone consideration in the assembly.[7] Only the assassination of Lincoln broke the stalemate. As Lincoln's funeral train approached Albany, Democrats feared for the party's reputation. How could they oppose an antislavery amendment in the presence of the martyred "Great Emancipator"? "From this point," one Democratic editor advised, "let us refuse to allow the Dem. party to ever *seem* in a disloyal position or as the defenders of Slavery."[8] On April 22, four days before Lincoln's casket arrived in the state capital, a Democratic faction led by Smith Weed (no relation to Thurlow) agreed to back the amendment, and the New York Assembly finally voted for ratification.[9] In death, as in life, Lincoln coaxed reluctant emancipators to embrace constitutional freedom.

In the Midwest, as in New York, Democrats had significant minorities in the legislatures, but here, the issue of loyalty had so severely split the state parties that reconciliation between propeace and prowar factions was nearly impossible. During the political campaigns of 1864, military authorities and Republican politicians in the Midwest had uncovered conspiracies and successfully linked them to Democratic organizations. By the time that midwestern states took up the Thirteenth Amendment, Democratic organizations there were still reeling from the conspiracy scares, leaving most War Democrats still firmly entrenched in state Union parties. In Indiana, for example, Republican propaganda against an allegedly treasonous Democratic organization known as the Sons of Liberty

---

6 *New York Daily News*, March 1, 1865, p. 4.
7 *New York Evening Post*, February 2, 1865, p. 2, February 3, 1865, p. 2.
8 Calvert Comstock to Manton Marble, April 21, 1865, Manton M. Marble MSS, LC.
9 *Journal of the Assembly of the State of New York*, 88th sess., 1865, pp. 1387–89; *New York Evening Express*, April 24, 1865, p. 1; *New York Herald*, April 24, 1865, p. 4.

had aggravated hostilities between the prowar and propeace wings of the state party. Instead of uniting with Peace Democrats to block ratification of the Thirteenth Amendment, War Democrats used the ratification debate to label Peace Democrats as traitors. State representative T. T. Wright, a lifelong Democrat who had joined the state Union party, accused those who opposed ratification of aiding the Confederates.[10] With the help of the War Democrats, the legislature in Indiana, as well as those in the other states of the Midwest, ratified the amendment only weeks after Congress had approved the measure.

In the far West, War Democrats also lined up with Republicans behind the amendment. But most of the western ratification debates took place much later than those in the Midwest and East, because the western governments often refused to consider the amendment until they received official word of congressional approval by mail. Lawmakers deemed notification by transcontinental telegraph untrustworthy.[11]

Although local circumstances shaped each state's ratification debate, some themes emerged in all of the debates. First, in those states where Democrats supported the amendment, they rarely renounced their party loyalty but instead claimed to be setting the Democracy right with slavery. As the Democratic Indiana assemblyman Henry Groves explained, a true Democrat was always for universal freedom – so long as it came constitutionally.[12]

Some Democrats went even further and argued that their party had in fact authored the amendment. By making this claim, Democrats hoped to reap the credit for the amendment's adoption and the authority for its interpretation. There was some truth to the Democrats' version of events. Democrats' objection to the Emancipation Proclamation as unconstitutional had helped prepare the ground for antislavery legislation more generally accepted as constitutional. After Democrat John B. Henderson had proposed the amendment in the U.S. Senate, the support of Democrats had carried the measure through the House of Representatives. Finally, Democrats could legitimately argue that, in matters of reform, their party had always favored constitutional revision over the broad use of legislative power. No wonder, then, that some Democrats in the California legislature claimed "paternity" of the amendment.[13] The

---

10 *Brevier Legislative Reports: Embracing Short-Hand Sketches of the Journals and Debates of the General Assembly of the State of Indiana,* vol. 7, 1865, House of Representatives, 190.

11 See Senate, Misc. Doc. 240, p. 4; *Documentary History of the Constitution,* 2:552–55, 570–72; 593–94, 617–23, 630–33; *Sacramento Daily Union,* December 7, 1865.

12 *Brevier Legislative Reports,* 207.

13 San Francisco *Daily Alta California,* December 16, 1865, p. 1.

case for Democratic authorship was made most eloquently by Jackson Hadley, a Democratic state legislator in Wisconsin:

> [The Democratic party] always believed that the institution of slavery, abstractly considered, was a great wrong . . . but for prudential reasons, it did not choose to meddle with it, in any way, outside of the Constitution of the United States. . . . It has always contended for the integrity of the Constitution, its inviolability, and the right of the people to amend it – not to break and destroy it. Those who now abandon their efforts to evade it, to violate it, to disregard its sacred provisions . . . come to the time-honored position occupied by the Democratic party.[14]

The cooperation between War Democrats and Republicans on the amendment had been heartening to those disgusted with partisan bickering, but when War Democrats at the state level chose to claim the amendment for their old party rather than for the coalition Union party, they revealed the weakness of their wartime bond to the Republicans and foreshadowed the postwar schism between the two groups.

Simultaneous with the struggle over authorship of the amendment was a related contest to determine the effect of the measure on former masters and slaves. In the border states of Maryland and Missouri, both of which had recently abolished slavery by state action, legislatures approved the amendment with ease. In Maryland, however, lawmakers took the additional step of declaring that former loyal slave owners should be compensated for their ex-slaves by the federal government. Congress had rejected compensation proposals, but border state emancipationists nonetheless expected Lincoln to deliver on the promise of compensation that he had made in 1861 and 1862.[15] Meanwhile, at least a few Maryland assemblymen attempted to attach to ratification a resolution promising to preserve "inviolate the purity and supremacy of the white race."[16] In this state, where control of a large free black population had always been high on lawmakers' agenda, legislators used ratification as a forum to read racial equality out of freedom. The white supremacy resolution was a promise to prevent the amendment from authorizing state or federal civil rights legislation.

Legislators in Kentucky had similar objectives. Ultimately, the Bluegrass State joined Delaware, the only other remaining Union slave state, in voting against ratification. In both states, the vote was a token act of

---

14 *Wisconsin State Journal,* February 25, 1865, p. 2.
15 *Journal of the Proceedings of the House of Delegates of Maryland,* January session, 1865, pp. 310–11, 340, 371.
16 Ibid., 125. The resolution was approved by a majority of the assembly, but it fell short of the two-thirds majority required for adoption.

defiance, a howl against the destruction of slavery wrought by federal armies and the ex-slaves they enlisted. As one Union officer in Kentucky put it, "the devotees of the barbarism cling to [slavery's] putrid carcass with astonishing tenacity."[17] Before voting against ratification, however, Kentucky considered a proposal for *conditional* ratification. Perhaps on the advice of Lincoln, Thomas E. Bramlette, the unionist governor, recommended ratifying the amendment on the condition that the federal government pay Kentucky $34 million, a sum based on the 1864 valuation of the state's slaves.[18] But members of the conservative majority in the legislature announced that they would not be appeased by compensation. In a last-ditch effort to reconcile Bramlette and the conservatives, a moderate faction in the Kentucky legislature offered an illuminating resolution: ratification would be contingent not only on compensation but on federal acceptance of state legislation granting ex-slaves "all the liberties and civil privileges . . . of free-born colored persons." Because freeborn blacks in Kentucky were still denied all social rights, such as the right of intermarriage, all political rights, such as the right to vote, and even some civil rights, such as the right to testify in cases against whites, the provision would act as a safeguard against any future federal attempt to use the amendment to overturn discriminatory state laws. The legislature's proposal also required that, in compliance with the state's manumission law, blacks freed by the amendment had to vacate Kentucky within ten years. The only new right the state would grant to African Americans was official recognition of marriages and parental relationships, a nod to the Victorian tradition that recognized the primacy of conjugal and filial bonds.[19]

The resolution failed. Nonetheless, it was a remarkable and revealing piece of legislation, representing the first attempt by a law-making body

---

17 Clinton B. Fisk to O. O. Howard, July 20, 1865, in Ira Berlin et al., eds. *Freedom: A Documentary History of Emancipation, 1861–1867*, ser. 1, vol. 2, *The Wartime Genesis of Free Labor: The Upper South* (Cambridge: Cambridge University Press, 1993), 706.

18 *Journal of the Senate of the Commonwealth of Kentucky, 1863–4*, 274–77. See *New York Tribune*, April 27, 1865, p. 8.

19 *Journal of the Senate of Kentucky, 1863–4*, 389–90; *Journal of the House of Representatives of the Commonwealth of Kentucky, 1863–4*, 576–77; Victor B. Howard, *Black Liberation in Kentucky: Emancipation and Freedom, 1862–1884* (Lexington: University Press of Kentucky, 1983), 77. See Nancy Isenberg, *Sex and Citizenship in Antebellum America* (Chapel Hill: University of North Carolina Press, 1998), 155–90; Elizabeth B. Clark, "Matrimonial Bonds: Slavery and Divorce in Nineteenth-Century America," *Law and History Review*, 8 (Spring 1990), 25–54; Amy Dru Stanley, *From Bondage to Contract: Wage Labor, Marriage, and the Market in the Age of Slave Emancipation* (Cambridge: Cambridge University Press, 1998), esp. 175–217; and Stanley, "Conjugal Bonds and Wage Labor: Rights of Contract in the Age of Emancipation," *Journal of American History*, 75 (September 1988), 471–500.

to specify the scope and power of the antislavery amendment. Especially striking was the implication that if the constitutional amendment were adopted without explicit restrictions, Congress might use it to overturn discriminatory state laws. Such fears led the Kentucky State Senate to take the further step of rewriting the ratification resolution to include an outright rejection of the amendment's second clause, which gave Congress the power to enforce emancipation.[20] In the debates in Congress, the meaning of the enforcement clause rarely had appeared as an issue. When the clause was discussed, defenders of the amendment – particularly War Democrats – had assured opponents that it merely assured the abolition of chattel slavery (ownership of a person), not the extension of civil, political, or social rights. Now, in the ratification debates, a broader interpretation of the second clause threatened to be the amendment's undoing, at least in Kentucky. Significantly, lawmakers in the Bluegrass State seemed to think that the first clause of the amendment, the simple declaration of slavery's end, posed no threat to discriminatory state laws. State officials could face the transformation of their slave labor into free labor so long as they retained their untrammeled power to shape the contours of black freedom.

In the free states as well, opponents of the amendment feared that the enforcement clause might undermine the authority of state governments. In Ohio and Indiana, critics of ratification warned that federal authorities would use the clause to rewrite state constitutions or abolish state courts and state legislatures.[21] Critics were especially fond of using the image of a desecrated body to convey the ill effects of enforcement. The new constitutional provision, one Michigan state senator warned, invested the federal government with "a despotic power that will most assuredly, ultimately eat out the vitals of the States."[22] An Illinois state senator was equally graphic; he predicted that enforcement would "emasculate" the states.[23] In an era when white Americans commonly equated federal mandates for racial justice with a dissipation of white male authority and honor, it was natural for antiamendment legislators to identify ratification with castration. Opponents of ratification in the free states, no less than those in the slave states, believed they were witnessing the twilight of state power.

---

20 *Journal of the Senate of Kentucky, 1863–4*, 390–91.
21 *Cincinnati Enquirer*, February 1, 1865, p. 1, February 11, 1865, p. 2; *Brevier Legislative Reports of the State of Indiana*, 212 (Cyrus L. Dunham).
22 "Protest of the Hon. Loren L. Treat," Senate Doc. 38, *Documents accompanying The Journal of the Senate of the State of Michigan at the Biennial Session of 1865*, 4.
23 *Speech of Hon. William H. Green, on the Proposed Amendment of the Federal Constitution, Abolishing Slavery* (Springfield, Ill.: Baker and Phillips, Printers, 1865), 9.

For the advocates of ratification – and, later, for most historians – the states' rights rhetoric of the opposition seemed little more than a mask for racial anxiety. According to the amendment's defenders, their opponents were driven by an irrational belief that emancipation would subvert white supremacy. Such racial fears were unwarranted, a Republican Indiana state senator explained: the Anglo-Saxons were a superior breed, so there was no danger in letting "all have a fair chance in the race of life." Only "the man who really feared negro equality," the legislator argued, "was in danger of being overtaken by the dreadful calamity."[24]

Racism was certainly a part – though only a part – of the antiratification position. A Michigan legislator, for example, proclaimed that the amendment gave freedom too quickly to black Americans, all of whom were "without intelligence, without habits of industry or economy, [and] without self-reliance."[25] Occasionally, a free-state legislator even took the outmoded stance that slavery was the natural state of African Americans. Because "God has stamped upon the negro a mark of inferiority that could not be removed by legislation," one Democratic Indiana assemblyman argued, "there would be American slavery in these States so long as the two races remained together."[26] The ratification debates revealed just how firmly northern Democrats were committed to white supremacy.

But opposition to ratification was born from more than deep-seated racial prejudice. At stake was not simply white purity but the whole order of society. In the Democratic mind-set, power was delicately balanced between federal and state authorities, and to realign that distribution even slightly was to invite complete social and political collapse. Fears of constitutional change and fears of racial disorder were mutually reinforcing, and for many Democrats, the yearning to keep the Constitution pure, to keep the text of the document unadulterated, was even more profoundly felt than the related desire to maintain white purity. "The question of the negro is at most but a collateral one," an Illinois Democrat told his colleagues in the legislature. "If you can convince me by argument, I will accept the modern doctrine that the negro represents the *ideal* and the white man the *actual,* and that miscegenation is the highest good of man . . . but I do not wish to be convinced that the Federal constitution is wrong."[27]

Had the fears of opposition legislators not been so magnified, had their resistance to constitutional change not been so visceral, they might have seen that they shared with many of the amendment's defenders a belief

24 *Brevier Legislative Reports of the State of Indiana,* 182 (Thomas W. Bennett).
25 "Protest of the Hon. Loren L. Treat," 6.
26 *Brevier Legislative Reports,* 191 (Stephen G. Burton).
27 Green, *Speech on the Proposed Amendment of the Federal Constitution,* 7, 5–6.

that the federal government should respect the authority of the states, especially when it came to racial issues. Republicans were not yet united behind the belief that the abolition amendment curtailed a loyal state's prerogative to restrict civil, political, and social rights. Those Kentucky Republicans who were part of the majority in the legislature that tried to attach legal disabilities for blacks to ratification obviously assumed that the states would continue to define the status of African Americans after emancipation. Similarly, Illinois Republicans who pushed through a repeal of the state's notorious black laws just days after carrying ratification of the Thirteenth Amendment justified their action with only *state* constitutional provisions; they said nothing of the amendment or its enforcement clause.[28] Of course, because the amendment was not yet ratified, Illinois Republicans would have been reluctant to invoke the measure. But the fact that no one made a connection between the amendment and the black laws, even as the legislature voted on both issues at nearly the same time, suggests that Illinois Republicans shared Democrats' assumption that the amendment should not affect states' authority over African Americans – at least in loyal regions of the Union.

The most prolonged debate over the effect of the amendment on state laws took place in Indiana, the northern state with the most restrictive racial laws. Democratic legislators charged that the amendment would allow the federal government to grant state citizenship – and, implicitly, national citizenship – to African Americans. "If I vote for the amendment," a Democratic assemblyman announced, "I shall feel constrained to follow out the principle to its natural, logical and legitimate results, and give to the African race the rights they will be entitled to. . . . They shall be elevated to the character of citizens of the commonwealth."[29] Indiana Republicans rejected the argument. Or, more precisely, they denied that, as a result of the amendment, African Americans would become *first-class* citizens. Because certain classes of people in the North such as male African Americans and females of every color had long been living as free "citizens" without some of the political and social rights associated with citizenship, it was a simple matter for Republicans to promise their opponents that an amendment assuring freedom did not necessarily assure full citizenship. A. C. Downey, a Republican state senator, distinguished between the "natural rights" of citizenship secured by the amendment and backed by the federal government, which he listed as "the right to live, to be free and to enjoy the fruits of one's labor," and the "relative rights" of citizenship still to be regulated by the states: "the right to vote, to sit on a

28 Springfield *Illinois State Register,* February 1, 1865, p. 2; February 2, 1865, p. 2; February 8, 1865, p. 2.
29 *Brevier Legislative Reports of the State of Indiana,* 189 (Samuel H. Buskirk).

jury or to hold an office." "It does not follow," Downey explained, "that if you recognize and secure to the colored man his natural rights, that you must confer upon him all those relative rights which you have conferred upon the white man."[30] Another Republican legislator, William W. Foulke, told Democrats that he saw no contradiction in supporting the amendment while approving of a state's "legal restrictions against inter-marriage with the inferior race."[31] The prevailing notion that a state could confer different types of citizenship, combined with Republicans' long-standing belief that people's citizenship status in a state determined their citizenship status in the nation, allowed Indiana Republicans to deflect the charge that the amendment made blacks and whites equal citizens.

There was an important difference between the way that state-level Republicans and congressional Republicans spoke on behalf of the amendment. At both levels, Republicans shared a similar vision of the civil rights that inhere in freedom: the right to labor under contract for wages, the right to rent or own property, the right to be free from arbitrary physical harm, the rights of marriage and child rearing, and the right to sue in court should any of those other rights be denied. Also, Republicans at both levels tended to assume that the amendment did not go so far as to guarantee political or social rights. Yet, state-level Republicans curtailed the scope of the amendment in a way that Republicans at the federal level had not explicitly done. In the congressional debates, Republicans had merely implied that the amendment would affect the status of blacks in the seceded states only; they unwittingly left open the possibility of federal enforcement of civil rights in the loyal states as well. In the ratification debates, state-level Republicans revealed more clearly their belief that the amendment would not affect a loyal state's power to regulate rights. They made the point not only in their positive statements but in their silences. Republicans in Illinois said nothing about the amendment when they repealed that state's black laws. Nor did Republicans in the Indiana legislature acknowledge the amendment in their failed attempt in 1865 to abolish their state's black laws. In large part because the ratifiers were *state* lawmakers, they resisted reading the amendment as a measure yielding their authority to the federal government, particularly in the making of racial laws.

By the time of the northern state ratification debates, Republican lawmakers did not yet expect the Thirteenth Amendment to confer citizenship on all African Americans. At the very least, Republicans thought that

30 Ibid., 180.
31 Ibid., 222.

the measure empowered the federal government to ensure that blacks in the former seceded states receive some civil rights, most importantly the right to make contracts and to sue in state and federal courts. At most – and this position was rare – some Republicans thought that the amendment granted full citizenship, but only to African Americans in the former seceded states because only in these states did federal authority trump that of the states. This position was best expressed by General Benjamin F. Butler, the proslavery Democrat turned radical Republican. A week after Congress passed the amendment, Butler declared that the measure made "every negro slave . . . a citizen of the United States, entitled as of right to every political and legal immunity and privilege which belongs to that great franchise."[32] Butler did not say whether free African Americans in the loyal states could expect the same treatment. Regardless of how Republicans understood the effect of the amendment on ex-slaves in the South, none seemed ready to argue that the measure affected northern states' power to confer and define citizenship. Certainly, many Republicans wanted African Americans to be granted equal citizenship, including equal voting rights, but they did not see the Thirteenth Amendment as the vehicle for doing so. The ratification debates helped Republicans define for themselves and for others the distinction between freedom and citizenship. As a result, more Republicans began to say publicly what Horace Binney had written privately more than a year before: that an abolition amendment might give ex-slaves access to the courts, but it would not confer full citizenship rights; only an additional amendment could do that.[33]

Securing the Union: The Confederate States and Ratification

Even if all twenty-two states that went for Lincoln in the election of 1864 voted for ratification, the amendment would be five states short of the twenty-seven needed for ratification. That number of twenty-seven, however, was based on the assumption that thirty-six states were in the Union. If one assumed instead that the eleven seceded states were out of the Union, then ratification required the approval of only seventeen states. As federal lawmakers faced the reality of the ratification process, they were forced to confront an issue they had barely considered, and certainly not

---

32 *New York Tribune,* February 6, 1865, p. 8. Butler's speech was a slightly revised version of the one he delivered in Lowell, Massachusetts, the week before; see *Speech of Maj.-Gen. Benj. F. Butler, upon the Campaign Before Richmond, 1864. Delivered at Lowell, Mass., January 29, 1865* (Boston: Wright and Potter, 1865).
33 Binney to Francis Lieber, March 11 and 14, 1864, Francis Lieber MSS, HEH.

resolved, during their debates on the amendment: were the southern states to be counted in ratification?

Unionists in the seceded states certainly believed that their states should be included in ratification. Within weeks of Congress adopting the amendment, the unionist legislatures of Louisiana, Tennessee, and Arkansas recorded unanimous or near unanimous votes in favor of ratification. Also voting for the amendment was the tiny unionist "legislature" of Virginia, a body that had convened in Alexandria early in the war and had helped create the free state of West Virginia. The State Department duly accepted all of the ratifications by the southern states. The Lincoln administration seemed to accept the legitimacy of southern ratification.

If we believe Alexander H. Stephens, the vice-president of the Confederacy, Lincoln and Secretary of State Seward explicitly condoned southern ratification even before the southern unionist legislatures took up the amendment. Stephens was one of the three Confederate envoys who traveled north to meet Lincoln during the last days of January and, unwittingly, jeopardized the final passage of the amendment in Congress. The president agreed to meet with Stephens and his associates, but only after hearing from James W. Singleton, an Illinois Peace Democrat who had recently met with Confederate authorities, that the Confederates might return to the Union if they were promised "*a fair compensation* [for their freed slaves] coupled with other liberal terms of reconstruction secured by Constitutional Amendments."[34] Lincoln surely doubted that the Confederates would renounce their aim of independence, but he could not turn back the peace mission without appearing intractable. On February 2, 1865, two days after the passage of the amendment, Lincoln and Seward met the Confederates on a ship anchored off of Hampton Roads, Virginia. No reliable record of the meeting survives. However, according to Stephens's later account of the conversation, Lincoln said that Georgia, Stephens's home state, might be readmitted to the Union if the state legislature recalled the state's troops, elected members to Congress, and ratified the antislavery amendment "*prospectively,* so as to take effect – say in five years."[35]

34 *New York Tribune,* February 6, 1865, p. 8.
35 Alexander H. Stephens, *A Constitutional View of the Late War between the States* (Philadelphia: National Publishing Company, 1870), 2:613–14. Besides Stephens, the other major source for the meeting is John A. Campbell, *Reminiscences and Documents Relating to the Civil War during the Year 1865* (Baltimore: John Murphy, 1887), 11–17. For commentary on these and other sources on the conference, as well as on historians' treatment of the conference, see William C. Harris, "The Hampton Roads Peace Conference: A Final Test of Lincoln's Presidential Leadership," *Journal of the Abraham Lincoln Association,* 21 (Winter 2000), 31–61.

Stephens's account is suspicious. A steadfast defender of states' rights writing during the period of military reconstruction, he wanted his readers to believe that Lincoln was ready to grant southern state governments complete control over emancipation and the freed people. In the absence of any evidence corroborating Stephens's story, it is difficult to believe that Lincoln would accept as constitutional the unprecedented action of "prospective" ratification. But it is possible that the president suggested that Georgia would be allowed – if not expected – to vote on ratification. Such a policy would have been consistent with the way that the administration handled ratification by unionist legislatures in other seceded states.

Another reason not to reject Stephens's report entirely is that he reported Lincoln saying that the federal government should pay slave owners as much as $400 million for the loss of their slaves.[36] When Lincoln returned to Washington from Hampton Roads, he did in fact propose to his cabinet a plan for distributing $400 million to the rebellious states, each state receiving funds in proportion to its slave population of 1860. (Half of the funds would be distributed by April 1 if the rebellion had ceased; the other half would be given by July 1 if the antislavery amendment had been ratified.) The cabinet rejected the proposal because it thought, quite rightly, that Congress would not adopt it, and that only military victories, not financial incentives, would end the war. The president, who had hoped to use the compensation plan to attract more southerners to the Union cause, regretfully accepted the cabinet's advice.[37] Compensation, it seemed, was as outdated as colonization, a solution to slavery that Lincoln already had rejected.[38] The conventions of property law – at least on the question of "just compensation" for slaves – had been ground down by the friction of four years of destructive war.

Regardless of what exactly was discussed at Hampton Roads, everyone who attended seems to have expected that the southern states would participate in the ratification of the Thirteenth Amendment. It was natural that Lincoln and Seward would take this position. Both had argued consistently that the southern states had not gone out of the Union and had not lost their status as states. Moreover, both hoped that the ratification of

---

36 Stephens, *A Constitutional View,* 2:617.
37 Michael Burlingame, ed., *An Oral History of Abraham Lincoln: John G. Nicolay's Interviews and Essays* (Carbondale: Southern Illinois University Press, 1996), 65–66; Francis Fessenden, *Life and Public Services of William Pitt Fessenden* (Boston: Houghton Mifflin, 1907), 2:8; *CW,* 8:260–61. See Johnson, "Lincoln's Solution to the Problem of Peace Terms," 582–86; and H. Clay Reed, "Lincoln's Compensated Emancipation Plan and Its Relation to Delaware," *Delaware Notes,* 7th ser. (1931): 60–61.
38 Michael Vorenberg, "Abraham Lincoln and the Politics of Black Colonization," *Journal of the Abraham Lincoln Association,* 14 (Summer 1993), 41–42.

the amendment by loyal legislatures in the southern states would quicken the process of reunion.

Some radical Republicans in Congress, however, took the opposite view. The leading spokesman of the radical position was Senator Charles Sumner of Massachusetts. Because the southern states had lost their official status as states, Sumner argued, they could not be included in calculating the number of states needed for ratification, and they could not vote on ratification until Congress confirmed their status as states. In other words, Sumner believed that congressional reconstruction must precede southern ratification. Lincoln and Seward thought that the two processes should be independent of one another. That view was shortsighted, for reconstruction and ratification were bound to collide. At the moment that state legislatures took up ratification, the Senate began to consider a bill recognizing the Union government of Louisiana. Sumner opposed the bill because Louisiana's new state constitution denied suffrage to African Americans. Naturally, the Massachusetts senator was reluctant to accept Louisiana's vote for ratification while denying its membership in the Union. Three days after Congress approved the Thirteenth Amendment, Sumner proposed a resolution keeping the seceded states out of any calculation regarding ratification.[39]

Logic was on Sumner's side. As the senator pointed out, when Congress debated the amendment, it demanded approval from only two-thirds of the congressmen then in attendance; it did not figure in the senators and representatives who had joined the Confederacy and left their chairs vacant. Congress would act inconsistently, therefore, if it included the rebellious states among the total number of states needed for ratification. Some fellow radicals agreed. William S. Robinson, a reporter and an old ally of Sumner, thought it particularly absurd that the "borough 'Virginia' has ratified the constitutional amendment," and he urged the senator to press his resolution.[40]

Most of Sumner's Republican colleagues in Congress, however, refused to lend their support. Senator Lyman Trumbull, who, as the amendment's sponsor the year before, had assumed that the southern states were to be included for the sake of ratification, dismissed Sumner's point as irrelevant.[41] Trumbull's opposition came as little surprise to Sumner, for the

---

39 *CG*, 38th Cong., 2d sess. (February 4, 1865), 588; Michael Les Benedict, *A Compromise of Principle: Congressional Radicals and Reconstruction, 1863–1869* (New York: W. W. Norton, 1974), 88–96; Herman Belz, *Reconstructing the Union: Theory and Policy during the Civil War* (Ithaca: Cornell University Press, 1969), 267–74.
40 Robinson to Sumner, February 10, 1865, Charles Sumner MSS, HL.
41 *CG*, 38th Cong., 1st sess. (March 28, 1864), 1314; ibid., 2d sess. (February 23, 1865), 1010–11. The leading argument against Sumner on the ratification question was made by James R. Doolittle of Wisconsin; see ibid. (February 23, 1865), 1010.

senator from Illinois was also leading the fight to readmit Louisiana over Sumner's objections.[42] More unsettling to Sumner must have been the resistance from one of his radical allies, Jacob M. Howard of Michigan, who suggested that the matter be dropped, as "it is not of so much importance."[43] If Sumner expected to receive help from radicals in the other chamber of Congress, he was likewise disappointed. The manager of the amendment in the House, James M. Ashley, had originally stated that the southern states were to be omitted from the ratification process, but now the Ohioan was noticeably silent.[44] Eventually, Sumner accepted what friends like the historian George Bancroft had told him, that public opinion was against him, and that the southern states might ultimately challenge the amendment's legitimacy if they were denied the chance to ratify it.[45] The normally relentless New England senator decided not to force his point, and he let the resolution die on the table. The Thirty-eighth Congress adjourned on March 3, 1865, having made no official pronouncement on either the status of the rebellious states or the number of states needed for ratification of the Thirteenth Amendment.

That left the oversight of ratification in the hands of the Lincoln administration, at least until the new Congress convened in December. But the president was not as active in securing the amendment's ratification as he had been in ensuring its approval by Congress. In his second inaugural address of March 1865, he delivered his most powerful message so far predicting the doom of slavery: that the war might continue "until every drop of blood drawn with the lash, shall be paid by another drawn with the sword."[46] But Lincoln said nothing of the antislavery amendment in particular. The war still weighed heavily on him, and he knew that outlawing slavery was meaningless in the absence of military triumph. Not until Robert E. Lee surrendered the Army of Northern Virginia to Ulysses S. Grant on April 9, 1865, did Lincoln turn his attention to seeing the amendment through to ratification.

Two days after Lee's surrender, the president delivered the first of many anticipated postwar addresses on reconstruction. The speech was mostly a restatement of his desire to restore the seceded states to "practical relations" with the Union without adhering to a single plan of reconstruction. Lincoln did have some new things to say, however. First, he made public an opinion he had held privately for at least a year, that black veterans and

42 David Donald, *Charles Sumner and the Rights of Man* (New York: Alfred A. Knopf, 1970), 197–205.
43 *CG*, 38th Cong., 2d sess. (February 23, 1865), 1011.
44 Ibid. (January 6, 1865), 140.
45 Bancroft to Sumner, February 27, 1865, Charles Sumner MSS, HL.
46 *CW*, 8:333.

"the very intelligent" of the race in Louisiana should be granted voting rights by the unionist government of that state. By extension, the president seemed to approve of limited black suffrage everywhere, a truly revolutionary step. Also, he tried to rally popular support for the bill recognizing Louisiana, which the Senate had just rejected.

Finally, Lincoln addressed the issue of the antislavery amendment, a subject he had said nothing about since Congress voted for it more than two months before. Without mentioning Sumner by name, the president challenged the senator's claim that only three-fourths of the *loyal* states were needed for ratification. As in all matters, Lincoln thought it was "a merely pernicious abstraction" to question whether the seceded states were still in the Union and thus qualified to ratify. A ratification by only three-fourths of the loyal states "would be questionable," said Lincoln, "while a ratification by three fourths of all the States would be unquestioned and unquestionable." He noted that Louisiana had already voted for ratification, and "if we reject Louisiana, we also reject one vote in favor of the proposed amendment." Once again, the president used the amendment to encourage a speedy reconstruction.[47]

Lincoln never had the chance to see the amendment through to ratification. Three days after his speech on reconstruction, he was assassinated.

The new president, Andrew Johnson, adopted Lincoln's policy toward southern ratification. Relying heavily on the advice of Seward, still the secretary of state, Johnson accepted ratifications from former Confederate states not yet recognized by Congress. Although Johnson's first proclamations on reconstruction said nothing about the amendment, he later implored the provisional governors in the South to endorse ratification at their state constitutional conventions.[48]

Johnson's reconstruction terms included a requirement that ex-Confederate states abolish slavery by their new constitutions, so why did he desire their ratification votes as well? One reason was to use southern ratification to keep Congress from undermining Johnson's conservative reconstruction program, which offered liberal terms of amnesty to ex-Confederates (except those owning more than $20,000 in property), and which allowed southern state governments to prohibit black suffrage. If, by the time Congress convened in December, the amendment had been ratified with the help of southern states, Johnson's Republican opponents might think twice about denying the southern states their place in the Union. Excluding these states might come at the embarrassing price of

47 *CW*, 8:399–405.
48 Hans L. Trefousse, *Andrew Johnson: A Biography* (New York: W. W. Norton, 1989), 218–19; Michael Perman, *Reunion without Compromise: The South and Reconstruction: 1865–1868* (Cambridge: Cambridge University Press, 1973), 74–75.

nullifying constitutional emancipation. Also, the amendment would assure the death of slavery in the border states, which were exempt from the reconstruction proclamations, and it would outlaw slavery in those southern states that refused to comply with Johnson's reconstruction terms. Finally, a constitutional amendment jointly recognized by sections recently in conflict would carry much symbolic value for the reconstructed Union. Like Abraham Lincoln, Andrew Johnson saw the amendment not only as a legal weapon against slavery but as a tool for sectional reconciliation.

But former Confederates were reluctant to accept the amendment as the salve of reunion. For a few recalcitrant ex-Confederates, opposition to constitutional emancipation was a form of collective denial. By refusing to make even the minimum admission that slavery was destroyed, southern whites could avoid the dishonor of conceding total defeat to the North. Some South Carolinians, according to a planter from that state, believed that "if the people of the South will watch and wait, take no oaths and remain as they are, slavery will yet be saved."[49] Yet most white southerners accepted the ultimate destruction of slavery. Those who opposed the emancipation amendment generally did so not because they hoped to preserve the antebellum institution, but because they saw the amendment, particularly its enforcement clause, as a revolutionary device surrendering their states to the control of federal authorities and African Americans. When the provisional governor of Mississippi, William L. Sharkey, followed Johnson's directive and recommended the amendment to his state's constitutional convention, delegates demanded to know the meaning of the measure's enforcement provision. "That section gives to Congress broad, and almost, I may say, unlimited power," said one speaker. "I am not willing to trust to men who know nothing of slavery the power to frame a code for the freedmen of the State of Mississippi."[50]

The southern ratification debates, then, were but minor variations on the debates in the North and in the border states. In the eyes of conservatives determined to preserve social order and states' rights, the amendment was nothing short of a license for social and political revolution. Not one southern state convention endorsed the amendment. Instead, all the conventions postponed the issue. Many of the conventions justified postponement by reasoning that ratification by convention would be illegitimate because the congressional resolution sending the amendment to

---

49   George W. Williams to Benjamin F. Perry, cited in Perman, *Reunion without Compromise,* 87. See Dan T. Carter, *When the War Was Over: The Failure of Self-Reconstruction in the South, 1865–1867* (Baton Rouge: Louisiana State University Press, 1985), 82–85.

50   *Journal of the Mississippi Constitutional Convention of 1865,* cited in Howard Devon Hamilton, "The Legislative and Judicial History of the Thirteenth Amendment" (Ph.D. diss., University of Illinois, 1950), 29.

the states specified ratification by *legislatures*. In fact, because the Constitution allowed states to ratify amendments by legislature or convention, and because there was no precedent for rejecting one of these methods of ratification, the State Department would most likely have treated ratification votes in convention as legitimate. The crucial point here was that, regardless of whether ratification could take place in a convention, the decision by southern conventions to postpone ratification jeopardized the amendment. Because most of the southern legislatures were not scheduled to meet until the end of the year, chances were slim that the amendment would be ratified by the time Congress convened. That was unacceptable to Johnson and Seward, both of whom feared that at the next meeting of Congress, which was a new, more radical body than the one before, the southern states would be disqualified from ratification.

Desperate for the amendment's adoption, the Johnson administration in late summer supplemented its demand for ratification with assurances of the measure's limited scope. To the governors of North Carolina and Mississippi, the president sent messages recommending that, in addition to pressing for ratification, they should also propose "such laws . . . for the protection of freedmen, in person and property, as justice and equity demand."[51] Johnson obviously expected the freed people to enjoy at least some civil rights, including, as he specified, the right to testify in court, but he wanted state lawmakers to know that the power to confer such rights would remain with the states. In a similar vein, Secretary of State Seward tried to defuse the enforcement clause. When Benjamin F. Perry, the provisional governor of South Carolina, informed the president that his state would never consent to the clause, which "may be construed to give Congress power of local legislation over the negroes, and white men," Seward responded that the objection was "querulous and unreasonable." The enforcement clause, the secretary wrote, "is really restraining in its effect, instead of enlarging the powers of Congress."[52]

One had to squint hard to read a provision that gave Congress the power to enforce emancipation, a power it had never had before, as "restraining in its effect." Seward's message infuriated the radical ex-general Ben Butler, who had welcomed the amendment as the foundation of legal equality between the races. Butler immediately wrote to the radical congressman Thaddeus Stevens that when Congress met, it should adopt a broad civil rights bill "so that hereafter no sophistry can claim that the word 'appropriate' is a *restrained* word."[53] Seward, a veteran

---

51 Perman, *Reunion without Compromise,* 78.

52 "Messages from the President of the United States," Senate Exec. Doc. 26, 39th Cong., 1st sess., 1966, 254, 198.

53 Butler to Stevens, November 20, 1865, Thaddeus Stevens MSS, LC.

lawyer and legislator, knew very well that Congress might use the second clause to authorize new legislation on behalf of African Americans. But he was also a practical politician, a master at shading the truth just enough to secure his objective. When he drafted his message on enforcement to South Carolina, his primary goal had been to appease southern fears about federal power, not to resolve with finality the meaning of constitutional freedom. As he had said before – but carefully omitted now – the ultimate decisions on slavery would be made not by the executive, but by Congress and the courts. Seward was simply acting like Lincoln before him: instead of trying to resolve the amendment's ambiguity, he capitalized on it to restore the Union.

The Johnson-Seward strategy met with only moderate success. When the Mississippi legislature convened, it rejected ratification, stating that the amendment's enforcement clause was "a dangerous grant of power . . . which, by construction, might admit federal legislation in respect to persons, denizens and inhabitants of the state."[54] South Carolina's legislature voted for ratification, but only on the basis of Seward's message eviscerating the amendment's second clause. The South Carolina legislature attached to its ratification a declaration that "any attempt by Congress toward legislating upon the political status of former slaves, or their civil relations, would be contrary to the Constitution of the United States, as it now is, or as it would be altered by the proposed amendment."[55] In the South, as in the North, state lawmakers used the ratification debates as opportunities to offer a distinctive interpretation of the amendment. In declaring the enforcement clause ineffectual, the states maintained their pose of defiance.

A more immediate motive also lay behind the southern renunciation of the amendment's second section. By the end of 1865, two southern states, Mississippi and South Carolina, had adopted "black codes," a set of vagrancy laws, legal apprenticeships, and broad local police powers that forced ex-slaves to enter into labor contracts against their will. Every other southern state adopted such codes during the following year.[56] The black codes were a violation of freedom of contract, one of the civil rights that Republicans expected to flow from the amendment. Because South Carolina and other states anticipated that congressional Republicans

54 "Report of the Joint Standing Committee [of Mississippi] on State and Federal Relations," cited in George H. Hoemann, *What God Hath Wrought: The Embodiment of Freedom in the Thirteenth Amendment* (New York: Garland, 1987), 156.
55 *Documentary History of the Constitution*, 2:606.
56 Eric Foner, *Reconstruction: America's Unfinished Revolution, 1863–1877* (New York: Harper and Row, 1988), 198–210; Perman, *Reunion without Compromise*, 68–109; Donald G. Nieman, *To Set the Law in Motion: The Freedmen's Bureau and the Legal Rights of Blacks, 1865–1868* (Millwood, N.Y.: KTO Press, 1979), 72–102.

would try to use the Thirteenth Amendment to outlaw the codes, they made the preemptive strike of declaring in their ratification resolutions that Congress could not use the amendment's second clause to legislate on freed people's civil rights.

What southern lawmakers feared most, however, was Congress using the enforcement clause to grant suffrage rights to ex-slaves. In Alabama's ratification resolution, for example, the legislature qualified the amendment's effect only on political rights, not civil rights; it ratified the amendment with the "understanding that it does not confer upon Congress the power to Legislate upon the political status of Freedmen in this State."[57] When Johnson and Seward announced that the second clause "restrained" congressional power, they probably were most interested in pacifying conservative fears, North and South, that the amendment would empower the federal government to force states to give African Americans the vote. Of all the fears expressed during the ratification debates, this one was perhaps the most unfounded. Regardless of how they felt about African Americans securing the vote, supporters of the amendment had consistently argued that this measure alone would not lead to black suffrage. Now, in the ratification debates, proamendment legislators again declared that the states would continue to regulate the vote. A New Jersey War Democrat who voted for ratification said that if "the second clause conferred upon Congress the right to interfere with suffrage in the States, he would allow his right arm to be cut off." James Scovel, the most prominent Republican in the legislature, concurred.[58] In Kentucky, Governor Bramlette, who had failed to carry the amendment through the legislature in early 1865, at the end of that year tried again with the promise that "the adoption of the proposed amendment will give us perpetual indemnity against the attempt to control the question of suffrage through the Federal power."[59] That was the same message that Johnson and other conservatives had delivered to the seceded states: ratifying the amendment meant retaining control of the suffrage; opposing the amendment meant inviting congressional interference.

But at the same time that Bramlette promised noninterference with voting rights, he revealed that he now had a broader interpretation of the amendment than he had had when he addressed the legislature on the subject ten months before. In his early message, he went along with those who said that the amendment would have no effect on Kentucky's pro-

57 *Documentary History of the Constitution,* 2:610.
58 Trenton *State Gazette,* January 24, 1866, p. 2. See William Gillette, *Jersey Blue: Civil War Politics in New Jersey, 1854–1865* (Brunswick, N.J.: Rutgers University Press, 1995), 318–26.
59 *Journal of the Senate of the Commonwealth of Kentucky,* 1865–66, 20–21.

scriptions against free blacks. Now he told the legislature that the amendment protected all people's "right to *life, liberty* and *property*," and therefore that the measure would empower the federal government to outlaw the Mississippi black codes and the Indiana black law barring African American immigration (and, implicitly, Kentucky's law requiring freed people to leave the state).[60] In one respect, Bramlette's statement was unusual: rarely did people prior to ratification suggest that the amendment might affect civil rights in a loyal state like Indiana. Yet, in another respect, the message did reflect popular views. There was a growing sense among northerners and border state unionists that the federal government would and should use the amendment to ensure the civil rights of African Americans in the seceded states. Political rights, however, were another matter. Bramlette, like most in the Union, was not ready to equate constitutional freedom with the vote.

The promise of noninterference with suffrage did little to change the minds of legislators determined to block ratification. The Kentucky legislature rejected Bramlette's appeal and voted against ratification. The border state of Delaware joined Kentucky, as did New Jersey, which still had a powerful majority of conservative Democrats in its legislature.[61]

As it turned out, ratification by these three Union states was unnecessary. Two weeks before Congress convened in December 1865, Secretary of State Seward, knowing that congressional Republicans might dictate their own terms of ratification, launched a final offensive to secure the amendment's adoption. If Seward thought that the conditional ratifications delivered by the ex-Confederate states were illegitimate, he did not show it. He accepted the ratifications without challenge or comment. Meanwhile, to the governor of every state that had not yet recorded a vote, Seward wrote a letter requesting the state's verdict "as soon as convenient."[62] Some states that had already approved the measure, including New Hampshire, now sent in their official notice to the State Department. Meanwhile, Oregon, which had been slow to ratify, hurried its endorsement through the legislature so that it might have the honor of

---

60 Ibid., 19.
61 New Jersey ratified in 1866 – after the amendment had been declared adopted. It appears that Kentucky never ratified the amendment; certainly it had not done so by 1868, when the Fourteenth Amendment was ratified. Delaware finally ratified the Thirteenth Amendment, along with the Fourteenth and Fifteenth, in 1901. See *Enrolled Bills of Delaware,* 1901, vol. 1, Senate Joint Resolution 13, Delaware State Archives, Hall of Records, Dover, Delaware; and Patience Essah, *A House Divided: Slavery and Emancipation in Delaware, 1638–1865* (Charlottesville: University Press of Virginia, 1996), 186–90.
62 See, for example, Seward to Gove Saulsbury, November 18, 1865, Executive papers, Delaware State Archives, Hall of Records, Dover, Delaware.

giving the last vote required for adoption.[63] The free state of Oregon, however, was edged out by the former slave state of Georgia, which, on December 6, 1865, became the twenty-seventh state to ratify. On December 18, Seward issued a proclamation declaring the amendment adopted.[64] "No event of this period, or any other period, is so remarkable or so grand," reported the *Cincinnati Gazette*.[65] William Canby, a Delaware resident, wrote in his diary, "I am glad, for one, that I have *lived to this day*."[66]

As if by divine arrangement, on the day of Seward's ratification proclamation, Thomas Corwin died. Almost five years before, the former Ohio senator had sponsored the "first" Thirteenth Amendment, which prohibited the adoption of an antislavery amendment. Appropriately, on the day Corwin died, so, finally, did slavery.

Enacting the Amendment: Congress and Civil Rights

With the end of ratification and the convening of Congress in December 1865, abstract speculation about enforcing the amendment gave way to actual legislation. Already, members of the Republican party, which held a majority in the new Thirty-ninth Congress, had offered a hint of what was to come. The Ohio congressman James A. Garfield told a July 4 rally that the new Congress would use the amendment to outlaw the new black codes in the South, for freedom meant more than "the bare privilege of not being chained."[67] President Johnson and Secretary of State Seward had tried to counter such statements with assurances that the amendment signaled only partisan and sectional healing.[68] They worked with prowar Democratic editors like Manton Marble and James G. Bennett to send the message to Congress and the South that the ratification of the amendment forestalled further federal intervention in the southern states. Marble's *New York World* announced that the amendment put an end to disputes "respecting rights acquired by the negroes."[69] Bennett's *New York Herald* added that Congress could no longer exclude states that had ratified the amendment: to do so "upsets the great constitutional amendment – an amendment which the people of all parties and all sections accept as a

63 Hoemann, *What God Hath Wrought*, 156, 165 n. 59.
64 *Documentary History of the Constitution*, 2:636–37.
65 *Cincinnati Gazette*, December 21, 1865, p. 2.
66 William Canby diary, December 19, 1865, HSD.
67 "Oration delivered at Ravenna, Ohio, July 4, 1865," in Burke A. Hinsdale, ed., *The Works of James Abram Garfield* (Boston: J. R. Osgood, 1882), 1:86.
68 See LaWanda Cox and John H. Cox, *Politics, Principle, and Prejudice, 1865–1866: Dilemma of Reconstruction America* (New York: Free Press, 1963), 50–67, 88–106.
69 *New York Daily World*, December 20, 1865, p. 4.

fixed fact."[70] The new Congress was quick to put the lie to this conservative reading of the amendment. Led by Lyman Trumbull, one of the sponsors of the amendment, congressional Republicans passed and eventually
adopted over President Johnson's veto the Freedmen's Bureau Act, which
enlarged the power and extended the life of the bureau, and the Civil
Rights Act of 1866, which offered African Americans federal protection
from discriminatory treatment by the states. By invoking the Thirteenth
Amendment's enforcement clause to pass these measures, Republicans
confirmed that, regardless of how they saw the amendment before, they
now considered it the foundation, not the capstone, of federal legislation
on behalf of African Americans.

The Freedmen's Bureau Act and Civil Rights Act offered unprecedented
legal protection to African Americans, yet historians remain divided over
whether they were truly revolutionary. The dispute is due in part to the
fact that the acts did two things at once, one of which the Republican
backers of the Thirteenth Amendment had largely anticipated, and one of
which they had not.[71]

On the nonrevolutionary side, the acts made explicit those civil rights
secured by the amendment that had so far been only implied or briefly
mentioned. African Americans could make and enforce contracts (including labor contracts), buy and sell property, and testify and sue in court.
These rights were to be enforced by federal judges (under the Civil Rights
Act) and Freedmen's Bureau agents (under the Freedmen's Bureau Act).
Although the acts might be read today as a promise of aggressive federal
intervention on behalf of civil rights, not all lawmakers saw them that way
in 1866. States could still discriminate on the basis of sex, age, mental
capacity, and place of birth. Also, the acts did not specify how far the
federal courts could go in upholding the law. Certainly the federal courts
could intervene when state laws or judicial rulings were explicitly
discriminatory, but in the absence of explicit discrimination, the federal
government's role was ambiguous. Many judges and lawmakers, including a good number of Republicans, expected federal authorities to allow

---

70 *New York Herald,* December 21, 1865, p. 4.
71 For an interpretation that leans toward the acts as revolutionary, see Robert J. Ka-
    czorowski, "To Begin the Nation Anew: Congress, Citizenship, and Civil Rights after
    the Civil War," *American Historical Review,* 92 (February 1987), 45–68. For the
    opposite view, see Earl M. Maltz, *Civil Rights, the Constitution, and Congress, 1863–
    1869* (Lawrence: University Press of Kansas, 1990), 61–78. The most balanced assess-
    ments may be found in Herman Belz, *A New Birth of Freedom: The Republican Party
    and Freedmen's Rights, 1861 to 1866* (Westport, Conn.: Greenwood Press, 1976),
    157–82; and Michael Les Benedict, "Preserving the Constitution: The Conservative
    Basis of 'Radical Reconstruction,'" *Journal of American History,* 61 (June 1974): 65–
    90.

state courts to oversee much of enforcement rather than removing to federal courts all legal matters concerning African Americans.[72]

The revolutionary aspect of the new legislation lay in the first section of the Civil Rights Act, which declared: "all persons born in the United States and not subject to any foreign power, excluding Indians not taxed, are hereby declared to be citizens of the United States."[73] This clause was meant to resolve the ambiguity of citizenship and to reverse the *Dred Scott* decision of 1857, which denied national citizenship to African Americans. Black citizenship might have been a logical sequel to emancipation, but it was rarely something envisioned by the original backers of the Thirteenth Amendment as embodied in the amendment itself. In those rare instances during the passage and ratification of the amendment when Republicans spoke of the rights secured by the measure, they almost always distinguished between "natural" rights that the amendment conferred and "citizenship" rights or "relative" rights that it did not. "Natural" rights were those civil rights that one enjoyed simply by reason of one's freedom. The right to the fruit of one's labor was the natural right most commonly mentioned by Republicans. "Citizenship" rights or "relative" rights, by contrast, were thought of as privileges that had to be secured by positive legislation – at least for white women and nonwhites of both sexes. These might include the political right of suffrage or the social right of unrestricted access to public conveyances.[74] Although Republicans during the passage and ratification of the amendment had expressed different ideas about which exact rights were natural, most understood that it was these sorts of rights, as opposed to citizenship rights, that the amendment was meant to confer. Many Republicans had wanted to establish equal citizenship for blacks, but they had seen that quest as separate from, albeit related to, the goal of constitutional emancipation.

Together, the Civil Rights Act and the Freedmen's Bureau Act were less than a pure revolution in law but more than a mere clarification. They simultaneously looked backward to the Thirteenth Amendment and forward to the Fourteenth Amendment, which Congress would soon adopt

---

72 Robert J. Kaczorowski, *The Politics of Judicial Interpretation: The Federal Courts, Department of Justice and Civil Rights, 1866–1876* (New York: Oceana Publications, 1985), esp. 1–48; Kaczorowski, "To Begin the Nation Anew," 55–59; Patricia Allan Lucie, *Freedom and Federalism: Congress and the Courts, 1861–1866* (New York: Garland, 1986), 166–77; Nieman, *To Set the Law in Motion*, 106–15; Belz, *A New Birth of Freedom*, 161–70; Benedict, "Preserving the Constitution," 78–81.

73 *Statutes at Large*, 14 (1866), 27 (chap. 31, sec. 1).

74 For the difference between civil, political, and social rights during this period, see Harold M. Hyman and William M. Wiecek, *Equal Justice under Law: Constitutional Development, 1835–1875* (New York: Harper and Row, 1982), 386–438.

and which engrafted the principle of birthright citizenship onto the Constitution.

The debates over the Civil Rights Act and the Freedmen's Bureau Act were part of an inevitable effort to map out rights in the postwar nation, but, in another sense, they were part of a less foreseeable struggle about the nature of original meanings – in this case, the original meaning of the Thirteenth Amendment. Senators Trumbull and Howard, Republican members of the Judiciary Committee that drafted the amendment, made assertions about the amendment's purpose that they had not mentioned during the initial amendment debate. Trumbull said that the measure was meant to abolish not only slavery but "all provisions of State or local law" that infringed on a person's right to property, freedom of movement, and education.[75] Howard went even further and claimed that the Judiciary Committee had originally intended that the amendment give "to persons who are of different races or colors the same civil rights."[76]

Certainly this understanding of the amendment was only inchoate rather than clearly expressed when the Judiciary Committee had met in early 1864. And even if Howard and Trumbull had originally thought of the amendment in this way, their reading of the measure slighted the interpretation originally offered by War Democrats and conservative Republicans who had helped secure the amendment's adoption. In the initial congressional consideration of the amendment, and again in the state ratification debates, conservatives like Senator John B. Henderson of Missouri, the measure's sponsor, had assured their colleagues that the amendment affected no state laws other than the law of slavery. Two years after Henderson proposed the amendment, however, freedom had developed a clearer meaning to most Republicans. Because of the appearance of southern black codes, the majority of Republicans could now see that freedom must mean not simply the absence of bondage but of other legal disabilities as well. The earlier, narrower reading of constitutional freedom now found only a small following among Democrats and a few conservative Republicans like Senator Edgar Cowan of Pennsylvania, who accused Trumbull and Howard of distorting the amendment's original meaning and attempting to use the measure to "revolutionize all the laws of the states everywhere."[77]

So whose reading of the Thirteenth Amendment, Cowan's or Trumbull's, was truest to the measure? Did Trumbull and Howard purposefully exaggerate the scope of the amendment as it was initially perceived? Was Cowan's reading of the amendment truer to history? And what about the

75 CG, 39th Cong., 1st sess. (January 19, 1866), 322.
76 Ibid. (January 30, 1866), 503–4.
77 Ibid., 499.

reading given by the Peace Democrats? They originally criticized the amendment for granting broad powers to the federal government but now joined Cowan in saying that the measure authorized only minimal federal intervention.

The quest to determine which interpretation of the Thirteenth Amendment is most credible or most authoritative is endless and, to a certain extent, pointless, for the measure *never* had a single, fixed meaning. Those who initially approved of the amendment had diverse, competing motivations as well as disparate notions about freedom, many of which were not fully formed or, for political purposes, not explicitly stated. And even before the amendment had been approved by Congress and ratified by the states, congressmen, like all Americans, had begun to reevaluate the measure in new social, political, and legal contexts. In 1864 Trumbull did not foresee the need for specific civil rights legislation, and therefore he was mute on the question of enforcement. But between the time of the Senate's approval of the amendment in that year and state ratification at the end of the next, the appearance of black codes in the South made him better appreciate and articulate the potential of the enforcement clause. In 1864 Peace Democrats believed that the federal government would use the amendment to undermine the authority of the states. A year later, seeing that some measure of states' rights would survive the amendment's adoption, they could believe that restrained federal enforcement was possible. Political posturing surely played a role in people's shifting positions on the amendment. But changing attitudes also represented a natural adjustment to unforeseen circumstances.

If they had not done so before, Americans now understood that freedom did not materialize magically out of legal abolition. But, even for many Republicans, this clearer sense of the meaning of freedom was still circumscribed by a limited vision of racial justice and a narrow understanding of federal power. Conservative Republicans preferred that the states rather than the federal government uphold civil rights. And Republicans as a whole ignored the amendment's potential impact on African Americans' legal status in the North.[78] Party members also tended to draw a clear line between the amendment and suffrage rights, although many Republicans worked assiduously for black suffrage at the same time

78 Because the Senate voted down Senator Cowan's proposal that the civil rights bill be limited to those states "such as have lately been in rebellion" (ibid., January 22, 1866, 374), it might seem that Republicans meant the bill to apply to the northern as well as the southern states. In fact, it was not the northern states but the border states that Republicans had in mind when they rejected Cowan's proposal. The Pennsylvania senator's provision would have thwarted the federal government's ability to enforce the Thirteenth Amendment in the slave states that had not seceded: Missouri, Kentucky, Maryland, and Delaware.

that they tried to secure the amendment's adoption.[79] Finally, Republicans did not explore what specific legal rights non-African Americans might gain as a result of the amendment. Republicans continued to champion the abstract ideal of free labor, but they did not yet seem to realize that the constitutional abolition of "involuntary servitude" might authorize legislation protecting workers of all colors.[80]

The struggle over the meaning of constitutional freedom revealed the ideological evolution not only in the Republican party but also in the Democracy. States' rights and white supremacy were still staples of Democratic ideology. But no longer as hardy was the onetime Democratic adherence to the "Constitution as it is." Democrats opposed the Fourteenth and Fifteenth Amendments as inexpedient and ultrarevolutionary, but they rarely dredged up the argument they had made against the Thirteenth Amendment: that the very process of constitutional revision could itself be illegitimate. Indeed, even the most notorious Peace Democrat of the era, Clement L. Vallandigham, began to embrace the idea of amending the Constitution as a means of reform. "If we cannot have the 'Constitution as it is,'" Vallandigham wrote to an old party ally in 1866, "let us accept the demand of the Republicans, and have the 'Constitution as it ought to be'; but let *us* determine what it 'ought to be.' Let *us* make the issues, and *agitate* till we accomplish our objects. Let us once more be 'the progressive Democracy.'" Unsurprisingly, the "progressive" plan Vallandigham had in mind included "a white man's government."[81]

The Civil Rights Act and Freedmen's Bureau Act briefly established the Thirteenth Amendment as the most powerful constitutional weapon protecting equal rights. The antithesis of slavery, proclaimed the Republican majority of the Thirty-ninth Congress, was more than the privilege of not having one's body or labor owned by another. Freedom from bondage carried additional federally protected civil rights. But the same Congress that endorsed a broad interpretation of the amendment unwittingly un-

---

79 Xi Wang, *The Trial of Democracy: Black Suffrage and Northern Republicans, 1860-1910* (Athens: University of Georgia Press, 1997), 15–18. Most Republicans believed suffrage should be secured at the state level, but some radicals already envisioned federal protection of suffrage rights. Frederick Douglass, for example, announced on January 13, 1865, almost three weeks prior to congressional passage of the Thirteenth Amendment, that "every colored man [is] bound in virtue of his manhood to demand of the American Government the elective franchise." "Black Freedom Is the Prerequisite of Victory: An Address Delivered in New York, New York, on 13 January 1865," in John W. Blassingame et al., eds., *The Frederick Douglass Papers* (New Haven: Yale University Press, 1991), ser. 1, 4:59.

80 Lea S. VanderVelde, "The Labor Vision of the Thirteenth Amendment," *University of Pennsylvania Law Review*, 138 (December 1989), 437–504.

81 Vallandigham to George W. Morgan, December 11, 1866, Vallandigham and Laird family MSS, WRH.

dermined the measure's effect on future civil rights law. By approving the Fourteenth Amendment, which granted citizenship to all persons born or naturalized in the United States, and which prohibited any state from denying a person "due process of law" or "equal protection of the laws," Congress diminished the significance of the Thirteenth Amendment in the eyes of future lawmakers. For a hundred years after the ratification of the Fourteenth Amendment in 1868, legislators and judges searching for constitutional guidelines on civil rights slighted the Thirteenth Amendment in favor of its younger sibling.

Legacies Denied: The Thirteenth Amendment in the Gilded Age

In the years following the Civil War, most Americans, perhaps out of shame for having allowed slavery to survive so long, chose to regard the Thirteenth Amendment only as an obvious end to the Civil War or a small first step toward legal equality. They failed to remember that the amendment was once seen as the pinnacle of freedom instead of a mere precursor to the Fourteenth and Fifteenth Amendments.

The two crucial acts spawned by the amendment, the Civil Rights Act of 1866 and the Freedmen's Bureau Act, were largely forgotten in the post-Reconstruction era. The Freedmen's Bureau dissolved as the federal troops that supported the institution left and southern states returned to "home rule." The Civil Rights Act of 1866 was preserved, but its component parts were separated during revisions of the U.S. statutes in the early 1870s, making the act very difficult to use by lawyers in civil rights cases.[82]

The clearest sign of the amendment's withering legacy was the neglect it received from the Supreme Court. Usually the Court treated constitutional abolition simply as a predestined consequence of a war caused by slavery. To his credit, Chief Justice Salmon P. Chase invoked the amendment to strike down discriminatory black apprenticeships as part of the *In Re Turner* case of 1866. But even Chase tended to play down the revolutionary quality of the amendment. Like many of his friends in the antislavery cause, Chase read the measure as a mere declaratory supplement to a Constitution that had always been antislavery and egalitarian. In his dissent in *Osborn v. Nicholson,* an 1871 case of slave warranty involving compensation for the former owner of an emancipated bondsman, he wrote that the amendment may have annulled all "positive law" uphold-

---

82   Harold M. Hyman, *The Reconstruction Justice of Salmon P. Chase: In Re Turner and Texas v. White* (Lawrence: University Press of Kansas, 1997), 132.

ing slavery, but even without the amendment the law of slavery was "against sound morals and natural justice." Therefore, Chase noted, the amendment merely restored "the common law of all the States . . . to its original principles of liberty, justice, and right."[83]

The Court was always willing to concede that the amendment guaranteed freedom from slavery, but it took an increasingly narrow view of the breadth of this freedom and the power invested in the federal government to uphold freedom. After suggesting in some early decisions that the amendment assured a wide slate of federally protected civil rights to African Americans, the Supreme Court in 1872 began to chip away at federal protection. In that year, the Court ruled in *Blyew v. U.S.* that a state court did not violate the Thirteenth Amendment when, in a criminal case against a white person, black witnesses were denied the right to testify. The majority of the justices rejected the argument of justices Joseph P. Bradley and Noah H. Swayne that such discrimination against African Americans represented "a badge of slavery" – the first use of that phrase by the Court.[84] The next year, in the *Slaughterhouse Cases*, the Court was more explicit: the amendment was relevant only in cases of chattel slavery, not in those involving other types of civil rights violations, where only the Fourteenth Amendment would apply. For the next three decades, from *Slaughterhouse* to the *Civil Rights Cases* in 1883 to *Plessy v. Ferguson* in 1896, the majority of the Court continued to argue along this line as dissenters, most notably Justice John M. Harlan, protested that the Thirteenth Amendment should guarantee African Americans all of the "civil rights as belong to freemen of other races."[85] Finally, in the 1906 case *Hodges v. United States*, the Court dealt its strongest blow against the measure. It declared that the state courts were the exclusive arbiters of violations of the Thirteenth Amendment.[86]

---

83 U.S. Supreme Court, *United States Reports,* 80 (1871), 663–64. See Hyman, *The Reconstruction Justice of Salmon P. Chase,* 123–31. On the debate over the amendment as declaratory or truly amendatory, see Jacobus tenBroek, *Equal under Law* (1951; repr., New York: Collier Books, 1965), 170–73.

84 *United States Reports,* 80 (1871), 644. The phrase "badge of servitude" already had appeared in Congress – Lyman Trumbull used it when he proposed the Civil Rights Act of 1866 to the Senate; see *CG,* 39th Cong., 1st sess. (January 29, 1866), 474.

85 *United States Reports,* 109 (1883), 848.

86 I have cited only those cases from which I have taken quotations; for summaries of and citations to the other cases mentioned here, as well as others relevant to the Thirteenth Amendment, see G. Sidney Buchanan, "The Quest for Freedom: A Legal History of the Thirteenth Amendment," *Houston Law Review,* 12 (1974–75), 1–34, 331–78, 592–639, 843–89, 1069–85. See also Aviam Soifer, "The Paradox of Paternalism and Laissez-Faire Constitutionalism: United States Supreme Court, 1888–1921," *Law and History Review,* 5 (Spring 1987), 249–79; and Soifer, "Status, Contract, and Promises Unkept," *Yale Law Journal,* 96 (July 1987), 1916–59.

The Court's narrow reading of the Thirteenth Amendment was coupled with an evisceration of the Fourteenth Amendment. By 1900 the Court had left the regulation of citizenship rights mostly to the states and allowed federal intervention only when state actions or state laws overtly violated the amendment, a principle that became known as the "state action" doctrine. The doctrine rested on the wording of the amendment, which prohibited states from denying "due process" and "equal protection" rights rather than explicitly granting those rights to all citizens. Because the Thirteenth Amendment had no state action wording, it could have become an even more powerful weapon than the Fourteenth in securing federally protected civil rights. That possibility made the Court's treatment of the Thirteenth Amendment even more tragic.

The Thirteenth Amendment fared little better in cases involving the rights of labor. The constitutional prohibition of involuntary servitude might well have been used to protect workers of all colors, North and South, from harsh labor practices. At first, it seemed that the amendment might have precisely such an effect. In 1867 Congress invoked the measure to pass an antipeonage statute, which prohibited any law or private contract allowing employers to render debtors into forced laborers. In other words, Congress ruled that debt was not one of the crimes under the Thirteenth Amendment that was punishable by involuntary servitude. In an era when debt plagued most laborers, particularly agricultural workers, and employers systematically practiced "debt slavery," champions of worker rights welcomed the antipeonage statute. Yet Congress and the courts failed to enforce the statute, and the practice of peonage, particularly against African Americans in the South, continued largely undeterred and unchallenged until the first two decades of the twentieth century.[87] Meanwhile, the amendment's prohibition against "involuntary servitude" offered little legal recourse to laborers in cases not involving peonage. Again and again in the late nineteenth and early twentieth centuries, labor leaders invoked the amendment as a source of their rights against the interests of capital. Occasionally the courts agreed, at least when the issue was a union's right to strike. But in most other respects, the amendment failed to become a constitutional bedrock for the rights of labor. Lawmakers and jurists usually held that if laborers still possessed the right to quit, then they were not in a condition of involuntary servitude. Even today, the Supreme Court continues to read "involuntary" narrowly. In 1988 the Court ruled that the Thirteenth Amendment did not

87 Daniel A. Novak, *The Wheel of Servitude: Black Forced Labor after Slavery* (Lexington: University Press of Kentucky, 1978), 45–46. See Pete Daniel, *The Shadow of Slavery: Peonage in the South, 1901–1969* (1972; 2d ed., Urbana: University of Illinois Press, 1990).

assure laborers any rights beyond freedom from physical or legal coercion.[88]

As it failed to become the foundation of justice originally envisioned by its most radical advocates, the Thirteenth Amendment also languished as the catalyst for partisan realignment touted by its more conservative backers. Following the lead of Lincoln and Seward, Andrew Johnson had drawn southern unionists and northern Democrats behind the amendment, but he so alienated moderates and radicals that he was impeached and nearly convicted by them. Meanwhile, Democrats and Republicans who had united to promote constitutional abolition split on the issue of civil and political rights for African Americans. As hopes of political realignment faded during the last years of Reconstruction, the role of the amendment in partisan cooperation withered in American memory.

Only occasionally in the late nineteenth century did Republicans try to gloss over party differences by crediting wartime Democrats and border state unionists for the amendment. Two such politicians were Lyman Trumbull and James Ashley. During losing bids for political office late in their lives, Trumbull, who oversaw the amendment in the Senate, and Ashley, who managed it in the House, both tried to broaden their appeal by touting the opposition's role in securing the amendment.[89] In the same way, the former Republican congressman James G. Blaine, who published his memoir in the midst of his presidential campaign of 1884, carefully softened partisan antagonism by praising those Democrats who had supported the amendment and thus "gained for the cause of emancipation a whole year."[90]

More commonly, however, speakers and writers dismissed the temporary bipartisan alliance as the result of mere opportunism, if not illicit bargaining. Such was the verdict of the Republican Henry Wilson, whose

88 "United States v. Kozminski," *United States Reports,* 487 (October 1987), 931–76. See VanderVelde, "Labor Vision of the Thirteenth Amendment"; James Gray Pope, "Labor's Constitution of Freedom," *Yale Law Journal,* 106 (January 1997), 941–1031, esp. 962–66, 981–84; and William E. Forbath, *Law and the Shaping of the American Labor Movement* (Cambridge, Mass.: Harvard University Press, 1991), 135–39.

89 For Trumbull, who was then running as a Democrat, see Ralph Roske, *His Own Counsel: The Life and Times of Lyman Trumbull* (Reno: University of Nevada Press, 1979), 169–70; Horace White, *The Life of Lyman Trumbull* (Boston: Houghton Mifflin, 1913), 412; and John A. Logan, *The Democratic Party: Did it Abolish Slavery and Put Down the Rebellion?* (Chicago, 1881). For Ashley, see "Address before the Ohio Society of New York, February 20, 1890," in Benjamin W. Arnett, ed., *Orations and Speeches: Duplicate Copy of the Souvenir from the Afro-American League of Tennessee to Hon. James M. Ashley of Ohio* (Philadelphia: A.M.E. Church, 1894), 713; and Robert F. Horowitz, *The Great Impeacher: A Political Biography of James M. Ashley* (Brooklyn: Brooklyn College Press, 1979), 168.

90 James G. Blaine, *Twenty Years of Congress: From Lincoln to Garfield* (Norwich, Conn.: Henry Bill Publishing Company, 1884), 539.

monumental *Rise and Fall of the Slave Power in America* looked dubiously upon the congressional coalition that approved the amendment: "Many acted from the highest convictions of religious obligation. . . . Others were prompted mainly by humane considerations and a natural detestation of slavery. . . . But a larger number still, it is probable, acted from prudential considerations merely."[91] Other Republicans went further. In reminiscences published long after the war, former Republican congressmen George S. Boutwell, Albert G. Riddle, and George Julian all pointed to sinister intentions on the part of opposition congressmen who supported the amendment. Thanks in large part to such unflattering and politically motivated accounts, the amendment was permanently tainted with the mark of corruption.[92]

Instead of denying the corruption charge, Democrats usually took up the muckrake and swung it at Republicans. When Samuel S. "Sunset" Cox, a former Democratic congressman from Ohio, first published his memoirs in 1865, he mentioned nothing about crooked dealings behind the Thirteenth Amendment. But after rumors circulated casting a villainous light on the amendment's non-Republican supporters, Cox changed his story. In 1885, when he published his second autobiography, the former Ohioan, now living in New York, had just won a seat in Congress by campaigning against the financial misdealing of the Republican administration. Cox accordingly revised his tale of the Thirteenth Amendment's approval to include an episode in which a roguish, unnamed, "radical" Republican tried without success to reap a $1,000 payoff by securing Cox's vote.[93]

Regardless of the actual extent of corruption behind the passage of the Thirteenth Amendment – and certainly there was some – the later accounts of illicit activity did poor service to the cause of constitutional abolition. The widespread story that the Thirteenth Amendment was the offspring of expedient if not illegal politicking, combined with the judicial disuse of the measure, diminished the amendment in the eyes of the Amer-

91 Henry Wilson, *Rise and Fall of the Slave Power in America* (Boston: Houghton Mifflin, 1877), 3:453.
92 George S. Boutwell, *Reminiscences of Sixty Years in Public Affairs* (New York: McClure, Phillips, 1902), 36; Albert Gallatin Riddle, *Recollections of War Times: Reminiscences of Men and Events in Washington, 1860–1865* (New York: G. P. Putnam's Sons, 1895), 324–25; George W. Julian, *Political Recollections, 1840 to 1872* (Chicago: Jansen, McClurg, 1884), 249.
93 Samuel S. Cox, *Union – Disunion – Reunion: Three Decades of Federal Legislation, 1855–1885* (1885; repr., Freeport, N.Y.: Books for Libraries Press, 1970), 329; compare with the earlier memoir: Cox, *Eight Years in Congress, From 1857 to 1865* (New York: D. Appleton, 1865), 396–98. See David Lindsey, *"Sunset" Cox: Irrepressible Democrat* (Detroit: Wayne State University Press, 1959), 234–40.

ican people. For nearly a century after the measure's adoption, the amendment was all but effaced from public memory.

Legacies Preserved: The Thirteenth Amendment in the Twentieth Century

During its years of dormancy, the amendment was never entirely forgotten. African Americans in particular, denied many of the basic rights that they assumed would follow emancipation, strove to keep alive the memory of the amendment and of all other events marking the end of slavery. During the Civil War, African Americans had shown less interest in the amendment than in legislation more explicitly guaranteeing legal equality, but by the early twentieth century, the amendment began to play a stronger role in their historical memory. For African Americans, the amendment carried both negative and positive symbolic power. On the negative side, the amendment stood for the country's defaulted commitment to its black citizens. The writer and activist W. E. B. Du Bois, in his classic 1903 work *The Souls of Black Folk,* invoked the measure on behalf of rural African Americans still at the mercy of white landowners: "In those vast stretches of land beyond the telegraph and the newspaper, the spirit of the Thirteenth Amendment is sadly broken."[94] Thirty years later, when he wrote his *Black Reconstruction in America,* Du Bois again pointed to the contrast between the amendment's promise and its actual impact. "Slavery was not abolished even after the Thirteenth Amendment," he declared.[95]

Other African Americans embraced the measure as a positive reminder of their glorious progress, as yet unfinished, toward equality. In Philadelphia, for example, the African American community endeavored to preserve the amendment – or at least its memory – through "Freedom Day" observances. Celebrated on February 1, the day in 1865 when Abraham Lincoln signed the Thirteenth Amendment, Freedom Day was one of many local festivals held throughout the country to commemorate the day that slavery ended.[96]

Philadelphia's observance of the Thirteenth Amendment was in large part due to Richard R. Wright. Wright, not to be confused with the famous novelist of the same name, was a ten-year-old slave in rural Georgia when the amendment was ratified. His father served in the Union

---

94 W. E. B. Du Bois, *The Souls of Black Folk* (1903; repr., Chicago: A. C. McClurg, 1953), 152.
95 Du Bois, *Black Reconstruction in America* (1935; repr., New York: Russell and Russell, 1963), 188.
96 William H. Wiggins, Jr., *O Freedom! Afro-American Emancipation Celebrations* (Knoxville: University of Tennessee Press, 1987), 20–24.

army. After the Thirteenth Amendment was ratified, Wright's mother enrolled her son in one of the new, free black schools in Atlanta. Eventually, Wright moved to Philadelphia and became a prominent, successful banker. The former slave never forgot the moment of final freedom, and he spent much of his life trying to rehabilitate the Thirteenth Amendment in American memory. First he spearheaded the effort to have the United States postal service issue a three-cent "Thirteenth Amendment" postage stamp. Then, in the early 1940s, he organized "Freedom Day" celebrations in Philadelphia. Finally, in 1947, he pressed Congress to make February 1 an annual holiday: "National Freedom Day." With the help of a few congressmen, including the freshman senator from Wisconsin, Joseph McCarthy, the ex-slave was again successful, although he died before President Harry S. Truman signed the final act in 1948. Asked frequently to explain the relevance of the Thirteenth Amendment, Wright said that it was "the key to the door of our freedom, the corner-stone of our liberty," that "it not only freed the black man legally, but laid the ground work for the white man's [freedom] also," and that its observance would "promote . . . good will between the races."[97]

Most people in Wright's day could not claim such a personal involvement with the amendment, but that did not stop them from reading the measure in ways that served their own personal and political causes. In an effort to rally lagging patriotism, President Franklin D. Roosevelt, when endorsing the Thirteenth Amendment postage stamp in 1940, asked Americans to remember that while slavery was outlawed "under the American flag," liberty was still "under violent attack" by fascist governments abroad.[98] The *Daily Worker,* an organ of the American Communist party, predictably claimed that the amendment broke "the handicap on all labor."[99] Senator James "Cyclone" Davis, who had worked in steel mills since the age of eleven, agreed with the *Worker* and said that "Labor as well as the Negro was freed" by the Thirteenth Amendment.[100] Adam

97 *Chicago Defender,* October 26, 1940, in "Emancipation Celebrations," in John W. Kitchens, ed., *The Tuskegee Institute News Clippings File,* microfilm edition (Tuskegee, Ala.: Tuskegee Institute, 1981) (hereafter cited as EC); Elizabeth Ross Haynes, *The Black Boy of Atlanta* (Boston: Edinboro, 1952), 210; and testimony of Richard Robert Wright, Congress, Senate, Committee on the Judiciary, "S. J. Res. 37: National Freedom Day," File 80A-E12, 46, NA, p. 4. See Hanes Walton, Jr., et al., "R. R. Wright, Congress, President Truman and the First National Public African-American Holiday: National Freedom Day," *PS: Political Science and Politics,* 24 (December 1991), 685–88; Wiggins, *O Freedom!,* 20–24; "Slave to Banker," *Ebony,* 1 (November 1945), 43–47; Webb Waldron, "Massa, Tell 'Em We're Rising," *Reader's Digest,* April 1945, pp. 53–56.
98 *New York Times,* October 21, 1940, EC.
99 *Daily Worker,* January 25, 1942, EC.
100 *Philadelphia Tribune,* February 7, 1942, EC.

Clayton Powell, Jr., one of the two African Americans then serving in Congress, used the occasion of a Freedom Day rally in 1947 to emphasize the African American role in precipitating emancipation: "we of this generation should be happy in the fact that freedom has not been handed to us, but rather that whatever freedom we shall enjoy shall be freedom that we must obtain for ourselves."[101]

These attempts to make the Thirteenth Amendment conform to disparate political agendas were less well known and had less impact on actual law than similar efforts in the immediate post Civil War period. Yet the contests over the amendment in the 1940s, no less than those in the 1860s, revealed that the amendment's meaning was still pliable, its language still suggestive of some higher cause beyond the abolition of simple chattel slavery. The amendment's capacity to produce divergent, sometimes divisive, interpretations became apparent again in the late 1960s and early 1970s, when two African Americans, acting independently, made national headlines by bringing a distinctive reading of the Thirteenth Amendment to the federal courts.

The first case involved Joseph Lee Jones, who claimed that he had been denied housing in a private development because of his color. His lawyers resurrected the method of declaring that their client had been branded with a "badge of slavery" prohibited by the Thirteenth Amendment. By invoking the Thirteenth instead of the Fourteenth Amendment, Jones's lawyers avoided the potential objection that the discrimination in question was legal because it was a private rather than a state action. In 1968 the Supreme Court took up the case and ruled in Jones's favor. According to the Court, the Thirteenth Amendment protected African Americans from private as well as statutory discrimination, for the "promise of freedom" included "freedom to buy whatever a white man can buy, the right to live wherever a white man can live."[102] The *Jones* case attracted much public attention and awakened scholarly interest in a measure that, according to one writer, had previously "seemed an unserviceable constitutional antique." Now lawmakers, judges, and legal theorists rejoined the battle over the reach of freedom secured by the amendment.[103]

---

101 *Louisiana Weekly*, February 15, 1947, EC.
102 "Jones v. Alfred H. Mayer Co.," *United States Reports*, 392 (1968), 443. The case did not mention whether the amendment might apply to other victims of discrimination besides African Americans.
103 "The 'New' Thirteenth Amendment: A Preliminary Analysis," *Harvard Law Review*, 82 (April 1969), 1294 (quotation). For samples of the debate over the Jones decision and its use of history, see Arthur Kinoy, "The Constitutional Right of Negro Freedom Revisited: Some First Thoughts on *Jones* v. *Alfred H. Mayer Company*," *Rutgers Law Review*, 22 (1968), 537–52; Gerhard Casper, "Jones v. Mayer: Clio, Bemused and Confused Muse," *Supreme Court Review*, 1968, 89–132; and Charles Fairman, *His-*

Four years after the *Jones* ruling, a second case concerning the Thirteenth Amendment, one that received even more public notice, came before the Supreme Court. Curt Flood, an African American baseball player earning $90,000 a year, claimed that he was being treated like a slave. For twelve years, Flood had played center field for the St. Louis Cardinals, but in 1969 he was traded to the Philadelphia Phillies. The athlete refused to abide by the trade and wished instead to offer his services to the highest bidder. Flood was not the first player to challenge baseball's infamous "reserve system," which prohibited players from acting as free agents and required them to go where the owners of their contracts demanded, but he was the first to make the Thirteenth Amendment part of his case. Represented by former Supreme Court justice Arthur J. Goldberg, Flood contended that he was "a piece of property" and the reserve system a form of slavery. The Thirteenth Amendment, Goldberg argued, should allow baseball players, like other employees, to control the terms of their labor.[104] Some Americans sympathized with Flood's plight. The fact that he was African American lent particular legitimacy to his claim of enslavement. But most people rejected Flood's reading of the amendment, and Flood himself asked in his memoir, "Who ever heard of a $90,000-per-year slave?"[105] The Court rejected Flood's suit and ignored his Thirteenth Amendment claim. In a dissenting opinion, Thurgood Marshall, the one African American justice, admitted that there were some who might regard Flood as having been "virtually enslaved."[106] But even Marshall thought that the baseball player was stretching the amendment too far, and that other laws besides that measure should be the basis for prohibiting the reserve system. In the modern era, the members of the Court, and Americans in general, might regard discrimination on the basis of race a "badge" of slavery. But most were still reluctant to concede that slavery might also include discriminatory practices that were not necessarily about race.[107]

In recent years, however, a new generation of legal scholars has stepped in to reassert that vestiges of slavery still exist – and in situations that do

tory of the Supreme Court of the United States, vol. 6, *Reconstruction and Reunion, 1864–1888: Part One* (New York: Macmillan, 1971), 1257–60.

104 "Flood v. Kuhn et al.," *United States Reports*, 407 (1971): 258–96. See Leonard Koppett, "Baseball's Exempt Status Upheld by Supreme Court," *New York Times*, June 20, 1972, p. 1, 45; Roger I. Abrams, *Legal Bases: Baseball and the Law* (Philadelphia: Temple University Press, 1998), 64–69.

105 Curt Flood, with Richard Carter, *The Way It Is* (New York: Trident Press, 1971), 139.

106 "Flood v. Kuhn et al.," 289.

107 It should be noted that the modern Supreme Court still has left some room for litigants to use the amendment to buttress claims not involving racial discrimination. See Laurence H. Tribe, *American Constitutional Law*, 2d ed. (Mineola, N.Y.: Foundation Press, 1988), 332–34.

not always involve racial discrimination. The Thirteenth Amendment, they argue, should protect exploited workers, abused women, neglected children, and all other victims of relationships reminiscent of slavery. Such innovative interpretations have reawakened slumbering interest in the amendment and revived the debate about the meaning of constitutional freedom. In a sense, this scholarly movement is simply the latest episode in a recurrent struggle to define the meaning of freedom, a struggle that began even before the amendment was adopted.[108]

But there is something different about this particular effort to make sense of the Thirteenth Amendment. Unlike those jurists, legislators, and ordinary Americans of the late nineteenth and early twentieth century who based their understanding of the Thirteenth Amendment on a highly

108   The following articles, an incomplete list to be sure, suggest the expansive view of the Thirteenth Amendment taken by legal scholars in the past twenty years: Larry J. Pittman, "Physician-Assisted Suicide in the Dark Ward: The Intersection of the Thirteenth Amendment and Health Care Treatments Having Disproportionate Impacts on Disfavored Groups," *Seton Hall Law Review,* 28 (1998), 776–896; Douglas L. Colbert, "Liberating the Thirteenth Amendment," *Harvard Civil Rights–Civil Liberties Law Review,* 30 (Winter 1995), 1–55; Lauren Kares, "The Unlucky Thirteenth: A Constitutional Amendment in Search of a Doctrine," *Cornell Law Review,* 80 (January 1995), 372–412; Michael A. Cullers, "Limits on Speech and Mental Slavery: A Thirteenth Amendment Defense against Speech Codes," *Case Western Reserve Law Review,* 45 (Winter 1995), 641–59; David P. T. Tedhams, "The Reincarnation of 'Jim Crow': A Thirteenth Amendment Analysis of Colorado's Amendment 2," *Temple Political and Civil Rights Law Review,* 4 (October 1994), 133–65; Neal Kumar Katyal, "Men Who Own Women: A Thirteenth Amendment Critique of Forced Prostitution," *Yale Law Journal,* 103 (December 1993), 791–826; Donald C. Hancock, "The Thirteenth Amendment and the Juvenile Justice System," *Journal of Criminal Law and Criminology,* 83 (Fall 1992), 614–43; Joyce E. McConnell, "Beyond Metaphor: Battered Women, Involuntary Servitude and the Thirteenth Amendment," *Yale Journal of Law and Feminism,* 4 (Spring 1992), 207–53; Andrew Koppelman, "Forced Labor: A Thirteenth Amendment Defense of Abortion," *Northwestern University Law Review,* 84 (Winter 1990), 480–535; Lorraine Stone, "Neoslavery – 'Surrogate' Motherhood Contracts v. the Thirteenth Amendment," *Law and Inequality,* 6 (July 1988), 63–73; Carol Baldwin, "The Thirteenth Amendment as an Effective Source of Constitutional Authority for Affirmative Action Legislation," *Columbia Journal of Law and Social Problems,* 18 (Winter 1983), 77–114; George S. Swan, "The Thirteenth Amendment Dimensions of *Roe* v. *Wade,*" *Journal of Juvenile Law,* 4 (1980): 1–33.

Akhil Reed Amar has led the way in much of the new scholarship on the Thirteenth Amendment. See, for example, "The Case of the Missing Amendments: *R.A.V.* v. *City of St. Paul,*" *Harvard Law Review,* 106 (November 1992), 124–61; "Forty Acres and a Mule: A Republican Theory of Minimal Entitlements," *Harvard Journal of Law and Public Policy,* 13 (Winter 1990), 37–43; "Remember the Thirteenth," *Constitutional Commentary,* 10 (Summer 1993), 403–8; and Amar and Daniel Widawsky, "Child Abuse as Slavery: A Thirteenth Amendment Response to DeShaney," *Harvard Law Review,* 105 (April 1992), 1359–85.

For some recent works that challenge expansive readings of the amendment, see Maltz, *Civil Rights, the Constitution, and Congress,* 13–28; and Herman Belz, "The Civil War Amendments to the Constitution: The Relevance of Original Intent," *Constitutional Commentary,* 5 (Winter 1988), 115–41.

selective reading of history, today's legal scholars are more careful and more self-conscious about the way they use history. Much better informed than their predecessors about historical methods and modes of historical understanding, legal scholars studying all issues, not only the Thirteenth Amendment, are less capricious than they once were when using history to make their case. They are more likely than they were in the past to offer rich descriptions of the historical context in which particular legal provisions were created. Other scholars, equally informed by the historical record, then put forward an alternative version of the historical context. And at the fray of the intellectual battle stand critics who challenge the authenticity of any version of events purporting to be "contextual." Simply put, the participants in this most recent struggle over the meaning of the Thirteenth Amendment (as well as similar struggles over other laws) are better historians than their predecessors.[109]

Nonetheless, an unfortunate though understandable teleological quality taints this new scholarship on the Thirteenth Amendment. Regardless of their personal understanding of the meaning of freedom or their preferred method of practicing history, the scholars who have turned to history all begin with one obvious premise, that the Thirteenth Amendment was ultimately adopted, and one primary question: what did people think they were adopting? The inquiry then becomes an exercise in examining the intentions and relative importance of the various groups involved in making the amendment. One scholar concludes that the radical Republicans were most important in making the amendment; another points to the crucial role of the proamendment Democrats; another reminds us of the integral role of feminist abolitionists; and still another casts our eye to the slaves themselves. What is lost in this sort of analysis is the contingency of events and ideas. By beginning with the premise that the amendment was adopted, these scholars flatten out the complexity of the historical process. We lose sight of the fact that the amendment emerged slowly, unpredictably as the preferred method of abolition, and that its adoption was contingent on developments that had nothing to do with slavery, emancipation, equal rights, or the law. And by asking what people thought they were adopting – or had adopted – these scholars make the participants in the amendment process seem more focused on the amendment than they actually were. People of the time were easily distracted from the amendment by other legislation, by elections, and, most importantly, by the Civil War. Their attitudes toward the amendment were never

---

109 See Laura Kalman, "Border Patrol: Reflections on the Turn to History in Legal Scholarship," *Fordham Law Review,* 66 (October 1997), 87–124; and William E. Nelson, "History and Neutrality in Constitutional Adjudication," *Virginia Law Review,* 72 (October 1986), 1237–96.

steady; they evolved in relation and in reaction to very different sorts of measures and events. The new scholarship on the Thirteenth Amendment makes good use of history in recovering some of the lost meanings of the amendment, but in the process something of the original historical moment is lost.

The struggle over the meaning of the amendment is far from over. Just as unforeseen circumstances during Reconstruction forced lawmakers to sharpen the definition of constitutional freedom, so will changing conditions in the future require a reconsideration of the Thirteenth Amendment's scope and meaning. As modern society becomes increasingly complex, unanticipated forms of oppression will surface, and the struggle for personal liberty will take on unexpected dimensions. Future interpreters of the amendment will continue to defy the prediction of Republican congressman James G. Blaine, who wrote that "the language of the Thirteenth Amendment is so comprehensive and absolute that vital questions of law are not likely at any time to arise under it."[110]

As every generation since the Civil War has discovered, the most striking aspect of the Thirteenth Amendment is the surprising subtlety that lies beneath its plain language. The measure's simplest message – that America's distinctive form of racial slavery was abolished – initially made it acceptable to disparate constituencies, but the amendment's larger meanings eventually divided its onetime adherents. One implication of the amendment was indisputable, however. Americans now understood that any generation could challenge and enlarge a previous generation's Constitution without violating the sanctity of the original charter. Richard Wright, the ex-slave who memorialized the Thirteenth Amendment in the 1940s, made good on that legacy by asking the people of his time to commemorate, and thus to reevaluate, constitutional freedom. The struggle to read new meanings into the amendment and into the new Constitution it created did not end in Wright's day. Nor will it end in our own.

110 Blaine, *Twenty Years of Congress*, 539.

Appendix: Votes on Antislavery Amendment

Senate Joint Resolution 16: A resolution submitting to the legislatures of the several States a proposition to amend the Constitution of the United States,

Resolved by the Senate and House of Representatives of the United States of America in Congress assembled (two thirds of both Houses concurring) that the following article be proposed to the legislatures of the several States as an amendment to the Constitution of the United States which, when ratified by three-fourths of said legislatures, shall be valid to all intents and purposes as a part of said Constitution, namely:

Section 1. Neither slavery nor involuntary servitude, except as a punishment for crime, whereof the party shall have been duly convicted, shall exist within the United States, or any place subject to their jurisdiction.

Section 2. Congress shall have power to enforce this article by appropriate legislation.

Table 1. *Vote on Antislavery Amendment, Senate, April 8, 1864*

Votes	Republican	Democrat	Union	Unconditional Union	Total
Yea	30	4	3	1	38
Nay	0	5	1	0	6
Absent	0	3	2	0	5
Abstain	0	0	0	0	0

Source: Vote on Senate Joint Resolution 16. CG, 38th Cong., 1st sess. (April 8, 1864), 1490.

Table 2. *Votes on Antislavery Amendment, House of Representatives, February 15 and June 15, 1864, and January 31, 1865*

Votes	Republican	Democrat	Union	Unconditional Union	Total
Vote 1[a]					
Yea	66	1	1	10	78
Nay	2	52	7	1	62
Absent	17	20	2	3	42
Abstain	1	0	0	0	1
Vote 2[b]					
Yea	78	4	0	11	93
Nay	1	58	6	0	65
Absent	6	10	4	3	23
Abstain	1	0	0	0	1
Vote 3[c]					
Yea	86	15	4	14	119
Nay	0	50	6	0	56
Absent	0	8	0	0	8
Abstain	0	0	0	0	0

[a]Test vote on resolution "That the Constitution shall be so amended as to abolish slavery in the United States wherever it now exists, and to prohibit its existence in every part thereof forever." CG, 38th Cong., 1st sess. (February 15, 1864), 659–60.
[b]Vote on Senate Joint Resolution 16. CG, 38th Cong., 1st sess. (June 15, 1864), 2995.
[c]Vote on Senate Joint Resolution 16. CG, 38th Cong., 2d sess. (January 31, 1865), 531.

Bibliography

Manuscript Collections

Albany Institute of Art and History, Albany, New York

Erastus Corning papers

Bowdoin College, Special Collections, New Brunswick, Maine

Fessenden family papers

Butler Library, Columbia University, New York, New York

August Belmont papers
John A. Dix papers
Sydney Howard Gay papers

Chicago Historical Society, Chicago, Illinois

Isaac N. Arnold papers
William Butler papers
David Davis papers
Stephen Douglas papers
Zebina Eastman papers
William Weston Patton papers
Logan Uriah Reavis papers
George Schneider papers

Cincinnati Historical Society, Cincinnati, Ohio

Murat Halstead papers
Alexander Long papers
William Lough papers
Caleb B. Smith papers
Isaac Strohm papers

Delaware Hall of Records, Dover, Delaware

Executive papers
Samuel Townsend collection

Eleutherian Mills Historical Library, Wilmington, Delaware

Samuel Francis DuPont papers

John Hay Library, Brown University, Providence, Rhode Island

Samuel S. Cox papers

Rutherford B. Hayes Historical Library, Fremont, Ohio

Rutherford B. Hayes papers
Robert C. Schenck papers

Historical Society of Delaware, Wilmington, Delaware

James A. Bayard papers
Thomas F. Bayard papers
William Canby diary
Gibbons family papers
George Read Riddle papers

Historical Society of Maryland, Baltimore, Maryland

Bond-McCullogh papers
A. W. Bradford papers
Anna Ella Carroll papers
J. W. Crisfield papers
Samuel A. Harrison diary
Reverdy Johnson papers
Brantz Mayer papers

Historical Society of Pennsylvania, Philadelphia, Pennsylvania

Salmon P. Chase papers
Thaddeus Stevens papers

Houghton Library, Harvard University, Cambridge, Massachusetts

Charles Eliot Norton papers
Wendell Phillips papers
Charles Sumner papers

Henry E. Huntington Library, San Marino, California

Samuel L. M. Barlow papers
Hiram Barney papers
Thomas Haines Dudley papers
Charles Halpine papers
Joseph Holt papers
Ward Hill Lamon papers

Francis Lieber papers
Allan Nevins papers
Charles H. Ray papers
Horatio Seymour papers
Isaac Sherman papers

Illinois Historical Survey, University of Illinois, Champaign-Urbana, Illinois

Arthur C. Cole notes
William W. Orme papers

Illinois State Archives, Springfield, Illinois

Richard J. Oglesby papers

Illinois State Historical Library, Springfield, Illinois

Nathaniel P. Banks papers
Sidney Breese papers
Orville Hickman Browning papers
Ichabod Codding papers
David Davis papers
Robert G. Ingersoll papers
Charles H. Lanphier papers
John A. McClernand papers
Nicolay and Hay papers
Richard Oglesby papers
John M. Palmer papers
Lewis B. Parsons papers
Lyman Trumbull papers
Yates family papers

Indiana Historical Society, Indianapolis, Indiana

Schuyler Colfax papers
John G. Davis papers
William H. English papers
John Lyle King diary
Henry S. Lane papers
Lew Wallace papers

Indiana State Library, Indianapolis, Indiana

Schuyler Colfax papers
William Dudley Foulke papers

Allen Hamilton papers
George W. Julian papers
Oliver P. Morton papers
Richard W. Thompson papers
John T. Wilder papers
Joseph A. Wright papers

Margaret I. King Library, University of Kentucky, Lexington, Kentucky

William Moody Pratt diary

Kentucky State Archives, Frankfort, Kentucky

Thomas E. Bramlette papers

Carl A. Kroch Library, Cornell University, Ithaca, New York

Francis Kernan papers

Lilly Library, University of Indiana, Bloomington, Indiana

J. A. Cravens papers
Hugh McCulloch papers

Manuscripts Division, Library of Congress, Washington, D.C.

Nathaniel P. Banks papers
Thomas F. Bayard papers
James Gordon Bennett papers
Jeremiah Black papers
James G. Blaine papers
Francis P. Blair family papers
Benjamin F. Butler papers
Zachariah Chandler papers
Salmon P. Chase papers
James A. J. Creswell papers
Caleb Cushing papers
Charles A. Dana papers
Henry Laurens Dawes papers
Anna Ella Dickinson papers
James Rood Doolittle papers
Frederick Douglass papers
William P. Fessenden papers
John W. Forney papers
James A. Garfield papers

Joshua Giddings and George W. Julian papers
Ulysses S. Grant papers
Horace Greeley papers
John Hay papers
Herndon-Weik papers
Robert G. Ingersoll papers
Thomas Allen Jenckes papers
Andrew Johnson papers
Reverdy Johnson papers
Francis Lieber papers
Robert Todd Lincoln collection
Manton M. Marble papers
George B. McClellan papers
Hugh McCulloch papers
Edward McPherson papers
Justin S. Morrill papers
Samuel F. B. Morse papers
John G. Nicolay papers
John Sherman papers
Caleb B. Smith papers
Edwin M. Stanton papers
Thaddeus Stevens papers
Ambrose Thompson papers
Lyman Trumbull papers
Benjamin Wade papers
Elihu B. Washburne papers
Gideon Welles papers
Levi Woodbury family papers
John Russell Young papers

Maryland State Archives, Hall of Records, Annapolis, Maryland

A. W. Bradford papers

Massachusetts Historical Society, Boston, Massachusetts

Adams family papers
John Andrew papers
George Bancroft papers
George S. Boutwell papers
Edward Everett papers
Winthrop family papers

Massachusetts State Archives, Boston, Massachusetts

John A. Andrew papers

New Jersey Historical Society, Newark, New Jersey

Joseph P. Bradley papers

New York Historical Society, New York, New York

Horace Greeley papers
Horatio Seymour papers
John A. Stevens papers
Theodore Tilton papers

New York Public Library, New York, New York

John Bigelow papers
Bryant-Godwin papers
Horace Greeley papers
Henry J. Raymond papers
Smith family papers
Samuel J. Tilden papers
Fernando Wood papers

New York State Library, Albany, New York

Edwin D. Morgan papers
John V. S. L. Pruyn journals
Horatio Seymour papers

Ohio Historical Society, Columbus, Ohio

John Bingham papers
Alexander S. Boys papers
William T. Coggeshall papers
Ewing family papers
Samuel Galloway papers
James A. Garfield papers
William Henry Smith papers
Isaac Strohm papers
John Allen Trimble papers

Rush Rhees Library, University of Rochester, Rochester, New York

George W. Patterson papers
William Henry Seward papers
Thurlow Weed papers

University of California at Los Angeles, Special Collections, Los Angeles, California

Cornelius Cole papers

Western Reserve Historical Society, Cleveland, Ohio

Warner M. Bateman papers
William P. Fessenden papers
Albert G. Riddle papers
Benjamin Summers journal
Milton Sutliff papers
Vallandigham and Laird family papers

Federal Archival Records, National Archives

U.S. Congress. House. Bill file, 37th–38th Congresses. RG 233.
  Joint Resolution file, 37th–38th Congresses. RG 233.
  Committee on the Judiciary. Minutes. 37th–38th Congresses. RG 233.
  Committee on the Judiciary. Petitions and Papers. 37th–38th Congresses. RG 233.
  Select Committee on Emancipation. Petitions and Papers. 38th Congress. RG 233.
U.S. Congress. Senate. Bill file, 37th–38th Congresses. RG 46.
  Joint Resolution file, 37th–38th Congresses. RG 46.
  Committee on the Judiciary. Minutes. 37th–38th Congresses. RG 46.
  Committee on the Judiciary. Petitions and Papers. 37th–38th Congresses. RG 46.
  Committee on the Judiciary. *Requesting the President to Proclaim February 1 as National Freedom Day.* 80th Cong., 1st sess., May 13, 1947.
U.S. Department of Justice. Attorney General's Official Letter Books. RG 60.

Published Federal and State Records

Biographical Dictionary of the United States Congresses, 1774–1989. Bicentennial ed. Washington, D.C.: Government Printing Office, 1989.
Delaware. *Enrolled Bills of Delaware,* 1901.
  Journal of the House of Representatives of the State of Delaware, 1863–65.
  Journal of the Senate of the State of Delaware, 1863–65.
Illinois. *Journal of the House of Representatives of Illinois,* 1863–65.
  Journal of the Senate of the State of Illinois, 1863–65.
Indiana. *Brevier Legislative Reports: Embracing Short-Hand Sketches of the Journals and Debates of the General Assembly of the State of Indiana,* 1863–65.
  Journal of the House of Representatives of Indiana, 1863–65.
  Journal of the Indiana State Senate, 1863–65.
Kentucky. *Journal of the House of Representatives of the Commonwealth of Kentucky,* 1863–66.

Journal of the Senate of the Commonwealth of Kentucky, 1863–66.

Maryland. *The Debates of the Constitutional Convention of the State of Maryland, Assembled at the City of Annapolis.* Annapolis: Richard P. Bayly, 1864.

Journal of the Proceedings of the House of Delegates of Maryland, 1863–65.

Journal of the Proceedings of the Senate of Maryland, 1863–65.

Missouri. *Journal of the Missouri State Conventions,* 1862, 1863, 1865.

New York. *Journal of the Assembly of the State of New York,* 1863–65.

Journal of the Senate of the State of New York, 1863–65.

Ohio. *Journal of the House of Representatives of the State of Ohio,* 1863–65.

Journal of the Senate of the State of Ohio, 1863–65.

Richardson, James D. *A Compilation of the Messages and Papers of the Presidents, 1789–1897.* Washington, D.C.: Government Printing Office, 1896–99.

U.S. Congress. *Congressional Globe,* 37th–39th Congresses.

House Executive Documents, 37th–39th Congresses.

House Miscellaneous Documents, 37th–39th Congresses.

House Reports, 37th–39th Congresses.

Senate Executive Documents, 37th–39th Congresses.

Senate Miscellaneous Documents, 37th–39th Congresses, 71st Congress.

Senate Reports, 37th–39th Congresses.

Statutes at Large, 37th–39th Congresses.

U.S. Department of Justice. *Official Opinions of the Attorneys General of the United States.*

U.S. Department of State. *Documentary History of the Constitution of the United States of America.* Washington, D.C., 1894.

U.S. Supreme Court. *United States Reports.*

War of the Rebellion: The Official Records of the Union and Confederate Armies. 128 vols. Washington, D.C.: Government Printing Office, 1880–1901.

Contemporary Documents

Diaries, Letters, Memoirs, and Memorials

The American Annual Cyclopedia and Register of Important Events of the Year 1862, 1863, 1864, 1865. New York: D. Appleton, 1863–70.

Ames, Jessie Marshall. *Private and Official Correspondence of Gen. Benjamin Butler during the Period of the Civil War.* 5 vols. Norwood, Mass.: privately published, 1917.

Arnett, Benjamin W., ed. *Orations and Speeches: Duplicate Copy of the Souvenir from the Afro-American League of Tennessee to Hon. James M. Ashley of Ohio.* Philadelphia: A.M.E. Church, 1894.

Arnold, Isaac N. *The History of Abraham Lincoln and the Overthrow of Slavery.* Chicago: Clarke, 1866.

The Life of Abraham Lincoln. Chicago: Jansen, McClurg, 1885.

Ashley, James M. "Abraham Lincoln." *Magazine of Western History,* 14 (May 1891), 23–36.

Baker, George E., ed. *The Works of William H. Seward.* 5 vols. Boston: Houghton Mifflin, 1884.

Barnes, Thurlow Weed, and Harriet Weed. *Life of Thurlow Weed, Including His Autobiography and a Memoir.* 2 vols. Boston: Houghton Mifflin, 1883–84.

Basler, Roy P., ed., and Marion Dolores Pratt and Lloyd A. Dunlap, asst. eds. *The Collected Works of Abraham Lincoln.* 9 vols. New Brunswick, N.J.: Rutgers University Press, 1953–55.

Beale, Howard, ed. *The Diary of Gideon Welles: Secretary of the Navy Under Lincoln and Johnson,* 3 vols. New York: W. W. Norton, 1960.

ed. *The Diary of Edward Bates, 1859–1866.* Washington, D.C.: Government Printing Office, 1933.

Blaine, James G. *Twenty Years of Congress: From Lincoln to Garfield.* 2 vols. Norwich, Conn.: Henry Bill Publishing Company, 1884–86.

Blassingame, John W., et al., eds. *The Frederick Douglass Papers.* 5 vols. to date. New Haven: Yale University Press, 1979–.

Boutwell, George S. *Reminiscences of Sixty Years in Public Affairs.* 2 vols. New York: McClure, Phillips, 1902.

Speeches and Papers Relating to the Rebellion and the Overthrow of Slavery. Boston: Little, Brown, 1867.

Brooks, Noah. *Abraham Lincoln and the Downfall of Slavery.* New York: G. P. Putnam's Sons, 1894.

Washington in Lincoln's Time. New York: Century Company, 1895; revised and edited by Herbert Mitgang, Chicago: Quadrangle Books, 1971; reprint, Athens: University of Georgia Press, 1989.

Brown, George Rothwell, ed. *Reminiscences of Senator William M. Stewart.* New York: Neale Publishing Company, 1908.

Bryant, William Cullen, II, and Thomas G. Goss, eds. *The Letters of William Cullen Bryant.* 4 vols. to date. New York: Fordham University Press, 1984–.

Burlingame, Michael, ed. *An Oral History of Abraham Lincoln: John G. Nicolay's Interviews and Essays.* Carbondale: Southern Illinois University Press, 1996.

Burton, Sir Richard. *A Mission to Gelele, King of Dahome,* 2 vols. London: Tinsley Brothers, 1864.

Butler, Benjamin F. *Autobiography and Personal Reminiscences of Major General Benjamin F. Butler.* Boston: A. M. Thayer, 1892.

Campbell, John A. *Reminiscences and Documents Relating to the Civil War During the Year 1865.* Baltimore: John Murphy and Co., 1887.

Carpenter, F. B. *Six Months at the White House with Abraham Lincoln.* New York: Hurd and Houghton, 1866.

Clay, Cassius M., ed. "Selections from the Brutus J. Clay Papers, 1861–1865." *Filson Club History Quarterly,* 32 (1958), 3–24, 136–50.

Cole, Cornelius. *Memoirs of Cornelius Cole.* New York: McLoughlin Brothers, 1908.

Conway, Moncure. *Autobiography.* 2 vols. Boston: Houghton Mifflin, 1904.

Cox, Samuel S. *Eight Years in Congress, From 1857 to 1865.* New York: D. Appleton, 1865.

Union – Disunion – Reunion: Three Decades of Federal Legislation. Providence, R.I.: J. A. and R. A. Reid, 1885; reprint, Freeport, N.Y.: Books for Libraries Press, 1970.

Dana, Charles A. *Recollections of the Civil War.* New York: D. Appleton, 1898.

Dennett, Tyler, ed. *Lincoln and the Civil War in the Diaries and Letters of John Hay.* New York: Dodd, Mead, 1939.

Donald, David, ed. *Inside Lincoln's Cabinet: The Civil War Diaries of Salmon P. Chase.* New York: Longmans, Green, 1954.

Eaton, John. *Grant, Lincoln, and the Freedmen: Reminiscences of the Civil War.* New York: Longmans, Green, 1907.

Fessenden, Francis. *Life and Public Services of William Pitt Fessenden.* 2 vols. Boston: Houghton Mifflin, 1907.

Foner, Philip S., ed. *The Life and Writings of Frederick Douglass.* 4 vols. New York: International Publishers, 1950–55.

Ford, Worthington C., ed. *A Cycle of Adams Letters, 1861–1865.* 2 vols. Boston: Houghton Mifflin, 1920.

Graf, Leroy P., Ralph W. Haskins, and Patricia P. Clark, eds. *The Papers of Andrew Johnson.* 15 vols. to date. Knoxville: University of Tennessee Press, 1967–.

Gray, John Chipman, ed. *War Letters, 1862–1865, of John Chipman Gray . . . and John Codman Ropes.* Boston: Houghton Mifflin, 1927.

Gurowski, Adam. *Diary: From March 4, 1861 to 1865.* 3 vols. Boston: Lee and Shepard, 1866.

Hayes, John D., ed. *Samuel Francis DuPont: A Selection from His Civil War Letters.* 3 vols. Ithaca: Cornell University Press, 1969.

Henderson, John B. "Emancipation and Impeachment." *Century Magazine,* 85 (December 1912), 196–209.

Hoar, George Frisbie, ed. *Charles Sumner: His Complete Works.* 20 vols. Boston: Lee and Shepard, 1873.

Hinsdale, Burke A., ed. *The Works of James Abram Garfield.* 2 vols. Boston: J. R. Osgood, 1882–1883.

Holland, Patricia G., and Ann D. Gordon, eds. *Papers of Elizabeth Cady Stanton and Susan B. Anthony.* Wilmington, Del.: Wilmington Scholarly Resources, 1989.

Houzeau, Jean-Charles. *My Passage at the New Orleans Tribune: A Memoir of the Civil War Era.* Edited by David C. Rankin. Translated by Gerard F. Denault. Baton Rouge: Louisiana State University Press, 1984.

Hughes, Sarah F., ed. *Letters and Recollections of John Murray Forbes.* 2 vols. Boston: Houghton Mifflin, 1899.

Johannsen, Robert W., ed. *The Letters of Stephen A. Douglas.* Urbana: University of Illinois Press, 1961.

Johnson, Donald Bruce, ed. *National Party Platforms.* Vol. 1, *1840–1956.* Urbana: University of Illinois Press, 1978.

Julian, George W. *Political Recollections, 1840 to 1872.* Chicago: Jansen, McClurg, 1884.

Laas, Virginia Jeans, ed. *Wartime Washington: The Civil War Letters of Elizabeth Blair Lee.* Urbana: University of Illinois Press, 1991.

Lieber, Francis. *Miscellaneous Writings*. 2 vols. Philadelphia: J. B. Lippincott, 1881.

Logan, John A. *The Great Conspiracy: Its Origins and History*. New York: A. R. Hart, 1886.

Marshall, Jessie A., ed. *Private and Official Correspondence of General Benjamin F. Butler During the Period of the Civil War*. 5 vols. Norwood, Mass.: Plimpton Press, 1917.

McClure, Alexander K. *Abraham Lincoln and Men of War-Times*. Philadelphia: Times Publishing Company, 1892.

Meltzer, Milton, and Patricia G. Holland, eds. *Lydia Maria Child: Selected Letters, 1817–1880*. Amherst: University of Massachusetts Press, 1982.

Merrill, Walter M., and Louis Ruchames, eds. *The Letters of William Lloyd Garrison*. 6 vols. Cambridge, Mass.: Harvard University Press, 1971–81.

Nevins, Allan, and Milton Halsey Thomas, eds. *The Diary of George Templeton Strong*. 4 vols. New York: Macmillan, 1952.

Niven, John, ed. *The Salmon P. Chase Papers*. 3 vols. to date. Kent, Ohio: Kent State University Press, 1993–.

Palmer, Beverly Wilson, ed. *The Selected Letters of Charles Sumner*. 2 vols. Boston: Northeastern University Press, 1990.

Pease, Theodore C., and James G. Randall, eds. *The Diary of Orville Hickman Browning*. 2 vols. Springfield: Illinois State Historical Library, 1925–33.

Phillips, Wendell. *Speeches, Lectures, and Letters*. Boston: Lee and Shepard, 1891.

Raymond, Henry J. *The Life and Public Services of Abraham Lincoln*. New York: Derby and Miller, 1865.

Rice, Allen Thorndike, ed. *Reminiscences of Abraham Lincoln by Distinguished Men of His Time*. New York: North American Review, 1886.

Riddle, Albert Gallatin. *Recollections of War Times: Reminiscences of Men and Events in Washington, 1860–1865*. New York: G. P. Putnam's Sons, 1895.

Rowland, Dunbar. *Jefferson Davis, Constitutionalist: His Letters, Papers and Speeches*. 10 vols. Jackson: Mississippi Department of Archives and History, 1923.

Schurz, Carl. *The Reminiscences of Carl Schurz*. 3 vols. New York: McClure, 1907–08.

Scovel, James M. "Personal Recollections of Abraham Lincoln." *Lippincott's Monthly Magazine*, 44 (August 1889), 244–51.

"Recollections of Abraham Lincoln." *Lippincott's Monthly Magazine*, 63 (February 1899), 277–82.

"Recollections of Seward and Lincoln." *Lippincott's Monthly Magazine*, 51 (February 1893), 237–42.

"Thaddeus Stevens." *Lippincott's Monthly Magazine*, 61 (1898), 545–51.

Sears, Stephen W., ed. *The Civil War Papers of George B. McClellan: Selected Correspondence, 1860–1865*. New York: Ticknor and Fields, 1989.

Simon, John Y., ed. *The Papers of Ulysses S. Grant*. 15 vols. Carbondale: Southern Illinois University Press, 1967–90.

Smart, James G., ed. *A Radical View: The "Agate" Dispatches of Whitelaw Reid*. 2 vols. Memphis: Memphis State University Press, 1976.

Smith, Gerrit. *Speeches and Letters of Gerrit Smith.* 2 vols. New York: J. A. Gray and Green (vol. 1) and American News Company (vol. 2), 1864–65.

Staudenraus, P. J., ed. *Mr. Lincolns Washington: Selections from the Writings of Noah Brooks, Civil War Correspondent.* South Brunswick, N.J.: Thomas Yoseloff, 1967.

Stephens, Alexander H. *A Constitutional View of the Late War between the States.* 2 vols. Philadelphia: National Publishing Company, 1868–70.

Teillard, Dorothy Lamon, ed. *Recollections of Abraham Lincoln, 1847–1865.* Chicago: A. C. McClurg, 1895.

Thorndike, Rachel Sherman, ed. *The Sherman Letters: Correspondence between General and Senator Sherman from 1837 to 1891.* New York: Scribner's, 1894.

Turner, Justin G., and Linda Levitt Turner. *Mary Todd Lincoln: Her Life and Letters.* New York: Alfred A. Knopf, 1972; reprint, New York: Fromm International Publishing Corporation, 1987.

Wainwright, Nicholas B., ed. *A Philadelphia Perspective: The Diary of Sidney George Fisher Covering the Years, 1834–1871.* Philadelphia: University of Pennsylvania Press, 1967.

Welles, Gideon. "Lincoln and Johnson: Their Plan of Reconstruction and the Resumption of National Authority." *Galaxy,* 13 (April 1872), 521–32.

Wilson, Rufus Rockwell, ed. *Intimate Memories of Lincoln.* Elmira: Primavera Press, 1945.

Pamphlets and Speeches

Reproductions of many fine pamphlets may be found in Frank Freidel, ed., *Union Pamphlets of the Civil War,* 2 vols. (Cambridge, Mass.: Harvard University Press, 1967). All pamphlets included in those volumes are excluded from the following list. Also excluded are reprints of congressional speeches originally printed in the *Congressional Globe.* Place and date of publication are given for a pamphlet only if that information is readily available from the pamphlet itself.

The Abolition Conspiracy to Destroy the Union; or A Ten Years' record of The "Republican" Party (Anti-Abolition Tracts no. 3). New York: Van Evrie, Horton, 1863.

Alvord, Thomas G. *Remarks of Hon. Speaker Alvord in reference to Resolutions proposing to define the Policy of the General Government in regard to the question of Slavery. In Assembly, March 28, 1865* (Union Campaign Document no. 9).

Andrew, John A. *Address of His Excellency John A. Andrew, to the Two Branches of the Legislature of Massachusetts, January 6, 1865.* Boston: Wright and Potter, 1865.

An Argument against the Abolition of the Constitution of the United States. 1864.

Blair, Montgomery. *On the Causes of the Rebellion and in Support of the President's Plan of Pacification.* Baltimore: Sherwood, 1864.

Speech of Montgomery Blair, on the Revolutionary Schemes of the Ultra Aboli-

tionists, and in Defence of the Policy of the President. New York: D. W. Lee, 1863.

Boutwell, George S. *Reconstruction: Its True Basis. Speech of Hon. George S. Boutwell, at Weymouth, Mass., July 4, 1865*. Boston: Wright and Potter, 1865.

Bross, William. *Legend of the Delaware: An Historical Sketch of Tom Quick*. Chicago: Knight and Leonard, 1887.

Brough, John. *Inaugural Address of John Brough, Governor of Ohio, delivered before the Senate and House of Representatives, Jan. 11, 1864*. 1864.

Brown, B. Gratz. *Freedom and Franchise Inseparable. Letter of the Hon. B. Gratz Brown*. Washington, D.C.: Gibson Brothers, 1864.

Butler, Benjamin F. *Speech of Maj.-Gen. Benj. F. Butler, upon the Campaign Before Richmond, 1864. Delivered at Lowell, Mass., January 29, 1865*. Boston: Wright and Potter, 1865.

Child, David L. *The Despotism of Freedom*. Boston: Young Men's Anti-Slavery Association, 1833.

["Copperskin"]. *An Argument against the Abolition of the Constitution of the United States*. (Originally printed in *Sangamon* [Illinois] *Tribune*, September, 27, 1864.)

Country Before Party: The Voice of Loyal Democrats (Union Campaign Document no. 4). Albany: Weed and Parsons, 1864.

Cox, Samuel S. *Puritanism in Politics*. New York: Van Evrie, Herton, 1863.

[Croly, David, and George Wakeman]. *Miscegenation: The Theory of the Blending of the Races, Applied to the American Man and Negro*. New York: H. Dexter, Hamilton, 1864.

Curtis, George Ticknor. *Address of George Ticknor Curtis* (in Philadelphia, September 30, 1864).

The True Conditions of American Loyalty (Papers from the Society for the Diffusion of Political Knowledge no. 5).

Defrees, John D. *The War Commenced by the Rebels. Copperheads of the North Their Allies. Speech of John D. Defrees, in Washington, D.C., Monday Evening, August 1, 1864*. Washington, D.C.: Lemuel Towers, 1864.

Drake, Charles D. *Speech of Charles D. Drake, delivered before the National Union Association, at Cincinnati, October 1, 1864*.

Edgerton, Henry. *Great Speech of Hon. Henry Edgerton, at the Union Mass Meeting, held at Platt's Hall, San Francisco, Wednesday Evening, Sept. 21, 1864*.

Emancipation and its Results (Society for the Diffusion of Political Knowledge no. 6).

Everett, Edward. *The Duty of Supporting the Government in the Present Crisis of Affairs. Address by Edward Everett Delivered in Faneuil Hall, October 19, 1864*.

Fenton, Reuben E. *Resources of the Country. How Peace Can Be Obtained. Remarks of Hon. Reuben E. Fenton, at Jamestown, N.Y., Tuesday Evening, September 8, 1864* (Union Campaign Document no. 3). Albany: Weed, Parsons, 1864.

["Fernando the Gothamite"]. *Copperhead Catechism for the instruction of such politicians as are of tender years.* New York: Sinclair Tousey, 1864.

Fisher, Sidney George *The Trial of the Constitution.* Philadelphia: J. B. Lippincott, 1862.

Garrison, William Lloyd, ed. *The Abolition of Slavery: The Right of the Government under the War Power.* Boston: R. F. Wallcut, 1862.

Green, William H. *Speech of Hon. William H. Green, on the Proposed Amendment of the Federal Constitution, Abolishing Slavery.* Springfield, Ill.: Baker and Phillips, Printers, 1865.

Hamilton, James Alexander. *The Constitution Vindicated: Nationality, Secession, Slavery.* 1864.

Handbook of the Democracy. [1864].

Howland, Charles H. *Remarks on the Joint Resolution Recognizing the "Equality of all Men before the Law," delivered in Senate of Missouri, January 13, 1865.*

Jay, John. *The Great Issue. An Address delivered before The Union Campaign Club, of East Brooklyn, New York, on Tuesday Evening, Oct. 25, 1864.* New York: Baker and Godwin, 1864.

Johnson, Reverdy. *Speech of Hon. Reverdy Johnson J of Maryland, delivered before the Brooklyn McClellan Central Association, October 21, 1864.* Brooklyn, N.Y.: Brooklyn McClellan Association, 1864.

Kelley, William D. *Replies of the Hon. William D. Kelley to George Northrop, Esq., in the Joint Debate in the Fourth Congressional District.* Philadelphia: Collins, 1864.

Kirkland, Charles P. *A Letter to the Hon. Benjamin R. Curtis, Late Judge of the Supreme Court of the United States.* New York: Latimer Bros. and Seymour, 1862.

Lane, James H. *The People's Choice. Speech of Hon. James H. Lane, Before the Union Lincoln Campaign Club, at the Cooper Institute, New York, March 30, 1864.* Washington, D.C.: William H. Moore, 1864.

Lieber, Francis. *A Letter to Hon. E. D. Morgan, Senator of the United States, on the Amendment of the Constitution Abolishing Slavery* (Loyal Publication Society no. 79). New York, 1865.

Logan, John A. *The Democratic Party. Did it Abolish Slavery and Put Down the Rebellion?* Chicago, 1881.

  Great Speech of Major Gen. John A. Logan, Delivered at Carbondale, Ill., Oct. 1, 1864. Chicago: *Chicago Tribune* Campaign Document no. 3, 1864.

Mack, A. W. *Speech of Hon. A. W. Mack, on the Slavery Question in the State Senate.* Springfield, Ill.: Baker and Phillips, Printers, 1865.

Miscegenation Indorsed by the Republican Party: Campaign Document no. 11. New York, 1864.

Morse, Samuel F. B. *An Argument on the Ethical Position of Slavery in the Social System, and its Relation to the Politics of the Day* (Society for the Diffusion of Political Knowledge no. 12). 1863.

Nordhoff, Charles, ed. *America for Free Working Men.* Loyal Publication Society no. 80. New York, 1865.

Owen, Robert Dale. *The Wrong of Slavery, The Right of Emancipation, and the Future of the African Race in the United States.* Philadelphia: J. B. Lippincott, 1864.

Parker, Joel. *Revolution and Reconstruction, two lectures delivered in the Law School of Harvard College.* New York: Hurd and Houghton, 1866.

Phelps, Amos A. *Lectures on Slavery and its Remedy.* Boston: New-England Anti-Slavery Society, 1834.

Phillips, Wendell. *Review of Lysander Spooner's Essay on the Unconstitutionality of Slavery.* Boston: Andrews and Prentiss, 1847.

Potts, William D. *Campaign Songs for Christian Patriots and True Democrats.* New York: privately published, 1864.

Proofs for Workingmen of The Monarchic and Aristocratic Designs of the Southern Conspirators and Their Northern Allies. 1864.

Pruyn, John V. S. L., et al. *Reply to President Lincoln's Letter, of 12th June, 1863* (Society for the Diffusion of Political Knowledge no. 10).

Pugh, George. *Speech of Mr. Pugh at Columbus Convention* (Society for the Diffusion of Political Knowledge no. 9).

Seaman, L. *What Miscegenation is! and What we are to Expect Now that Mr. Lincoln is Re-elected.* New York: Waller and Willetts, 1864.

Treat, Loren L. "Protest of the Hon. Loren L. Treat." Senate Doc. 38, *Documents accompanying The Journal of the Senate of the State of Michigan at the Biennial Session of 1865.*

Upham, N. G. *Rebellion – Slavery – Peace* (Loyal Publication Society no. 52). Concord, N.H.: E. C. Eastman, 1864.

Vallandigham, Clement L. *Speeches, Arguments, and Addresses of Clement L. Vallandigham.* New York: O. J. Walter, 1864.

Van Evrie, John. *Subgenation (The Theory of the Normal Relations of the Races; An Answer to "Miscegenation").* New York: J. Bradburn, 1864.

Weed, Thurlow. *The Presidential Question. Letter from Thurlow Weed* (to Abraham Wakeman, Albany, October 13, 1864).

Wells, David A. *Our Burden and our Strength* (Loyal Publication Society no. 54). New York, 1864.

Whiting, William. *The Return of Rebellious States to the Union. A letter to the Union league of Philadelphia.* Philadelphia: C. Sherman, Son, 1864.

The War Powers of the President, Military Arrests, and the Reconstruction of the Union. Boston: J. L. Shorey, 1864.

Winthrop, Robert C. *Great Speech of Robert C. Winthrop at New London, Connecticut, October 18, 1864.*

Speech of Robert C. Winthrop at Great Ratification meeting in Union Square, New York, September 17, 1864.

Yates, Richard. *Gov. Yates' Speech, Delivered at Bryan Hall, Chicago, Thursday Evening, November 4, 1864. War for the Union – Our National Crisis – The Duty of the Hour. Our Home Traitors – Illinois and the War – The Retributions of History.* 1864.

Message of His Excellency, Richard Yates, Governor of Illinois, to the General Assembly. January 2, 1865. Springfield, Ill.: Baker and Phillips, 1865.

Newspapers and Periodicals

Atlantic Monthly
Baltimore *Sun*
Boston Evening Transcript
Chicago Times
Chicago Tribune
Christian Recorder
Cincinnati Enquirer
Cincinnati Gazette
Cleveland Leader
Continental Monthly
Forney's War Press
Harper's Weekly
Indianapolis *Daily Journal*
Indianapolis *State Sentinel*
Liberator
National Anti-Slavery Standard
New York Evening Express
New York Evening Post
New York Herald
New York Times
New York Tribune
New York Daily World
North American Review
Ohio State Journal
Philadelphia Inquirer
Rochester Democrat and American
Sacramento Daily Union
San Francisco *Daily Alta California*
Springfield *Illinois State Journal*
Springfield *Illinois State Register*
Trenton *State Gazette*
Washington *Daily National Intelligencer*
Wisconsin State Journal

Secondary Works

Books

Abbott, Richard H. *Cobbler in Congress: The Life of Henry Wilson, 1812–1875.* Lexington: University Press of Kentucky, 1972.
    The Republican Party and the South: The First Southern Strategy, 1855–1877. Chapel Hill: University of North Carolina Press, 1986.
Abrams, Roger I. *Legal Bases: Baseball and the Law.* Philadelphia: Temple University Press, 1998.

Abzug, Robert H., and Stephen E. Maizlish, eds. *New Perspectives on Race and Slavery in America: Essays in Honor of Kenneth M. Stampp*. Lexington: University Press of Kentucky, 1986.

Ackerman, Bruce. *We the People*. 2 vols. to date. Cambridge, Mass.: Harvard University Press, 1991–.

Ambrosius, Lloyd E, ed. *A Crisis of Republicanism: American Politics in the Civil War Era*. Lincoln: University of Nebraska Press, 1990.

Ames, Herman V. *The Proposed Amendments to the Constitution of the United States during the First Century of Its History*. Washington, D.C.: American Historical Association, 1896; reprint, New York: Burt Franklin, 1970.

Anderson, Eric, and Alfred A. Moss, Jr., eds. *The Facts of Reconstruction: Essays in Honor of John Hope Franklin*. Baton Rouge: Louisiana State University Press, 1991.

Attie, Jeannie. *Patriotic Toil: Northern Women and the American Civil War*. Ithaca: Cornell University Press, 1998.

Baker, Jean H. *Affairs of Party: The Political Culture of Northern Democrats in the Mid-Nineteenth Century*. Ithaca: Cornell University Press, 1983.

  The Politics of Continuity: Maryland Political Parties from 1858 to 1870. Baltimore: Johns Hopkins University Press, 1973.

Baum, Dale. *The Civil War Party System: The Case of Massachusetts, 1848–1876*. Chapel Hill: University of North Carolina Press, 1984.

Bederman, Gail. *Manliness and Civilization: A Cultural History of Gender and Race in the United States*. Chicago: University of Chicago Press, 1995.

Beeman, Richard, Stephen Botein, and Edward C. Carter II, eds. *Beyond Confederation: Origins of the Constitution and American National Identity*. Chapel Hill: University of North Carolina Press, 1987.

Bell, Howard Holman. *Minutes of the Proceedings of the National Negro Conventions, 1830–1864*. New York: Arno Press and the New York Times, 1969.

Belz, Herman. *Abraham Lincoln, Constitutionalism, and Equal Rights in the Civil War Era*. New York: Fordham University Press, 1998.

  Emancipation and Equal Rights: Politics and Constitutionalism in the Civil War Era. New York: W. W. Norton, 1978.

  A New Birth of Freedom: The Republican Party and Freedmen's Rights, 1861 to 1866. Westport, Conn.: Greenwood Press, 1976.

  Reconstructing the Union: Theory and Policy during the Civil War. Ithaca: Cornell University Press, 1969.

Benedict, Michael Les. *A Compromise of Principle: Congressional Republicans and Reconstruction, 1863–1869*. New York: W. W. Norton, 1974.

Bennett, Lerone. *Forced into Glory: Abraham Lincoln's White Dream*. Chicago: Johnson, 1999.

Bensel, Richard Franklin. *Yankee Leviathan: The Origins of Central State Authority in America, 1859–1877*. Cambridge: Cambridge University Press, 1990.

Berlin, Ira, Barbara Jeanne Fields, Steven F. Miller, Joseph P. Reidy, and Leslie S. Rowland. *Freedom: A Documentary History of Emancipation*. 4 vols. to date. Cambridge: Cambridge University Press, 1982– .

Slaves No More: Three Essays on Emancipation and the Civil War. Cambridge: Cambridge University Press, 1992.

Bernstein, Richard B., with Jerome Agel. *Amending America: If We Love the Constitution So Much, Why Do We Keep Trying to Change It?* New York: Times Books, 1993.

Berry, Mary Frances. *Military Necessity and Civil Rights Policy: Black Citizenship and the Constitution, 1861–1868.* Port Washington, N.Y.: Kennikat Press, 1977.

Bilotta, James D. *Race and the Rise of the Republican Party, 1848–1865.* New York: Peter Lang Publishing, 1992.

Binney, Charles Chauncey. *The Life of Horace Binney.* Philadelphia: J. B. Lippincott, 1903.

Blight, David W., and Brooks D. Simpson, eds. *Union and Emancipation: Essays on Politics and Race in the Civil War Era.* Kent, Ohio: Kent State University Press, 1997.

Blight, David W. *Frederick Douglass' Civil War: Keeping Faith in Jubilee.* Baton Rouge: Louisiana State University Press, 1989.

Bloch, J. M. *Miscegenation, Melaleukation, and Mr. Lincoln's Dog.* New York: Schaum Publishing, 1958.

Blue, Frederick J. *Salmon P. Chase: A Life in Politics.* Kent, Ohio: Kent State University Press, 1987.

Bogue, Allan G. *The Congressman's Civil War.* Cambridge: Cambridge University Press, 1989.

The Earnest Men: Republicans of the Civil War Senate. Ithaca: Cornell University Press, 1981.

Bonadio, Felice A. *North of Reconstruction: Ohio Politics, 1865–1870.* New York: New York University Press, 1970.

Boritt, Gabor S. *Lincoln and the Economics of the American Dream.* Memphis: Memphis State University Press, 1978.

ed. *The Historian's Lincoln: Pseudohistory, Psychohistory, and History.* Urbana: University of Illinois Press, 1988.

ed. *Lincoln, the War President: The Gettysburg Lectures.* New York: Oxford University Press, 1992.

ed. *Why the Civil War Came.* New York: Oxford University Press, 1996.

Brandon, Mark E. *Free in the World: American Slavery and Constitutional Failure.* Princeton: Princeton University Press, 1998.

Brock, W. R. *An American Crisis: Congress and Reconstruction, 1865–1867.* New York: St. Martin's Press, 1963; reprint, New York: Harper Torchbooks, 1966.

Brodie, Fawn M. *Thaddeus Stevens: Scourge of the South.* New York: W. W. Norton, 1959.

Brotherhood of Liberty. *Justice and Jurisprudence: Inquiry concerning the Constitutional Limitations of the Thirteenth, Fourteenth, and Fifteenth Amendments.* Philadelphia: J. B. Lippincott, 1889; reprint, New York: Negro Universities Press, 1969.

Brummer, Sidney D. *Political History of New York State during the Period of the Civil War.* New York: Columbia University Press, 1911.

Buck, Paul H. *The Road to Reunion, 1865–1900*. Boston: Little, Brown, 1937; reprint, New York: Vintage Books, 1959.

Burlingame, Michael. *The Inner World of Abraham Lincoln*. Urbana: University of Illinois Press, 1994.

Cain, Marvin R. *Lincoln's Attorney General: Edward Bates of Missouri*. Columbia: University of Missouri Press, 1965.

Carman, Harry J., and Reinhard Luthin. *Lincoln and the Patronage*. New York: Columbia University Press, 1943.

Carter, Dan T. *When the War Was Over: The Failure of Self-Reconstruction in the South, 1865–1867*. Baton Rouge: Louisiana State University Press, 1985.

Cimprich, John. *Slavery's End in Tennessee, 1861–1865*. University: University of Alabama Press, 1985.

Clinton, Catherine, and Nina Silber, eds. *Divided Houses: Gender and the Civil War*. New York: Oxford University Press, 1992.

Cohen, William. *At Freedom's Edge: Black Mobility and the Southern White Quest for Racial Control, 1861–1915*. Baton Rouge: Louisiana State University Press, 1991.

Cole, Arthur C. *The Era of the Civil War, 1848–1870*. Springfield: Illinois Centennial Commission, 1918; reprint, Urbana: University of Illinois Press, 1987.

Cornish, Dudley T. *The Sable Arm: Negro Troops in the Union Army, 1861–1865*. New York: Longmans, Green, 1956.

Coryell, Janet L. *Neither Heroine nor Fool: Anna Ella Carroll of Maryland*. Kent, Ohio: Kent State University Press, 1990.

Coulter, Ellis M. *The Civil War and Readjustment in Kentucky*. Chapel Hill: University of North Carolina Press, 1926.

Cover, Robert M. *Justice Accused: Antislavery and the Judicial Process*. New Haven: Yale University Press, 1975.

Cox, LaWanda. *Lincoln and Black Freedom: A Study in Presidential Leadership*. Columbia: University of South Carolina Press, 1981; reprint, Urbana: University of Illinois Press, 1985.

Cox, LaWanda, and John H. Cox. *Politics, Principle, and Prejudice, 1865–1866: Dilemma of Reconstruction America*. New York: Free Press, 1963.

Current, Richard Nelson. *Arguing with Historians: Essays on the Historical and the Unhistorical*. Middletown, Conn.: Wesleyan University Press, 1987.

⸻. *The Lincoln Nobody Knows*. New York: McGraw-Hill, 1958.

⸻. *Old Thad Stevens: A Story of Ambition*. Madison: University of Wisconsin Press, 1942.

Curry, Leonard P. *Blueprint for Modern America: Non-Military Legislation of the First Civil War Congress*. Nashville: Vanderbilt University Press, 1968.

Curry, Richard O., ed. *Radicalism, Racism, and Party Realignment: The Border States during Reconstruction*. Baltimore: Johns Hopkins Press, 1969.

Daniel, Pete. *The Shadow of Slavery: Peonage in the South, 1901–1969*. 2d ed. Urbana: University of Illinois Press, 1990.

Davis, David Brion. *From Homicide to Slavery: Studies in American Culture*. New York: Oxford University Press, 1986.

Dell, Christopher. *Lincoln and the War Democrats: The Grand Erosion of Conservative Tradition*. Rutherford, N.J.: Fairleigh Dickinson University Press, 1975.

Dennett, Tyler. *John Hay: From Poetry to Politics.* New York: Dodd, Mead, 1933.

Diffley, Kathleen. *Where My Heart Is Turning Ever: Civil War Stories and Constitutional Reform, 1861–1876.* Athens: University of Georgia Press, 1992.

Donald, David Herbert. *Charles Sumner and the Coming of the Civil War.* New York: Alfred A. Knopf, 1960.

   Charles Sumner and the Rights of Man. New York: Alfred A. Knopf, 1970.

   Lincoln. New York: Simon and Schuster, 1995.

   Lincoln Reconsidered: Essays on the Civil War Era. New York: Alfred A. Knopf, 1947; reprint, New York: Vintage Books, 1956.

   The Politics of Reconstruction, 1863–1867. Baton Rouge: Louisiana State University Press, 1965; reprint, Cambridge, Mass.: Harvard University Press, 1984.

Dorris, Jonathan. *Pardon and Amnesty under Lincoln and Johnson.* Chapel Hill: University of North Carolina Press, 1953.

DuBois, Ellen C. *Feminism and Suffrage: The Emergence of an Independent Women's Movement in America, 1848–1869.* Ithaca: Cornell University Press, 1978.

Du Bois, W. E. B. *Black Reconstruction in America.* New York: Russell and Russell, 1935.

   The Souls of Black Folk. Chicago: A. C. McClurg, 1903; reprint, Chicago: A. C. McClurg, 1953.

Durden, Robert F. *The Gray and the Black: The Confederate Debate on Emancipation.* Baton Rouge: Louisiana State University Press, 1972.

   James Shepherd Pike: Republicanism and the American Negro, 1850–1882. Durham: Duke University Press, 1957.

Dusinberre, William. *Civil War Issues in Philadelphia, 1856–1865.* Philadelphia: University of Pennsylvania Press, 1965.

Edwards, Laura. *Gendered Strife and Confusion: The Political Culture of Reconstruction.* Urbana: University of Illinois Press, 1997.

Edwards, Rebecca. *Angels in the Machinery: Gender in American Party Politics from the Civil War to the Progressive Era.* New York: Oxford University Press, 1997.

Essah, Patience. *A House Divided: Slavery and Emancipation in Delaware, 1638–1865.* Charlottesville: University Press of Virginia, 1996.

Fairman, Charles. *History of the Supreme Court of the United States.* Vol. 6, *Reconstruction and Reunion, 1864–1888: Part One.* New York: Macmillan, 1971.

Faust, Drew Gilpin. *The Creation of Confederate Nationalism: Ideology and Identity in the Civil War South.* Baton Rouge: Louisiana State University, 1988.

Fehrenbacher, Don E. *Chicago Giant: A Biography of "Long John" Wentworth.* Madison, Wisc.: American History Research Center, 1957.

   The Dred Scott Case: Its Significance in American Law and Politics. New York: Oxford University Press, 1978.

   Lincoln in Text and Context. Stanford, Calif.: Stanford University Press, 1988.

Fehrenbacher, Don. E., and Virginia Fehrenbacher, eds. *Recollected Words of Abraham Lincoln.* Stanford, Calif.: Stanford University Press, 1996.

Fellman, Michael. *Citizen Sherman: A Life of William Tecumseh Sherman.* New York: Random House, 1995.

Inside War: The Guerrilla Conflict in Missouri during the American Civil War. New York: Oxford University Press, 1989.

Ferguson, John L. *Arkansas and the Civil War.* Little Rock: Arkansas Civil War Centennial Commission, 1962.

Fermer, Douglas. *James Gordon Bennett and the New York Herald: A Study of Editorial Opinion in the Civil War Era, 1854–1867.* New York: St. Martin's Press, 1986.

Fessenden, Francis. *Life and Public Services of William Pitt Fessenden.* 2 vols. Boston: Houghton Mifflin, 1907.

Field, Phyllis F. *The Politics of Race in New York: The Struggle for Black Suffrage in the Civil War Era.* Ithaca: Cornell University Press, 1982.

Fields, Barbara J. *Slavery and Freedom on the Middle Ground: Maryland during the Nineteenth Century.* New Haven: Yale University Press, 1985.

Finkelman, Paul. *An Imperfect Union: Slavery, Federalism, and Comity.* Chapel Hill: University of North Carolina Press, 1981.

Finkelman, Paul. *Slavery and the Founders: Race and Liberty in the Age of Jefferson.* Armonk, N.Y.: M. E. Sharpe, 1996.

Flood, Curt, with Richard Carter. *The Way It Is.* New York: Trident Press, 1971.

Fogel, Robert W. *Without Consent or Contract: The Rise and Fall of American Slavery.* New York: W. W. Norton, 1989.

Foner, Eric. *Free Soil, Free Labor, Free Men: The Ideology of the Republican Party before the Civil War.* New York: Oxford University Press, 1970.

Nothing but Freedom: Emancipation and Its Legacy. Baton Rouge: Louisiana State University Press, 1983.

Politics and Ideology in the Age of the Civil War. New York: Oxford University Press, 1980.

Reconstruction: America's Unfinished Revolution, 1863–1877. New York: Harper and Row, 1988.

Forbath, William E. *Law and the Shaping of the American Labor Movement.* Cambridge, Mass.: Harvard University Press, 1991.

Forgie, George B. *Patricide in the House Divided: A Psychological Interpretation of Lincoln and His Age.* New York: W. W. Norton, 1979.

Frank, Joseph Allan. *With Ballot and Bayonet: The Political Socialization of American Civil War Soldiers.* Athens: University of Georgia Press, 1998.

Franklin, John Hope. *The Emancipation Proclamation.* Garden City, N.Y.: Doubleday, 1963; reprint, Wheeling, Ill.: Harlan Davidson, 1995.

From Slavery to Freedom. 5th ed. New York: Alfred A. Knopf, 1990.

Frederickson, George M. *The Arrogance of Race: Historical Perspectives on Slavery, Racism, and Social Inequality.* Middletown, Conn.: Wesleyan University Press, 1988.

The Black Image in the White Mind: The Debate on Afro-American Character and Destiny, 1817–1914. New York: Harper and Row, 1971; reprint, Middletown, Conn.: Wesleyan University Press, 1987.

The Inner Civil War: Northern Intellectuals and the Crisis of the Union. New York: Harper and Row, 1965.

Freehling, William W. *The Reintegration of American History: Slavery and the Civil War.* New York: Oxford University Press, 1994.
  The Road to Disunion: Secessionists at Bay, 1776–1854. New York: Oxford University Press, 1990.
Freehling, William W., and Craig M. Simpson, eds. *Secession Debated: Georgia's Showdown in 1860.* New York: Oxford University Press, 1992.
Freidel, Frank. *Francis Lieber: Nineteenth-Century Liberal.* Baton Rouge: Louisiana State University Press, 1947.
Gallman, J. Matthew. *Mastering Wartime: A Social History of Philadelphia during the Civil War.* Cambridge: Cambridge University Press, 1990.
  The North Fights the Civil War: The Home Front. Chicago: Ivan R. Dee, 1994.
Gambill, Edward L. *Conservative Ordeal: Northern Democrats and Reconstruction.* Ames: Iowa State University Press, 1981.
Gerber, David A. *Black Ohio and the Color Line, 1860–1915.* Urbana: University of Illinois Press, 1976.
Gerteis, Louis S. *From Contraband to Freedman: Federal Policy toward Southern Blacks, 1861–1865.* Westport, Conn.: Greenwood Press, 1973.
  Morality and Utility in American Antislavery Reform. Chapel Hill: University of North Carolina Press, 1987.
Gienapp, William E. *The Origins of the Republican Party, 1852–1856.* New York: Oxford University Press, 1987.
Gillette, William. *Jersey Blue: Civil War Politics in New Jersey, 1854–1865.* New Brunswick, N.J.: Rutgers University Press, 1995.
Glatthaar, Joseph T. *Forged in Battle: The Civil War Alliance of Black Soldiers and White Officers.* New York: Free Press, 1990.
Glickstein, Jonathan A. *Concepts of Free Labor in Antebellum America.* New Haven: Yale University Press, 1991.
Goodman, Paul. *Of One Blood: Abolitionism and the Origins of Racial Equality.* Berkeley: University of California Press, 1998.
Gray, Wood. *The Hidden Civil War: The Story of the Copperheads.* New York: Viking Press, 1942.
Hall, Kermit. *The Magic Mirror: Law in American History.* New York: Oxford University Press, 1989.
Hall, Kermit L., Harold M. Hyman, and Leon V. Sigal, eds. *The Constitutional Convention as an Amending Device.* Washington D.C.: American Historical Association and American Political Science Association, 1981.
Halttunen, Karen. *Confidence Men and Painted Women: A Study of Middle-Class Culture in America, 1830–1870.* New Haven, Yale University Press, 1982.
Hancock, Harold. *Delaware during the Civil War: A Political History.* Wilmington: Historical Society of Delaware, 1961.
Hansen, Stephen L. *The Making of the Third Party System: Voters and Parties in Illinois, 1850–1876.* Ann Arbor, Mich.: UMI Research Press, 1980.
Harding, Vincent. *There Is a River: The Black Struggle for Freedom in America.* New York: Harcourt Brace Jovanovich, 1981; reprint, New York: Vintage Books, 1983.
Harlow, Ralph Volney. *Gerrit Smith: Philanthropist and Reformer.* New York: Henry Holt, 1939.

Harris, William C. *With Charity for All: Lincoln and the Restoration of the Union.* Lexington: University Press of Kentucky, 1997.

Harrison, Lowell. *The Civil War in Kentucky.* Lexington: University Press of Kentucky, 1975.

Hattaway, Herman, and Archer Jones. *How the North Won.* Urbana: University of Illinois Press, 1983.

Haynes, Elizabeth Ross. *The Black Boy of Atlanta.* Boston: Edinboro, 1952.

Hendrick, Burton J. *Lincoln's War Cabinet.* Boston: Little, Brown, 1946.

Henig, Gerald S. *Henry Winter Davis: Antebellum and Civil War Congressman from Maryland.* New York: Twayne Publishers, 1973.

Herndon, William H., and Jesse W. Weik. *Herndon's Lincoln: The True Story of a Great Life.* 3 vols. Chicago: Belford, Clarke, 1889. Revised as *Abraham Lincoln: The True Story of a Great Life.* New York: D. Appleton, 1892; reprint, 1913.

Hess, Earl J. *Liberty, Virtue, and Progress: Northerners and Their War for the Union.* New York: New York University Press, 1988.

Hesseltine, William B. *Lincoln and the War Governors.* New York: Alfred A. Knopf, 1948.

———. *Lincoln's Plan of Reconstruction.* Tuscaloosa, Ala.: Confederate Publishing, 1960; reprint, Chicago: Quadrangle Books, 1967.

Hicken, Victor. *Illinois in the Civil War.* Urbana: University of Illinois Press, 1989.

Hodes, Martha. *White Women, Black Men: Illicit Sex in the Nineteenth-Century South.* New Haven: Yale University Press, 1997.

Hoemann, George H. *What God Hath Wrought: The Embodiment of Freedom in the Thirteenth Amendment.* New York: Garland, 1987.

Hofstadter, Richard. *The American Political Tradition and the Men Who Made It.* New York: Alfred A. Knopf, 1948; reprint, New York: Vintage Books, 1974.

———. *The Idea of a Party System: The Rise of Legitimate Opposition in the United States, 1780–1840.* Berkeley: University of California Press, 1969.

———. *The Paranoid Style in American Politics and Other Essays.* New York: Alfred A. Knopf, 1965; reprint, Chicago: University of Chicago Press, 1979.

Hollister, O. J. *Life of Schuyler Colfax.* New York: Funk and Wagnalls, 1886.

Holt, Michael F. *The Political Crisis of the 1850s.* New York: John Wiley and Sons, 1978; reprint, W. W. Norton, 1983.

Horner, Harlan H. *Lincoln and Greeley.* Urbana: University of Illinois Press, 1953.

Horowitz, Robert F. *The Great Impeacher: A Political Biography of James M. Ashley.* Brooklyn: Brooklyn College Press, 1979.

Horton, James Oliver. *Free People of Color: Inside the African American Community.* Washington, D.C.: Smithsonian Institution Press, 1993.

Howard, Victor B. *Black Liberation in Kentucky: Emancipation and Freedom, 1862–1884.* Lexington: University Press of Kentucky, 1983.

Howe, Daniel Walker. *The Political Culture of the American Whigs.* Chicago: University of Chicago Press, 1979.

Huggins, Nathan Irvin. *Black Odyssey: The African-American Ordeal in Slavery.* New York: Random House, 1977; reprint, New York: Vintage Books, 1990.

Hyman, Harold M. *Lincoln's Reconstruction: Neither Failure of Vision nor Vision of Failure*. Fort Wayne, Ind.: Louis A. Warren Lincoln Library and Museum, 1980.

A More Perfect Union: The Impact of the Civil War and Reconstruction on the Constitution. New York: Alfred A. Knopf, 1973.

The Reconstruction Justice of Salmon P. Chase: In Re Turner and Texas v. White. Lawrence: University Press of Kansas, 1997.

The Radical Republicans and Reconstruction, 1861–1870. Indianapolis: Bobbs-Merrill, 1967.

Hyman, Harold M., and William M. Wiecek. *Equal Justice under Law: Constitutional Development, 1835–1875*. New York: Harper and Row, 1982.

Isely, Jeter Allen. *Horace Greeley and the Republican Party, 1853–1861*. Princeton: Princeton University Press, 1947; reprint, New York: Octagon Books, 1965.

Isenberg, Nancy. *Sex and Citizenship in Antebellum America*. Chapel Hill: University of North Carolina Press, 1998.

Jeffrey, Julie Roy. *The Great Silent Army of Abolitionism: Ordinary Women in the Antislavery Movement*. Chapel Hill: University of North Carolina Press, 1998.

Jimerson, Randall C. *The Private Civil War: Popular Thought during the Sectional Conflict*. Baton Rouge: Louisiana State University Press, 1988.

Johannsen, Robert W. *Lincoln, the South, and Slavery: The Political Dimension*. Baton Rouge: Louisiana State University Press, 1990.

Stephen A. Douglas. New York: Oxford University Press, 1973.

Johnson, Donald B. *National Party Platforms*. Urbana: University of Illinois Press, 1978.

Jones, Howard. *Abraham Lincoln and a New Birth of Freedom: The Union and Slavery in the Diplomacy of the Civil War*. Lincoln: University of Nebraska Press, 1999.

Union in Peril: The Crisis over British Intervention in the Civil War. Chapel Hill: University of North Carolina Press, 1992.

Kaczorowski, Robert J. *The Politics of Judicial Interpretation: The Federal Courts, Department of Justice and Civil Rights, 1866–1876*. New York: Oceana Publications, 1985.

Kammen, Michael. *A Machine That Would Go of Itself: The Constitution in American Culture*. New York: Alfred A. Knopf, 1986; reprint, New York: Vintage Books, 1987.

Karcher, Carolyn L. *The First Woman in the Republic: A Cultural Biography of Lydia Maria Child*. Durham, N.C.: Duke University Press, 1994.

Katz, Irving. *August Belmont: A Political Biography*. New York: Columbia University Press, 1968.

Kettner, James H. *The Development of American Citizenship, 1608–1870*. Chapel Hill: University of North Carolina Press, 1978.

King, Willard L. *Lincoln's Manager, David Davis*. Cambridge, Mass.: Harvard University Press, 1960.

Kirkland, Edward C. *The Peacemakers of 1864*. New York: Macmillan, 1927.

Kitchens, John W., ed. *The Tuskegee Institute News Clippings File*. Microfilm edition. Tuskegee, Ala.: Tuskegee Institute, 1981.

Klement, Frank L. *The Copperheads in the Middle West*. Chicago: University of Chicago Press, 1960.

Dark Lanterns: Secret Political Societies, Conspiracies, and Treason Trials in the Civil War. Baton Rouge: Louisiana State University Press, 1984.

The Limits of Dissent: Clement L. Vallandigham and the Civil War. Lexington: University of Kentucky Press, 1970.

Kleppner, Paul. *The Cross of Culture: A Social Analysis of Midwestern Politics, 1850–1900*. New York: Free Press, 1970.

The Third Electoral System, 1853–1892: Parties, Voters, and Political Cultures. Chapel Hill: University of North Carolina Press, 1979.

Knapp, Charles Merriam. *New Jersey Politics During the Period of the Civil War and Reconstruction*. Geneva, N.Y.: W. F. Humphrey, 1924.

Knupfer, Peter. *The Union As It Is: Constitutional Unionism and Sectional Compromise, 1787–1861*. Chapel Hill: University of North Carolina Press, 1991.

Kousser, J. Morgan, and James M. McPherson. *Region, Race, and Reconstruction*. New York: Oxford University Press, 1982.

Kraditor, Aileen. *Means and Ends in American Abolitionism: Garrison and His Critics on Strategy and Tactics, 1834–1850*. New York: Pantheon Books, 1969.

Krug, Mark M. *Lyman Trumbull: Conservative Radical*. New York: A. S. Barnes, 1965.

Kull, Andrew. *The Color-Blind Constitution*. Cambridge, Mass.: Harvard University Press, 1992.

Kutler, Stanley I. *Judicial Power and Reconstruction Politics*. Chicago: University of Chicago Press, 1968.

Kyvig, David E. *Explicit and Authentic Acts: Amending the U.S. Constitution, 1776-1995*. Lawrence: University Press of Kansas, 1996.

Leech, Margaret. *Reveille in Washington, 1860–1865*. New York: Harper and Brothers, 1941; reprint, New York: Time, 1962.

Levinson, Sanford, ed. *Responding to Imperfection: The Theory and Practice of Constitutional Amendment*. Princeton: Princeton University Press, 1995.

Linden, Glenn M. *Politics or Principle: Congressional Voting on the Civil War Amendments and Pro-Negro Measures, 1838–1869*. Seattle: University of Washington Press, 1976.

Lindsey, David. *"Sunset" Cox: Irrepressible Democrat*. Detroit: Wayne State University Press, 1959.

Litwack, Leon F. *Been in the Storm So Long: The Aftermath of Slavery*. New York: Borzoi, 1979.

North of Slavery: The Negro in the Free States, 1790–1860. Chicago: University of Chicago Press, 1961.

Long, David E. *The Jewel of Liberty: Abraham Lincoln's Re-Election and the End of Slavery*. Mechanicsburg, Penn.: Stackpole Books, 1994.

Lott, Eric. *Love and Theft: Blackface Minstrelsy and the American Working Class*. New York: Oxford University Press, 1993.

Lucie, Patricia Allan. *Freedom and Federalism: Congress and Courts, 1861–1866*. New York: Garland, 1986.

Mabee, Carleton. *Black Freedom: The Nonviolent Abolitionists from 1830 through the Civil War.* London: Macmillan, 1970.

Magdol, Edward. *Owen Lovejoy: Abolitionist in Congress.* New Brunswick, N.J.: Rutgers University Press, 1967.

A *Right to the Land: Essays on the Freedmen's Community.* Westport, Conn.: Greenwood Press, 1977.

Maier, Pauline. *American Scripture: Making the Declaration of Independence.* New York: Alfred A. Knopf, 1997.

Maizlish, Stephen E., and John J. Kushma, eds. *Essays on American Antebellum Politics, 1840–1860.* College Station: Texas A&M University Press, 1982.

Maltz, Earl M. *Civil Rights, the Constitution, and Congress, 1863–1869.* Lawrence: University Press of Kansas, 1990.

Martin, Waldo E. *The Mind of Frederick Douglass.* Chapel Hill: University of North Carolina Press, 1985.

McCormick, Richard L. *The Party Period and Public Policy: American Politics from the Age of Jackson to the Progressive Era.* New York: Oxford University Press, 1986.

McCrary, Peyton. *Abraham Lincoln and Reconstruction: The Louisiana Experiment.* Princeton: Princeton University Press, 1978.

McFeely, William S. *Frederick Douglass.* New York: W. W. Norton, 1991.

Grant: A Biography. New York: W. W. Norton, 1981.

Yankee Stepfather: General O. O. Howard and the Freedmen. New Haven: Yale University Press, 1968; reprint, New York: W. W. Norton, 1970.

McInerney, Daniel J. *The Fortunate Heirs of Freedom: Abolition and Republican Thought.* Lincoln: University of Nebraska Press, 1994.

McJimsey, George T. *Genteel Partisan: Manton Marble, 1834–1917.* Ames: Iowa State University Press, 1971.

McKay, Ernest. *The Civil War and New York City.* Syracuse, N.Y.: Syracuse University Press, 1990.

Henry Wilson, Practical Radical: Portrait of a Politician. Port Washington, N.Y.: Kennikat Press, 1971.

McKitrick, Eric L. *Andrew Johnson and Reconstruction.* Chicago: University of Chicago Press, 1960.

McPherson, Edward. *The Political History of the United States of America during the Great Rebellion.* 2d ed. Washington: Philp and Solomons, 1865; reprint, New York: Da Capo Press, 1972.

McPherson, James M. *Abraham Lincoln and the Second American Revolution.* New York: Oxford University Press, 1991.

Battle Cry of Freedom: The Civil War Era. New York: Oxford University Press, 1988.

For Cause and Comrades: Why Men Fought in the Civil War. New York: Oxford University Press, 1997.

The Struggle for Equality: Abolitionists and the Negro in the Civil War and Reconstruction. Princeton: Princeton University Press, 1964.

What They Fought For, 1861–1865. Baton Rouge: Louisiana State University Press, 1994.

ed. *The Negro's Civil War: How American Negroes Felt and Acted during the*

War for the Union. New York: Pantheon Books, 1965; reprint, Urbana: University of Illinois Press, 1982.

McPherson, James M., and William J. Cooper, Jr., eds. *Writing the Civil War: The Quest to Understand.* Columbia: University of South Carolina Press, 1998.

Melish, Joanne Pope. *Disowning Slavery: Gradual Emancipation and "Race" in New England, 1780–1860.* Ithaca: Cornell University Press, 1998.

Miller, William Lee. *Arguing about Slavery: The Great Battle in the United States Congress.* New York: Alfred A. Knopf, 1996.

Mitchell, Reid. *The Vacant Chair: The Northern Soldier Leaves Home.* New York: Oxford University Press, 1993.

Montgomery, David. *Beyond Equality: Labor and the Radical Republicans, 1862–1872.* New York: Alfred A. Knopf, 1967.

Citizen Worker: The Experience of Workers in the United States with Democracy and the Free Market during the Nineteenth Century. Cambridge: Cambridge University Press, 1993.

Morrison, Michael A. *Slavery and the American West: The Eclipse of Manifest Destiny and the Coming of the Civil War.* Chapel Hill: University of North Carolina Press, 1997.

Mushkat, Jerome. *Fernando Wood: A Political Biography.* Kent, Ohio: Kent State University Press, 1990.

The Reconstruction of the New York Democracy, 1861–1874. London: Associated University Presses, 1981.

Neely, Mark E., Jr. *The Fate of Liberty: Abraham Lincoln and Civil Liberties.* New York: Oxford University Press, 1991.

The Last Best Hope of Earth: Abraham Lincoln and the Promise of America. Cambridge, Mass.: Harvard University Press, 1993.

Nelson, Larry E. *Bullets, Ballots, and Rhetoric: Confederate Policy for the United States Presidential Contest of 1864.* University: University of Alabama Press, 1980.

Nelson, William E. *The Fourteenth Amendment: From Political Principle to Judicial Doctrine.* Cambridge, Mass.: Harvard University Press, 1988.

Nevins, Allan. *Fremont: Pathmarker of the West.* New York: Appleton-Century, 1939; reprint, New York: Longmans, Green, 1955.

Ordeal of the Union. 8 vols. New York: Scribner's, 1947–71.

Nichols, Roy F. *The Disruption of American Democracy.* New York: Macmillan, 1948; reprint, New York: Free Press, 1967.

Nicolay, John, and John Hay. *Abraham Lincoln: A History.* 10 vols. New York: Century Co., 1890.

Nieman, Donald G. *Promises to Keep: African Americans and the Constitutional Order, 1776 to the Present.* New York: Oxford University Press, 1990.

To Set the Law in Motion: The Freedmen's Bureau and the Legal Rights of Blacks, 1865–1868. Millwood, N.Y.: KTO Press, 1979.

ed. *Black Southerners and the Law, 1865–1900.* New York: Garland, 1994.

ed. *The Constitution, Law, and American Life: Critical Aspects of the Nineteenth-Century Experience.* Athens: The University of Georgia Press, 1992.

Niven, John. *Gideon Welles: Lincoln's Secretary of the Navy.* New York: Oxford University Press, 1973.

   Salmon P. Chase: A Biography. New York: Oxford University Press, 1995.

Noonan, John T. *Bribes.* New York: Macmillan, 1984.

Novak, Daniel A. *The Wheel of Servitude: Black Forced Labor after Slavery.* Lexington: University Press of Kentucky, 1978.

Oates, Stephen B. *Abraham Lincoln: The Man behind the Myths.* New York: Harper and Row, 1984.

   With Malice toward None: The Life of Abraham Lincoln. New York: Harper and Row, 1977.

Onuf, Peter S. *Statehood and Union: A History of the Northwest Ordinance.* Bloomington: Indiana University Press, 1987.

Paludan, Phillip Shaw. *A Covenant with Death: The Constitution, Law, and Equality in the Civil War Era.* Urbana: University of Illinois Press, 1975.

   "A People's Contest": The Union and Civil War, 1861–1865. New York: Harper and Row, 1988.

   The Presidency of Abraham Lincoln. Lawrence: University Press of Kansas, 1994.

Parrish, William E. *Missouri under Radical Rule, 1865–1870.* Columbia: University of Missouri Press, 1965.

   Turbulent Partnership: Missouri and the Union, 1861–1865. Columbia: University of Missouri Press, 1963.

Pease, Jane H., and William H. Pease. *They Who Would Be Free: Blacks' Search for Freedom, 1830–1861.* Urbana: University of Illinois Press, 1989.

Perman, Michael. *Reunion without Compromise: The South and Reconstruction, 1865–1868.* Cambridge: Cambridge University Press, 1973.

   The Road to Redemption: Southern Politics, 1869–1879. Chapel Hill: University of North Carolina Press, 1984.

Perry, Lewis, and Michael Fellman, eds. *Antislavery Reconsidered: New Perspectives on the Abolitionists.* Baton Rouge: Louisiana State University Press, 1979.

Peterson, Merrill D. *Lincoln in American Memory.* New York: Oxford University Press, 1994.

Porter, George H. *Ohio Politics during the Civil War Period.* New York: Columbia University Press, 1911; reprint, New York: AMS Press, 1968.

Potter, David. *The Impending Crisis, 1848–1861.* New York: Harper and Row, 1976.

   Lincoln and His Party in the Secession Crisis. New Haven: Yale University Press, 1942.

Pressly, Thomas J. *Americans Interpret Their Civil War.* Princeton: Princeton University Press, 1954; reprint, New York: Free Press, 1965.

Quarles, Benjamin. *Black Abolitionists.* New York: Oxford University Press, 1969.

   Frederick Douglass. Washington, D.C.: Associated Publishers, 1948.

   Lincoln and the Negro. New York: Oxford University Press, 1962.

   The Negro in the Civil War. Boston: Little, Brown, 1953.

Rakove, Jack N. *Original Meanings: Politics and Ideas in the Making of the Constitution.* New York: Alfred A. Knopf, 1996.

Randall, James G. *The Confiscation of Property during the Civil War.* Indianapolis: Bobbs-Merrill, 1913.

  Constitutional Problems under Lincoln. New York: D. Appleton, 1926; revised, Urbana: University of Illinois Press, 1951; reprint, Gloucester, Mass.: Peter Smith, 1963.

Randall, James G., and Richard N. Current. *Lincoln the President.* 4 vols. New York: Dodd, Mead, 1945–55; reprint vol. 4, *Lincoln the President: Last Full Measure,* Urbana: University of Illinois Press, 1991.

Ransom, Roger L. *Conflict and Compromise: The Political Economy of Slavery, Emancipation, and the American Civil War.* Cambridge: Cambridge University Press, 1989.

Rawley, James A. *Edwin D. Morgan, 1811–1883: Merchant in Politics.* New York: Columbia University Press, 1955.

  Turning Points of the Civil War. Lincoln: University of Nebraska Press, 1966.

  ed. *Lincoln and Civil War Politics.* New York: Holt, Rinehart, and Winston, 1969.

Renda, Lex. *Running on the Record: Civil War-Era Politics in New Hampshire.* Charlottesville: University Press of Virginia, 1997.

Rhodes, James Ford. *History of the United States from the Compromise of 1850 to the Restoration of Home Rule in the South in 1877.* 7 vols. New York: Harper and Brothers (vols. 1–3) and Macmillan (vols. 4–7), 1893–1906.

Richards, David A. J. *Conscience and the Constitution: History, Theory, and Law of the Reconstruction Amendments.* Princeton: Princeton University Press, 1993.

Richardson, Heather Cox. *The Greatest Nation of the Earth: Republican Economic Policies during the Civil War.* Cambridge, Mass.: Harvard University Press, 1997.

Ripley, C. Peter. *Slaves and Freedmen in Civil War Louisiana.* Baton Rouge: Louisiana State University Press, 1976.

Ripley, C. Peter, et al., eds. *The Black Abolitionist Papers.* 5 vols. to date. Chapel Hill: University of North Carolina Press, 1985–.

Ritchie, Donald A. *Press Gallery: Congress and the Washington Correspondents.* Cambridge, Mass.: Harvard University Press, 1991.

Roediger, David. *The Wages of Whiteness: Race and the Making of the American Working Class.* London: Verso, 1991.

Rose, Anne C. *Victorian America and the Civil War.* Cambridge: Cambridge University Press, 1992.

Roseboom, Eugene H. *The Civil War Era, 1850–1873.* Columbus: Ohio State Archaeological and Historical Society, 1944.

Roske, Ralph J. *His Own Counsel: The Life and Times of Lyman Trumbull.* Reno: University of Nevada Press, 1979.

Royster, Charles W. *The Destructive War: William Tecumseh Sherman, Stonewall Jackson, and the Americans.* New York: Alfred A. Knopf, 1991; reprint, New York: Vintage Books, 1991.

Ryan, Mary P. *Cradle of the Middle Class: The Family in Oneida County, New York, 1790–1865*. Cambridge: Cambridge University Press, 1981.

Women in Public: Between Banners and Ballots, 1825–1880. Baltimore: Johns Hopkins University Press, 1990.

Sandburg, Carl. *Abraham Lincoln*. 6 vols. New York: Harcourt, Brace, 1926–39.

Sánchez-Eppler, Karen. *Touching Liberty: Abolition, Feminism, and the Politics of the Body*. Berkeley: University of California Press, 1993.

Saxton, Alexander. *The Rise and Fall of the White Republic: Class Politics and Mass Culture in Nineteenth-Century America*. New York: Verso, 1990.

Sawrey, Robert D. *Dubious Victory: The Reconstruction Debate in Ohio*. Lexington: University Press of Kentucky, 1992.

Schmidt, James D. *Free to Work: Labor Law, Emancipation, and Reconstruction, 1815–1880*. Athens: University of Georgia Press, 1998.

Sewell, Richard H. *Ballots for Freedom: Antislavery Politics in the United States, 1837–1860*. New York: Oxford University Press, 1976; reprint, New York: W. W. Norton, 1980.

Shankman, Arnold M. *The Pennsylvania Antiwar Movement, 1861–1865*. Rutherford, N.J.: Fairleigh Dickinson University Press, 1980.

Silber, Nina. *The Romance of Reunion: Northerners and the South, 1865–1900*. Chapel Hill: University of North Carolina Press, 1993.

Silbey, Joel H. *The American Political Nation, 1838–1893*. Stanford, Calif.: Stanford University Press, 1991.

The Partisan Imperative: The Dynamics of American Politics before the Civil War. New York: Oxford University Press, 1985.

A Respectable Minority: The Democratic Party in the Civil War Era, 1860–1868. New York: W. W. Norton, 1977.

Silver, David M. *Lincoln's Supreme Court*. Urbana: University of Illinois Press, 1956.

Simpson, Brooks D. *Let Us Have Peace: Ulysses S. Grant and the Politics of War and Reconstruction, 1861–1868*. Chapel Hill: University of North Carolina Press, 1991.

Smith, Elbert B. *The Death of Slavery: The United States, 1837–1865*. Chicago: University of Chicago Press, 1967.

Francis Preston Blair. New York: Free Press, 1980.

Smith, William Benjamin. *James Sidney Rollins*. New York: DeVinne Press, 1891.

Smith, William E. *The Francis Preston Blair Family in Politics*. 2 vols. New York: Macmillan, 1933.

Stampp, Kenneth M. *America in 1857: A Nation on the Brink*. New York: Oxford University Press, 1990.

And the War Came: The North and the Secession Crisis. Baton Rouge: Louisiana State University Press, 1950.

Indiana Politics during the Civil War. Indianapolis: Indiana Historical Bureau, 1949.

Stanley, Amy Dru. *From Bondage to Contract: Wage Labor, Marriage, and the Market in the Age of Slave Emancipation*. Cambridge: Cambridge University Press, 1998.

Stanton, Elizabeth Cady, Susan B. Anthony, and Matilda Joslyn Gage. *The History of Woman Suffrage*. 6 vols. Rochester and New York: Fowler and Wells, 1881–1922; reprint, New York: Arno and New York Times, 1969.

Steiner, Bernard C. *Life of Reverdy Johnson*. Baltimore: Norman, Remington, 1914.

Steinfeld, Robert J. *The Invention of Free Labor: The Employment Relation in English and American Law and Culture, 1350–1870*. Chapel Hill: University of North Carolina Press, 1991.

Stokes, Melvyn, and Stephen Conway, eds. *The Market Revolution: Social, Political, and Religious Expressions*. Charlottesville: University Press of Virginia, 1996.

Strozier, Charles. *Lincoln's Quest for Union: Public and Private Meanings*. New York: Basic Books, 1982.

Suits, Linda Norbut, and George L. Painter, eds. *Abraham Lincoln and a Nation at War: Papers from the Ninth Annual Lincoln Colloquium*. Springfield, Ill.: Lincoln Home National Historic Site, 1996.

Summers, Mark Wahlgren. *The Era of Good Stealings*. New York: Oxford University Press, 1993.

——— *The Plundering Generation: Corruption and the Crisis of the Union, 1849–1861*. New York: Oxford University Press, 1987.

Swierenga, Robert P., ed. *Beyond the Civil War Synthesis: Political Essays of the Civil War*. Westport, Conn.: Greenwood Press, 1975.

Swisher, Carl B. *Roger B. Taney*. New York: Macmillan, 1935.

Taylor, Joe Gray. *Louisiana Reconstructed, 1863–1877*. Baton Rouge: Louisiana State University Press, 1974.

Taylor, John M. *William Henry Seward: Lincoln's Right Hand*. New York: HarperCollins, 1991.

tenBroek, Jacobus. *Equal under Law*. Berkeley: University of California Press, 1951 (originally published as *The Antislavery Origins of the Fourteenth Amendment*); reprint, New York: Collier Books, 1965.

Thomas, Benjamin P. *Abraham Lincoln: A Biography*. New York: Alfred A. Knopf, 1952.

Thomas, Benjamin P., and Harold M. Hyman. *Stanton: The Life and Times of Lincoln's Secretary of War*. New York: Alfred A. Knopf, 1962.

Thomas, John L. *The Liberator: William Lloyd Garrison*. Boston: Little, Brown, 1963.

——— ed. *Abraham Lincoln and the American Political Tradition*. Amherst: University of Massachusetts Press, 1986.

Thornbrough, Emma L. *Indiana in the Civil War Era, 1850–1880*. Indianapolis: Indiana Historical Bureau, 1965.

Toll, Robert C. *Blacking Up: The Minstrel Show in Nineteenth Century America*. New York: Oxford University Press, 1976.

Tredway, G. R. *Democratic Opposition to the Lincoln Administration in Indiana*. Indianapolis: Indiana Historical Bureau, 1979.

Trefousse, Hans L. *Andrew Johnson: A Biography*. New York: W. W. Norton, 1989.

Ben Butler: The South Called Him Beast! New York: Twayne Publishers, 1957.

Benjamin Franklin Wade: Radical Republican from Ohio. New York: Twayne Publishers, 1963.

Carl Schurz: A Biography. Knoxville: University of Tennessee Press, 1982.

The Radical Republicans: Lincoln's Vanguard for Racial Justice. New York: Alfred A. Knopf, 1969.

Thaddeus Stevens: Nineteenth-Century Egalitarian. Chapel Hill: University of North Carolina Press, 1997.

ed. *Lincoln's Decision for Emancipation.* Philadelphia: Lippincott, 1975.

Tribe, Laurence H. *American Constitutional Law.* 2 ed. Mineola, N.Y.: Foundation Press, 1988.

Tunnell, Ted. *Crucible of Reconstruction: War, Radicalism, and Race in Louisiana.* Baton Rouge: Louisiana State University Press, 1984.

Turner, Justin G. *The Thirteenth Amendment and the Emancipation Proclamation.* Los Angeles: Plantin Press, 1971.

Uya, Okon Edet. *From Slavery to Public Service: Robert Smalls, 1839–1915.* New York: Oxford University Press, 1971.

Van Deusen, Glyndon G. *Horace Greeley: Nineteenth-Century Crusader.* Philadelphia: University of Pennsylvania Press, 1953.

Thurlow Weed: Wizard of the Lobby. Boston: Little, Brown, 1947.

William Henry Seward. New York: Oxford University Press, 1967.

Venet, Wendy Hamand. *Neither Ballots nor Bullets: Women Abolitionists and the Civil War.* Charlottesville: University Press of Virginia, 1991.

Vile, John R. *The Constitutional Amending Process in American Political Thought.* New York: Praeger Publishers, 1992.

Contemporary Questions Surrounding the Constitutional Amending Process. Westport, Conn.: Praeger Publishers, 1993.

Vinovskis, Maris, ed. *Toward a Social History of the American Civil War: Exploratory Essays.* Cambridge: Cambridge University Press, 1990.

Voegeli, V. Jacque. *Free but Not Equal: The Midwest and the Negro during the Civil War.* Chicago: University of Chicago Press, 1967.

Wagandt, Charles Lewis. *The Mighty Revolution: Negro Emancipation in Maryland, 1862–1864.* Baltimore: Johns Hopkins Press, 1964.

Walters, Ronald G. *The Antislavery Appeal: American Abolitionism after 1830.* Baltimore: Johns Hopkins University Press, 1976.

Wang, Xi. *The Trial of Democracy: Black Suffrage and Northern Republicans, 1860–1910.* Athens: University of Georgia Press, 1997.

Ward, Geoffrey C., with Ken Burns and Ric Burns, eds. *The Civil War: An Illustrated History.* New York: Alfred A. Knopf, 1990.

White, Horace. *The Life of Lyman Trumbull.* Boston: Houghton Mifflin, 1913.

Wiecek, William M. *The Sources of Antislavery Constitutionalism in America, 1760–1848.* Ithaca: Cornell University Press, 1977.

Wiggins, William H. *O Freedom! Afro-American Emancipation Celebrations.* Knoxville: University of Tennessee Press, 1987.

Williams, T. Harry. *Lincoln and the Radicals.* Madison: University of Wisconsin Press, 1941.

Williamson, Joel. *The Crucible of Race: Black-White Relations in the American South since Emancipation.* New York: Oxford University Press, 1984.

  New People: Miscegenation and Mulattoes in the United States. New York: New York University Press, 1984.

Wills, Garry. *Lincoln at Gettysburg: The Words That Remade America.* New York: Simon and Schuster, 1992.

Wilson, Henry. *History of the Rise and Fall of the Slave Power in America.* 3 vols. Boston: Houghton Mifflin, 1875–1877.

Wilson, Major. *Space, Time, and Freedom.* Westport, Conn.: Greenwood Press, 1974.

Wood, Forrest G. *Black Scare: The Racist Response to Emancipation and Reconstruction.* Berkeley: University of California Press, 1968.

Woodward, C. Vann. *The Burden of Southern History.* 2d ed. Baton Rouge: Louisiana State University Press, 1968.

Wright, John S. *Lincoln and the Politics of Slavery.* Reno: University of Nevada Press, 1970.

Yellin, Jean Fagan, and John C. Van Horne, eds. *The Abolitionist Sisterhood: Women's Political Culture in Antebellum America.* Ithaca: Cornell University Press, 1994.

Zarefsky, David. *Lincoln, Douglas, and Slavery: In the Crucible of Public Debate.* Chicago: University of Chicago Press, 1990.

Zilversmit, Arthur. *The First Emancipation: The Abolition of Slavery in the North.* Chicago: University of Chicago Press, 1967.

Zornow, William Frank. *Lincoln and the Party Divided.* Norman: University of Oklahoma Press, 1954.

Articles

Abzug, Robert H. "The Copperheads: Historical Approaches to Civil War Dissent in the Midwest." *Indiana Magazine of History,* 66 (1970), 40–55.

Amar, Akhil Reed. "The Case of the Missing Amendments: *R.A.V. v. City of St. Paul.*" *Harvard Law Review,* 106 (November 1992), 124–61.

  "The Consent of the Governed: Constitutional Amendment outside Article V." *Columbia Law Review,* 94 (March 1994), 457–508.

  "Forty Acres and a Mule: A Republican Theory of Minimal Entitlements." *Harvard Journal of Law and Public Policy,* 13 (Winter 1990), 37–43.

  "Philadelphia Revisited: Amending the Constitution outside Article V." *University of Chicago Law Review,* 55 (Fall 1988), 1043–1104.

  "Remember the Thirteenth." *Constitutional Commentary,* 10 (Summer 1993), 403–8.

Amar, Akhil Reed, and Daniel Widawsky. "Child Abuse as Slavery: A Thirteenth Amendment response to DeShaney." *Harvard Law Review,* 105 (April 1992), 1359–85.

Baker, Jean Harvey. "Politics, Paradigms, and Public Culture." *Journal of American History,* 84 (December 1997), 894–99.

Baldwin, Carol A. "The Thirteenth Amendment as an Effective Source of Constitutional Authority for Affirmative Action Legislation." *Columbia Journal of Law and Social Problems,* 18 (Winter 1983), 77–114.

Bell, Howard H. "Negro Emancipation in Historic Retrospect: The Nation. The Conditions and Prospects of the Negro as Reflected in the National Convention of 1864." *Journal of Human Relations,* 9 (1963), 221–31.

Belz, Herman. "Abraham Lincoln and American Constitutionalism." *Review of Politics,* 50 (Spring 1988), 169–97.

"The Civil War Amendments to the Constitution: The Relevance of Original Intent." *Constitutional Commentary,* 5 (Winter 1988), 115–41.

"Henry Winter Davis and the Origins of Congressional Reconstruction." *Maryland Historical Magazine,* 67 (1972), 129–43.

"Origins of Negro Suffrage during the Civil War." *Southern Studies,* 17 (Summer 1978), 115–30.

"Protection of Personal Liberty in the Republican Emancipationist Legislation of 1862." *Journal of Southern History,* 42 (1976), 385–400.

Belz, Herman, et al. "Equality before the Law: The Civil War Amendments." *Center Magazine,* 20 (November–December 1987), 4–19.

Benedict, Michael Les. "Equality and Expediency in the Reconstruction Era: A Review Essay." *Civil War History,* 23 (December 1977), 322–35.

"Preserving the Constitution: The Conservative Basis of 'Radical Reconstruction.'" *Journal of American History,* 61 (June 1974), 65–90.

Bennett, Lerone, Jr. "The Day Slavery 'Died.'" *Ebony,* 31 (1976), 72–82.

"Was Abe Lincoln a White Supremacist?" *Ebony,* 23 (1968), 35–42.

Berlin, Ira. "Emancipation and Its Meaning in American Life." *Reconstruction,* 2 (1994), 41–44.

Berlin, Jean V. "Thaddeus Stevens and His Biographers." *Pennsylvania History,* 60 (April 1993), 153–62.

Berwanger, Eugene H. "Western Prejudice and the Extension of Slavery." *Civil War History,* 12 (September 1966), 197–212.

Bestor, Arthur. "The American Civil War as a Constitutional Crisis." *American Historical Review,* 69 (January 1964), 327–52.

"State Sovereignty and Slavery." *Journal of the Illinois State Historical Society,* 54 (Summer 1961), 327–52.

Binder, Guyora. "Did the Slaves Author the Thirteenth Amendment? An Essay in Redemptive History." *Yale Journal of Law and the Humanities,* 5 (Summer 1993), 471–505.

Blassingame, John W. "The Recruitment of Colored Troops in Kentucky, Maryland, and Missouri, 1863–1865." *Historian,* 29 (1967), 533–45.

"The Recruitment of Negro Troops in Maryland." *Maryland Historical Magazine,* 58 (1963), 20–29.

"The Recruitment of Negro Troops in Missouri during the Civil War." *Missouri Historical Review,* 58 (1964), 326–38.

Blight, David. "For Something beyond the Battlefield: Frederick Douglass and the

Struggle for the Memory of the Civil War." *Journal of American History*, 75 (March 1989), 1156–78.

"Frederick Douglass and the American Apocalypse." *Civil War History*, 31 (December 1985), 309–28.

Bluc, Frederick J. "Friends of Freedom: Lincoln, Chase, and Wartime Racial Policy." *Ohio History*, 102 (Summer–Autumn 1993), 85–97.

Bogue, Allan G. "The Radical Voting Dimension in the U.S. Senate during the Civil War." *Journal of Interdisciplinary History*, 3 (Winter 1973), 449–74.

Breiseth, Christopher N. "Lincoln and Frederick Douglass: Another Debate." *Journal of the Illinois State Historical Society*, 68 (February 1975), 9–26.

Brown, Thomas. "The Miscegenation of Richard Mentor Johnson as an Issue in the National Election Campaign of 1835–1836." *Civil War History*, 39 (March 1993), 5–30.

Brumgardt, John R. "Presidential Duel at Midsummer: The Peace Missions to Canada and Richmond, 1864." *Lincoln Herald*, 77 (Summer 1975), 96–102.

Buchanan, G. Sidney. "The Quest for Freedom: A Legal History of the Thirteenth Amendment." *Houston Law Review*, 12 (1974–75), 1–34, 331–78, 592–639, 843–89, 1069–85.

Bullard, Frederick L. "Abraham Lincoln and the Statehood of Nevada." *American Bar Association Journal*, 34 (1940), 210–13, 236, 313–17.

Casper, Gerhard. "Jones v. Mayer: Clio, Bemused and Confused Muse," *Supreme Court Review*, 1968, 89–132.

Cimprich, John, and Robert C. Mainfort, Jr. "The Fort Pillow Massacre: A Statistical Note." *Journal of American History*, 76 (December 1989), 830–37.

Clark, Elizabeth B. "Matrimonial Bonds: Slavery and Divorce in Nineteenth-Century America." *Law and History Review*, 8 (Spring 1990), 25–54.

Clubb, Jerome M., and Santa A. Traugott. "Partisan Cleavage and Cohesion in the House of Representatives, 1861–1974." *Journal of Interdisciplinary History*, 7 (Winter 1977), 375–401.

Cohen, William. "Negro Involuntary Servitude in the South, 1865–1940: A Preliminary Analysis." *Journal of Southern History*, 42 (February 1976), 31–60.

Colbert, Douglas L. "Liberating the Thirteenth Amendment." *Harvard Civil Rights–Civil Liberties Law Review*, 30 (Winter 1995), 1–55.

Cottrol, Robert J. "The Thirteenth Amendment and the North's Overlooked Egalitarian Heritage." *National Black Law Journal*, 11 (1989), 198–211.

Cox, LaWanda. "The Promise of Land for the Freedmen." *Mississippi Valley Historical Review*, 45 (December 1958), 413–40.

Crofts, Daniel W. "The Union Party of 1861 and the Secession Crisis." *Perspectives in American History*, 11 (1977–78), 325–76.

Cullers, Michael A. "Limits on Speech and Mental Slavery: A Thirteenth Amendment Defense against Speech Codes." *Case Western Reserve Law Review*, 45 (Winter 1995), 641–59.

Curry, Leonard P. "Congressional Democrats: 1861–1863." *Civil War History*, 12 (September 1966), 213–29.

Curry, Richard O. "Copperheadism and Ideological Continuity: The Anatomy of a Stereotype." *Journal of Negro History*, 57 (1972), 29–36.

Dumond, Dwight L. "Emancipation: History's Fantastic Reverie." *Journal of Negro History,* 49 (1964), 1–12.

Durden, Robert F. "A. Lincoln: Honkie or Equalitarian?" *South Atlantic Quarterly,* 71 (1972), 281–91.

Durrill, Wayne K. "The Struggle for Black Freedom before Emancipation." *Organization of American Historians Magazine of History,* 8 (Fall 1993), 7–10.

Fehrenbacher, Don. E. "The Making of a Myth: Lincoln and the Vice-Presidential Nomination in 1864." *Civil War History,* 41 (December 1995), 273–90.

Fellman, Michael. "Emancipation in Missouri." *Missouri Historical Review,* 83 (October 1988), 36–56.

Fields, Barbara J. "Slavery, Race and Ideology in the United States of America." *New Left Review,* no. 181 (May–June 1990), 95–118.

Finkelman, Paul. "The Nationalization of Slavery: A Counterfactual Approach to the 1860s." *Louisiana Studies,* 14 (1975), 213–40.

Fladeland, Betty L. "Compensated Emancipation: A Rejected Alternative." *Journal of Southern History,* 42 (May 1976), 169–86.

Foner, Eric. "The Meaning of Freedom in the Age of Emancipation." *Journal of American History,* 81 (September 1994), 435–60.

"Thaddeus Stevens and the Imperfect Republic." *Pennsylvania History,* 60 (April 1993), 140–52.

Foner, Philip S. "The Battle to End Discrimination against Negroes on Philadelphia Streetcars." *Pennsylvania History,* 40 (1973), 261–90, 355–79.

"The First Negro Meeting in Maryland." *Maryland Historical Magazine,* 66 (Spring 1971), 60–67.

Franklin, John Hope. "A Century of Civil War Observance." *Journal of Negro History,* 47 (1962), 97–107.

"The Civil War and the Negro American." *Journal of Negro History,* 48 (1962), 77–107.

Fuke, Richard Paul. "A Reform Mentality: Federal Policy toward Black Marylanders, 1864–1868." *Civil War History,* 22 (September 1976), 214–35.

Gerteis, Louis S. "Salmon P. Chase, Radicalism, and the Politics of Emancipation, 1861–1864." *Journal of American History,* 60 (June 1973), 42–62.

"Slavery and Hard Times: Morality and Utility in American Antislavery Reform." *Civil War History,* 29 (December 1983), 316–31.

Gienapp, William E. "Abraham Lincoln and the Border States." *Journal of the Abraham Lincoln Association,* 13 (1992), 13–46.

Gilliam, Will D., Jr. "Robert J. Breckinridge: Kentucky Unionist." *Kentucky Historical Society Register,* 69 (1971), 362–85.

Gillman, Howard. "The Collapse of Constitutional Originalism and the Rise of the Notion of the 'Living Constitution' in the Course of American State-Building." *Studies in American Political Development,* 11 (Fall 1997), 191–247.

Gordon, Sarah Barringer. " 'The Liberty of Self-Degradation': Polygamy, Woman Suffrage, and Consent in Nineteenth-Century America." *Journal of American History,* 83 (December 1996), 815–47.

Graebner, Norman L. "Thomas Corwin and the Sectional Crisis." *Ohio History,* 86 (1977), 229–47.

Haag, James Henry. "Involuntary Servitude: An Eighteenth-Century Concept in Search of a Twentieth-Century Definition." *Pacific Law Journal,* 19 (1988), 873–904.

Hancock, Donald C. "The Thirteenth Amendment and the Juvenile Justice System." *Journal of Criminal Law and Criminology,* 83 (Fall 1992), 614–43.

Harding, Vincent Gordon. "Wrestling toward the Dawn: The Afro-American Freedom Movement and the Changing Constitution." *Journal of American History,* 74 (December 1987), 718–39.

Harris, William C. "Conservative Unionists and the Presidential Election of 1864." *Civil War History,* 38 (December 1992), 298–318.

"The Hampton Roads Peace Conference: A Final Test of Lincoln's Presidential Leadership." *Journal of the Abraham Lincoln Association,* 21 (Winter 2000), 31–61.

Hartman, Linda. "The Issue of Freedom: Under Governor Richard Yates, 1861–1865." *Journal of the Illinois State Historical Society,* 57 (1964), 293–97.

Hershock, Martin J. "Copperheads and Radicals: Michigan Partisan Politics during the Civil War Era, 1860–1865." *Michigan Historical Review,* 18 (Spring 1992), 29–69.

Hesseltine, William B. "Abraham Lincoln and the Politicians." *Civil War History,* 6 (March 1960), 43–55.

Hood, James Larry. "For the Union: Kentucky's Unconditional Unionist Congressmen and the Development of the Republican Party in Kentucky, 1863–1865." *Register of the Kentucky Historical Society,* 76 (July 1978), 197–215.

"The Union and Slavery: Congressman Brutus J. Clay of the Bluegrass." *Kentucky Historical Society Register,* 75 (1977), 214–21.

Horowitz, Robert F. "Land to the Freedmen: A Vision of Reconstruction." *Ohio History,* 86 (Summer 1977), 187–99.

"Seward and Reconstruction: A Reconsideration." *Historian,* 47 (May 1985), 382–401.

Howard, Victor B. "The Civil War in Kentucky: The Slave Claims His Freedom." *Journal of Negro History,* 67 (1982), 246–56.

Hubbell, John T. "Politics as Usual: The Northern Democracy and Party Survival, 1860–1861." *Illinois Quarterly,* 36 (1973), 22–35.

Hurt, R. Douglas. "Historians and the Northwest Ordinance." *Western Historical Quarterly,* 20 (August 1989), 261–80.

Hyman, Harold M. "Abraham Lincoln, Legal Positivism, and Constitutional History." *Journal of the Abraham Lincoln Association,* 13 (1992), 1–12.

"Law and the Impact of the Civil War: A Review Essay." *Civil War History,* 14 (1968), 51–59.

"Lincoln and Congress: Why Not Congress and Lincoln?" *Journal of the Illinois State Historical Society,* 68 (1975), 57–73.

"Lincoln and Equal Rights for Negroes: The Irrelevancy of the 'Wadsworth Letter.'" *Civil War History,* 12 (September 1966), 258–66.

Jackson, W. Sherman. "Representative James M. Ashley and the Midwestern Origins of Amendment Thirteen." *Lincoln Herald,* 80 (Summer 1978), 83–95.

Jacobsohn, Gary J. "Abraham Lincoln 'On This Question of Judicial Authority':

The Theory of Constitutional Aspiration." *Western Political Quarterly*, 36 (1984), 52–70.

John, Richard R. "Governmental Institutions as Agents of Change: Rethinking American Political Development in the Early Republic." *Studies in American Political Development*, 11 (Fall 1997), 347–80.

Johnson, Ludwell H. "Lincoln and Equal Rights: The Authenticity of the Wadsworth Letter." *Journal of Southern History*, 32 (February 1966), 83–87.

"Lincoln and Equal Rights: A Reply." *Civil War History*, 13 (March 1967), 66–73.

"Lincoln's Solution to the Problem of the Peace Terms, 1864–1865." *Journal of Southern History*, 34 (November 1968), 576–86.

Kaczorowski, Robert J. "To Begin the Nation Anew: Congress, Citizenship, and Civil Rights after the Civil War." *American Historical Review*, 92 (February 1987), 45–68.

Kalman, Laura. "Border Patrol: Reflections on the Turn to History in Legal Scholarship." *Fordham Law Review*, 66 (October 1997), 87–124.

Kamphoefner, Walter D. "German-Americans and Civil War Politics: A Reconsideration of the Ethnocultural Thesis." *Civil War History*, 37 (September 1991), 232–46.

Kaplan, Sidney. "The Miscegenation Issue in the Election of 1864." *Journal of Negro History*, 34 (1949), 274–343.

Kares, Lauren. "The Unlucky Thirteenth: A Constitutional Amendment in Search of a Doctrine." *Cornell Law Review*, 80 (January 1995), 372–412.

Katyal, Neal Kumar. "Men Who Own Women: A Thirteenth Amendment Critique of Forced Prostitution." *Yale Law Journal*, 103 (December 1993), 791–826.

Kelley, Robert. "Ideology and Political Culture from Jefferson to Nixon." *American Historical Review*, 82 (June 1977), 531–82.

Kinoy, Arthur. "The Constitutional Right of Negro Freedom." *Rutgers Law Review*, 21 (1967), 387–441.

"The Constitutional Right of Negro Freedom Revisited: Some First Thoughts on *Jones v. Alfred H. Mayer Company.*" *Rutgers Law Review*, 22 (1968), 537–52.

Klement, Frank L. "Civil War Politics, Nationalism, and Postwar Myths." *Historian*, 38 (May 1976), 419–38.

"Midwestern Opposition to Lincoln's Emancipation Policy." *Journal of Negro History*, 49 (1964), 169–83.

"Ohio and the Knights of the Golden Circle: The Evolution of a Civil War Myth." *Cincinnati Historical Society Bulletin*, 32 (1974), 7–27.

Koppelman, Andrew. "Forced Labor: A Thirteenth Amendment Defense of Abortion." *Northwestern University Law Review*, 84 (Winter 1990), 480–535.

Kousser, J. Morgan. "Toward 'Total Political History': A Rational-Choice Research Program." *Journal of Interdisciplinary History*, 20 (Spring 1990), 521–60.

Krug, Mark M. "The Republican Party and the Emancipation Proclamation." *Journal of Negro History*, 48 (April 1963), 98–114.

Kurtz, Michael J. "Emancipation in the Federal City." *Civil War History*, 24 (September 1978), 250–67.

Law, Robin. "Dahomey and the Slave Trade: Reflections on the Historiography of the Rise of Dahomey." *Journal of African History,* 27 (1986), 237–67.

Lee, Bill R. "Missouri's Fight over Emancipation in 1863." *Missouri Historical Review,* 45 (April 1951), 256–74.

Lee, R. Alton. "The Corwin Amendment in the Secession Crisis." *Ohio Historical Quarterly,* 70 (January 1961), 1–26.

Linden, Glenn M. "A Note on Negro Suffrage and Republican Politics." *Journal of Southern History,* 36 (August 1970), 411–20.

Littlefield, Charles E. "The Insular Cases." *Harvard Law Review,* 15 (December 1901), 281–301.

Long, David E. "'I Am Aware That the Subject Creates Prejudice . . .': The Race Issue in the 1864 Election." *Lincoln Herald,* 94 (Winter 1992), 138–47 (part 1); 95 (Spring 1993), 2–11 (part 2); 95 (Summer 1993), 51–57 (part 3).

Lucas, Marion B. "Kentucky Blacks: The Transition from Slavery to Freedom." *Register of the Kentucky Historical Society,* 91 (Autumn 1993), 403–19.

Lucie, Patricia M. L. "Confiscation: Constitutional Crossroads." *Civil War History,* 23 (December 1977), 307–21.

"On Being a Free Person and a Citizen by Constitutional Amendment." *Journal of American Studies,* 11 (1978), 343–58.

Luthin, Reinhard H. "A Discordant Chapter in Lincoln's Administration: The Davis-Blair Controversy." *Maryland Historical Magazine,* 39 (1944), 25–48.

Maltz, Earl M. "The Idea of the Proslavery Constitution." *Journal of the Early Republic,* 17 (Spring 1997), 37–59.

McConnell, Joyce E. "Beyond Metaphor: Battered Women, Involuntary Servitude and the Thirteenth Amendment." *Yale Journal of Law and Feminism,* 4 (Spring 1992), 207–53.

McConnell, Stuart. "The Civil War and Historical Memory: A Historiographical Survey." *Organization of American Historians Magazine of History,* 8 (Fall 1993), 3–6.

McCurdy, Charles W. "Legal Institutions, Constitutional Theory, and the Tragedy of Reconstruction." *Reviews in American History,* 4 (June 1976), 203–11.

McMurtry, R. Gerald. "Lincoln Need Not Have Signed the Resolution Submitting the Thirteenth Amendment to the States." *Lincoln Lore,* no. 1604 (October 1971), 1–4.

McPherson, James M. "Abolitionist and Negro Opposition to Colonization during the Civil War." *Phylon,* 26 (Winter 1965), 391–99.

"Who Freed the Slaves?" *Reconstruction,* 2 (1994), 35–40.

Neely, Mark E., Jr. "Abraham Lincoln and Black Colonization: Benjamin Butler's Spurious Testimony." *Civil War History,* 25 (March 1979), 77–83.

"Was the Civil War a Total War?" *Civil War History,* 37 (March 1991), 5–28.

Nelson, Larry E. "Black Leaders and the Presidential Election of 1864." *Journal of Negro History,* 63 (1978), 42–58.

Nelson, Paul David. "From Intolerance to Moderation: The Evolution of Abraham Lincoln's Racial Views." *Register of the Kentucky Historical Society,* 72 (January 1974), 1–9.

Nelson, William E. "History and Neutrality in Constitutional Adjudication." *Virginia Law Review,* 72 (October 1986), 1237–96.

"The 'New' Thirteenth Amendment: A Preliminary Analysis." *Harvard Law Review*, 82 (April 1969), 1294–1321.

Owsley, Harriet C. "Peace and the Presidential Election of 1864." *Tennessee Historical Quarterly*, 18 (March 1959), 3–19.

Page, Catherine M. "*United States v. Kozminski:* Involuntary Servitude – A Standard at Last." *University of Toledo Law Review*, 20 (Summer 1989), 1023–45.

Paludan, Phillip S. "The American Civil War Considered as a Crisis in Law and Order." *American Historical Review*, 77 (1972), 1013–34.

"The American Civil War: Triumph through Tragedy." *Civil War History*, 20 (1974), 239–50.

"Lincoln, the Rule of Law, and the American Revolution." *Journal of the Illinois State Historical Society*, 70 (February 1977), 10–17.

Pease, William H., and Jane H. Pease. "Anti-Slavery Ambivalence: Immediatism, Expediency, Race." *American Quarterly*, 17 (Winter 1965), 682–95.

Pendergraft, Daryl. "Thomas Corwin and the Conservative Republican Reaction, 1858–1861." *Ohio State Archaeological and Historical Quarterly*, 57 (1948), 1–23.

Pittman, Larry J. "Physician-Assisted Suicide in the Dark Ward: The Intersection of the Thirteenth Amendment and Health Care Treatments Having Disproportionate Impacts on Disfavored Groups." *Seton Hall Law Review*, 28 (1998), 776–896.

Pomeroy, Earl S. "Lincoln, the Thirteenth Amendment, and the Admission of Nevada." *Pacific Historical Review*, 12 (1943), 362–68.

Pope, James Gray. "Labor's Constitution of Freedom." *Yale Law Journal*, 106 (January 1997), 941–1031.

Pratt, Harry E. "The Repudiation of Lincoln's War Policy in 1862 – the Stuart-Swett Congressional Campaign." *Journal of the Illinois State Historical Society*, 24 (1931), 129–40.

Pressly, Thomas J. "Bullets and Ballots: Lincoln and the 'Right of Revolution.'" *American Historical Review*, 67 (1962), 647–62.

Rankin, David C. "The Impact of the Civil War on the Free Colored Community of New Orleans." *Perspectives in American History*, 11 (1977–78), 379–416.

Rawley, James A. "Lincoln and Governor Morgan." *Abraham Lincoln Quarterly*, 6 (March 1951), 272–300.

"The Nationalism of Abraham Lincoln." *Civil War History*, 9 (1963), 283–98.

Reed, H. Clay. "Lincoln's Compensated Emancipation Plan and Its Relation to Delaware." *Delaware Notes*, 7th ser. (1931), 27–78.

Rhodehamel, John H., and Seth Kaller. "A Census of Copies of the Thirteenth Amendment to the U.S. Constitution Signed by Abraham Lincoln." *Manuscripts*, 44 (Spring 1992), 93–114.

Saxton, Alexander. "Blackface Minstrelsy and Jacksonian Ideology." *American Quarterly*, 27 (March 1975), 3–27.

Schwartz, Thomas F. "Salmon P. Chase Critiques *First Reading of the Emancipation Proclamation of President Lincoln*." *Civil War History*, 33 (March 1987), 84–87.

Sears, Stephen W. "McClellan and the Peace Plank of 1864: A Reappraisal." *Civil War History*, 36 (March 1990), 57–65.

Shade, William G. " 'Revolutions May Go Backwards': The American Civil War and the Problem of Political Development." *Social Science Quarterly*, 55 (December 1974), 753–67.

Shaffer, Dallas S. "Lincoln and the 'Vast Question' of West Virginia." *West Virginia History*, 32 (January 1971), 86–100.

Simpson, Brooks. " 'The Doom of Slavery': Ulysses S. Grant, War Aims, and Emancipation, 1861–1863." *Civil War History*, 36 (March 1990), 36–56.

"Land and the Ballot: Securing the Fruits of Emancipation?" *Pennsylvania History*, 60 (April 1993), 176–88.

"Slave to Banker." *Ebony*, 1 (November 1945), 43–47.

Smith, John D. "The Recruitment of Negro Soldiers in Kentucky, 1863–1865." *Kentucky Historical Society Register*, 72 (1974), 364–90.

Soifer, Aviam. "The Paradox of Paternalism and Laissez-Faire Constitutionalism: United States Supreme Court, 1888–1921." *Law and History Review*, 5 (Spring 1987), 249–79.

"Reviewing Legal Fictions." *Georgia Law Review*, 20 (Summer 1986), 871–915.

"Status, Contract, and Promises Unkept." *Yale Law Journal*, 96 (July 1987), 1916–59.

Spencer, Ivor D. "Chicago Helps to Reelect Lincoln." *Journal of the Illinois State Historical Society*, 63 (1970), 167–79.

Stampp, Kenneth M. "The Milligan Case and the Election of 1864 in Indiana." *Mississippi Valley Historical Review*, 31 (June 1944), 41–58.

Stanley, Amy Dru. " 'Beggars Can't Be Choosers': Compulsion and Contract in Postbellum America." *Journal of American History*, 78 (March 1992), 1265–93.

"Conjugal Bonds and Wage Labor: Rights of Contract in the Age of Emancipation." *Journal of American History*, 75 (September 1988), 471–500.

Starr, Stephen Z. "Was There a Northwest Conspiracy?" *Filson Club History Quarterly*, 38 (1964), 323–41.

Staudenraus, P. J. "The Popular Origins of the Thirteenth Amendment." *Mid-America*, 50 (1968), 108–15.

Stone, Lorraine. "Neoslavery – 'Surrogate' Motherhood Contracts v. the Thirteenth Amendment." *Law and Inequality*, 6 (July 1988), 63–73.

Strickland, Arvarh E. "The Illinois Background of Lincoln's Attitude toward Slavery and the Negro." *Journal of the Illinois State Historical Society*, 56 (Autumn 1963), 474–94.

Swan, George S. "The Thirteenth Amendment Dimensions of *Roe v. Wade*." *Journal of Juvenile Law*, 4 (1980), 1–33.

Tandler, Maurice. "The Political Front in Civil War New Jersey." *Proceedings of the New Jersey Historical Society*, 83 (1965), 223–33.

Tap, Bruce. "Race, Rhetoric, and Emancipation: The Election of 1862 in Illinois." *Civil War History*, 39 (June 1993), 101–25.

Tedhams, David P. "The Reincarnation of 'Jim Crow': A Thirteenth Amendment Analysis of Colorado's Amendment 2." *Temple Political and Civil Rights Law Review*, 4 (October 1994), 133–65.

Thornbrough, Emma L. "The Race Issue in Indiana Politics during the Civil War." *Indiana Magazine of History,* 47 (1951), 165–88.

Trask, David F. "Charles Sumner and the New Jersey Railroad Monopoly during the Civil War." *Proceedings of the New Jersey Historical Society,* 75 (October 1957), 259–75.

Trefousse, Hans L. "Zachariah Chandler and the Withdrawal of Frémont in 1864: New Answer to an Old Riddle." *Lincoln Herald,* 70 (1968), 181–88.

Turner, Justin G. "The Strohm Letters and Lincoln's Thirteenth Amendment." *Lincoln Herald,* 78 (Spring 1976), 24–26.

VanderVelde, Lea S. "The Labor Vision of the Thirteenth Amendment." *University of Pennsylvania Law Review,* 138 (December 1989), 437–504.

Vile, John R. "Francis Lieber and the Process of Constitutional Amendment." *Review of Politics,* 60 (Summer 1998), 525–43.

Volpe, Vernon L. "The Frémonts and Emancipation in Missouri." *Historian,* 56 (Winter 1994), 339–54.

Vorenberg, Michael. "Abraham Lincoln and the Politics of Black Colonization." *Journal of the Abraham Lincoln Association,* 14 (Summer 1993), 23–46.

Wagandt, Charles L. "The Army versus Maryland Slavery, 1862–1864." *Civil War History,* 10 (June 1964), 141–48.

  ed. "The Civil War Journal of Dr. Samuel A. Harrison." *Civil War History,* 13 (June 1967), 131–46.

Waldron, Webb. "Massa, Tell 'Em We're Rising," *Reader's Digest,* April 1945, pp. 53–56.

Walton, Hanes, Jr., et al. "R. R. Wright, Congress, President Truman and the First National Public African-American Holiday: National Freedom Day." *PS: Political Science and Politics,* 24 (December 1991), 685–88.

Weisberger, Bernard A. "Horace Greeley: Reformer as Republican." *Civil War History,* 23 (March 1977), 5–25.

White, Shane. " 'It Was a Proud Day': African-Americans, Festivals, and Parades in the North, 1741–1834." *Journal of American History,* 81 (June 1994), 13–50.

Wickenden, Dorothy. "Lincoln and Douglass: Dismantling the Peculiar Institution." *Wilson Quarterly,* 14 (Autumn 1990), 102–12.

Wiecek, William M. "The Reconstruction of Federal Judicial Power, 1863–1875." *American Journal of Legal History,* 13 (October 1969), 333–59.

Williams, Gary L. "Lincoln's Natural Allies: The Case of the Kentucky Unionists." *South Atlantic Quarterly,* 73 (1974), 70–84.

Young, James Harvey. "Anna Elizabeth Dickinson and the Civil War: For and against Lincoln." *Mississippi Valley Historical Review,* 31 (June 1944), 59–80.

Zilversmit, Arthur. "Lincoln and the Problem of Race: A Decade of Interpretations." *Papers of the Abraham Lincoln Association,* 2 (1980), 22–45.

Zingg, Paul J. "John Archibald Campbell and the Hampton Roads Conference:

Quixotic Diplomat, 1865." *Alabama Historical Quarterly,* 36 (1974), 21–34.

Zoellner, Robert H. "Negro Colonization: The Climate of Opinion Surrounding Lincoln, 1860–65." *Mid-America,* 42 (July 1960), 131–150.

Zornow, William F. "The Cleveland Convention, 1864, and the Radical Democrats." *Mid-America,* 36 (January 1954), 39–53.

Zuckert, Michael P. "Completing the Constitution: The Thirteenth Amendment." *Constitutional Commentary,* 4 (Summer 1987), 259–84.

Unpublished Dissertations and Theses

Barton, Donald Scott. "Divided Houses: The Civil War Party System in the Border States." Ph.D. diss., Texas A&M University, 1991.

Boyd, Willis D. "Negro Colonization in the National Crisis, 1860–1870." Ph.D. diss., University of California at Los Angeles, 1954.

Cochrane, William G. "Freedom without Equality: A Study of Northern Opinion and the Negro Issue, 1861–1870." Ph.D. diss., University of Minnesota, 1957.

Cowden, Joanna. "Civil War and Reconstruction Politics in Connecticut, 1863–1868." Ph.D. diss., University of Connecticut, 1974.

Davis, Van M. "Individualism on Trial: The Ideology of the Northern Democracy during the Civil War and Reconstruction." Ph.D. diss., University of Virginia, 1972.

Endres, Fredric Franklin. "The Northern Press and the Civil War: A Study in Editorial Opinion and Government, Military and Public Reaction." Ph.D. diss., University of Maryland, 1975.

Gordon, Sarah Barringer. "The 'Twin Relic of Barbarism': A Legal History of Anti-Polygamy in Nineteenth-Century America." Ph.D. diss., Princeton University, 1995.

Hamilton, Howard Devon. "The Legislative and Judicial History of the Thirteenth Amendment." Ph.D. diss., University of Illinois, 1950.

Henry, George S. "Radical Republican Policy toward the Negro during Reconstruction, 1862–1872." Ph.D. diss., Yale University, 1963.

Henry, Milton L., Jr. "Henry Winter Davis: Border State Radical." Ph.D. diss., Louisiana State University, 1974.

Hubbard, Paul G. "The Lincoln-McClellan Presidential Election in Illinois." Ph.D. diss., University of Illinois, 1949.

Kamaras, Nicholas P. "George B. McClellan and the Election of 1864." Ph.D. diss., University of Delaware, 1976.

Kuebler, John B. "Montgomery Blair in the Lincoln Cabinet." M.A. thesis, University of Maryland, 1972.

McCarthy, John L. "Reconstruction Legislation and Voting Alignments in the House of Representatives, 1863–1869." Ph.D. diss., Yale University, 1970.

McLaughlin, Tom LeRoy. "Popular Reactions to the Idea of Negro Equality in Twelve Non-Slaveholding States, 1846–1869." Ph.D. diss., University of Washington, 1969.

Osher, David M. "Soldier Citizens for a Disciplined Nation: Union Conscription and the Construction of the Modern American Army." Ph.D. diss., Columbia University, 1992.

O'Sullivan, Katherine Emily. "Lincoln, Congress, and the Ideology of the Thirteenth Amendment." Senior thesis, Harvard University, 1993.

Owen, Thomas Louis. "The Formative Years of Kentucky's Republican Party, 1864–1871." Ph.D. diss., University of Kentucky, 1981.

Quigley, David. "Reconstructing Democracy: Politics and Ideas in New York City, 1865–1880." Ph.D. diss., New York University, 1997.

Reilley, George L. A. "The Camden and Amboy Railroad and New Jersey Politics." Ph.D. diss., Columbia University, 1951.

Robinson, Armstead. "Day of Jubilo: Civil War and the Demise of Slavery in the Mississippi Valley, 1861–1865." Ph.D. diss., University of Rochester, 1976.

Simon, John Y. "Congress under Lincoln, 1861–1863." Ph.D. diss., Harvard University, 1960.

Syrett, John. "The Confiscation Acts: Efforts at Reconstruction during the Civil War." Ph.D. diss., University of Wisconsin, 1971.

Zaeske, Susan Marie. "Petitioning, Antislavery and the Emergence of Women's Consciousness." Ph.D. diss., University of Wisconsin, 1997.

Index

abolitionists: in National Union party (1864), 122–5; petitions of, 12, 38–40, 61–2; in Radical Democratic party, 119–21, 126; view of Constitution, 11–14; view of Thirteenth Amendment, 81
Ackerman, Bruce, 54
Adams, Charles Francis, 20, 59
Adams, John Quincy, 12, 15, 51
African Americans: Confederate recruitment policy for, 185; efforts to gain equal rights, 81–4, 103; efforts to gain freedom, 23–4, 80–1, 103, 246; efforts to gain voting rights, 84–6, 119, 188–9; land for, 84, 120–1, 179, 190; military service in Civil War, 37–8, 82; national convention (1864), 158–9; at National Union party convention, 124; observe passage of Thirteenth Amendment, 205, 207; rights under Freedmen's Bureau Act of 1866 and Civil Rights Act of 1866, 233–9; rights under Thirteenth Amendment, 55–6, 99–107, 130–3, 186–91, 216–22; role in emancipation policy making, 79–81, 103, 131, 188–9; status in the North, 82; Union recruitment policy for, 27–8; view of Thirteenth Amendment, 61, 81–8, 244–6; *see also* citizenship; civil rights; colonization; equality; voting rights
Alabama: ratification debate on Thirteenth Amendment, 231
Alley, John B., 198
American Anti-Slavery Society, 125
Anthony, Henry B., 90
Anthony, Susan B., 38
Antietam (battle), 37
anti-Puritanism, 95–6
antislavery amendment: *see* Thirteenth Amendment
apprenticeship, 47, 174, 230, 239
Arnold, Isaac N., 48, 59, 70–1, 91–2, 131
Ashley, James M., 242; in election of 1864, 141, 151, 171; reconstruction legislation of, 49–50, 128–9, 190, 226;

on Thirteenth Amendment, 49–51, 53, 139, 141, 171, 179–80, 199, 204–6
Atlanta, 154, 155, 179
Augusta, A. T., 83

Bancroft, George, 51n, 203, 226
Banks, Nathaniel P., 34
Barlow, Samuel L. M., 78–9, 179, 183–4
Barnett, T. J., 120
Bates, Edward, 40, 56, 68, 179
Battery Wagner, 37
Bayard, Thomas F., 167
Belz, Herman, 49
Benedict, Michael Les, 49, 138n
Bennett, James Gordon, 77, 86, 233; on black suffrage in Montana territory, 101–2; criticism of Abraham Lincoln, 72, 116; for Ulysses S. Grant as Republican nominee for president, 117; on peace mission to Jefferson Davis, 147; on Thirteenth Amendment, 72–3, 92
Bertonneau, Arnold, 85
Bilbo, William N., 182, 183, 197
Bill of Rights, 10, 107
Binney, Horace, 66–70, 87, 105, 222
Black, Jeremiah S., 134, 160
black codes (southern states), 230, 237
black laws (northern states), 166, 170, 188, 220–1, 232
Blaine, James G., 145, 242
Blair, Francis P. (Frank), Jr., 42n, 46, 118, 172n
Blair, Francis P., Sr., 46, 182, 186, 205; peace missions of, 206–7
Blair, Montgomery, 46, 86; on emancipation and reconstruction, 41–2, 78–9; in Abraham Lincoln's cabinet, 118, 123, 155; Maryland Union party of, 173; in promoting Thirteenth Amendment, 183–5
Blyew v. U.S. (1872), 240
border states: antislavery movement in, 37–8, 97; compensated emancipation in, 27, 216; confiscation policy in, 23; conscription in, 168–9; under Emancipation Proclamation, 31, 33;